WARS AND SOLDIERS IN THE EARLY REIGN OF LOUIS XIV

Volume I – The Army of the United Provinces of the Netherlands, 1660–1687

Bruno Mugnai

'This is the Century of the Soldier', Fulvio Testi, Poet, 1641

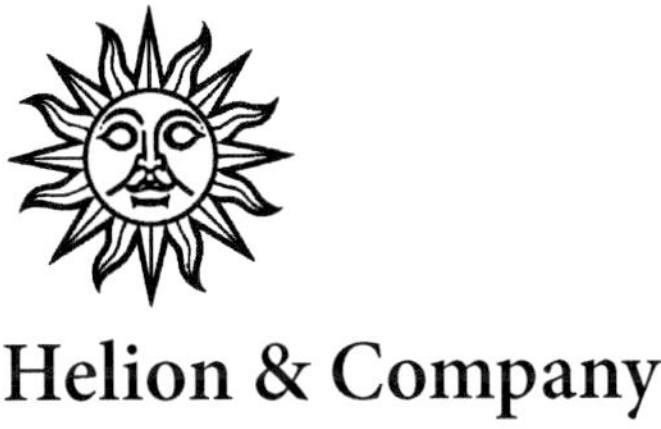

Helion & Company

Helion & Company Limited
Unit 8 Amherst Business Centre
Budbrooke Road
Warwick
CV34 5WE
England
Tel. 01926 499 619
Fax 0121 711 4075
Email: info@helion.co.uk
Website: www.helion.co.uk
Twitter: @helionbooks
Visit our blog at http://blog.helion.co.uk/

Published by Helion & Company 2019
Designed and typeset by Serena Jones
Cover designed by Paul Hewitt, Battlefield Design (www.battlefield-design.co.uk)
Printed by Henry Ling Limited, Dorchester, Dorset

ISBN 978-1-911628-59-0

British Library Cataloguing-in-Publication Data.
A catalogue record for this book is available from the British Library.

Contents

List of Illustrations & Maps 4
Foreword 9
Acknowledgements 10
Chronology 11

1. Armies of the *Grand Siècle* 16
   - Introduction 16
   - The Rise of the Modern Standing Armies 20
   - The Golden Age of the Dutch Republic 32
2. *Het Staatsche Leger* 47
   - The Dutch Army before and after 'the Disaster' 47
   - Command and Military Administration 64
   - Supply and Logistics 78
   - Infantry Organisation 81
   - Cavalry and Dragoons Organisation 89
   - Artillery Organisation 91
   - Provincial Militias 92
3. The Dutch Army on Campaign 99
   - Warfare in the Netherlands 99
   - Wars Against Cologne and Münster (1660–1664) 101
   - The Second Anglo-Dutch War (1665–1667) 105
   - *La Guerre d'Hollande* (1672–1678) 111
4. Uniforms, Equipment, and Ensigns 163
   - Infantry 171
   - Cavalry 187
   - Artillery 199
   - Militia 203
   - Ensigns 204

Appendix I: Orders of Battle and Army Lists 212
Appendix II: Companies, Squadrons and Regiments, 1660–1687 222

Colour Plate Commentaries 249
Bibliography 255

List of Illustrations & Maps

Illustrations

1. Scene of a military camp in the Spanish Low Countries, by Joshua de Grave, 1675. (Rijksmuseum Library, Amsterdam) 17
2. From the series of Illustrated Proverbs issued by Giuseppe Maria Mitelli, 1670. (Author's archive) 21
3. Prince Willem II, 1651, by Gerard van Honthorst (Rijksmuseum, Amsterdam) 38
4. The young Prince William III of Orange, by Cornelius Johnson. (Yale Center for British Art, New Haven, CT) 38
5. Johan de Witt (1625–1672). (Engraving by Romain de Hooghe, Rijksmuseum, Amsterdam) 45
6. The drawings of Hoynck van Papendrecht, commissioned by F.J.G. ten Raa, illustrating the *Garde te voet* (Foot Guards) in the 1680s. 53
7. Items of the *Gardes te voet*. a: Grenadier's coat after de Hooghe (1690); b: Musketeer's coat after Papendrecht-ten Raa (1680-89) ; c: Grenadier fur cap, after engraving by anonymous (1690), d: Grenadier mitre cap after de Hooghe (1689) (Author's illustration) 53
8. A detail from the landing of the Medway, by Romeyn de Hooghe. Note the private marines in short coats and the officers wearing the fashionable long *justaucorps* and laced baldrics 57
9. Godard van Reede-Ginkel (1644–1703), later Earl of Athlone. (Author's archive) 58
10. The siege and capture of Naarden, 1673 (Romeyn de Hooghe) 60
11. Coerland dragoons, 1673. (Author's illustration) 61
12. The States' Army chain of command 64
13. View of a Dutch army's encampment, showing tents, supply waggons, sentinel with pike and other troops and officer; late 17th century. Unsigned ink and wash drawing, about 1680. (Author's archive) 76
14. Dutch infantry, c.1655, by Gerbrand van den Eeckhout (1621–1674) 79
15. This is the only known picture depicting English infantry in Dutch service 84

17. Another unusual weapon, a flintlock holster pistol manufactured entirely of steel, Dutch or German *c.*1660. (Private collection) 85
16 A pair of Dutch early flintlock holster pistols with pre-charged turn-off barrels, *c.*1665-70; a double barrel cavalry flintlock pistol, with turn-over barrels formed in two stages, probably Dutch 1660. (Private collection) 85
18. Willem Frederik van Nassau-Dietz (1613–1664), painting by Pieter Nazon 87
19. Two portraits painted by Jacob Fransz van der Merck, representing the captains of two of the six companies of the civic guards of Leiden, dated 1657 94
20. Detail from the painting 'Playing Card' by Pieter de Hooch, dated 1672 95
21. Reconstruction of the officer's *justaucorps* after 'Playing Card' by Pieter de Hooch 95
22. Infantry regiments comprised a variable number of boys and soldiers' sons – *enfants de troupe* – who served as junior adjutants or, the lucky ones, as apprentices to the senior officers. 95
23. Cover illustration from the *Nieuwe Jaars aan de Manhafte Schuttery van Nederland* of 1672 96
24. Coat patterns after the *Nieuwe Jaars Gift aan de Manhafte Schuttery van Nederland*, dated 1672 (opposite); a: ensign; b: drummer 97
25. A map of the city of Groningen made after the siege in 1672, showing the Munster and Cologne trenches and approaches. 100
26. Johan Maurits Count of Nassau-Siegen (1604-1679), here portrayed during his mandate as Governor of Brazil from 1634 to 1644. Engraving by unknown artist. (Author's archive) 102
27. Henri Charles de La Trémoille (1620–1672). Engraving by Jean de Baen. (Author's archive) 104
28. Het Rampjar: 1672 was a true year of disaster (*rampjaar* in Dutch), which seemed to provoke the bitter end of the Republic 117
29. The attack on Coevorden, 1672 118
30. Prince William III of Orange by Caspar Netscher. (Rijksmuseum, Amsterdam) 120
31. Carl Rabenhaupt (Lambert Visscher) 120
32. Willem Frederik van Nassau-Zuylenstein (1624–1672). (Portrait by Peter Lely, Private Collection) 125
33. The Looting of Zwammerdam 128
34. The Dutch seizure of New York in 1673, anonymous engraving 130
35. The siege of Grave. Anonymous engraving. (Author's archive) 137
36. The Battle of Seneffe, fought on 11 August 1674 between the French and the Dutch–Imperial–Spanish army 140
37. The Battle of Seneffe. Note the baggage wagons in the foreground. (Collection of print of the University of Leyden, NL) 141
38. The Battle of Mont Cassel, fought on 11 April 1677, in a contemporary Dutch print 153

39. Brunswick-Lüneburg born, Count Georg Friedrich of Waldeck-Pyrmont (1620–1692). Copper Engraving of unknown artist, dated 1682. (Author's archive) 154
40. Hendrik Casimir II of Nassau-Dietz (1657–1696) was the second Dutch Statholder in charge of the province of Friesland and Groningen 155
41. Veldmaarschalk Pauls Wirtz (also Würz or Würtz, 1612–1676), German-born freelance officer who at various times was in Swedish, Brandenburg, Danish, and Dutch service 156
42. Colonel Hans Willem van Aylva (1633–1691). (Engraving by Lambert van den Bos and Lieuwe van Aitzema, Fries Museum, Leeuwarden, NL) 157
43. Saint-Denis, 1678 158
44. A notary act 164
45. Dutch marinier, 1665–67, Moses Ter-Borch. (Metropolitan Museum of Art, New York) 167
46. Marine soldier, regiment *Vrijbergen* (I-35), 1678–80, after de Wilde and Nicolas. (Author's illustration) 167
47. The marine regiment embarking at Texel in 1671, Ludolf Bakhuysen 168
48. Veldtwaibels (NCOs) of the regiment Holstein-Norburg (I-88) and Nassau-Friesland (I-27), dated 1672–75, copies by Hoynck van Papendrecht after de Rydder-Robitschek 174
49. Musketeers and pikeman in training, from the *Vertoogh van de krijghs-oeffeninge* by Johan Boxel, published in 1672, but datable in the previous decade 175
51. Dutch musketeers and pikemen from the *Vertoogh van de Kryghs-Oeffeninge* by Johan Boxel 175
51. Armour and pot helm, Dutch manufacture, mid 17th century. (Private collection) 175
52. Musketeers and pikemen by Hendrick Cornelissen van Buren (1736–1703), from the *Dril Konst* printed in Utrecht in 1672 for the manual of training of the province's infantry 177
53. Dutch infantrymen of the late 1660s, from the Ordres van Batailljen, published in 1672. Musketeer and drummer wear open-sleeve cassocks, while the pikeman has armour and buff coat 177
54. Dutch soldier wearing cassock, 1665–68, by Gerard ter Borch (Collection of prints of the Libreria Reale of Turin) 178
55. Another fine detailed cassock is represented in this painting by Jacob Duck, entitled 'The Distraint', 1658–60 178
56. Dutch cassock patterns, 1: after Boxel's manual, 1663–69; 2: after Jacob Duck, 1658–60; 3: after Gerhard ter Borch, 1665–68 (Author's illustration) 178
57. A very good detailed image representing an early *justaucorps* worn by this smoking Dutch soldier, by Jacob Duck, dated 1660–65. Note the pattern of flap cuffs and the straight collar 179
58. The reading man in the painting by Pieter de Hooch, executed after 1672, well shows the evolution of the justaucorps, which complete sleeves and large flap cuffs 179

59. Early *justaucorps*; 1: after Jacob Duck, 1660-65; 2: after Gerard ter Borch; early 1670s; 3: after Jan Verkolje 1670; 4: after anonymous, 1672 179
60. Dutch cavalry officers, 1662–65, by Gerard ter Borch and Pieter de Hooch. They wear the same kind of buff leather coat with sleeves piped of silver or gold lace 180
61. The officer portrayed by Jan Verkoljein the early 1670s wears a fashionable buff kolder with dark blue cloth cuffs and red fringes 181
62. Dutch buff coat, 1660–70, Collection of the Centraal Museum in Utrecht 181
63. The Battle of the Boyne, anonymous artist, 1690 184–185
64. A Dutch cavalry sword, second half of the 17th century (Private collection) 187
65. A very fine engraving by Jan van Troyen, after Gerbrand van den Eeckhout, representing a Dutch cavalry officer of 1660–64. (Author's archive) 190
66. Dutch cavalrymen, 1672–78, after de Hooghe and Belagering der Stad Grave (1674) by anonymous. (Author's illustration) 188
67. Dutch cavalry trooper, 1665–68, reconstruction after Philips Wouverman. Buff leather coat with white metal armour; orange sash and grey-brown headgear. (Author's illustration) 188
68. Left: a: cassocks, after the 'Battle of the Boyne' by anonymous; b: waistcoat (For more details see colour plate F) 190
69. Below: private guard in casaque, after de Hooghe 190
70. Portrait of Jacob de Graeff (1642–1690), by Gerard ter Borch, Rijksmuseum collection, Amsterdam 191
71. Above: cavalry *surtout* or greatcoat, after the painting by Pieter de Hooch 192
72. Four interesting and well-detailed Dutch cavalrymen by Pieter de Hooch, all datable to the 1660s 192
73. Dutch cavalrymen with girl outside tent, from a collection of copper-engravings after Philips Wouwerman (1619–68), dated approximately 1660 194
74. Four Dutch infantrymen dateable to *c.*1688, in this anonymous print preserved in the Royal Library in Windsor Castle 196
75. Cavalryman and trumpeter, 1660. 196
76. The trumpeter as main subject in the painting appears again in the works of Jan Verkolje. Note the elaborate gallon of the livery and the coat with false sleeves 197
77. Pattern of the coat of the 1674 trumpeter. (Author's illustration. For more details see colour plate E) 197
78. Dutch Artillery, 1668–80; illustration by Richard Knötel from *Die Grosse Uniformenkunde* 200
79. The arrest of the de Witt brothers by The Hague militia in 1672, by Pieter Frits (1627–1708) 201
80. The Hague Town Militia by Martinus Lengele, dated early 1660s 202

81. Courland's cavalry standard, probably the life colour, with the motto VIGILANTER ET CONSTANTER, today preserved in the Military Museum of Stockholm 205
82. Colonel's ensign, infantry regiment *Reede* (I-86), 1673; Scots infantry ensigns are described in 1686 in red or blue with the white St. Andrew cross 206
83. Company ensign, infantry regiment *Rabenhaupt* (I-6) 1672; Colonel's ensign, infantry regiment *Wijnbergen* (I-99), 1690 206
84. Company standard, cavalry regiment *Nassau-Saarbrücken*, 1690; Company standard, cavalry regiment *Berlo* (C-28) 207
85. Company standards, regiment *Waldeck* (C-9), 1690 207
86. Reconstruction of the ensign belonging to the Civic Guard of Kampen, Overijssel, dated 1672 210

Maps

1. The Seven Provinces of the Dutch Republic 33
2. Holland's *waterlinie* 115
3. Friesland's *waterlinie* 116

Dutch Currency

The early *guilder* (a 10.61 gram. 910 silver coin) was divided into 20 *stuivers*, each of 8 *duiten* or 16 *penningen*. The *guilder* gradually replaced other silver coin denominations circulating in the Dutch Republic: the *florijn* (28 *stuivers*), the *daalder* (1.5 *guilders* or 30 *stuivers*), the *rijksdaalder* (2.5 *guilders* or 50 *stuivers*), the 'silver ducat' (same value as the *rijksdaalder*) and the 'silver rider ducaton' (3 *guilders* or 60 *stuivers*).

Foreword

I am not sure when I first became aware of the work of Bruno Mugnai, probably from one of the beautiful illustrations he often produced of Central European Soldiers, in a variety of groundbreaking publications.

All that can be said was that I was stunned.

I loved the clarity of his line and his vibrant use of colour, which managed to be full and lustrous, without at anytime modern and jarring. His work is a throw back to the classic military draftsmen of the late 19th and early 20th Century, such as Meissonier, Detaille, and Leloir. Anyone wishing to recreate his plates, in either model or re-enactment clothing form, would, always, have a superb clear image to work from, and this sharpness, is his defining characteristic.

This new series is not only a joy, because it is an excuse to view Bruno's artwork, but also to see the fruits of his original research, in a period which is also one of my loves, and across subject matter that has received little proper coverage.

I commend this, and look forward to future publications with great anticipation.

Mark Allen
Redditch 2019.

Acknowledgements

This book, the first of the series *Wars and Soldiers in the Early Reign of Louis XIV*, has been written thanks to two fortunate coincidences. The first is the publication of the research carried out by Olaf van Nimwegen: *The Dutch Army and the Military Revolutions 1588–1688*, which has been a formidable source of consultation and guide in the intricate history of the Dutch Army after the Peace of Westphalia.

I could never have written this book without the research done by Edwin Groot: the second fortunate coincidence. His extraordinary constancy in the search for sources on the State's army is worthy of unconditional admiration. I should also add that the idea of embarking on this adventure through the armies of this age was born precisely when I discovered his research.

Also my thanks go to Serena Jones, who has patiently edited my manuscript in the most difficult enterprise to make my 'Italenglish' understandable.

Florence, 30 November 2018.
BM

Chronology

1660	
February 27	Under Holland's insistence, the States General decrease the Dutch army to 24,000 men in total
1663	
December	Münster troops invade the princedom of East Friesland; the States General mobilise the army to expel the invaders.
December 23	English corsairs under Robert Holmes bombard the Dutch fortress of Gorée in the Gold Coast, West Africa.
1664	
Jan–Feb	English corsairs seize the Dutch ports on the Gold Coast.
April 12–14	English corsairs conquer the Dutch fortresses of Cape Coast and Elmina in West Africa.
June 6	The Dutch under Johan Maurits of Nassau-Siegen conquer Fort Dijlerschans in East Friesland hold by Münster troops.
August 27	English naval squadron in North America seizes the Dutch colony of Nieuw Amsterdam (today New York) in North America.
Sep–Oct	The Dutch fleet under de Ruyter expels the English from West Africa, except the Cape Coast.
1665	
February 22	The States General declare war on England (Second Anglo-Dutch war).
June 13	The English fleet prevails over the Dutch fleet at the Battle of Lowestoft.
June	Münster's preparation for war alarms the States General.
September 19	The Dutch Republic enters into an alliance with Brunswick-Lüneburg and Osnabrück.
September 25	Münster army cross the border with Overjissel and Groningen
Sep–Oct	The towns of Achterhoek and Twente surrender to the Prince-Bishop of Münster's troops.
November 15	The French auxiliary corps joins the Dutch army on the River Ijssel.
December 7	The Dutch–French army begins the offensive against Münster.
1666	
April 15	As allies of the Dutch Republic, France declares war on England.

April 11 Peace of Cleves between the Republic and the Prince-Bishop of Münster.

June 1–4 Four Days Battle fought off the east coast of England results in a Dutch victory.

July 25–26 English victory at the naval battle of Saint James.

July 27–28 English fleet destroys the harbours in the Frisian islands of Vlieland and Terschelling.

Aug–Sep The French fleet seizes the English ports in the Caribbean of Saint Kitts, Antigua, and Montserrat.

1667

May 20 French–Dutch assault on Nevis Island, in the Caribbean, is repulsed by the English fleet.

May–June Peace negotiations open in Breda – the Dutch fleet under Abrahm Crijnssen occupies the English colony of Surinam.

May France invades the Spanish Low Countries, begins the War of Devolution.

June The English fleet attacks the French in Martinique sinking 21 enemy ships, and then conquers the French colony of La Cayenne.

June 20–22 The Dutch fleet successfully lands troops near the Medway estuary and destroys English naval installations and ships at Chatham.

July 31 Peace treaty is signed at Breda between England, France, and Dutch Republic.

1668

January The Triple Alliance is signed by England, Sweden, and the United Provinces.

May 2 Treaty of Aix-la-Chapelle, end of the War of Devolution.

1672

February 24 Prince William III of Orange is appointed as Captain-General of the Dutch army.

March 12 England declares war on the Dutch Republic. The English fleet attacks a Dutch return fleet, sailing from the Levant.

April 8 France declares war on the Republic.

May 17 The French army assembled in the Ardennes crosses the Meuse under Marshall Turenne.

May 28 French troops march to Kaiserswerth for joining the armies of the Prince-Bishop of Münster and the Elector of Cologne.

June 1 Münster and Cologne troops, approximately 30,000 men, occupy Lingen and Overdinkel, then march through Twente, where they conquer Enschede and besiege Groenlo, which surrenders on 10 June.

June 12 The French army cross the Rhine at Lobith, first field engagement between the French and Dutch armies; Marshall Condé is injured during the action. Turenne takes command and splits the army in two corps; Arnhem is besieged. The French corps under Louis XIV moves to Doesburg, his brother Philippe marches to Zutphen. Münster artillery shells Bredevoort.

June 13	The Dutch field army under Prince William III marches on Utrecht.
June 16	Surrender of the major stronghold of Arnhem – the States General order evacuation of Utrecht.
June 18–22	Prince-Bishop of Münster conquers Bredevoort; days later Lochem, Hattem, Elburg, Harderwijk, Deventer, and Zwolle also surrender.
June 20	Naarden surrenders to the French.
June 21	Johan de Witt is severely wounded in an attack.
June 23	The French enter Utrecht – the towns of Kampen, Hasselt, Rouveen, De Lichtmis, Zwartsluis, and Staphorst surrender without fighting.The Dutch open the dikes to inundate the polders to form the *waterlinie* (waterline).
June 24	In Friesland and Groningen also, the Dutch inundate the countryside.
June 25	The city of Zutphen is conquered by the French.
June 26	The Dutch fortresses of Steenwijk, Blokzijl, and Kuinre surrender after brief resistance.
June 28	French blockade of Maastricht.
June 30	French vanguards appear in front of Gorkum.
July 4	In Haarlem, the house of the regent Cornelis Ascanius van Sypesteyn is looted because of rumours that his cousin, Grand Pensionary Johan de Witt, is hidden inside.
July 5	Delegates of the capitulated city of Overijssel, convened in the Ommerschans, recognise the sovereignty of the Holy Roman Empire; the province accepts to submit to Münster, declaring dissolved the bond with the Dutch Republic.
July 8	The States General appoint Prince William III to Captain-General of the army and Admiral-General of the fleet.
July 9	Nijmegen surrenders after six days of siege.
July 11	The town of Coevorden falls after a six day siege: the resistance has lasted much longer than expected. The French siege fails at Bourtange.
July 18	Bernhard van Galen, Bishop of Münster, orders shelling of the city of Groningen.
July 23	Dutch lieutenant-general Hans Willem van Aylva retreats with the troops under his command to the north of Groningen.
August 4	Johan de Witt resigns as Grand Pensionary.
August 12	Johan de Witt and his brother Cornelis are murdered by the populace in The Hague.
Sep 27–28	The Dutch fail in the assault on Naarden.
October 11	Battle of Woerden, William III fails to seize the towns, but inflicts heavy casualties on the French relief corps.
November 27	French troops conquer Ameide, a village on the *waterlinie*, but withdraw after plundering the countryside.
December 15	The Dutch–Spanish army under William III besiege Charleroi, but are forced to raise the camp the day after.
December 30	Dutch troops from Groningen reconquer by surprise attack the fortified town of Coevorden.
Dec 29–31	French under the Duke of Luxembourg march to cross the frozen waterline but the ice proves too thin to support the passage of cavalry and carts.

1673

January 3–4	French troops seize control of Zwammerdam and Bodegraven, going on devastating lootings.
April 7	Elector of Brandenburg signs separate peace with France (Peace of Vossen).
June 7 and 14	The Dutch fleet defeats the French-English in the battles of Schoneveld.
June 17–18	The French lay siege to Maastricht; the Dutch garrison surrenders after 13 days.
July 1	Austrian emperor Leopold I signs alliance with Spain against France.
August 9	Dutch fleet under Vice-Admiral Evertsen seizes New York.
August 21	Admiral de Ruyter again defeats the Anglo-French fleet.
August 30	The Triple Alliance treaty is concluded by Austria, Spain, and the Dutch Republic.
September 3	Successful Dutch raid on Ferryland in Virginia.
September 13	The Dutch–Spanish army under William III recapture Naarden.
November 11	Bonn, in the Electorate of Cologne, surrenders to the Allied army.
December	The French evacuate Utrecht and other major towns in Overijssel and Gelderland, except Grave.

1674

February 13	The French under the Count of Navailles invade Franche-Comté.
February 19	Peace of Westminster, England retires from the war.
April 22	Bernhard von Galen, Prince-Bishop of Münster, signs peace with the Dutch Republic.
May 11	Elector of Cologne leaves the French side and signs for peace.
May 15	French army of the Franche-Comté seizes Besançon.
May 16	French army under Condé invades the Spanish Low Countries.
June 27	Dutch Admiral Tromp lands troops in Bretagne and plunders the suburbs of Dieppe and Bayonne.
July 20	de Ruyter's attempt to seize French possession of French Martinique is repulsed with heavy losses.
July 29	Prince William III besieges Grave; the French garrison surrenders on 27 October.
August 11	The battle engaged at Seneffe between Dutch–Spanish Imperialists and French results in heavy casualties for both sides.
September 16	The Allies besiege Oudenarde.
September 19	Condé crosses the River Scheldt at Tournay; the Allied army interrupts the siege of Oudenarde.

1675

February	Sweden invades Brandenburg.
March 31	French troops occupy Liège.
April	The Dutch navy seizes La Cayenne.
May 29	French conquests Dinant in the Spanish Low Countries.
June 6	Huy surrenders to the French.
June 10	Condé besieges Limburg, which surrenders on 21 June.
June 28	Elector of Brandenburg defeats the Swedes at Fehrbellin.
July 27	Turenne's death at Salzbach.

August 11 The French are defeated at the Battle of Konzer Brücke near Trier.
September 6 French garrison of Trier surrenders to Duke Charles IV of Lorraine.

1676
February French fleet retakes control of La Cayenne.
April 26 The town of Condé surrenders to the French.
May 2 The French besiege Bouchain, which falls nine days later.
July 8 The Allied army under William III lays siege to Maastricht, but he is forced to retreat on 27 August.
September 8 The Imperialists conquer Philippsburg.

1677
February 26 French admiral d'Estrées fails to seize Tobago.
March 3 French fleet of the Caribbean defeats the Dutch Squadron of Tobago.
April 11 Dutch–Spanish are defeated in the battle of Mont Cassel.
April 17–22 French army under Louis XIV and his brother Philippe seizes Cambrai and Saint-Omer.
August 10 Prince William III besieges Charleroi a second time, but he is forced again to leave the siege by Luxembourg's relief.
September Charles II of England promotes negotiation for a peace.
December 7 d'Estrées seizes Tobago.

1678
March 5 Ghent surrenders to the French.
March 26 Ypres is conquered by the French army.
May Conference to negotiate the peace opens at Nijmegen.
June 29 French blockade of Mons.
July 26 England and the States General sign alliance against France.
August 10 Charles II of England and the States General send an ultimatum to Louis XIV to accept the peace terms.
August 14 France and the Dutch delegates at Nijmegen sign a peace; the Battle of Saint-Denis is won by the Dutch–Spanish under William III.

1

Armies of the *Grand Siècle*

Introduction

The long reign of Louis XIV is usually referred in France as the 'Great Century'. With similar terms, the same period is conventionally celebrated as the 'Golden Age' of the United Provinces of the Netherlands. Both states reached the top of political supremacy, trade and arts, and constituted two opposing models in 17th century Europe. Important historians have written valuable works on this age, concentrating their research on both political and military subjects, which the latter, as everyone knows, represents the natural continuation of the first. Research has focused the final phase of this era, which includes fundamental events for the history of Europe, such as the War of the Grand Alliance and the Spanish Succession. However, both for France and for the Dutch Republic, these latter conflicts coincide with the beginning of their decline. On the other hand, the years from 1660 to 1687 have not been properly cleared, especially with regard to the evolution of armies, their development in modern permanent institutions, the evolution of equipment, weapons, and tactics, the variety of ensigns, and field signs. In fact, apart from the wars of the late 17th century, military recent historiography has rarely dealt with the conflicts fought after the Thirty Years' War and before the Grand Alliance of 1688–97.

It is harder to explain why historians of a more general cast of mind have not discussed military institutions and wars of this age to any great degree. Generations of military historians have claimed the age between the Thirty Years' War and the wars of the French Revolution as a period of 'limited warfare', and no historian laid more emphasis on this notion than did John Ulrich Nef.[1] The contention is that warfare, after a period typified by irrational, primarily religious, motivations, and fought with little constraint against enemy soldiers and unfortunate civilians alike, became more rational in its goals and more humane in its conduct. As religion ceased to be a primary motivation, war

1 'For Western Europe as a whole, years of war were still the rule, years of peace the exception. Yet there was more or less continuous moderation in the fierceness of the fighting.' John U. Nef, *War and Human Progress* (Cambridge, MA: W.W. Norton & Company, 1950), p. 155. The period he is discussing is 1640–1740 in a chapter entitled, 'Less Blood and More Money'.

1. Scene of a military camp in the Spanish Low Countries, by Joshua de Grave, 1675. (Rijksmuseum Library, Amsterdam)
After the Peace of Westphalia the armies of the major European powers became permanent. Manpower consumed the greater part of the military budgets. Although the soldier's life was nasty, brutish, ill-rewarded and short, it was no worse than the world he had left behind, where landless peasants starved in bad times. Joining up, with the prospect of wages, food and plunder might even have represented an improvement. Pay was so beggarly, and frequently months in arrears, that a soldier could not have supported himself from the basic daily remuneration, but it was augmented by an array of ***ex gratia*** payments. Officers were expected to support their men financially during times of hardship. Although a soldier's remittance was eaten into by deductions to his officers to pay for clothes, basic equipment and medicine, the average infantryman could accumulate sufficient money to buy food and drink from the authorised seller, gamble, if permitted, and some voluntuary items like shoes, undercoat and cloak.

became more a question of dynastic politics, and regimes fought not to destroy one another but simply for limited territorial or economic gain. At the same time, better military administration relieved the pressures that drove soldiers to prey on towns and villages just to survive, and laws of war regulated the conduct of armies towards civilians. This thesis encountered success in the more recent historiography too,[2] and the popular vulgate continued to consider this period like the age of the *guerre en dentelle* ('war in lace').

Only a few historians turn seriously to this matter writing as something other than a means of memorialising the past, mining it for moral examples, or employing it to abstract rules and principles. Authoritative scholars studied the *Grand Siècle* and produced major biographies, histories, and collections of documents, while the increasing accessibility to the archives facilitated the research of unpublished sources and original accounts. Now the scenario appears more complex: wars continued to be frequent, religion

2 See Alessandro Barbero, *La Guerra in Europa dal Rinascimento a Napoleone* (Roma: Carocci, 2003), p. 39: 'The war, in this era, shows very different characteristics from the fierce religious wars of the previous age. This is partly because the Enlightenment culture deeply influences the actions of the governments and the commanders themselves: increasingly, the war between European countries is fought by common accord and following formal rules that aspire to be scientific and civilized.'

retained its importance in the eastern conflicts between Poles, Swedes and Russians, and much more religious hate moved Austria and her allies against the Ottomans, or the Dukes of Savoy against the Valdese. On some fronts, the exercise of violence reached an intensity not less than that in darkest periods in the European history. Hungarian, Bosnian, Serbian and Greek peasants and townsmen would not agree to consider the Ottoman campaigns of 1683–99 as a low-intensity conflict, and not even the inhabitants of the Valdese valleys could subscribe to this version after the persecution of 1688–89, with its corollary of destruction and cruelty, surely not inferior to the excesses committed during the Thirty Years' War. Also with regard to the strategic-political aspects, these formulations appear wrong if referring to the whole European context. Historians' critics point to the assault on the United Provinces of the Netherlands in 1672, as one designed to eliminate the Dutch Republic, not simply to defeat it. Similarly, in 1684 Austria, Poland, Russia, and Venice joined them in the Holy League to expel the Ottomans from Europe and conquer Constantinople.

After 1660, wars changed in intensity but not in some simple sense of moving from 'total war' to 'controlled war'.[3] Possibly these conflicts, coldly planned by governments in the secrecy of their cabinets, no longer give rise to the same passions as the campaigns of the Thirty Years' War or the Napoleonic era. Late 17th-century warfare is often seen as a cumbersome and antiquated procedure, with almost theatrical cadences. Actually, in this age, war is conceived above all as an instrument available to the state, a perfectly legitimate means of resolving international disputes. Ideally, war becomes a branch of politics, a resource to be used wisely and trying to avoid negative conequences as much as possible for society and the economy: war becomes a matter for professional actors.

Changes within the army during the period 1660–1687 are thought not to be seen as isolated developments but as part of an important evolution that affected several European powers. If we observe what has happened in terms of technological innovations and tactical experimentation, and how many European societies have been affected by radical processes of economic and political transformation, it becomes impossible not to consider this period as one of the most interesting and complex in the whole of military history.

The idea to write about the armies of this age started after the reading of the John Albert Lynn's classic *Giant of the Grand Siècle*. This ambitious programme wants to represent the ideal continuation and expansion of the concept expressed in 1997 by this authoritative work. With great effectiveness, Lynn described the French army of the Sun King as 'The Great Unknown'.[4] Despite the interest in this historical period, which also recently attracted the attention of novelists and screenwriters, the French army of the Sun King, as a subject for historical inquiry, has attracted the attention of only a few diligent

3 John A. Lynn, *Giant of the Grand Siècle. The French Army, 1610–1715* (Cambridge: Cambridge University Press, 1997), pp. 10–11.

4 *Ibid*, p. ix: 'It is easier to prove that few have seen the giant than to explain why. An understanding of this disregard, such selective blindness, must account for, first, those with a predisposition to regard the history of war as something of inherent interest or practical value and, second and more importantly, those with a broader view of the past for its own sake.'

scholars and talented amateurs, but it has never been in the spotlight.[5] Such neglect seems all the more bizarre given the self-evident importance of the subject and same destiny has occurred with the other armies of this age with few exceptions.[6]

This series focuses the years between 1660 and 1687 for several reasons. This age registers the coming of age of Louis XIV, personality who marked deeply this period and established the structure of the French army for almost two centuries. Though the great king actually begun his personal reign in 1661, after the death of Prime Minister Mazzarino, in 1659 he took his first steps in European Diplomacy with the Peace of the Pyrenees. Moreover, we should not forget that, some years before, the young prince had appeared in the role of the sun in the *Ballet de la Nuit*, joining indissolubly to the star his image as monarch: his royal person becomes an element of political propaganda, a concept that today appears of extraordinary modernity. Nevertheless, 1660 is also a deliberate citation. The choice refers to authoritative works,[7] and is adopted without any suggestion that the period was either radically different to what had come before and crucial to the development of modern warfare. The period includes a lapse of time that is the natural prelude to this age: in 1654 was signed the peace between England and the Dutch Republic, which fought for conquering the naval supremacy and the control of worldwide trade in the first of their three wars; while in 1655, the First Northern War involved in a few years several states not only of northern Europe, but saw the significant participation of a Central European power like Austria. This latter conflict provoked the intervention of the Ottoman Empire, while the First Anglo-Dutch War saw both greater interaction between different parts of the world and the rise of European influence and power in America and Asia.[8] Moreover, these two wars were strictly linked, as demonstrated by the Dutch decision to attack the Swedish fleet that was besieging Copenhagen. The year

5 Apart from the contributions of John Lynn and André Courvoisier, more recently some research about the army in the age of Louis XIV have been the subject of extensive works. Among the most considerable there are Jean-Philippe Cénat, *Le Roi Stratège: Louis XIV et la direction de la guerre (1661–1715)* (Rennes: Pu Rennesm 2010); Olivier Chaline, *Les Armées du Roi: Le grand chantier, XVIIe–XVIIIe siècle* (Paris: Armand Colin, 2016), and Rémi Masson, *Défendre le Roi: La Maison Militaire au XVIIe siècle* (Ceyzérieu: Champ Vallon, 2017).

6 Lynn, *Giant of the Grand Siècle*, p. xiii: 'The 17th century brought constant and important evolution in military institutions and practices, but attempts to study this change only through examinations that deal with it during a short time span distort its coherent and often gradual nature. Perhaps such distortion comes as a nearly unavoidable by product of the emphasis on biographies, since such works try to encompass a major subject within the decades of an individual's active life. Biography not only encapsulates history; the biographer tends to champion his or her subject.'

7 The most significant works which use this dates as watershed are: Christopher Duffy, *Siege Warfare vol. 1: The Fortress in the Early Modern World, 1494–1660* and the following *Siege Warfare vol. 2: The Fortress in the Age of Vauban and Frederick the Great, 1660–1789*. Among the authors who pointed out several works on this period, there are Robert A. Doughty and Ira D. Gruber, *Warfare in the Western World. Military Operations from 1660 to 1871* and Jeremy Black with his *European Warfare, vol. 1* and *2*, *European Warfare in a Global Context, 1660–1815* and (with Stephen Morillo and Paul Lococo) *War in World History Vol. 1* and *2*.

8 'It was through the projection of European power that the "Old World" and the "New World" were connected, and indeed that the "New World" was created as an idea as first, Spain and Portugal, and later, England, France and the Dutch conquered and settled important portions of North and South America.' Black, *European Warfare, vol. I, 1494–1660* (London: UCL Press, 1994), p. ix.

1659 saw the end of a 24-year conflict between the Bourbon kings of France and the Habsburg rulers of Spain, as well as the end of the aforementioned First Northern War, and with it Swedish expansion, as well as republican rule in the British Isles. Finally, the year 1660 also marks the end of the military revolution originally discerned by Michael Roberts. The series closes in 1687, and this year is exactly the eve of the 'Glorious Revolution' of England and the War of the Grand Alliance.

This choice is provocative, because with these two events starts a phase that marks the beginning of the decline of Louis XIV's dominance and, above all, closes the phase of consolidation of the modern standing armies.

The Rise of the Modern Standing Armies

> War is no longer an accident but a trade, and they that will be anything in it must serve a long apprenticeship to it. Human wit and industry has raised it to such a perfection, and it is grown to such a piece of manage that it requires people to make it their whole employment. (Daniel Defoe, *A Brief Reply to the History of Standing Armies in England*, 1698, p. 1)

During the 17th century, Europe experienced only four years of general peace: 1610 and 1680–82. This scenario of almost continuous strife provided the terrain for the rise of the standing professional armies. The states were eager to avoid a repetition of the chaos and destruction that had plagued Europe during the Thirty Years' War, and therefore invested in these larger, more powerful armies to reduce the risks and costs of war. Some historians considered this act as one of the most important institutional developments of the early modern world.[9] The permanent armies became an organic feature of the Old Regime, a symbol of power, and strength, the means by which the prince could defend his interests and play an active role in international policy. This change dates from approximately the first half of the 17th century, although the first standing armies are much older.[10] Some monarchs and rulers in the ancient era instituted the first professional armies, with soldiers, and cavalrymen paid for their service, rather than a militia of

9 'The bitter experience of the Thirty Years' War had taught the monarchs that they could not entrust the protection of their states to unreliable feudal levies or disorderly bands of mercenary soldiers who were recruited only during a military emergency and dismissed immediately at its conclusion. What was required was an army of systematically trained and well-disciplined professionals, maintained both in peace and in war, in winter as well as in summer, with a regular means of obtaining supplies and replacement, bound directly and indissolubly to the state and paid by it.' John Anthony Mears, 'The Emergence of the Standing Professional Army in Seventeenth-Century Europe', in *Social Science Quarterly*, vol. 50, No 1, June 1969, p. 106.

10 The first known standing armies in Europe were in Ancient Greece and Macedon. The male citizen body of ancient Sparta functioned as professional soldiers, unlike all other *poleis* (city states), whose armies were citizen militias. The existence of an enslaved population of Helots liberated the Spartiates from the need to work for the subsistence, enabling them to focus their time and energy on military training. Philip of Macedonia raised the most successful professional army of the ancient era, and Rome is also considered to have been a standing army since the late Republican age.

2. From the series of Illustrated Proverbs issued by Giuseppe Maria Mitelli, 1670. (Author's archive)

Poor pay, remorseless drill and brutal conditions of service further increased the 'proletarianisation' of the army. Little wonder that voluntary enlistment in return for a substantial bounty was less and less adequate for filling the ranks. Trickery, brute force and, eventually, a new system of conscription, which pressed increasingly hard on the ruler's own subjects, were all employed to provide rank-and-file soldiers. These conditions and the consequent lack of motivation made soldiers desert in unexpectedly high numbers. During the Thirty Years' War soldiers deserted to try their luck with the supposedly better-paid, better-supplied or victorious enemy. From the second half of the century, military service became the main reason why deserters wanted to escape service and potential recruits to avoid it, for instance, with self mutilation. However, the army continued to be a place of refuge for overwhelming problems in civilian life. On the whole, it was the new forms of compulsory recruitment which created a negative attitude towards service in the army. Deserters, if recruited from the province, were now welcomed back by the population and even protected from persecution, in contrast to the attacks on army stragglers by peasants during the Thirty Years' War.

men who mostly farmed the land for subsistence and occasionally mustered for campaigns. According to the conditions expressed before, the ancient Greek and Roman armies were both true standing armies also for their role in society: a key factor for the concept of 'modern standing armies'.[11]

Some scholars affirm that Spain created Europe's first standing army of the modern era through the creation of the infantry *tercios* by Emperor Charles V of Habsburg (otherwise known as Charles I of Spain). Certainly, the *tercios* revolutionised modern warfare in Europe and became the most prestigious and undefeated military force during the era of Spanish Habsburg dominance in Europe. Eventually, all European armies would try to adopt style and tactics of fighting introduced by the *tercios* because of their constant innovative evolution that was sparked by creative veteran soldiers and their officers. However, in several aspects, the *tercios* should be considered permanent corps, and not standing armies,[12] which usually

11 See also John Keegan, *A History of Warfare*, 'Rome: Mother House of the Modern Armies' (New York: Vintage Books, 1993), p. 263.

12 In Western Europe, the first actual standing army was established by Charles the Bold, the Duke of Burgundy, in 1471, after the creation of the *Compagnies d'Ordonnance*. In addition, in the 1460s the Hungarian king, Matthias Corvinus, created a considerable standing army called *Fekete Sereg*.

included also cavalry, artillery, and logistics. Furthermore, just as there were limitations on the creation of true standing armies before the 17th century, there were similar limitations on the professionalisation of officers and the standardisation of armies.[13] Cash shortages often limited the standardisation of equipment and contributed significantly to poor standards of discipline. Unpaid mercenaries deserted or turned into a plundering mob at the first opportunity on campaign. Revolts by armies were almost non-existent, but mutinies – essentially, strikes – were common: the Spanish army in the Low Countries mutinied almost annually in some periods of the war there.

More convincingly, other authors suggest that the first modern standing army in Europe was the *kapikulu* corps of the Ottoman Empire, which included several specialties of soldiers and logistic apparatus too, paid for their service month-round. Interestingly, some coeval observers contrasted European standards of discipline in the 16th century unfavourably with those of the Porte's soldiers. The Ottoman army continued to be for centuries a redoubtable enemy to the Christian states, as well as its role in the society became more and more relevant, but never was a model in Europe, except for some life guard corps and tactics.[14] An actual standing army is a permanent, often professional, army. It is composed of full-time soldiers who may be either career soldiers or conscripts, and overall is not disbanded during times of peace. It differs from army reserves, which are enlisted for the long term, but activated only during wars or political crisis, and temporary armies, which are raised from the civilian population only during a conflict or threat of war and disbanded once the war or threat is over. Standing armies tend to be better equipped, better trained, and better prepared for emergencies, defensive deterrence, and particularly, war campaigns.

Although France, Sweden, Spain, and Austria had founded permanent corps during the later 16th and early 17th centuries, after 1648 the formation of standing armies intensified. By the middle of the 17th century, the first standing armies had been formed, more or less made up of professional soldiers, completing a process begun in the 16th century and providing a permanent army of social prestige and relevance. In the opinion of many contemporaries, it offered an opportunity to exploit strategic knowledge, to examine the effectiveness of military tactics and become aware of the increasing importance of the overall organisation of the army. It would allow the military classes to occupy a significant place inside the major European powers. Even the poorest recruit could rise through the social ranks thanks to his occupation in the army and the prestige that could arise from his military career.

---

13 'Mercenary service also undermined standardization in terms of uniforms, as independent mercenary soldiers objected to the servile implications of uniform dress.' Jeremy Black, *War in World History, Society, Technology, and War from Ancient Times to the Present* (New York: McGraw-Hill, 2009), p. 309.

14 In 1670, Poland raised a Janissary corps as palace guard for the King, while in the 16th century the Hungarian *huszár* light cavalry adopted and improved the Ottoman tactics introduced by *akincy* and *dely* raiders.

Alongside the rise of the standing armies and the birth of a new social class, burst into this scenario the military leaders: the commanders. History claims a long series of successful military leaders since the antique age. In this regard, it is interesting to outline Napoleon's opinion about the greater commanders of the past. He considered Alexander the Great, Hannibal, Julius Caesar, Gustavus Adolphus, Prince Eugene of Savoy, and Frederick I of Prussia as the best military commanders of the history. It is significant that, after Julius Cesar, and before Gustavus Adolphus, he considered any captain worthy of being celebrated alongside the aforementioned personalities. Equally significant, the first commander reputed as a great military leader is one who lived in the 17th century. The long pause between the ancient age and the 17th century in the matter of military leaders denotes the subordinate role embodied by soldiers in the coeval society compared to the princes and the aristocracy, and their limited influx in the cultural context throughout the Middle Ages and Renaissance. Moreover, in the second half of the 17th century, the military professions experienced a further transformation and now armies consisted not only of 'professional' soldiers but also of 'specialists', like grenadiers, dragoons, engineers, and artillerymen, managed by officers who applied the new scientific theory ranging from physics and mathematics: after being an art, now war began to be considered a science. In the same period, the fleets achieved equally important success in armament, sailing technique, and tactics. It is no coincidence that from the middle of the century there was a blossoming of scientific and theoretical treaties related to war and the way of conducting armies according to criteria derived from experimentation and direct experience. War was now analysed according to principles coherent with the modern scientific investigation inaugurated by Galileo, to get to the astonishing aphorisms of Raimondo Montecuccoli and his visionary insights on the functions of armies and their management.[15] In the same way, the theoretical investigation in matter of siegecraft produced the fundamental studies of Vauban and van Coehoorn, which not only influenced coeval warfare but also that of the following century.

Usually, in Western Europe, we find at least two prerequisites for the creation of a standing army. The first was a centralised political power capable not only of overcoming opposition from the local representatives of the Estates, often reluctant to grant a prince the powers of taxation required for the maintenance of permanent troops. In this process, the prince had also to subdue the mercenary colonels who were expected to relinquish their rights as free recruiting masters and subordinate themselves to the monarch's authority.[16] The second was adequate financial resources, dependent upon the wealth of the prince's territories and his ability to collect taxes without the consent of the Estates. Wars remained frequent and protracted, rendering reliance upon mercenaries, expensive, but garrisoning

15 See in Raimondo Luraghi, in *Edizione critica delle Opere di Raimondo Montecuccoli* (Ufficio Storico SME, Rome: vol. I and II, 1988). Today, it is factual that Montecuccoli's thought, as well as Sun Tzu, can be apply not only with politics, but also even with the corporate management and marketing.

16 Mears, 'The Emergence of the Standing Professional Armies', p. 106.

sophisticated fortifications and defending frontiers. The concept of a linear border had emerged already during the late 16th century, and presented rulers with the new problem of meeting extensive peacetime commitments. The solution was to raise permanent troops and pay the bill from taxation. Throughout Europe, social, and political development was uneven and diverse. States' constitutional paths were shaped as much by prior political structures, economic developments, and internal bargaining as by defensive necessity, and military innovation issued from not just strong central monarchies, as in France, or Spain, but smaller German states of varying political persuasions and decentralised polities like the Dutch Republic. The advance and limitations of government power especially to 1660 are well illustrated by the history of standing armies, where permanently maintained forces have continuity in units and administration.

There is a direct correlation between the reappearance of economic growth and the formation of disciplined military force in Europe, because war has been always matter of money, and whoever has more wins.[17] To face an external threat becomes now an exercise of financial balances, taxes, and resources useful for raising disciplined military forces. This process involved several aspects, such as organisation, tactics, equipment and dress: standing armies are now expansive states' instruments, which require to be identified among the civilians, avoiding the risk of desertion, with special symbols like ensigns and, of course, uniforms. Under certain aspects, the dawn of uniform marked the final stage of the birth of the standing armies, and despite the differences existing in the establishment of armies in the various European states, the uniform, also in its primitive appearance, constitutes the most evident sign of the beginning of a new age.

Social bonds among soldiers were strengthened further by the fact that after 1648 standing armies encouraged long-term enlistment and reenlistment. Once assigned to a particular unit, a soldier might therefore spend many years in the ranks, sharing experiences with long-time comrades. This allowed sentiments of group solidarity to become firmly fixed and transformed small army units into effective primary communities: every experienced commander knew that a single company composed of veterans was more effective than two of new recruits.

Reciprocity, fashion, and necessity also accounted for the spread of the standing army. Within a few years of the Peace of Westphalia, most states began to organise permanent defence forces, sometimes recruited from militias, which remained useful as local police forces, alongside old feudal levies. Mercenaries continued to be employed, but under contractual bases.[18]

17 *Ibid.*

18 Some authors point out that several aspects of the standing armies' management after 1648, had been anticipated by the Italian states of the Renaissance, such as Milan, Venice and Florence. Government control of salary and supplies, regular payment of the soldiers with funds derived from tax revenues, along with differentiation and tactical coordination of infantry, cavalry and artillery all were shared between 15th century Italian city states, and the same goal was achieved by Le Tellier and his son Louvois after 1661: 'The French Secretary of War, in supplying the army, regularizing its structure and standardizing equipment, can be closely paralleled by the work of the little known Venetian *provveditore* Belpetro Masselini (in office 1418–55), who did the same

The military establishment was now transformed into some kind of public institution. What had been a private business regulated by bilateral contracts became service to the prince, even for the ordinary soldier, who rather than volunteering for a limited period, was increasingly forced to serve for life or until he became unfit. The traditional obligation for the subject to hold the defence of the state, for a limited period, and within the borders, turned into an obligation to serve in the standing army without any geographical restrictions as a home defence system and the regular armed forces began to merge.

With the most numerous population in Europe, in the mid 17th century France fielded one of the largest armies of this age. Short before the Peace of the Pyrenees, in 1659, the young Louis XIV disposed approximately 120,000–125,000 soldiers.[19] Even in the 1660s many regiments had been licensed, and Louis XIV's army could still count on being a formidable instrument of war, which represented the most significant fighting force in Europe.[20] It might indeed appear that the French army of the later 17th century had moved away from the murky motivations and private enterprise of warlords and general contractors, to be replaced by forces whose state-controlled organisational and operational characteristics would be recognisable into the following centuries. Following his announcement in 1661 that he would henceforth rule in person, Louis XIV's highest priority was the reform of the army to bring it under direct royal authority and to make it an effective instrument of government policy.

The results purportedly represent one of the great military success stories of early modern Europe. In 1667, 70,000 infantry and 35,000 cavalry swept aside the defences of the Spanish Low Countries, while between 1672 and 1678 the army, expanded up to an operational strength of 250,000, almost conquered the United Provinces in a single campaign, then held its own against a strong European coalition for a further six years. The French army expanded to become the largest military institution in the world, surpassing even the Ottoman army in the next 30 years. As a dominant political and cultural power, and because Louis XIV expressed his power also through the medium of his military strength, the French model was soon followed by other monarchs, and this despite being done through his pursuit of personal glory. Louis XIV was perceived by neighbour states as an enemy intent on amending the Peace of Westphalia. France, attacking with ever-larger armies, was opposed by states obliged to augment their own military forces. Smaller states, which could raise only limited numbers of troops, sheltered within anti-French coalitions whose major powers recruited, or hired, large contingents of troops to face the French army that climbed above 400,000 men in the last decade of the century.

Since the earlier phase, French lines inspired most of the European powers in the formation of permanent forces. In 1645, England's New Model

for the troops that defended the Republic of Saint Mark.' William McNeill, *The Pursuit of Power: Technology, Armed Force, and Society Since A.D. 1000* (Chicago: Chicago University, 1984), p. 135.

19 Lynn, *Giant of the Grand Siècle*, p. 7.

20 General L. Susane, *Histoire de l'Infanterie Française* (Paris, 1853), vol. I, p. 192.

Army initially consisted of 7,600 cavalry, including one regiment of dragoons, and 14,400 infantry.[21] The execution of Charles I in 1649 ushered in 11 years of republican rule during which the New Model Army was the pillar of political authority. By July 1652, the Commonwealth government had over 70,000 men in arms in England, Scotland, and Ireland, reducing to 53,000 in 1654, 42,000 in 1658, and 28,342 in 1660.[22] The restored monarch, Charles II Stuart, disbanded the New Model in 1660 and 1661, but to secure his regime raised a new standing army of two foot and two cavalry regiments, plus a considerable number of garrison companies, for an overall total of 8,865 professional soldiers by 1685, 19,778 in 1686, and 22,364 in 1687, while to face William of Orange's invasion in November 1688, the royal army was increased to 34,320.[23]

Not much different the trajectory followed by Spain. After the Peace of the Pyrenees in 1659, King Philipp IV maintained on the paper a regular force of 29,000 foot and 14,000 horse.[24] This core continued to increase with new regiments under his son Charles II, in order to face the external threats in Portugal, Low Countries, and colonies, while in the same period, the *tercios fijos* (fixed regiments) for the first time were introduced on a territorial basis. Financial shortage and declining policy as major powers, caused the disbanding of several units, but in 1668, when France opened the War of Devolution, the Spanish army theoretically numbered 41,000 infantrymen and 18,000 cavalrymen and dragoons,[25] after the enlistment of native Spanish or Walloon recruits and foreign mercenaries in Germany, Italy, Ireland, England, and even in Lorraine. When in 1669 the Peace of Aix-la-Chapelle closed hostilities, the Spanish army deployed about 70,000 men,[26] who had faced – with poor results – enemies in Catalonia, Franche-Comté, Low Countries, and Portugal. Here in 1659, the Portuguese fielded about 18,000 foot and 5,000 horse, formed by mixture of peasant conscripts and mercenaries, foreigners included. Two years after, the field army in Alentejo numbered about 10,000 men, able to successfully face the Spanish army alongside the garrisons along the wide border between the states.[27]

Further major enemy powers of France constituted peculiar cases, such as Austria, which took its own path to the formation of the standing army. At the end of the Thirty Years' War, the House of Austria maintained a fighting force of just 25,000 men, comprising infantry, cavalry, and artillery. It was a relatively small but well-experienced force, which had been campaigning for

21 J.W. Fortescue, *A History of the British Army* (London: Macmillan, 1906), vol. I, p. 249.

22 R. Manning, *An Apprenticeship in Arms – The Origin of the British Army 1585–1702* (Oxford University Press: Oxford, 2006), pp. 186–188.

23 *Ibid.*, p. 201.

24 Conde de Clonard, *Historia Orgánica de las Armas de Infanteria y Caballeria* (Madrid, 1853), vol. IV, pp. 458–463.

25 *Ibid.*, p. 468

26 C. Storrs, *The Resilience of the Spanish Monarchy, 1665–1700* (Oxford: Oxford University Press, 2006), p. 17.

27 Arquivo Nacional da Torre do Tombo, *Conselho de Guerra, Consultas*, 1661, maço 21, 'Relação dos Officiais, e Soldados da Infantaria e Cauallaria deste Ex[érci]to que se acha effectiua, Conforme consta dos roes de Lista da ultima m[ost]ra, que se lhes passou na maneira seguinte.'

many years under skilled commanders like Piccolomini and Montecuccoli. Some regiments had already been in existence for many years and certain units continued to be part of the Habsburg army until its dissolution in 1918. The Austrian army began its expansion in 1655–58 through the formation of new infantry regiments, followed one year later by further new units. This significant rise was a direct reaction to the emergency unfolding with the proximity of the First Northern War in the Baltic (1655–60). When in February 1658 the Habsburg Emperor was setting up his contingent to support Poland against Sweden, the army marching to Pomerania deployed 14,447 men.[28] Further troops were in Italy to support Spain against the French. The larger part of this force was licensed between 1659 and 1660, following the decreasing emergency in Poland and the Peace of the Pyrenees, but soon new regiments were formed or hired from other German states. In 1662, the theoretical force of the Austrian Habsburgs army was 30,345 infantrymen, 10,180 cuirassiers and 2,754 dragoons.[29] In 1663, when the war against the Ottoman Porte seemed inevitable, the army increased its strength again with more troops, included the first 'regular' regiments of Croatian light horsemen, and Hungarian *huszár*, with both opening a long and dense history in the Imperial army.

Alongside Austria, Holy Roman-Germanic Empire represented a very creative laboratory in the formation of standing armies. Though most of the states deployed little contingents compared to Austria, Germany became the European forge of soldiers. In the second half of the 17th century, Germany became the most militarised region of Europe, surpassing Switzerland for the quantity of mercenaries serving in other states. This trading of men affected several rulers, from the major electors to small princes like Ansbach-Bayreuth and Hohenlohe.

All the German armies raised in this period contained features that could trace their origins to the previous century, combined with town militias, paid professional garrison troops, and feudal levies. These forces were primarily defensive, reflecting not only the inability of any ruler to maintain large, combat-ready field forces, or the deeply rooted belief that starting offensive wars was unchristian, but especially because the strong political limitations imposed by the Westphalia Treaty. Campaigns to punish wrongdoers or fight the Ottomans were mounted by mobilising the levies, augmented by additional professional soldiers. These latter became more important with the spread of new weapons technology, requiring large disciplined units to be truly effective. However, such professionals were expensive, and princes pressed their estates to increase their tax grant to cover the escalating costs of war. In Austria and Bohemia as well as in Bavaria and Tyrol, old feudal obligations were gradually modified, transforming limited personal service by noble vassals and peasants into either cash payments or enlistment in militias, organised, and trained in new tactics. In northern Germany, militiamen were incorporated as field units to supplement the mercenaries

28 *Theatrum Europeum*, vol. 8 (Frankfurt am Main, 1693), pp. 1051–1052.

29 Alphons von Wrede, *Geschichte der K. und K. Wehrmacht* (Wien, 1898–1901), vol. I, pp. 34–37.

or increasingly, from the 1660s onwards, used as a recruitment pool for what were becoming permanent field formations. In the same period, the Münster Bishopric emerged alongside Brandenburg and the Guelph duchies (Brunswick-Wolfenbüttel, Brunswick-Lüneburg Celle and Brunswick-Lüneburg Kalemberg) as states capable of fielding 18,000–25,000 men, though the normal average strength was closer to 5,000. The electorates of Bavaria, Saxony and Palatinate each had 2,000–3,500 men more or less permanently under arms by the mid 1660s and retained the capacity to double these figures with additional recruits and militia. The Duchy of Holstein-Gottorp displayed 1–2,000 permanent troops, while other middling secular principalities such as Pfalz-Neuburg, Württemberg, Hessen-Kassel, Mecklenburg, Würzburg, and the Ernestine Duchies of Saxony were beginning to add professional soldiers to their garrison companies. Most Imperial cities also maintained permanent infantry units, although only Bremen, Hamburg and to a lesser extent Nuremberg and Augsburg had much more than 800–1,000 men at any one time. Several ecclesiastical states too were at the forefront of these developments, with Mainz, Cologne, Trier, and the aforementioned Bishopric of Münster emerging as those maintaining the most powerful forces. The three electorates were linked by personal rule to other bishoprics, expanding their resource base and permitting the maintenance of 1,500–2,000 permanent troops by the 1670s, along with the construction of modern fortifications. In addition, the minor bishoprics such as Würzburg, Salzburg, and Osnabrück followed this path in matter of permanent troops, but with smaller contingents. This scenario caused a deep separation in the *Reich*, obviously regarding the relevance, and political weight of the armed princes against the unarmed ones.[30]

Alongside the permanent units recruited by the states, the Holy Roman-Germanic Empire continued to deploy a relic from the past like the troops of the *Reichskreise* (Imperial Circles): Franconian, Swabian, Bavarian, Upper Rhenish, Electoral Rhenish, Westphalian, Lower Saxon, Upper Saxon, Austrian, and Burgundian circle. These ancient institutions constituted an autonomous way to maintain the original military force of the Empire, notwithstanding the limitation of Westphalia. It is surprising how the *Kreise* survived despite the changed political conditions which occurred after 1648. However, the persistent and only apparently anachronistic existence of the *Kreis* was due principally to the growing threat from France than from the strengthening of Imperial authority. The need to face France to the west and the Ottoman Empire to the south-east favoured a development of the *Kreis* system. At the same time, a distinction between armed, and unarmed territories was beginning to emerge, as many of the weaker princes paid stronger neighbours to take over their obligations for raising the contingents. This occurred in Swabia, for instance, where Württemberg, Baden, Fürstenberg, Ulm, Augsburg, and Esslingen all fielded small corps of permanent troops on behalf of other *Kreis* members, many of whom had been reluctant to contribute at all; while in the Franconian

30 Peter Wilson, *German Armies, War and German Politics, 1648–1806* (London: Routledge, 1998), pp. 26–28.

Circle the association of even small states was able to field a sufficiently trained contingent, and to enter in campaign like the regiments of larger states with a more deeply rooted military tradition. Nonetheless, the composite formation of the contingents remained a characteristic of the corps raised by the circles. The basic establishment of the circles of 24,000, known as the *simplum*, was revised upwards to 12,000 horse and 28,000 foot in 1681; when more troops were required, the *simplum* became *duplum* (double) or, more rarely, *triplum* (triple). This latter was invoked in 1664 to counter the Ottoman advance in Hungary and again in 1683, when Merzifonlu Kara Mustafa besieged Vienna. Part of the contingent coming from Swabia, Franconia, Upper Rhine, and Lower Saxony, the army of the Circles was normally ill trained, badly disciplined, and indifferently commanded. Larger states donated their worst regular units because they were usually under some political obligation or mercenary treaty opposed to Imperial interests. Consequently, most of the contingents of the Imperial circles were destined to garrison or reserve tasks, influencing the strategy of the Imperial commanders, especially on the Rhenish front in all wars against France.

Alhough in Germany wars conditioned and developed the formation of the standing armies, in other European regions were experienced different solutions. In Italy, the Duchy of Savoy-Piedmont developed a significant field army of approximately 6,700 men in 1664, which constantly increased to 26,178 men in 1672 for the war against Genoa. Despite the limitations due to French interference, the Savoy-Piedmont army continued to strengthen its force. Because it controlled the Alpine passes from France and Switzerland into the Po valley, the Duchy required means of self-defence as it was continually exposed to and involved in disputes between France and the Spanish holdings in northern Italy. Alongside Savoy-Piedmont, also Venice deployed a significant standing force formed by professional soldiers. In the mid 17th century, the 'Most Serene' Republic was engaging in the bitter struggle against the Porte for the possession of Crete, and therefore maintained the largest army in Italy, with more than 25,000 professional soldiers in the 1660s, including native recruits, Italians from other states, and foreign mercenaries from Switzerland, the Grisons, France, and Germany. The composite army, formed mainly by footmen, was employed until 1669 in Crete, Dalmatia, Italy, or was embarked on the fleet, which was reputedly one of the most powerful in the Mediterranean.

Apart these two major powers, most of the smaller Italian states disposed of troops unable to march and perform an active campaign. During the last decades of the 17th century, the Papal States maintained a garrison army of approximately 4,500 soldiers, including the ancient corps of the Pope's Life Guards formed by Swiss recruited in the Catholic cantons, while between 1660 and 1670 Genoa possessed 3,500 garrison troops, and Tuscany 2,500 on average. Further standing troops for garrison duty and life guards, usually formed by professional soldiers or nobles, were raised by Modena with 260, Parma and Piacenza 200, Mantua 100, and Lucca approximately 110. Status symbols of this size were of limited utility, although they provided the ruler with a police force and a reservoir of patronage. Though governed by the international order of the Knights of Saint John, Malta belonged to the Italian geo-strategic scenario and unlike the Italian states, the island remained constantly belligerent through the century. The Order, for its struggle against the Ottomans and their North African allies, had deployed a standing force already in the beginning of the 17th century. In 1660s, the Maltese Grand Master managed a force of 2,000 foot soldiers and about 400 knights, who sailed each year on board the fleet for their campaign in the Eastern Mediterranean, as Venice's allies, or in autonomy.[31]

Despite the limited forces deployed, the Italian scenario shows the most original solutions in fact of standing troops, even just for defensive tasks. With a population of about 12,500,000 of inhabitants, the Italian states managed a force of 250,000 militiamen.[32] The male population was enlisted in different proportion from one state to another, with a status that varied in relation to the service required; however the arrangement was in some cases very close to a standing force, such as happened in the ancient Tuscan *Bande* or the Venetian *Cernide*, *Craine* and *Proli*, until the most recent Savoy-Piedmont *Battaglioni*. Usually, the militia's ranks were obviously conditioned by the physiological setback of strength and effectiveness, but these figures represent an interesting example of compulsory military service in the early modern age.[33]

The Italian militia system was not affected by shortage of manpower, however even more diffused forms of conscription were introduced in less populous countries. Lacking sufficient economic and human resources, Scandinavian states were the first to regularise conscription in both peace and war. Every 10 peasant farms on royal lands, or 20 on estates belonging to the aristocracy, were arranged into a *rota* (file). Commissioners supervised an annual conscription assembly, which had to be attended by all inhabitants; absentees were automatically drafted. Men who could be spared from agriculture were preferred, such as younger sons of farmers, although there were numerous exempt categories including miners, armaments workers, and the only sons of widows. In the 1660s, the *rota* system had to allow the formation of an army of 40–45,000 men. The results were below expectations, because conscripts were reluctant to serve; therefore, Sweden continued to rely upon mercenaries. However, the *rota* system, which actually created a territorial rather than a standing army, probably inspired later schemes in some German states, in Austria, and in Denmark.

Between 1663 and 1679, Denmark relied upon a mixture of peasant conscripts and mercenaries. However, in the last years of the century, Frederick IV possessed a standing army of 33,500, mostly German mercenaries: 23,000 were stationed in Denmark and 10,500 in Norway.

Two major powers not directly involved in the Thirty Years' War, Poland, and Russia, also created their own standing armies. Poland's vast territories stretched from the Baltic in the north to the borders of Hungary in the

31 Fr. Bartolomeo F. Piloni, *Historia della Sacra Religione Militare di S. Giovanni Gerosomilitano, detta di Malta* (Venice, 1715), pp. 368–401.

32 Luciano Pezzolo, ' *"Le Arme Proprie" in Italia nel Cinque e nel Seicento*', in T. Fanfani (ed.) *Saggi di storia economica. Studi in onore di Amelio Tagliaferri* (Pacini: Pisa 1998), p. 56.

33 On this topic see Livio Antonelli and Claudio Donati (eds.), *Corpi armati e ordine pubblico in Italia (XVI–h XIX sec.)* (Rubettino: Catanzaro, 2003).

south and from Muscovy in the east, to Brandenburg–Prussia in the west. Paradoxically, Polish society was substantially militarised, yet the state was unable to defend itself adequately against these highly predatory neighbours. The principal difficulty was the size and political independence of the Polish nobility.[34] Although royal rents financed a standing force, founded in 1564 – the *Sejm* (the noble diet) – fearful that the elected monarch would institute military rule, ensured that he was starved of additional funds. Thus, this 'Crown Army', rarely larger than 30,000 men, was confined to frontier defence and never grew sufficiently to enhance royal authority. When King Jan III Sobieski (1674–96) raised new troops to succour Vienna during the Ottoman siege in 1683, his 25,000 troops were collected very slowly from among the feudal noble cavalry, foreign mercenaries, and the infantry of the Crown Army. The Polish 'military' retained anachronistic features for a long time, such as the preponderance of cavalry, recruited from the ubiquitous nobility, instead of cheaper, and more flexible infantry. By the early 18th century, the ratio was as high as four horsemen to each foot soldier, when most European armies enjoyed an inverse proportion.

Further east, Ivan the Terrible founded a personal standing army in 1556, but the social institutions on which it was based had stagnated by the mid 17th century. Subsequent expansion to the west and towards the Baltic demanded a larger and more effective force. Regiment-size units were established, trained in Western methods, and commanded by foreign mercenaries. In 1640, half the Muscovite army was composed of these 'new formation' units. In 1647, some new regiments were raised through conscription based on the census returns and often officered by foreigners. These regiments, plus numerous mercenaries, served in the Russo-Polish war of 1654–67. By the 1670s Russia could field huge numbers, but with poor training, and low discipline. A new impulse for the modernisation of the army came after the alliance with the Holy League against the Ottomans. In 1687 and 1689, Russian armies of over 100,000 men marched south to Crimea but were unable to force the Isthmus of Perekop against only 15,000 Tatars and Ottomans. Around 1689, Czar Peter I formed two modern and fully Westernised regiments, the *Preobrazhenski*, and the *Semionovski* Guards, the basis of the organisational exemplars for the Westernisation of the Russian army.

By slow degrees, tax collection for the support of standing armed forces began to conform to bureaucratic regularity over wider areas of Europe. The modern administration of armies moved in the same direction. Louis XIV's army is regularly presented as the paradigm of this transformation, and with a few exceptions the major standing armies resulted to be products of absolutism. However, the most valuable exceptions is represented by Dutch Republic, which deployed a large permanent army, although being a state unrelated with

34 In the 17th century, about 12 percent of Poles claimed noble status, and in some provinces, there were more aristocrats than peasants. Not that there was much to distinguish one from the other: most nobles were as poor as peasants, and sought protection by joining the private armies of the few rich magnates. The King could not compete, hence in Poland the 'monopoly of violence' remained with the nobility and did not migrate to the sovereign. See also in Aleksander Gieysztor, *Storia della Polonia* (Milan: Bompiani, 1983).

the coeval monarchies. Since the beginning of the 17th century, the United Provinces pioneered important improvements in military administration and training, and their army was long considered a model by other European state.[35] The result was the creation of an entirely original instrument of war unlike any other European armies. A result which was probably not the best possible one, but surely the most appropriate way to face any political contingency and war emergency. In this context, the Republican atavistic conservationism contributed to slow the development of military armed forces in the modern meaning, but the deadly conflict against France of 1672–78 proved even more crucial in the evolution of the field army. The technological escalation generated by a conflict against a modern European army forced the government to reconsider its military policy. This conflict represented a formidable challenge for the Republic, because the centre of gravity moved deeply to the ground, leaving the fleet to face English and French squadrons or to launch raids far from the metropolitan territory. After 1672 there were choices which the Republic could not escape, and in the fierce struggle against Louis XIV would require even more drastic changes of its military institutions.

The Golden Age of the Dutch Republic

In 1650, the Republic of the Seven Provinces of the Netherlands had reached a level of economic expansion such as to be considered the richest state in Europe. At the zenith of power and splendour, the Republic had grown from small and besieged confederation of cities and provinces to global empire. Many contemporaries tried to explain the apparent contradiction of a state of small size, governed by a republican government that founded its power on the federalism, when the norm was instead the absolute monarchy.[36] Between 1550 and 1650, the population had tripled, while in many other European states it had remained unchanged or had decreased due to plague epidemics or military campaigns. During the Thirty Years' War, Dutch cities had always been regularly procured with all kinds of goods, when instead many urban centres in Europe had suffered famine and increased prices. The Republic's fleets crossed all the seas of the globe and its navigators extended

35 In 1645, the Republic of Venice's decision to maintain a standing army below 10,000 men found comfort assuming as model the army of the United Provinces of the Netherlands. Although Venice adapted the Dutch military policy to itself in a rather incongruous way, all facts and events regarding both the Dutch army and fleet were held in high regard. Therefore, since the beginning of the 17th century, the government subscribed to the declaration of Maurice of Nassau, who considered a well-trained force of 8,500 foot soldiers and 1,500 cavalrymen, supported by a powerful fleet and a modern network of fortresses, as able to stand up to any opponent. See Contarini's relation, cited in Ian Heath *Armies of the Sixteenth Century* (Guernsey: A Foundry Book Publications, 1997), p. 107. Further analogies can be found with the army of the Swiss Confederation, in coincidence of the common federalist and bourgeois ascendant.

36 In 1650, a member of the Royal Society wrote: 'there is no subject that is treated with equal frequency by the talented men. The marvellous progress of this small state that in only a hundred years has grown to a level not only superior to the ancient republics of Greece, and not much less than greatest monarchies of our time.' Cit. by Simon Schama, *The Dutch Culture of the Golden Age* (New York: Alfred Knopf, 1988), p. 225.

Map 1. The Dutch Republic was a confederation of seven provinces governed by the States-General (***Staten-Generaal*** in Dutch), the federal government. The States-General were seated in The Hague, but each province had its own Provincial State. The provinces of the republic were, in official feudal order: the Duchy of Gelderland, the County of Holland, the County of Zealand, the Lordship of Utrecht (formerly the Episcopal principality of Utrecht), the Lordship of Overijssel, the Lordship of Friesland, the Lordship of Groningen and Ommelanden. There was an eighth province, the County of Drenthe, but this area was the poorest and therefore iwas exempt from paying federal taxes and as a consequence was denied any representation in the States General. The last areas under Republican rule were the Generaliteitslanden (Generality Lands). They represented about one fifth of the territories of the Republic, directly governed by the States-General. During the Eighty Years' War, the Generality Lands came under control of the United Provinces, and this situation was consolidated by the Treaty of Westphalia in 1648. The Republic held also colonies in Asia, Africa and the Americas. In the mid 17th century the population was approximately estimated at 2,000,000 inhabitants.

the geographical knowledge even to the antipodes. This achievement was ostentatiously exhibited on the decoration of the *Burgerzaal* floor in the new City Hall of Amsterdam, where Abel Janszoon Tasman's recent discoveries were proudly designated as 'New Holland'. In many respects, the Dutch Republic was the great exception of the 17th century. No wonder if its citizens considered themselves as the most lucky and protected by God. Actually, the Republic had shown good elasticity in the most dramatic moments and had prevented political struggles from degenerating into a civil war.[37]

The comment of foreign observers was often severe and described the complications of federalism as a 'governmental chaos',[38] but this kind of affirmation testifies to the incidence of critics of the Republic to understand the Dutch exception.[39] The conservatism of the Dutch and all the late-medieval aspects that remained in the civil society of each province, each proud of their independence, alienated them from the rest of the world. Their prosperity, regarded as exceptional in a period of recurring economic crises, their tolerance in matters of religion, the freedom of the bourgeois class, equated with the aristocracy, were poorly suited to the coeval scenario, yet their antiquated institutions predicted the Enlightenment.

In the 17th century, even the greatest enemies of Dutch commercial prosperity, such as Louis XIV's minister, Colbert, or the English ambassador, Sir George Downing, assiduously imitated Dutch methods, and sought to attract Dutch skills. Inseparably entwined with Dutch primacy in world trade, the Republic was also the technological leader of Europe and many visitors, included Czar Peter the Great of Russia, concentrated on the technical inventions, from new practices in shipbuilding to improved sluices, harbour cranes, timber-saws, textile looms, windmills, clocks, and street lamps. Relatively few foreigners showed interest also in agricultural innovation; nevertheless, those who studied the Dutch technique of drainage, horticulture, fodder crops, and methods of soil replenishment could, applied them with profit elsewhere.[40] With science, the Republic supported also arts and philosophy. The major Dutch cities registered a constant stream of visitors more inclined to scholarly and artistic pursuits among them several of the greatest philosophers

37 The sense of the internal tension is well described by Jonathan Israel in *The Dutch Republic, Its Rise, Greatness and Fall, 1477–1806* (Oxford: Clarendon Press, 1995): 'During most of the history of the United Provinces, allegiance and identity were based on provincial, civic, and sometimes also local rural sentiment rather than attachment to the Republic as a whole. In this respect, the loose federal structure which evolved was well suited to the disposition, and attitudes, of its population. In particular, politics frequently revolved around the tension between the dominant province of Holland, and the rest of the provinces, which continually strove to protect their local interests and avoid being dominated.', p. vi.

38 *Ibid.*, p. 226.

39 The isolation of the United Provinces became even more profound: 'The very existence of the Republic, which heralded enlightenment despite its antiquated structure, with its irritating prosperity, constituted for the principles of countries in which the absolutism and the raison d'état of the baroque age, a paradox and a challenge, prevailed.' *The New Cambridge Modern History*: vol. 5, 'The Ascendency of the French (1648–1688)', Chapter 12, The Dutch Republic (Cambridge: Cambridge University Press, 1968), p. 365.

40 A large part of the agricultural revolution in England, in the 18th century was based on techniques and innovations borrowed from the United Provinces. See in Israel, *Dutch Republic*, p. 2.

of early modern times: Descartes, Locke, and Bayle who were attracted by the abundance of libraries, scientific collections, and publishers in the United Provinces and, above all, the intellectual, and religious freedom to be found there. There was no other country, averted Descartes, 'où l'on puisse jouir d'une liberté si entière.'[41] Other observers were struck by the orderliness of Dutch civic life, the effectiveness of the welfare system, prisons, and penal practice, and the remarkably low levels of crime characterised Dutch society.[42]

However, wealth, progress, and glory were not enough to eliminate ambiguity and tension from the republican political system, which mined the state's cohesion. The complexity of Dutch domestic politics makes it difficult to form a homogeneous scenario of the country. The differences between the Seven Provinces that formed the Republic were of such magnitude that any generalisation risks likely appearing arbitrary. The differences were considerable if we take as a reference the aristocratic society of Friesland, still linked to the rural world, or that of Gelderland, which still boasted extensive feudal privileges, both very different from the dynamic and enterprising patricians of Holland. Proceeding to the lower levels of society, the differences appear equally considerable. The peasant farmers of Gelderland and Overijssel, settled in sparsely populated areas and devoted to subsistence farming, had to face problems far different from those of Holland's peasants, who produced a huge variety of crops destined to trade and industry. The political weight of the different classes also seemed different between one locality and another. In Holland, the province by far the richest, and one of the most densely populated regions in Europe, the structure of class was very simple. The nobility had an irrelevant demographic weight and formed a rigidly closed caste: it did not exercise political or economic powers and most of the lands had long been under the control of the capitalists of the cities. The aristocracy of Holland had no connection with the great bourgeois families and normally did not contest its function as a predestined ruling class. By the middle of the 17th century, the great bourgeois families had definitively affirmed themselves, which had been enriched with the trade and exploitation of the lands, and they held the responsibilities of government. The ruling class constituted an oligarchy that dominated the life of the state. From their ranks were the men who held the highest offices in the city administrations, took part in the assemblies of the States-Provincial and on the boards of commercial companies. These men had the right to appoint the minor offices in the cities and in the countryside. This class had taken the name of *regenten* ('regents') and eventually ended up forming a homogeneous group often hostile to dividing the exercise of power with exponents of other families. Although they sometimes bought noble titles and built sumptuous country residences worthy of a prince, they remained the bourgeois devoted to the characteristic occupations of their social class. Only a few great aristocratic families could dispute their power: among them the Orange and the Nassau.

The Republic's power structure was cumbersome and complicated. The Republic did not represent a single state, but a federation of seven sovereign

41 Descartes, *Lettres à Jean Luis G. dit Balzac*, in Amsterdam, dated 5 May 1631.

42 Israel, *Dutch Republic*, p. 3.

provinces, each jealous of its own prerogatives.[43] The great differences between one province and another and the composite social structure that existed produced this complicated form of government based on a federal system, which to foreign observers appeared weak, conditioned by the laws that obliged him in every decision to reach unanimity.

The most important federal organs were the *Staten-Generaal* (States General), officialy designated in every act with the prestigious appellation *Leurs Hautes Puissances*, to which each province sent a delegation obliged to vote according to the constraint given them by the provincial assembly. Every deliberation of the States General had to be voted unanimously and therefore every vote was often preceded by long and exhausting negotiations. The States General met in The Hague and among the most important tasks were those relating to foreign policy, federal taxes, divided between the provinces according to pre-established rates and that had as largest contributor the province of Holland that alone paid 58 percent. One of the most important function performed by the States General was the appointment in wartime of the commander-in-chief of the army and the admiral-general of the Union.

However, the States General were not a sovereign body, because sovereignty belonged to the individual States-Provincial. Moreover, the composition of these assemblies was different between one province and another. For instance, the States of Holland were formed by 19 delegations, each of which had only one vote, representing the 18 major cities, plus a delegation for the nobility. The States-Provincial, like the General ones, took decisions unanimously, because the inspiring principle of the Republic was that none of its members could be forced to bow to the wishes of the majority. In practice, every decision was licensed only after long negotiations and thanks to the action of the ablest politicians.

Given these premises, the politics of the Republic were exposed to non-negligible centrifugal forces. Also for this reason, two offices of government were established to offset the autonomy of the provinces, namely the *Raad Pensionaris* (Grand Pensionary) and the *Stadhouder* (Stadtholder). The first of these two important dignitaries was the legal advisor of the States-Provincial, among whom the Grand Pensioner of Holland (at first called *landsadvocaat*) was the most powerful. His duty was to prepare and execute decisions of his States. He was then a kind of legal advisor to the Republic, who presided over the States General and the various commissions and often took care of the diplomatic relations of the state with the ambassadors abroad and received correspondence. As such, he was a central figure in policymaking, especially of foreign relations. A charge like the Grand Pensioner required an intelligent and energetic politician who enjoyed the confidence of the provinces.[44] Formally, his office included only civil functions within the province of Holland, but by the middle of the century the Grand Pensioner

43 *Ibid.*, p. 368. The United Provinces, as Johan de Witt outlined, were not a single *respublica*, but more *respublicae*.

44 Joop W. Koopmans and Arend H. Huussen Jr., *Historical Dictionary of the Netherlands* (Lanham, Maryland – Toronto – Plymouth UK :The Scarecrow Press, Inc., 2007), p. 97.

had become the dominant political figure of the Republic and, in fact, he exercised power over the entire government apparatus.

Relations between civil power and the army were regulated by the *Raad van State* (Council of State), which included political personalities, and military advisors. This assembly met every time an important administrative decision was proposed by the States General. The Council addressed the military policy of the Republic; all resolutions were taken by common agreement and therefore binding for all the provinces. Because of its military feature, the Council of State was considered by the regents an instrument of the Stadtholders.

Compared to the Grand Pensionary, the function of the Stadtholder appeared to be much more ambiguous. This office, whose literal meaning was 'lieutenant', had already taken on different meanings throughout Dutch history. Originally, the Stadtholder was just the lieutenant of the prince during his absence, but in Holland, he occupied a prominent place in the civil government too, gaining support from a considerable part of provinces, especially when the Orange family held the office in Holland and Zealand. The growing popularity of the exponent of this family could represent a problem for the maintenance of the balance of power in the Republic, also because at the same time, the Stadtholder held the office of commanders of the troops of the province under his jurisdiction.[45] Each province appointed its own Stadtholder in charge with the military affairs, choosing from a very shortlist of candidates. Although a function attributed by the States-Provincial and then theoretically subject to the respective sovereign organs, the Stadtholder could hold the same office in more than one province. In fact, the provinces of Holland, Zealand, Utrecht, Overijssel and Gelderland gave the title to a Prince of Orange for some time, and also Groningen and the region of Drenthe (which however did not send representatives to the States General) joined the other provinces standardising their appointment to the same candidate. Only Friesland remained far towards the Orange, constantly giving the charge to a member of the Nassau family. However, the importance of the Princes of Orange compared to their colleagues was incomparable. In fact, they simultaneously held the functions of Captain-General of the army and General Admiral of the fleet, so it was natural that he occupied a pre-eminent place in domestic politics and in the elaboration of government action. Moreover, the enormous prestige enjoyed by the Orange house gave to the Stadtholder an influence and a power not defined by any law, but they did not appear to be less relevant. The important role of military leader covered by the Stadtholder and the aversion that the most orthodox republican exponents had towards his figure, exploded in open contrast when the States General examined the army's reduction plan in response to the States of Holland.

In the decade 1640–50, relations between the Stadtholder and the regents had been very tense and the delegates of Holland had strongly opposed

45 In 1581, declaring the king deposed, William 'the Silent' of Orange and the Stadtholders of the other provinces considered themselves lieutenants of the new sovereign: François de Valois, Duke of Anjou. On the death of William, for lack of a sovereign, were the states of the individual provinces to choose a new Stadtholder, which in Holland was Maurice of Nassau. If, therefore, before the Stadtholder as the representative of the sovereign was above the States General, over time he became the owner of the military affairs of the Republic. See Israel, *Dutch Republic*, p. 152.

3. Prince Willem II, 1651, by Gerard van Honthorst (Rijksmuseum, Amsterdam)

Prince William II of Orange (1626–1650), Statholder of five of the seven provinces: Holland, Zealand, Utrecht, Guelders and Overijssel. Prince William had inherited 30 territories all over Europe: in Franche-Comté, Nassau, Katzenelnbogen, Dietz, Vianden, Meurs, Lingen, Buren, Veere, Flushing, Doesburg, Lingdam, Naaldwijk, Breda, Grave, Willemstadt, Geertruidenburg; and in the Spanish Netherlands, Diest, Herstal and St. Vith, as well as in France the Principality of Orange, from which he took his title. Orange became a principality and fief of the Holy Roman Empire in the 12th century. Under the house of Nassau it became a Protestant stronghold, nestled curiously in an enclave surrounded by the Papal State of Avignon. The Principality suffered its first incursion by the French. The governor of the Principality of Orange, Frederick von Dohna, surrendered Orange to France for a bribe on 20 March 1660. Shortly thereafter, on 9 March 1661, Louis XIV took personal control and in 1664 William's grandmother Amelia accepted a Roman Catholic governor for Orange so that on 25 March 1665 the French withdrew.

4. The young Prince William III of Orange, by Cornelius Johnson. (Yale Center for British Art, New Haven, CT)

The young Prince William III of Orange, by Cornelius Johnson. The prince was born on 4 November 1650, three weeks after the death of his father, Prince William II. In 1653, when the Holland's States were discussing the appointment of the Statholder, William III was only three years old. By tradition, only a blood descendant of Prince William I of Orange was eligible for this most senior military office. However, for the 'State faction' his appointment as Captain-General was out of the question under any circumstances. On 5 August 1667, Grand Pensioner Johan de Witt had a 'Perpetual Edict' passed whereby Holland and the other states were never to appoint a Captain-General or an Admiral-General as Statholder. The war against England and Münster increased the influence of the Orangist party and de Witt proposed that the province of Holland should not only charge itself with William's education, but should adopt him as a 'Child of State.' After the 'adoption' of the young prince, the States of Holland had voted for the appointment of William III as Statholder after his majority age, established when aged 23, but on 24 February 1672 the Prince was appointed at this charge, a year and a half earlier than planned.

the militaristic and dynastic policy of Prince Frederik Hendrik of Orange. Supported by the pro-Orange towns of Leiden and Haarlem, the Prince was the principal instigator for the continuation of the war against Spain, and thanks to his position of prestige, he tried to strengthen his family's position by intensifying relations with the European monarchies. The marriage of the Stadtholder's son, William II, with the daughter of Charles I of England resulted in the support of the Prince of the Stuart cause in the English Civil War: a fact nothing short of surprising for a leading exponent of a Republic. Frederik Hendrik's attitude aroused great indignation in the government and the conflicts did not cease even with his death in 1647. However, the disappearance of the Prince allowed the representatives of the Seven Provinces to conclude peace with Spain. The Münster treaty of 1648 reflected in the internal politics of the Republic to strengthen the position of the bourgeois and the weakening of the military and aristocratic classes. The son of the late Stadtholder, William II, was invested with all the posts of his father and supported by loyalist forces to his family openly challenged the Republican government. Soon a serious and dangerous internal conflict loomed, caused by the military policy of the States General.

The bitter quarrel exploded in 1650, and involved William II against the province of Holland and the powerful regents of Amsterdam, Andries Bicker, and Cornelis de Graeff. The regents' plan to reduce the size of the army was felt by the Prince to be a reduction of authority and of prestige. The tension between the opposed sides did not decrease, and requests of intervention coming from sectors of army convinced William II to intervene with a coup. In early summer 1650, the prince convinced the States General to send him with a delegation to the cities of Holland to try to convince them to change their vote for military reduction in the provincial assembly. This manoeuvre was fiercely opposed by Holland as an unprecedented attack on the constitution and on the province's sovereignty. On 30 July, William denounced the representatives of Holland's cities, which had rejected his overtures, and reacted by imprisoning eight members of the States of Holland in the castle of Loevestein. In addition, he sent his cousin, Willem Frederik of Nassau-Dietz with 10,000 troops to seize Holland by force. Bad weather foiled the campaign, but Amsterdam did give in on 6 August 1650. Once the attack plans failed, William compromised with the States General. He released the representatives he had taken prisoner and Amsterdam agreed to replace some of the magistrates who had opposed him. Suddenly, on 6 November William II died of smallpox, leaving his only one-year-old son William III as his heir. It was around the person of this prince, and the main adversary of his family, the Grand Pensioner Johan de Witt, that the main events of the Republic were played out between the Anglo-Dutch wars and the Grand Alliance.

Another fact of political relevance happened immediately following the death of William II, when the States of Holland abolished the offices of Stadtholder and provincial Captain-General. They took effective control over the nomination of officers and the moving of troops paid by Holland. With the exception of Friesland and Groningen, all the other provinces followed Holland's example. The States General were now faced with a completely new fact: the absence of the Stadtholder. The proposal to transfer to the

Stadtholder of Friesland the offices held by the Prince of Orange were accepted only by Groningen and Drenthe. This situation determined the undisputed affirmation of the most intransigent republican sectors, strongly determined to maintain the balance of powers both in the government and the army. The States-Provincial agreed the opening of negotiations to proceed with a reform from the foundations of the form of government. In January 1651, the 'Great Assembly' was convened in The Hague, which, at the suggestion of the Dutch representatives, had to assume all the powers held by the Council of State, considered a government organ still largely dominated by Orange supporters. The negotiations continued until August, but the proposal, too ambitious, and revolutionary, remained just a project: 'leaving the great assembly unable to formulate any proposal and turned into a theatre of empty theoretical speculations'.[46] The only important decision was that relating to the army. The assembly established that military matters would be subordinated to the will of each of the Seven Provinces, with the result that the army risked of becoming seven small provincial armies.[47] However, in July 1652, the First Anglo-Dutch War erupted, turning the government in a new difficult position. In the course of the complex events that characterised the years of the First Anglo-Dutch War, the government proved to possess a considerable political capacity, especially through the action of the Johan de Witt. Surviving the Orangist surge, in May 1653 he was appointed as Grand Pensionary of Holland and soon mastered the difficult Dutch political arena, imposing his leadership on the States General, but despite these personal achievements, he encountered great difficult in managing the foreign affairs, which fatally turned against him in 1672.

The Peace of Westminster, signed on 15 April 1654, closed the expensive naval conflict against England. During the negotiations, de Witt made any concession to England's maritime and colonial interests. The Grand Pensionary had to accept only the 'Act of Exclusion', which suspended the appointment of the Orange family as Stadtholder, in order to exclude the Prince from becoming King of England. The following years were known in the history of the Republic as the age without Stadtholder,[48] ended only in 1672 with the appointment of Prince William III of Orange, which occurred after the French invasion of the state.

The Westminster peace was a success for de Witt and Republic's sense of purpose and solidarity, but this result was not welcomed in all provinces.[49]

46 The New Cambridge Modern History: vol. 5, p. 368.

47 At the start of the 18th century, the Dutch statesman Simon van Singelandt commented in retrospect that it was as if 'the militia repartioned among the respective provinces in the State of War is actually … the militia of the province by which they are paid, in such a manner, however, that this province is obliged to use and to allow it to be used for the Common Defence', in Olaf Nimwegen, *The Dutch Army and the Military Revolutions, 1588–1688* (English Edition, Woodbridge, Suffolk: Boyden Press, 2010), p. 305.

48 The assignment was suspended a second time in 1702, and then definitively reinstated, in hereditary way, in 1747 as military governor of all the seven provinces. The office was finally abolished in 1795 following the French occupation.

49 To justify his conduct, de Witt compiled a lengthy text where he presented first to the States of Holland and then distributed widely, in the name of the States: 'Nevertheless, it left a bad taste in the mouth of the public. The official festivities held at the end of May, to mark the peace with England, were a frigid affair by comparison with the celebrations for the peace with Spain, in 1648,

Some regents vehemently criticised de Witt, deploring the 'Exclusion' as an usurpation of the powers of '[the] Generality, and collectivity of the provinces, which alone have responsibility for making peace'. De Witt held that when tested against the 'touchstone of true and unfalsified freedom', the 'true aims' of his critics were manifestly damaging to 'our dearly bought freedom'.[50]

Now the Republic was in a strategically delicate situation, because, as a European power, it was called to play a leading role that was ill suited to the attitude of their ruling class, which was not to get involved in international tensions. For this reason, de Witt's action appears conditioned by the need to share the most important choices. When the First Northern War began, the United Provinces remained strictly neutral, despite during the conflict against England, Denmark had supported the Republic. However, the change of attitude matured after the government understood the risk to remain excluded by the commercial routes in the Baltic Sea. In early 1656, Carl Gustav X of Sweden ordered the investment of Danzig. For the Republic this represented a highly dangerous development, because the Swedes, once they conquered the city, and gained the control of the mouth of the Vistula River, could exclude the Dutch trade from the large and vital Polish grain market. In the spring of 1656, the States General voted for the expedition to break through the Swedish blockade. The Dutch fleet appeared before the besieged city in late July, whereupon the Dutch soldiers joined Danzig's garrison. Then, de Witt persuaded the States General that a Swedish victory would transform the Baltic Sea into a Swedish lake and the loss of the Öresund strait could turn into serious damage to trade with Denmark. Therefore, when in the summer of 1658 the Swedish fleet besieged Copenhagen, the States General authorised the expedition of the fleet with 2,000 soldiers in the Öresund to defeat the Swedes, freeing the Danish capital from the siege. Sweden and Denmark put an end to hostilities with the peace of Roskilde and after intense diplomatic activity came to The Hague concert. Here England, France and the United Provinces declared that the treaty had to form the basis of international relations in the Baltic. For the first time in history, the Dutch Republic held the role of great power. This new phase marked the end of the illusion nourished by the Republican bourgeois classes, who hoped to maintain a neutral conduct, avoiding being involved in major international conflicts. The regents, reluctantly, had to adapt to the

---

with which they were widely compared. As on the earlier occasion, Leiden refused to participate in the celebrations at all. The inhabitants of Rotterdam, an Englishman reported: "*burnt pitch barrels but it was slightly done, most of the understanding people being dissatisfied with the conditions of peace. Not one citizen or particular person did make any bonfire or demonstration of joy*, it was alleged, *but only those who either depended upon the magistrate or the admiraltie.' At Dordrecht, the young men were so bold as to sett up the Prince of Orange his colours upon the street and De Witt durst not pull them downe.* Only at Amsterdam was there more zest in the festivities with *thousands of people abroad in the streetes to heare and see the showes upon the Dam. The text of the peace was read out to the multitude with the sound of trompets and the discharging of the great guns*, after which came *bonfires and fireworks throughout the cittie*."' Israel, *The Dutch Republic*, p. 726.

50 *Ibid.*, p. 724: Discoursing on past republics, especially Florence under the Medici, de Witt insisted that 'everyone should realize that, according to the judgement of all political writers of sound mind, high positions cannot be assigned, in a republic, to those whose ancestors held these posts, without considerable peril to freedom.' The hereditary principle, and that of the 'eminent head', he argued, 'had destroyed the Florentine republic and was inherently dangerous to republics.'

fact that the Republic would be forced to assume tasks and responsibilities deriving from the new status assumed, and the extensive commercial interests unavoidably forced the Republic to defend this relevant position on the world stage. Then, in order to sustain a policy of great power it was necessary to have not only an efficient fleet, but also an army capable of this task, and consequently accept the rise of the military class. This was another source of concerns, because most of the high officers possessed an extensive net of links with a multitude of foreign ruling houses, from the largest to the ones of limited size. The hostility to foreign monarchies was always strong in the Seven Provinces, and with the appointment of important military charges to the supporters of the Orange family, de Witt impended the risk of arousing the reaction of the most intransigent republicans. The Grand Pensionary knew this scenario weakened the Republic. The vulnerability of the United Provinces forced him to seek foreign aid, and on the other hand, the persistent hostility of England, the weakness of Spain, and Austria limited the possibilities of choice in terms of alliances. In some respects, the Franco-Dutch treaty signed in 1662 was an important success for de Witt in domestic politics, as both Mazzarino before, and the young Louis XIV after, had maintained close relations with William II and the Orangist party, looking suspiciously at the republican sectors. The treaty recognised the political strength of the state by strengthening the stability of the Grand Pensionary. The policy of alliance with France, however unavoidable, was full of shadows, and dangers. A Franco-Dutch collaboration was in fact quite unnatural because from the Dutch point of view, French foreign policy and Colbert's economic measures in matter of trade were equally unacceptable like the Spanish presence of the previous century. Already in the first weeks after the Peace of Münster, Spain had continually invited the United Provinces to sign a secret alliance in an anti-French key. The States General well understood that the French annexation of the Spanish Low Countries would inevitably lead the Republic to a confrontation with Paris.[51] In 1664, the Dutch attempt to restrain the growing French ambitions on the Spanish Low Countries by a concerted solution failed, despite the tenacity, cleverness, and ability of the Grand Pensionary.

However, the alliance was attractive for Louis XIV, who hoped to put the Dutch under an obligation to him in view of the conquest of the Spanish Low Countries, as well as for the Republic, which received the King's promise to assist the United Provinces with 6,000 French troops in the event of enemy attack. The agreement revealed its utility in the Second Anglo-Dutch War. The conflict of 1652–54 had been fought essentially on sea, but now England had found an ally in the Prince-Bishop of Münster, Christoph Bernhard von Galen. The warlike bishop had faced the Dutch army already in 1657 and 1661, during the crisis of Münster, however without arriving at the armed confrontation. In 1663, a new crisis had pushed the Republic to intervene in support of the Prince Georg Christian of East Friesland, menaced by von

51 See John H. Elliot, *Imperial Spain* (London: Penguin, 1990), p. 464: 'Spain's principal delegate at Westphalia, the Count of Peñaranda. Was able to play on growing Dutch fears of the rising power of France, and succeeded in frightening the Dutch by revealing a secret offer made by Richelieu's successor, cardinal Mazarin, to return Catalonia to Spain in exchange for Flanders.'

Galen who claimed territorial gains. In May 1664, the Dutch army had entered East Friesland, forcing the Münster troops to withdraw. Disappointed by this failure, in 1665 the Prince-Bishop had set up a very respectable army, capable of invading the Dutch eastern provinces. In June 1665, Charles II Stuart, and Christoph Bernhard von Galen signed their alliance and on 23 September, Münster troops moved the offensive on the ground invading the province of Groningen. The invasion found the Dutch army unprepared, despite a modest rearmament voted by the States General in early 1665. As had happened during the First Anglo-Dutch War, the government seemed unprepared to face an unprecedented strategic situation. A naval re-armament policy had to be planned in great urgency, for which considerable sums had been necessary, but these were found in a short time thanks to the large availability of low-interest loan money. The army presented more problems, but mercenary troops could be enlisted by turning to Protestant states such as the duchies of Brunswick and the reformed Prince-Bishop of Osnabrück. In the following months, the French decision to join the Dutch army represented one more good reason to persuade von Galen to sign a separate peace with the United Provinces. The French participated in the war against Münster with a small corps, then in January 1666 Louis XIV declared war on England and his support for the Dutch Republic contributed to isolate Charles II. The war against England lasted one year more, and closed on 31 July 1667 with the Treaty of Breda. The outcome of the war was a great success for the United Provinces and for de Witt in particular. The victories gained by the fleet and the overwhelming raid on the Medway River confirmed the role of great power of the Dutch Republic, despite a military policy that seemed incongruous for that role.

England and the United Provinces signed the Peace of Breda just before the French invasion of the Spanish Low Countries. This act constituted the turning point for the United Provinces and for de Witt too. Historians have considered the Grand Pensionary as the most responsible for the isolation of the Republic and the following invasion of 1672. According to 19th century historians, he would not understand the danger of war against France, and acted imprudently towards England, refusing any commercial concession. However, before criticising the imprudent conduct of de Witt on foreign affairs, it is necessary to remember that the Dutch did not realise the envy and hatred aroused by the wealth of their state and the radical republicanism of their politicians, who acted according to principles incomprehensible to the chancelleries of other countries. During the peace negotiations of Breda, the foreign ambassadors considered it surprising that the Dutch diplomats, so obstinately defending their commercial interests, did not understand how this behaviour irritated their adversaries.[52] The Dutch did not know much

52 Some historians reply to these critics by pointing out that not even the Dutch interlocutors appeared less arrogant and provocative. Louis XIV's minister Hughes de Lionne contemptuously called the Dutch 'herring traders.' However it is a mistake to define this attitude as arrogant, because it was a vision of the world deeply inculcated in the aristocratic society of the 17th century: 'Thus, the crude, sometimes brutal, insolent, and presumptuous behaviour of the Dutch ambassador van Benningsen profoundly offended the French diplomats and prejudices even more in their sovereign.' John B. Wolf, *Louis XIV* (New York: W.W. Norton & Company, 1974), p. 245.

about the other countries, despite being great navigators and although The Hague was the centre of 17th century European journalism, and ultimately remained unrelated to many of the contemporary cultural trends. The political constitution, the structure of their commerce, the bourgeois dimension of society and several aspects of Dutch culture appeared once more as the great anomaly in the European scenario and fatally favoured the isolation of the state and the French decision to invade the Republic.

Already in 1667, Louis XIV seemed less disposed to maintain the alliance with the United Provinces, and not having understood it had been considered de Witt's resounding political error, as well as not guessing how high was the hostility of the neighbouring states. Actually, de Witt, and the Republican government were fully aware that the situation was rapidly changing. Signals of the ambiguous French attitude were not lacking. The Grand Pensionary knew what to expect from Prince-bBshop Christoph Bernhard von Galen, a prince 'always ill-intentioned for the States', as the French ambassador at The Hague expressed it.[53] Obviously, von Galen's actions in matter of religion and territorial claims were supported by Louis XIV. In 1668 the Prince-Bishop, exploiting dissension in the Calvinist county of Bentheim, persuaded the Count, previously a client of the Dutch, to convert to Catholicism, occupied the county, and reintroduced the Catholic faith. Louis XIV also egged on the Elector of Cologne to demand Dutch evacuation of Rheinberg and the transfer of part of the Overmaas to the bishopric of Liège, which had the same ruler, and encouraged the Elector's efforts to master the Imperial Free City of Cologne, which was surrounded by his territory. To counter French influence, the Republic backed the city of Cologne. Just as in 1661 the States General tried to save the city of Münster from the encroaching absolutism of the Prince-Bishop, so now they sought to defend Cologne's autonomy against the Elector. Arrangements were made for Cologne to accept a Dutch garrison should the Elector threaten force.

These actions, alongside plans to increase the army's strength, show that de Witt was not so blind to the external threats. During the War of Devolution, Louis XIV, and de Witt had several talks to agree a compromise on the Spanish Low Countries. The negotiations proved to be difficult and slow, and when they failed, Charles II succeeded in inducing de Witt to adopt an intransigent line about the French invasion of that region. Thus, in January 1668, the Triple Alliance of England, Sweden, and the United Provinces was formed, in order to force France to suspend the war against Spain. De Witt had always been very careful to prevent good relations with France from being threatened but, evidently, it was not possible this time. The alliance, which appeared a victory of the Anglo-Dutch diplomacy, as it had arrested the French expansionism in the Spanish Low Countries, was unwillingly signed by the Grand Pensionary, because it marked the end of the prudent policy of friendship with France and aggravated the danger of isolation. After all, there were few alternatives: Charles II and the States General were extremely irritated by the customs war

53 Israel, *The Dutch Republic*, p. 726.

inaugurated by Colbert and these arguments forced de Witt to accept the political line of the Triple Alliance.[54]

In domestic politics, de Witt's action remained incisive, but ultimately his successes turned into damage for his charge. The way he had dealt with the question of the Orange's house had been masterly. In addition, the Stuarts' Restoration was destined to cause repercussions in the United Provinces. Charles II was the uncle of William III and the English king was hostile to the Act of Exclusion, because it was imposed by Cromwell. In fact, the act was abolished in 1660, and the provinces of Zealand, Friesland and Groningen, influenced by the Orangist propaganda, demanded for William the charges of his ancestors. Holland maintained its hostility to this motion, and de Witt and his collaborators were able to prevail by convincing the States General that such a decision would have offered to the Stuarts an instrument to exercise their influence in the United Provinces. The dynastic questions were destined to return to the foreground, and this was precisely what de Witt wished to avoid. However, a compromise was reached, which stipulated that the province of Holland had to bear the burden of educating the young prince to the duties of his ancestors. The House of Orange would have held a major role in the state, on terms that would accept the strictly republican form of the government and sever its ties with foreign princes. This plan had already been rejected for the first time in 1663, but three years later, following seasons of political agitation and propaganda, the proposal was accepted by Orange supporters. No doubt, it was thanks to this initiative if in the following years, Prince William III showed that he had strayed from the dynastic and ingenuously pro-Stuart tradition of his supporters.

5. Johan de Witt (1625–1672). (Engraving by Romain de Hooghe, Rijksmuseum, Amsterdam)

Johan de Witt (1625–1672), here portrayed with his brother Cornelis. Grand Pensionary of Holland from 1653 to 1672, de Witt has entered history as the founder of the new Dutch war fleet. He paid less attention to the army, and above all had too much confidence with the Republic's defences in the case of war against France. According to historian S.B. Baxter, the Grand Pensionary deliberately ignored abuses in the land-based force because the only means of improving the army would have been to appoint the Orange family in the rank of Captain-General of the Union, and de Witt feared that this would lead to the restoration of the Statholderate in Holland. This assertion is mostly incorrect, though it is true that de Witt underestimated the problems in the army. De Witt became the target of the people's anger in spite of the unanimous vote of the Estates declaring him free of all blame on 23 July. Accused of plotting against the Prince, he resigned and was replaced as Grand Pensionary by Caspar Fagel on 23 August. De Witt was sentenced to banishment and loss of all his offices. This did not satisfy the populace, which on 20 August 1672 assaulted and killed him and his brother Cornelis.

To seal the favourable scenario, the States of Holland decreed the incompatibility between the office of Stadtholder, Captain-General, and General Admiral of the province. Then, they confirmed the abolition of the Stadtholder's office with the 'Perpetual Edict'.[55] This act was another political

54 The New Cambridge Modern History: vol. 5, p. 366.

55 In the version of the 'Act of Harmony' laid before the States of Holland, in July 1667, the Prince was deemed insufficiently prepared for the captaincy-general until he had reached 23, rather than 18 (or one year on), as the Orangists were insisting. However, the key feature of the 'Harmony', as it

victory for de Witt, but did not solved the problem on the constitutional aspect. The rigid separation of political power from the military one seemed incongruous to many of the regents, and also did not solve the problem of how to keep the Oranges far from power after having appointed many of them to the position of high commander. The other provinces did not agree to follow the example of Holland and it took a long time to let them accept the choice, which took place only in 1670. Two years earlier William III became a member of the States of Zealand as representatives of the nobility, and he entered the Council of State: two important political functions.

The fortune of de Witt had reached its peak in 1668–70, but now his prestige was wavering. Even in his province, the Grand Pensionary was opposed, and also the rich Amsterdam escaped from his control, moving under the influence of his major political adversary Gillis Valckenier. Though the popular vulgate unilaterally condemns de Witt, considering him as the main person responsible for the isolation of the Republic, several assertions are baseless, and some actions reveal that the Grand Pensionary was aware of the plans that threatened the Republic. His main mistake was not to have ignored this danger, but to have had too much trust in the navy and in the fortifications that had already successfully repulsed the Spaniards in the early part of the century. The offended pride of Louis XIV, hindered in his plans to conquer the Spanish Low Countries, was the main factor that moved the French king to the road of arms. Louis XIV and his ministers spent four years preparing the war against the Seven Provinces, strengthening the army, preparing magazines, and supplies, diverting the foreign chancelleries on its plans and concluding alliance. The commercial rivalry of the English and the unscrupulous politics of Charles II Stuart made possible the signing of the Dover Treaty in 1670, through which France, and England agreed to share out the United Provinces. England would have received some coastal towns and islands at the mouth of the Scheldt; other regions would be ceded to the Prince-Bishop of Münster and to the Elector of Cologne. France would have obtained the key forts across the River Ijssel, notwithstanding the advice of Colbert, who preferred to annex anything, in order to not allow the Dutch merchants, once they become subjects of the Bourbons, to jeopardise the growth of French trade. Once the anomaly of the Dutch Republic was removed from the maps of Europe, Prince William III would have obtained sovereignty over the remaining territory.

evolved in Holland, was the celebrated additional clause that abolished forever the stadholderate in the province. This addendum, introduced in one of the supreme ironies of the Republic's history not by De Witt but by Caspar Fagel, Pensionary of Haarlem, and Gillis Valckenier, later key figures in William III's regime, nevertheless came to be regarded as the constitutional centrepiece of de Witt's 'True Freedom'. In the summer of 1667, the Orangists were still in eclipse and there was scant opposition to the measure in the States of Holland. In their deliberations, on 2 August, the Leiden city council noted gloomily that while a few other towns as Enkhuizen, Alkmaar, Schoonhoven, and Edam were unenthusiastic, only Leiden categorically opposed abolition of the stadholderate on principle. See Israel, *The Dutch Republic*, p. 791.

2

Het Staatsche Leger[1]

> 'The Dutch army, more than any other at that time, obeyed the concept in which it was generally considered the 'Military', namely nothing more than a job and a trade. ... In this way the Dutch gathered their army with mercenaries, in which, beside the troops recruited in the Provinces, there were the most numerous ones recruited outside the borders and joined in strange mixture.'[2]

The author of the judgements expressed at the end of the 19th century, on the authoritative work of the Imperial-Royal war archive of Vienna, reveals the hostility still deeply rooted in the military structures of the republican governments. This aversion was not dictated only by ideological considerations but, above all, the criticism was directed to the control exercised by these governments over the professional soldiers and the balancing instruments of power used to grant this dominance. The military policy of the United Provinces of the Netherlands in the 17th century is a subject on which many inaccuracies have been and are repeated today. The current opinion is that of a state with an army managed by mercantile methods, incongruous with the age in which it was operating, assembled with foreign mercenaries led by foreign commanders under the asphyxiating control of the government. However, the reading of some texts and a minimum of reflection and knowledge of Dutch history reveal a very different scenario.

The Dutch Army Before and After 'the Disaster'

In the later 16th century, the Dutch Republic was one of the few states that managed a significant core of a standing army. By the late 1580s and early 1590s the troops had evolved from a loose band of militiamen into a highly disciplined corps of professional soldiers in which proficiency and obedience were valued above all else. This was a significant achievement, which has been ascribed by most historians solely to the reforms of Maurice of Nassau.

1 Literally: 'The States' Army'.

2 K.u.K. Kriegsarchiv, *Feldzüge des Prinzen Eugen of Savoyen* (Vienna, 1876), vol. I, p. 465–466.

His famous *Articles of War* of 1590 are said to have transformed the hastily recruited units into a reliable and efficient war machine. Afterwards the Dutch army was reputed to be the 'School of Mars', where discipline, organisation and the most effective tactics had been implemented so successfully in battlefield that the Republic could endure the assault of the most powerful armies.[3]

The Dutch case appeared even more interesting observing the structure of the army, conceived as a federal organisation. Each province held a large autonomy and joined the others only to defend the Republic against the external threats. The government offices involved in the direction of the army – the States of the Seven Provinces, the States General and the Council of State (*Raad van State*) – exercised a balanced power over the army, and no decision could be made without the consent of all. For the expenditures destined for the troops, a common trust was established to which all the provinces contributed according to their financial abilities. This arrangement was known as *Repartitiestelsel*, and was established for the first time in 1588. The rich province of Holland paid 57 percent of this budget, Friesland 11.4 percent, Zealand 11, Utrecht, and Groningen 5.7, Gelderland 5.5, Overijssel 3.5.

The federal structure of the Republic ensured that central revenues were limited. They consisted of a salt tax, fees for passports, and safeguards, along with the Generality stamp duty. Generality lands (the conquered areas in Flanders, Brabant, and Westerwolde) yielded some five percent of the revenues, mostly from taxes, and contributions. The admiralties collected the customs, which yielded around 12 percent of the total. But the bulk of the revenues (almost 82 percent) had to come from the provinces. They had to provide the funds for the most expensive part of the war budget, the army, and fortifications, plus sums for the navy, administration, and servicing of debts. Army represented always the high percentage of the war budget, with more than half of the total expenditure.[4]

At the eve of the Peace of Münster, the army of the United Provinces numbered 45,000 men, divided in 31 regiment of infantry and 12 of cavalry plus some independent companies, not included the Life Guards with one company of horse from Zealand and two companies of foot from Friesland and Groningen. The infantry was composed principally by indigenous professional soldiers, while 11 regiments were of foreign mercenaries: French, Walloons, Scots, and English. In the cavalry, except for some foreign colonels, the Dutch nationality was uniquely represented.

---

3 'Military men took a keen interest, especially in the period down to 1648, in the military revolution carried through in the United Provinces, since the 1590s, by the Stadholders Maurits and Frederik Hendrik, a revolution characterized not only by innovations in artillery, tactics, fortification, siege techniques, and military transportation, but by a vast improvement in the discipline and orderliness of the military. Together, the north and south Netherlands were the principal school of warfare of both Protestant and Catholic Europe from the 1580s down to the middle of the seventeenth century and were again one of the main schools of warfare, for Europe, from 1672 down to 1713, a period in which the Low Countries were the strategic hub of the great struggle between Louis XIV and the European coalition ranged against him.' Israel, *The Dutch Republic*, p. 42.

4 Marjolein't Hart, *The Dutch Wars of Independence. Warfare and Commerce in the Netherlands, 1570–1680* (New York: Routledge, 2014), p. 154.

For over half a century this organisation had proved to be the best possible for the United Provinces and had ensured the cohesion of the army, but just a few years after the Peace of Münster there was little evidence of the renowned discipline and high level of proficiency deployed in recent years. Historians have concluded that the cause of this crisis is to be attributed to the drastic reduction of strength which occurred after 1648. The political position of the dominant bourgeois classes caused not only the diminution of troops, but also a reduction in the number of officers, causing as a consequence a dispersion of military knowledge and synergy that resulted in deleterious effects.

The strength of the field army had been a point of controversy since 1643. In order to prevent massive bankruptcies and mutinies, the States of Holland forced Frederick Hendrik of Orange, Commander-in-Chief since 1625, to reduce the army from 80,000 to 60,000 men. The Hollanders argued that this would not reduce fighting strength, since one-quarter of the troops only existed on paper. In future, the remaining 60,000 effective troops would be paid on time, they assured Frederick Hendrik.[5] The reduction took effect on 1 March 1643. In the following years, the States of Holland, Zealand, and Friesland turned again on this matter devising for further diminution of the army strength. Prince Frederik Hendrik of Orange, as Stadtholder, and the Council of State had insisted on establishing the new army's strength, but the Provinces had preferred not to commit themselves at that time.

Nevertheless, the decrease of the external threat arrived just in time to solve the emergency represented by military expense, which was provoking the total collapse of the army finances. As a future peace strength, the Council of State proposed in 1647 to maintain in service 30,000 men,[6] but Holland's delegates considered this force excessive and reiterated new requests for a further reduction. A special committee was instituted in order to compose the differences. No agreement was found, but between 1648 and 1649 at least 10,000 soldiers were dismissed. After these reductions, only a further 5,095 men had to be licensed to obtain the intended size. The committee proposed the disbanding 1,340 cavalrymen and 55 infantry companies of 50 men each, as well as reducing 201 foot companies by five men apiece. The agreement could be signed after a further diminution demanded by Holland that brought the overall strength under 30,000 men in all.[7] This plan would interested principally the 11 foreign regiments, reducing French, English, and Scottish companies from 175 to 120, but preserving the strength of the Walloon regiment. Prince William II of Orange, succeeded in 1647 as Stadtholder of Holland, Gelderland, Zealand, Utrecht, Overijssel, and

5 It is interesting to note the debate that involved the Stadtholder and the government about the size of the army and its tactical capabilities. At a size of 60,000 men, the Dutch army was too small to achieve complete victory. A successful attack on the Spanish Low Countries required the conquest of Antwerp, because only then would the major rivers be available for transporting siege artillery and foodstuffs. See also in Nimwegen, *The Dutch Army*, pp. 223–225.

6 Frederik J.G. ten Raa, *Het Staatsche Leger, 1568–1795* (Breda: Koninklijke Militaire Academie, 1911), vol. IV, p. 138.

7 The States of Holland consented to sign the plan of reduction with a further dismissing of 300 horsemen, and the 55 infantry companies to be disbanded would have been selected from the foreign units.

Groningen, considered this reduction as unacceptable.[8] The debate lasted until 1650, when the States General submitted a new plan. The government proposed to reduce the army to 52 cavalry companies (about 3,000 men) and 410 infantry companies (26,415 men). This reduction interested mainly the companies' strength and not the number of units, which diminished slightly during this period. In fact, in 1650, the Dutch army numbered 30 infantry regiments after the disbanding of just one regiment in 1645.[9] The cavalry regiments were now 12, after the joining in a new regiment of the last independent companies. The payroll of this force saw the prosperous and densely populated province of Holland in a prominent position, with 16, and a half infantry regiments and eight cavalry regiments; then Gelderland with four and one; Friesland three infantry; Groningen two and one; Overijssel two infantry; Utrecht one and one, Zealand half an infantry regiment and one cavalry. The committee's chairman asserted that with this force would be possible to ensure 'the security and the reputation of the Republic'.[10]

On 4 June 1650, the States General acted accordingly: Holland notified William II and the Council of State that 31 French, English, and Scottish companies – exactly the province's quota of the 55 infantry companies considered in the reduction – would be disbanded within a fortnight.[11] The rich Holland could enact this decision thanks to her position of economic predominance, trying to force the law. The *Repartitiestelsel* system established that the army was apportioned to each of the provinces according to their economic means, but all troops remained under the command of the government. Therefore, the provinces were not allowed to license troops without the permission of the Generality. Though the States General consented unanimously to the strength of the army as desired by the Stadtholder, Holland delegates insisted on dismissing 55 infantry companies, selected exclusively among the 'foreign nations'. Days later, the States of Holland's proposal to dismiss only French, English and Scottish infantry companies was clearly intended to reduce William II's autonomy over the army and to reassert the authority of the provinces over the troops. In fact, this privilege was the main concern of the regents of Holland and this is unequivocally demonstrated by the provincial resolution already voted in June 1650 to proceed with further army reduction, if necessary on their own authority.

The assault on Amsterdam did not soften Holland's determination, and soon after the sudden death of William II left the province's delegates practically without opponents. Now English, Scottish, and French infantry

8 Several important military commanders of the Orange family had exploited the ousting of the *advocaat* van Oldenbarneveldt in 1618 to curtail the power of the States-Provincial in commissioning officers. As provincial captains-general, they had the final word in the appointment of officers of Dutch and German companies and of field officers. Their influence in the conferment of the patent of captain and lower-ranking office of foreign companies (French, English and Scottish) became even greater, because new officers for these units were commissioned without first consulting the State-Provincial. See also in Nimwegen, *The Dutch Army*, p. 302.

9 Infantry regiment *van den Berg*, raised in 1634 by Holland.

10 *Voorslagen en (de) consideratiën op den niewen Staet van Orlogh*, by Alexander van Capellen, president of the committee, cited in Nimwegen, *The Dutch Army*, p. 302.

11 This decision provoked William II's infamous assault on Amsterdam.

units were reduced to lesser terms, while just the *Gardes te voet* (Foot Guards) regiment maintained the full strength of 10 companies. Preserving regimental structures had not been taken into consideration at all in the army's peacetime establishment, and as a result there were several cavalry regiment formed by just two companies under captains 'who do not know whether they ranged under a regiment and under which regiment, which could then cause disorder during combat with the colours, drumbeat, and otherwise.'[12] However, the regents of Holland believed this force largely sufficient to maintain the synergy among ranks and files with new recruits in case of war that, however, was regarded as an unexpected event. Moreover, if the army was considerably reduced, the fleet could avert every external threat.[13]

In the 17th century, political contrasts were certainly not only a Dutch prerogative, but here the consequences were more serious than for other European states, given that the Republic had relied on a small army for her security since the Peace of Münster, and part of this force, calculated between 5,000 and 6,000 musketeers,[14] had to be deployed on the fleet because of the war with England of 1652–54. The war was fought above all on the sea, but the needs of ground troops persuaded in 1655 the reluctant States of Holland to raise a new infantry regiment, and another in 1660 recruited in Scotland.[15] At first, it seems a sharp inversion to the policy of army reduction supported by Holland, but this effort represented just a small percentage of military expense, which turned mainly on the fleet.[16] The energy demonstrated in the transformation of the navy into a standing war fleet in the 1650s and 1660s contrasts with the lethargy reigned in the army during the same period. Once the danger was over, the policy of reducing the army's strength resumed force. In February 1660, on Holland's insistence, the States General decided to reduce the army to just 24,000 men in all. As outlined by some historians, the explanation for this move is that on the sea, the Republic was confronted

12 Cited in Nimwegen, *The Dutch Army*, p. 301.

13 The Dutch historian Jap R. Bruijn estimated the extent of the fleet personnel during the three Anglo-Dutch Wars at between 20,000 or 25,000 sailors and soldiers, more than twice the size managed in 1642. However, this figure represented the wartime manpower of the fleet, more or less equal in number to the army in peacetime. Even the engagements of the Dutch East India Company, which needed at least 4,000 men, could modify this proportion. Further reading: J.R. Bruijn, *Varen verleden. De Nederlandse oorlogvloot in the zeventiende en achttiende eeuw* (Amsterdam: Uitgeverij Balans B.V., 1998).

14 Nimwegen, *The Dutch Army*, p. 318. In this figure are not included the private troops belonging to the Dutch West India Company and the Dutch East India Company, which totalled 10,000 soldiers and sailors in the 1660s.

15 The 'Dutch' regiment of Colonel Adriaan Cuyck van Meteren and the Scottish regiment of Colonel Lewis Erskine.

16 Navy-related business was wholly dominated by rich Holland, where three of the five admiralties were based, furthermore, the First Anglo-Dutch War caused the Republic considerable problems in the early stage of the conflict: 'The Dutch fleet was traditionally augmented with armed merchant during wartime, but such vessels were no match for specialized English warships, which were armed with many more guns. This pushed the States General to order the construction of sixty new warships in 1653, and in January 1654 they decreed that none of the new ships could be sold without the unanimous consent of the Seven Provinces, making the establishment of the Dutch permanent navy. In the 1660 the Dutch battle fleet was expanded substantially. Between 1664 and 1667 were raised the fund for a further sixty warships, including twelve very large ships of the line.' Bruijn, *Varen verleden*, p. 76.

6. Above and left: The drawings of Hoynck van Papendrecht, commissioned by F.J.G. ten Raa, illustrating the ***Gardes te voet*** (Foot Guards) in the 1680s in blue coat with yellow mustard facings and red neck cloth. The artist reconstructed these figures after contemporary engravings

Left: note, top, the musketeer still equipped with old items, replaced around 1688–89 with a sword belt and ammunition pouch.

Above: a Dutch foot guard positioning a wheeled screen padded with woolsacks. Note the detail of the pocket flap.

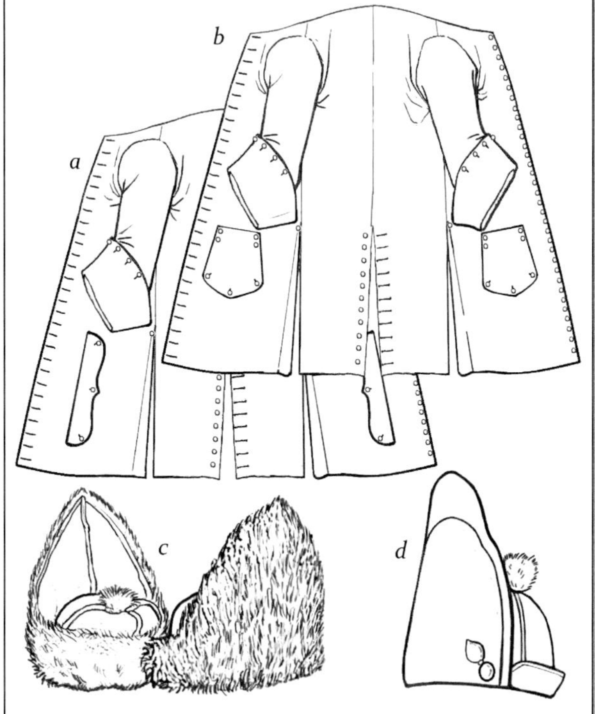

7. Right: Items of the ***Gardes te voet***. a: Grenadier's coat after de Hooghe (1690); b: Musketeer's coat after Papendrecht-ten Raa (1680-89) ; c: Grenadier fur cap, after engraving by anonymous (1690), d: Grenadier mitre cap after de Hooghe (1689), colours unknown, but possibly dark blue plate with yellow grenades and edge, yellow mustard cap with blue pompom. Before the 1690s there are very few example of mitre caps for the Dutch infantry. A part the iconographic sources, in a private collection in USA is preserved an authentic grenadier's cap, but it dates after 1690. The headdresses here represented are the most ancient documented example of grenadier's caps. They evidently mark the passage from the early fur caps to the typical 'Protestant' mitre headdress adopted in a later period. In this evolution, the Dutch infantry marked a style quickly imitated by other northern European armies. (Author's illustration)

with a superior opponent, while a comparable situation on land would not arise until 1667: 'the task of reforming the fleet followed a different path, both in magnitude, and nature, than the task of reforming the army.'[17]

After the crisis of East Friesland, in early 1665 the oncoming war with Münster and England necessitated the reinforcement of the field army. According to the Council of State, the frontiers could only be secured if all the Dutch infantry companies were reinforced with 25 or 36 men. Furthermore, the Council asked the recruitment of 4,000 *mariniers* infantrymen for the service on the fleet, where a whole regiment had been already in service since 1664.[18] This latter recruitment disengaged the ordinary soldiers to be deployed on the fleet, and brought two advantages: more troops became available for the army in the field and it facilitated recruitment in Germany, because among the Germans: 'the apprehension about going to sea was so tremendously great that no persuasions, oaths, yea even written assurances that they would be let go soon as there was the least appearance of going to sea, can be of any help.'[19] At the eve of the war against England and Münster, the Dutch army could deploy approximately 1,470 cavalrymen in 24 companies and 15,000 infantrymen in 191 companies. In March 1665, the provinces consented to a reinforcement of the infantry with 11,000 new recruits. Including the *mariners*, this act strengthened the Dutch army to 39,500 men on the paper,[20] but this force would be only temporary because Gelderland, Zealand, Utrecht, Friesland, Overijssel, and Groningen had consented in June 1665 to a further reinforcement of the companies apportioned to these six provinces. An overall total of 165 companies of infantry and 25 of cavalry were each strengthened, and by way of compensation, Holland financed the equipping of the fleet.[21]

However, in September 1665, the army actually numbered 25,790 infantrymen and 2,600 cavalrymen.[22] The States General tried to overcome the shortage of troops by establishing the recruitment of further 4,000 foot soldiers and 1,000 horsemen, but by mid November only 3,000 infantrymen had been enlisted.[23] The infantry's much greater numbers represented certainly the absence of a rational military policy, rather a strictly defensive strategy, but more important was the lack of a central authority to maintain oversight of all military affairs. In November 1665, the States General petitioned the Council of State to report on the expansion of the Dutch army, which had been decreed earlier that year. The Council of State apologised for being unable to provide any precise information, as such figures were not forthcoming from the province. In addition, it came to light that the states of Gelderland, Zealand, Utrecht, Friesland, Overijssel, and Groningen had been remiss in the reinforcement of the company of horse and foot with 31 troopers and 36 infantrymen to which they consented in June 1665.

17 Nimwegen, *The Dutch Army*, p. 307.
18 The infantry regiment of colonel Theodorus van Vrijbergen (I-35).
19 Ten Raa, *Het Staatsche Leger*, vol. V, p. 138.
20 *Ibid.*, pp. 139–142.
21 Nimwegen, *The Dutch Army*, p. 417.
22 *Ibid.*, p. 321.
23 *Ibid.*, p. 427.

The resulting scenario was therefore obvious. The muster rolls registered several units understrength and therefore the field army could deploy just 12,800 effectives at best.[24] Only eight of the 25 cavalry companies and just 55 of the 165 infantry companies had been strengthened and even then incompletely. The regiments deployed in the autumn 1665 for the incoming campaign against Münster were therefore highly uneven in number and often composed of companies that had been randomly cobbled together. Johan Maurits of Nassau-Siegen, the field commander-in-chief, wrote to the field deputies to inform them about the critical situation of the army, and therefore they turned to the States General specifying each unit's strength:

> From these Your High Mightiness shall be able to see the true constitution and endowment of the garrisons, which ... ought to be treated which the utmost care and without keeping any minutes thereof, much less making copies [but should only] be imparted by word of mouth in secret, and as an extra precaution and certainly torn up at once.[25]

The letter continued explaining the difficult to form an army from this force, without depriving garrisons, and towns and putting them in evident danger. Finally, the field deputies demanded as quickly as possible new recruitment, or otherwise, extra soldiers to send 'in order to obstruct the enemy's design'. Incomplete strength constituted a serious obstacle to the correct application of large-scale combat tactics. This handicap represented a major problem for the infantry, which performed very poorly in the open field. Instead, the cavalry seemed less affected by the lack of personnel, also because it was required to operate tactically in much smaller parties.

After the close of the 1665 campaign, Johan Maurits turned directly to the States General. He presented a report in which he made a whole raft of proposals aimed at improving the performance and the strength of the field army, so that the following year the Republic would be able to plan the war to her advantage. The war forced the government to raise 10 infantry and seven cavalry regiments between 1664 and 1665. The province of Holland contributed with the larger quote, equal to raise four infantry and three cavalry regiments, but also smallest and less wealthy provinces like Utrecht and Drenthe raised funds for the recruitment of more than some companies.[26]

The campaigns against Münster in 1665–66 and the French–Spanish War of Devolution (1667–68) brought about a growing awareness in the Republic that measures needed to be taken to improve the organisation of the army, but energetic measures were still not forthcoming. Thanks to the availability of auxiliary troops from Brunswick-Lüneburg, Osnabrück and Brandenburg, and the arrival of the French corps, the Bishop of Münster was forced to

24 *Ibid.*, p. 420.

25 *Ibid.* Letter of the field deputies to the States General, in Zwolle, 23 September 1665. According to the lines that the field deputies sent to The Hague, the effective strength of the available Dutch force was 60 troopers and soldiers per company, while the muster roll of Nassau-Siegen reveals an average effective strength of 70 men for infantry companies and 60 troopers per cavalry company.

26 Ten Raa, vol. V, p. 197.

stop his assault on the Republic after just one campaign and conclude a peace in the spring of 1666. Fortunately, the poor performance of the field army against Münster had gone unnoticed due to the limited engagements sustained. Critics outlined how experience of fighting in formation above company level was long forgotten and there were only a few Dutch officers who were prepared enough to follow and manage orders from superiors. However, the Second Anglo-Dutch War had created the framework for an army of 69,000 men, a figure that could be reached through the increase of company strength, avoiding the harmful dismissal of officers and NCOs.

The following establishment of the Triple Alliance between the Dutch Republic, England and Sweden seemed to be sufficient to dissuade Louis XIV from attempting further conquest in the Spanish Low Countries. Therefore, implementing radical, and forceful reforms in the army was deemed unnecessary. This decision represented a dangerous miscalculation. The Peace of Aix-la-Chapelle (2 May 1669) quickly dissolved the debate about the army. Plans and proposals for improving the quality of the troops remained only projects. Only the advice to organise the infantry and cavalry into regiments with identical strength was finally adopted. Holland delegates proposed that in peacetime the army should be assembled once a year in one or more suitable flat pieces of ground to be exercised there for several days. However, the positive effect of this measure was counterbalanced by the proposal to slash the strength of the army to 33,000 men, when the Council of State deemed a peacetime strength of 39,000 men to be essential. Reduction of costs was the main goal for Holland delegates and for de Witt too, but the adversaries criticised these measurers as false economy, because the regiments would soon have to be brought back up to wartime strength, causing high costs for recruitment. Moreover, the policy of reduction was detrimental to the quality of troops.[27]

Nevertheless, signals of rising began to be noticed and according to contemporary accounts, in early 1668 the Dutch army was improving in tactical discipline as well as in organisation.[28] This did not mean that there were not many problems remain unresolved,[29] but the general trend appeared positive. Though the most part of the regiments were not at full strength, officers, and soldiers had gained experience during the war and the brilliant action on the Medway, performed by the fleet but achieved thanks to skill and courage of the marine infantry, confirmed this improvement. The

27 The American historian Herbert Harvey Rowen rightly observes that Johan de Witt, Grand Pensionary of Holland from 1653 to 1672, 'failed to see… the importance of a specific army esprit developed over time; for him an army was a relative simple apparatus, something to be bought, used, and dismissed, as the occasion required.' In H.H. Rowen, *John de Witt, Grand Pensionary of Holland, 1625–1672* (Princeton, NJ: Princeton Legacy Library,1978) pp. 599–601.

28 The Dutch army was in better shape 'than she had been in many years', wrote an observer. In Nimwegen, *The Dutch Army*, p. 323.

29 *Ibid.*, p. 312. In June 1669, Major Joseph Bampfield, an offier who regularly advised Johan de Witt on military affairs, complained to the Grand Pensionary: 'I wish that all those who command in Your army were Caesars, Hannibals and Gustavus Adolphus, but in their present state an encampment lasting three months would be very much required to teach them the most necessary things before facing an enemy.'

8. A detail from the landing of the Medway, by Romeyn de Hooghe. Note the private marines in short coats and the officers wearing the fashionable long ***justaucorps*** and laced baldrics.

army remained always without a general commander, but two field marshals were finally appointed: Johan Maurits of Nassau-Siegen and Paulus Wirtz. The sudden conquest of the Spanish Low Countries achieved by the French prompted in 1668 the Council of State and Johan Maurits to propose further improvements. They recommended bringing all the regiments up to the same strength: the infantry regiments to 1,400 men in 14 companies and the cavalry regiments to 480 horse in six companies. Unfortunately, this reform was not yet sufficient. Regimental structures would have to be kept intact in times of war as well as in peace to maintain cohesion by billeting the companies that belonged to the same regiment in a single garrison and dividing the same regiment across the neighbouring garrisons when fewer companies are required there. Another proposal concerned training. The regiments were to be exercised *en corps* by the field officers themselves at least once a week and drill would have to be performed by all the troops in the same manner without regard to nation. Lastly, the generals and the Council of State underscored the importance of holding manoeuvres with an army corps at least once a year, to give the commanders the opportunity to try several battle formations. This latter proposal was implemented. Exercises of troops assembled in army corps became regular and lasted several weeks, as requested by Johan Maurits. In the spring of 1668, Cornelis de Witt attended the training of the troops assembled near Bergen op Zoom as a Field Deputy. He reported with satisfaction to his brother, the Grand Pensionary Johan de Witt: 'the militia [*sic*] of the State is generally complete

9. Godard van Reede-Ginkel (1644–1703), later Earl of Athlone. Colonel of a cavalry regiment and *Luitenant-Generaal* under William III, he left several interesting accounts on the campaign of 1672–78 in the correspondence with his father, who was an eminent regent of Holland. (Author's archive)

and well constituted as it has not been for many years heretofor.'[30] Despite the enthusiasm shown by Cornelis de Witt, musters registered that companies numbered in average 80 percent of the prescribed strength in rank and file, and the tactical size of the battalions remained under the hoped number. At the training camp of Bergen op Zoom the troops were divided among 20 battalions of 400 men in average instead of 700. The provinces failed to hasten the bringing of all regiments to regular strength until late 1671, when they could no longer have been any doubt that France, alongside Münster, and Cologne, was preparing an assault on the Republic. Already in 1670, the French occupation of Lorraine had alarmed the States General and made them aware that the decision to decrease the army had not been a wise one and now, in late 1671, the threat of war made military expansion increasingly urgent. To show their muscles, the States General ordered the mobilisation of two army corps: one of almost 11,000 men at Bergen op Zoom, and a second of 6,800 men at Zutphen, in order to control the strategic area along the River Ijssel.[31] The only immediate aid to the United Provinces could arrive from Spain throughout their domains in the Low Countries. On December 1671 de Witt, and the Spanish governor-general Juan Domingo Méndez de Haro y Fernández de Córdoba, Count of Monterrey, signed an alliance to provide reciprocal support. In accordance with the defensive treaty, the Dutch Republic had to send 10–12,000 men to Brabant, and Monterrey, in turn, kept a cavalry corps with an effective strength of 3,000 men ready to intervene in case these troopers should be requested.

The States General ordered the reinforcements of all the infantry and cavalry companies to 100 foot and 80 horse respectively, and the recruitment of 14,000 infantrymen in 10 regiments and 2,880 horsemen to form six new cavalry regiments. Holland financed the raising of five and a half infantry regiments and five cavalry regiments; Utrecht followed with two and half infantry, Friesland one infantry and one cavalry, Groningen one infantry. On paper, the army had to deploy 64,715 men, but soon this total was considered insufficient, because spies informed the government about the French preparations which continued to grow at an ever-increasing rate.[32] Between

30 *Ibid.*: 'The States-General followed this last piece of advice by immediately ordering exercises with 9,000 men to be held near Bergen op Zoom from April to June 1668.'

31 Ten Raa, *Het Staatsche Leger*, vol. V, p. 207.

32 The government was informed by Dutch traders in Cologne and Münster, but could receive more proofs on the French preparative, if the government had supervised the activity of some financiers who were acting in their homeland. In fact, considerable quantities of items and

February and April 1672, the provinces consented for three times further augmentations for 19,760, then 22,560 and finally 25,200 new recruits.[33] Once the augmentations had been completed, the army would have numbered no fewer than 132,000 men. Time ran out to complete the last recruitment before the enemy offensive was launched in June 1672, when the Republic could field only 80–85,000 men in all. This appeared a significant force, but the majority of troops were scattered across garrisons and, above all, largely formed by inexperienced soldiers and officers who could not match the French in quality. As complained in February 1672 by Colonel Godard van Reede-Ginckel, Earl of Athlone: 'It would have been better if one had taken on some pre-existing regiments, for I fear these recruitments shall be very sluggish and of poor men.'[34] The military commanders were aware on the poor condition of their forces and criticised the politicians for delays in government action. General Paulus Wirtz expressed clearly his opinion on the exasperating slowness of The Hague when he claimed that the regents were 'slow and take care of their own interest and therefore display negligence in defending the state.'[35]

In the same months, the oncoming French attack forced the de Witt faction to appoint the 21-year-old William III as commander-in-chief of the Dutch army. On 17 May, Louis XIV invaded the Republic with 110,000 men, not included the field forces fielded by his allies: the Prince-Bishop of Münster and the Elector of Cologne, which soon joined this very powerful army. England joined the fleet with the French one to tight the nose around the Republic. The discrepancy in numbers turned the French invasion into a triumphal march. The collapse of Dutch defences resulted in the murder of Johan de Witt and the elevation of William III to the stadtholderate of Holland and Zealand. The young prince wanted to counterattack as soon as possible, but the disheartened, and weakened army was yet unable to accomplish this aim. By half June, the enemies already occupied the Generality Lands, Utrecht, Overijssel, Drenthe, and Gelderland, and just the providential *waterlinie* halted further progress. Holland, Zealand, Friesland, and the city of Groningen stood their ground. The 'Existenzkampf'[36] compelled the Dutch to reform their army. That they succeeded in doing this in an astonishingly short space of about two years can be attributed to the collaboration between William III, the new Grand Pensionary Gaspar Fagel, and Field Marshals Johan Maurits of Nassau-Siegen and Georg Friedrich von Waldeck.

---

ammunition were purchased in the Electorate of Cologne thanks to the intermediation of the banker Sadoc of Amsterdam. Through similar connections, the French bought directly into the Dutch Republic gunpowder, lead and saltpetre that one year later they used to destroy the enemy country. See in Cénat, *Le Roi Stratège*, p. 100.

33 Nimwegen, *The Dutch Army*, p. 324.

34 *Ibid.*, p. 325. The criticism was aimed at the officers rather than the rank and file. Another colonel wrote: 'These troops are all brave men, but God grant that our military discipline might regain its former state and glory', and addressed these words to the Stadtholder of Friesland. His letter continued: 'Your Serene Highness would scarce believe what disorder and disobedience I am finding in my regiment among all the unexperienced young officers.'

35 M. Reinders, *Printed Pandemonium. Popular Print and Politics in the Netherlands, 1650–72* (Brill: Leiden-Boston 2013), p. 103.

36 The term 'Existenzkampf' was introduced by the German historian Werner Hahlweg, in his essay *Die Oranische Heeresreform und die Antike* (Vienna, 1941).

10. Above: the siege and capture of Naarden, 1673 (Romeyn de Hooghe).

Naarden was taken by the Dutch army under William III, on 13 September. Note on the right of the picture, the strangely uniformed dragoons, who are equipped with old-fashioned battle hammers and floppy pointed leather hats with fur brims (see close-up, right, and illustration opposite). These are soldiers from the Polish-Latvian ***Coerland*** dragoon regiments. On the left of the picture (and see close-up, left), a trooper of the ***Gardes te Paard*** examines some enemy property.

11. *Coerland* dragoons, 1673. (Author's illustration)

The measures introduced in July 1672 saved the Dutch army from disintegration, but they were still insufficient. After the flood of the country, and waiting for the involvement of the Empire and Spain alongside the Republic to change the strategic situation, turning the French onslaught around was only feasible if three conditions were met: re-establishing self-confidence in the troops; ensure their regular pay, and give financial support to the captains enabling them to recover their losses. This latter condition constituted a novelty. The government had always considered the company commanders as responsible for maintaining their units at full strength. The disastrous circumstances prevailing in 1672 forced a change in attitude. During the winter of 1672 and spring of 1673, the States of Holland took a number of decisions that fundamentally changed the relationship between the army and the state. These decisions affected the Dutch army in its entirety. The army had in effect become the 'Holland army' as a result of the French invasion. The occupation of Gelderland, Overijssel, and Utrecht had left the troops allocated to these three provinces without pay. The States of Holland decided to take on the responsibility of paying all these troops, until the enemy had been repulsed. Holland's share grew from 58 percent to nearly 69 percent of total Dutch army expenses, while the other shared the remaining 31 percent. During the winter of 1672, the Dutch troops lived from hand to mouth, especially the troops who had formally been paid by the occupied provinces. This situation hampered military operations. However, the new arrangement whereby losses were recompensed changed all of this. Within six weeks, a field army could be ready for battle again. Whereas before this time the Dutch army had to retire to its garrisons after heavy fighting, from 1673 onwards the Dutch army could stay in the field and after a short period of rest engage another battle. The second important measure entailed that infantry captains whose companies were mustered at 70 rank and file were paid the full complement. To make the situation less critical and to restore a proper fighting force, an unexpected, and fortunate event came to the aid of the Republic. At the end of the summer, after the payment of a moderate ransom, the French released over 20,000 Dutch prisoners, who in large numbers crossed the front to resume service in the army.[37] Nevertheless, in the autumn of 1672, namely the decisive moment in which the Republic seemed to be able to undertake a counter-offensive, only 25–27,000 men were available for the field army. The total number of

37 This was certainly a serious error, and for over two centuries the French historians considered this act the main reasons because was not possible to win the Dutch resistance. In recent times, also André Corvisier denounced this decision. Instead, John A. Lynn consider that in doing so, the French freed themselves of a mass of men to feed, and even if they returned to their regiments, they were soldiers without equipment, becoming a burden for the Dutch who had to take their maintenance. While it is true that releasing prisoners of war was an age-old military tradition, this does not detract from the fact that the king of France and his minister Louvois made another grave error, because they had not taken advantage of the opportunity to make political capital from the military victories over the Dutch Republic. Moreover, Louis XIV largely had himself to blame, because by demanding too high a price for peace, he forced the Dutch to continue the struggle to the bitter end. See in André Corvisier, *Louvois* (Paris: Fayard, 1983), p. 260 and John A. Lynn: *The Wars of Louis XIV, 1667–1714* (London: Addison Wesley Longman, 1999), p. 163.

troops able to fight was about 43,000 men, of whom 18,000 were assigned to the surveillance of the crucial line of defence on the *waterlinie*.[38] In addition, the States General ordered the raising of seven new infantry regiments and a regiment of dragoons. Speed was of the essence with this expansion of the army, because there was every indication that Louis XIV and Louvois were preparing a large-scale military offensive.

The military reforms carried out in the winter of 1672 and first half of 1673 yielded astounding results. Defeatism and despair were rooted out and replaced by defiance. One year after the enemy invasion, the number of troops available was nearly doubled, the only conquests still in the Sun King's hands were Grave and Maastricht, and his three allies – Münster, Cologne, and England – had abandoned the alliance. First, in December 1672 occurred the successful assault on Coevorden, then in the summer of 1673, the Dutch army started its longed-for counter-offensive. After a siege of just three days, the town of Naarden was retaken, and then William III in conjunction with the Imperial army captured Bonn in the Electorate of Cologne. The new strategic scenario forced the French commanders to withdraw, leaving the occupied territory, and moving their armies to new fronts.

In 1674, 30,000 Dutch troops were sent to the Spanish Low Countries, where they fought together with the Spaniards and Imperialists. Roughly, the same number of troops served there from 1675 to 1678, approximating 40 percent of the total number of Dutch forces, which may be estimated at 70,000 effective men. On paper the army of the States General should muster around 80,000 men, so that the difference between official and effective strength amounted to just 15 percent. This low percentage is comparable to that of the French army.[39] After the return of peace in 1678, the army was reduced to a peace establishment of 40,000 men. In contrast to 1648, however, much care was now taken to ensure that regimental structures were left intact, and that the experience gained during the last war was preserved. The year 1678 saw the birth of the actual Dutch modern standing army. The regiments exercised regularly on army corps level, and companies were mustered more frequently. Muster rolls show that the foot companies in 1680s had an effective strength of about 90 percent.[40]

Through the Caudine forks of the war of 1672–78, the Dutch army gained a reputation for steadfastness and reliability that was highly regarded by allies and enemies alike. Although the situation was favourable, the Dutch army was the instrument that allowed Prince William III to exploit the enterprise of the Glorious Revolution.

---

38 Nimwegen, *The Dutch Army*, p. 453.

39 Guy Rowlands, *The dynastic state and the army under Louis XIV*, p. 171.The author estimates the difference between real and paper strength of the French forces at between 10 and 20 percent.

40 Nimwegen, *The Dutch Army*, p. 353.

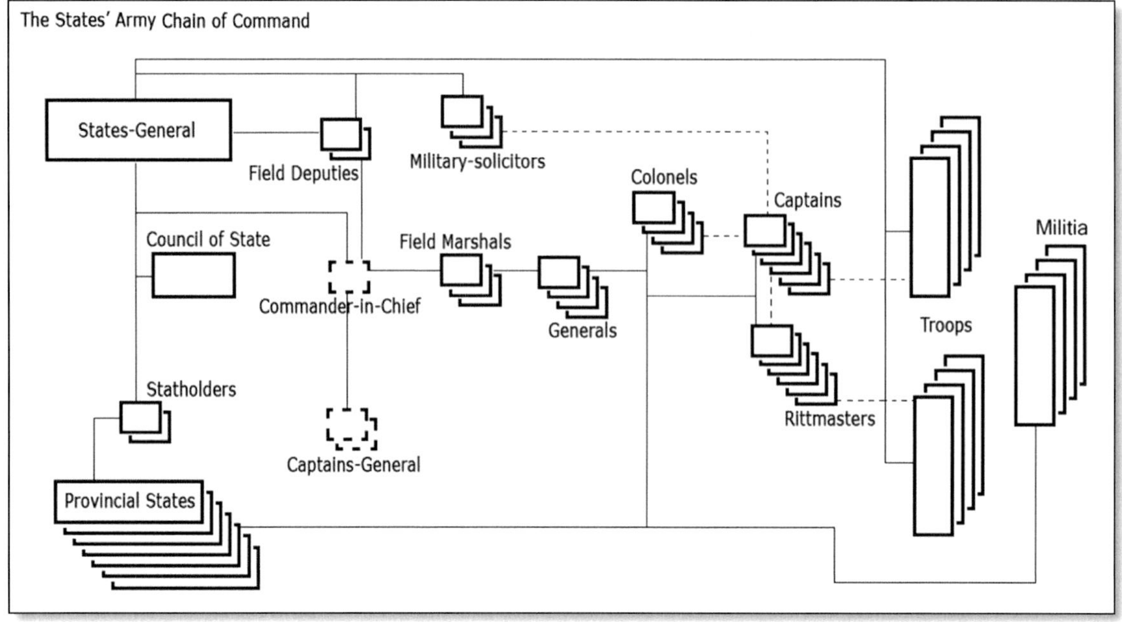

12. The States' Army chain of command.

Command and Military Administration

The balance of powers between the Republican institutions was the basis of sustaining the architecture of the state. Civil power exercised its dominance over all institutions, including the commanders of the army and navy. Also the Stadtholders were subordinated to the Generality, which exercised its authority in times of peace and war. Only in wartime, the Stadtholders exerted a more autonomous role as captain-generals of the provinces' troops. However, the supreme direction of the war belonged to supreme commander: the *Opperbevelhebber* or *Kapitein-Generaal der Unie* (Commander-in-Chief or Captain-General of the Union) appointed by the States General, which entrusted him with command functions in the field. In the first half of the 17th century, this charge was often coupled with the one of Admiral-General, but later the latter had assumed an honorific character and the conduct of naval operations was directed by a chief-admiral chosen from a list of candidates. Formally, the charge of Captain-General, and Admiral-General could not be attributed to the Stadtholders, but this event occurred several times since the origin of the Republic and it was source of great concern for internal political life. The commander-in-chief had a decisive role in the commissioning of the other commanders, natives as well as foreigners. Moreover, he could propose the appointment or promotion of officers and could order the licensing of companies and even regiments, dismissing also colonels. The rank hierarchy continued with the charge of *Generaal van Cavalerie* (General of Horse) and *Generaal van Infanterie*, who held the command of large corps of the respective troops. The other senior ranks were *Luitenant-generaal van Cavalerie* (Lieutenant-General of Cavalry), *Majoor General van Cavalerie* (Major-General of Cavalry), and the same ranks as for the infantry.[41]

The largest formation of the Dutch field army was the brigade of between eight and 12 battalions or squadrons. There were not yet independent divisions, although William III tried to assign the command of groups of brigades to a senior officer, and in some ways he anticipated the creation of divisions and army corps of the following century. However, a sort of rudimentary higher organisation of large numbers of troops for battle, march, or camp existed in the subdivision of armies into the usual two lines, and sometimes an additional reserve for action, divided in the centre, usually formed by infantry, and two mixed wings, each led by a commander.

As happened in several affairs, every act concerning the army was discussed collegially, but the formal authority over the army belonged always to the States General. For the conduct of ordinary affairs of the army, the Republic had instituted the Council of State. This office was comparable to a Secretary of War, formed by members appointed by the provinces. The Council of State acted also for the administrative control of the units, through the commissars who monthly mustered the troops. The responsibilities of the Council of State extended from ensuring that troops were properly fed, equipped, and quartered. Twelve articles governed the responsibilities of the representatives of the Council of State and in these tasks, they operated in the same way as the *Intendant* in the French army. Actor and eyes of the Council of State for these matters was the *Veldafgevaardigde* (Field Deputy). The responsibilities of this official ranged in the key role of controlling that troops were properly fed, equipped, and quartered. Before a war campaign, the Council of State appointed two field deputies who joined the commander of the army on the field. They participated in the war council and could intervene in the discussion like any other general. They also stood at the top of that army's disciplinary system. The nature of field deputies allowed them to concentrate on military affairs alone, freeing them from the need for a corps of sub-delegates working directly under their direction; instead, their most important assistants were the commissars. The field deputies supervised also the activity of the contractors entrusted by the government for the supply destined to the army.

The Council of State continued to appoint officers of any rank higher than colonel. The reason of this was that the authority of the general extended over all troops, irrespective of the province which financed them, but only if the States Generals could approve the appointment. The appointment of captains and senior officers had always been a sensitive matter in the Dutch army. Since 1588 the payment of most of the troops had for political and financial reasons, been devolved to the provinces using the *Repartitiestelsel* system. This meant that all the troops remained under the control of the Generality but they received their wages from the States-Provincial and the number of troops allocated to each province depended on its resources. For this reason, Holland considered the appointment of company commanders and junior officers to be a provincial

41 The rank of brigadier for the infantry and the cavalry was created in 1689 in order to manage the growing army's size on campaign.

prerogative. The other provinces soon subscribed to this standpoint. Either the Stadtholder, in his functions as provincial captain-general, or the States-Provincial, 'recommended' the appointment or the promotion of captain or *rethmaaster* (captain of cavalry) to the Council of State, which subsequently issued the commission in charge for military matters. The appointment to company commander of infantry or cavalry was from then on the preserve of the States assembly of the province to which the company belonged. In the resolution signed on 16 March 1651 the States of Holland had set out the procedure to be followed, which included the clause that 'in the appointment of the officers the procedure to be followed henceforth is by nomination of three persons and immediately thereafter to election, during the same session [of the States of Holland].' The lieutenant and the ensign or cornet were no longer automatically contenders for a captaincy or rittemastership that had been fallen vacant and the stipulation that candidates should have at least four years of military experience lapsed.[42] The Council of State concluded with the suggestion of modifying the function of the army's majors in such manner 'that it only came to extend over the infantry, and consequently that the said function is made parallel and equal to that of commissary-general of the cavalry.' The States General failed to heed the advice of the Council of State until almost three years later, when on 23 March 1671, the recommendations were adopted almost unamended. A transitional arrangement was struck to lessen the pain somewhat for the majors, *rittmasters*, lieutenants, and cornets of the cavalry. The cavalry officers who had received their commission prior to 23 March 1671 would have 'precedence' over majors, captains, lieutenants, and ensigns in the field, but within strongholds and fortified positions the 'seniority' of an officer's commission would be the deciding factor. The rank of 'sergeant-major' of the army and that of commissioner-general of the cavalry were put on the same footing – these general officers were subsequently designated as 'major-generals' and the distinction between captain-lieutenants and normal lieutenants also lapsed.

In 1650, after the death of William II, the States of Holland had left the rank of province's Stadtholder empty. This act favoured the successive abolition of the charge of Commander-in-Chief, voted by the States General in order to exclude the Oranges from any post in the government.[43] Therefore, the army remained entrusted to a *Veldmaarschalk* (field marshal) in the person of Johan Wolfert van Brederode (1599–1655). He was a veteran soldier of the war against Spain, but a less experienced officer for autonomous role and, overall, a feeble instrument for de Witt's policy. Brederode's power was very limited and though his command extended over the troops, for the rest he had very few functions when the army was not in the field. Historians claimed that the absence of a general commander was the main reason of

42 Nimwegen, *The Dutch Army*, p. 53.

43 In 1667, after Holland's insistence, the States-General proclaimed the 'Act of Harmony' which required that the same person could not be Commander-in-Chief and Stadtholder of any province, nor could accept the engagement of a foreign prince. See Herbert Harvey Rowen, *Johan de Witt, Grand Pensionary of Holland, 1652–1672* (Princeton, NJ: Princeton University Press, 2016), p. 805.

the decline of discipline in the Dutch army and certainly, it was a significant problem, however, the field marshal represented the continuity of the military tradition started with Maurits and Willem Lodevijk of Nassau.

The lack of a supreme commander was not necessary disadvantageous, however, the conduction of the army in campaign required a rapid response, when a captain-general of the Union would be indispensable, as he alone possessed sufficient authority to push through reforms effectively. The States General was not the appropriate office for taking rapid decision and the Dutch generals were wary of shouldering responsibility for drastic military innovations, in the battle array, for instance, 'because in case of defeat the blame would be attributed to that'. The generals were of the opinion that only a captain-general of the Union had a mandate to make such decisions.[44]

In this period, a crucial phase began not only for the army but also for the history of the Dutch Republic. After the death of Broderode in 1655, there were just two candidates for this rank: Willem Frederik of Nassau-Dietz, Stadtholder of Friesland. Groningen and Drenthe, and Lieutenant-General Johan Maurits of Nassau-Siegen. There were both valiant officer, but the powerful States of Holland considered it less prudent to place a cousin of the Prince of Orange at the head of the Dutch army. Two years later, when the States of Zealand alongside three other provinces persisted in pressing for the appointment of a field marshal, Holland's regents opposed resolutely to this proposal.[45] The question remained suspended until 1667 when the experience gained during the war against Münster and England had convinced the influential Haarlem regent, Gaspar Fagel, and the Amsterdam burgomaster, Gilles Valckenier, that the restoration of the Dutch army was feasible only if the troops stood under the permanent supervision of a Commander-in-Chief. But the appointment of a commander-in-chief required the amendment of the Act of Exclusion, because only descendants of William the Silent were eligible for the rank of Captain-General and Admiral-General of the Union. However, before 1667, Fagel, and Valckenier had declared that the functions of Stadtholder and Commander-in-Chief were irreconcilable. They thus hoped to allay the concern among the regents about a repetition of the events of 1618 and 1650. A majority of the Holland delegates were able to come to terms with their proposal. In a resolution of 5 August 1667 they had informed other provinces that they would no longer obstruct the appointment of a captain-general established in a resolution that he to whom 'the supreme command over the militia at sea and on land shall ever be tendered may not be nor remain Stadtholder of any province or provinces'.[46]

44 Nimwegen, *The Dutch Army*, p. 3017: Memorandum by Lieutenant-General Daniel de Savornin (1669–1739). Other factors contributed to maintain this opposition to a supreme commander. Having an Admiral-general of the Fleet was not a prerequisite for the Dutch navy's modernisation, because its organisation, financing, maintenance and deployment were assigned to the five admiralty colleges.

45 The regents of Holland declared: 'The army is provincial and no military chief can be imposed upon any province by the Generality.' Nimwegen, *The Dutch Army*, p. 309. The Holland's regents nor could accept the engagement of a foreign prince. See in Herbert, Harvey Rowen, *Johan de Witt, Grand Pensionary of Holland, 1652–1672* (Princeton: Princeton University, 1978), p. 807.

46 Nimwegen, *The Dutch Army*, p. 438.

In the 1670s, the development of European policy would have completely changed this scenario giving a decisive impulse for the transformation of the Republic's internal balance. The growing threat of war with France, by late 1671, had stirred a powerful new movement in the provinces for the appointment of the Prince of Orange as Captain- and Admiral-General of the Union. On 4 December, the Prince's supporters in the States of Holland proposed the appointment. Most of the provinces voted in favour over the next few days. De Witt tried at first to block the proposal outright, arguing that such an appointment would violate the Perpetual Edict, since the Prince already held high political office as a member of the Council of State. Then, seeing he could not prevent it, de Witt supported a proposal for a temporary appointment, for the coming campaign season only, rejecting the captaincy-general for life urged by the Orangist faction.[47] The issue of whether to nominate the Prince captain-general *ad tempus* or *ad vitam* was furiously debated in the provincial assemblies; the States of Utrecht, like most of the other lesser provinces, voted for the latter during December. In January 1672, the States General asked Holland to conform with the majority of provinces and proclaim the Prince permanent Captain-General of the Union. Holland, still dominated by the de Witt party refused, offering the Prince a temporary appointment only, but the Prince declined. The deadlock continued for a few more weeks; but finally, with the external situation continually worsening, Holland yielded, though initially his appointment was for just a single campaign. On 8 July 1672, the States General formally appointed William III Captain- and Admiral-General, albeit under strict supervision of the Generality. On 4 August 1672, de Witt resigned as Grand Pensionary, shortly before the appointment of William III as Stadtholder of Zealand, Gelderland, Overijssel, and Utrecht too. The States of Holland appointed Gaspar Fagel as Grand Pensionary that very same day. Fagel and many others were of the opinion that the struggle against France could be brought to a successful conclusion only if William III was able to pursue an autonomous military direction as commander-in-chief formulating the best strategy as possible.[48] Therefore, the States of Holland empowered their Stadtholder to change 'on this occasion' the law, namely to reconstitute the councils of the voting towns as he saw fit.[49] Eventually, some 130 of the 460 Holland regents were dismissed and replaced by personalities who were prepared to support William III's policy. At the same time, William III assumed overall military command; unlike his ancestors, who had always operated with a large war council, the Prince planned the campaigns himself, with a few close advisors. The field deputies diminished their powers and the Council of State was reduced to an executive body carrying out the Prince's orders. This went against every tradition of the Republic and its politics, but because of the war any opposition was soon silenced.

---

47 Israel, *The Dutch Republic*, p. 790.

48 The need to make the army less controlled by politics was clearly expressed on 20 June 1672, by the delegated member of Leyden, who declared that: 'the Republic should rely more on the Prince of Orange, because an army cannot be ruled by many heads.'. Cited in Reinders, *Printed Pandemonium*, p. 104.

49 States of Holland, dated 16 September 1672, in Nimwegen, *The Dutch Army*, p. 447.

However, in 1672 the 21-year-old Prince of Orange was still an unknown factor. The destiny of the Dutch Republic was now tied to this young Prince on whom residual hopes were placed as if he were a Messianic promise. The implications of the organisational revolution in the art of war surprised not only the Republics political and military leaders, but also Louis XIV himself. Nor could the Sun King have suspected that William III would prove to be an adversary to be reckoned with. The contribution of William III was primarily focused on restoring the morale of the Dutch troops. Apart from administrative reform, the Dutch army was able to get out of that dangerous situation thanks to the strategic and tactical choices of its leaders, who chose to operate offensively, and this against all logical prevision. The Prince enacted a deep reform in the general staff of the army, by rationalising ranks and functions. Field marshals were entruste with leading the army's wings when the command was held by the Prince, or as autonomous commanders in different war theatres, but he remained under the strategic direction of the commander-in-chief.

Like the majority of the 17th century armies' officers, aspiring Dutch officers began their career as volunteers in a colonel's company. More or less usually, on the insistence of some external supporter or for his personal merit, the volunteers obtained the rank of officer in a company when the place became available. This was exactly how Johan Maurits, Count of Nassau-Siegen (1604–1679) began his military career. In 1618, he entered in the company of the *Gardes Friesland* as pikeman, under the protection of his uncle Willem Lodewijk. In 1620, Johan Maurits accompanied his cousin Frederik Hendrik to the Palatinate as a rank-and-file trooper and the promotion to ensign followed later that year. Finally, in 1624, he received the commission as an infantry captain. In the following years, his career progressed swiftly: in 1626, he became a lieutenant-colonel, and three years later a colonel, closing his career as field marshal.[50] Volunteers and cadets who lacked a patron as powerful as those of Johan Maurits were reliant on a long record of service and bravery for their commission and career. Nor even a member of the Nassau family could be given preferential treatment at the expense of an older and more experienced officer, thought the right connections were still essential for someone who wanted to rise through the ranks of the Dutch army.

Foreign officers were usually welcomed in the Dutch army and the most represented were English with Scots and Germans in a prominent position. Since the 1650s several German officers served in the infantry and went up the hierarchy to the highest grade. Alongside fine German officers such as Paulus Wirtz, the Republic had in her service one of the most renowned tacticians and able theorists, Prince Georg Friedrich von Waldeck. In the same period there were also several French officers, included some with high rank, who came into Dutch service especially after the *Fronde*, such as Henri-Charles de La Trémoille and Armand de Caumont de la Force-Mountpouillon. The latter continued to serve under Prince William and was eventually appointed to the rank of Lieutenant-General of Cavalry. Other foreign nationalities in the

50 In the United Provinces, infantry was considered the best school of war, despite that cavalry could be more appropriate for a young aristocrat, but 'the infantry is the true training school of every young soldier'. Cited by Nimwegen, *The Dutch Army*, p. 25.

Dutch officers corps were the Walloons and the Flemish from the Spanish Low Countries, and even some Spaniards, who entered Dutch service after 1672.[51]

The quality of the Dutch officer had been usually highly considered in Europe and until the middle of the century several Dutch captains, and military technicians took service in foreign states.[52] This trend changed drastically after 1648. Several commentators related that the commissions to officer ranks were no longer decided by the experience and qualities of the candidates, but rather for their relationship with provincial and urban factions. Some commentators complained that in Holland commissions to lieutenant and ensign were 'given away in turns by the Delegated Councillors and subsequently assigned to cousins and nephews'.[53] Though he was exaggerating, this complaint was not unfounded. In December 1653, Field Marshal Brederode advised Grand Pensionary de Witt about the 'proficiency' of the Dutch officers, asking to reprimand them for the situation he found. He related that after the States General decided to join 21 Dutch cavalry companies into a field corps in the winter, at the review it came to light that only six *rittmasters* were actually present: 'there are companies among them that do not have a single officer with them, but are led only by a corporal.'[54]

Concerning the lower ranks in the infantry and cavalry and their competence, the Dutch government was involved in continuous reforms and published several regulations regarding the patents of the officers and their duties.[55] In the 1650s, the alternation of reforms caused several drawbacks with

51 This is the case of the Mallorcan 'colonel' Fullana. He took up military service for Spain in 1640 and was promoted to *Sargento Mayor* in 1652 (the equivalent of Major). Fullana specialised in fortifications, taking part in several sieges in Catalunia and Roussillon and finally left for the Low Countries in 1670. Two years later, he joined the Dutch Army in the Zealand regiment of Colonel Alexander Colins d'Aheree. In 1672 his company moved to Amsterdam where he was ordered to man the fortress of Uithoorn. In the waterline near Waverveen, he commanded seven companies and a *uitlegger*, a gun boat, but his troops were to far spread out to make an effective defence and risking being cut off, he retired to Uithoorn again. On the 9 November, he was ordered by Maurice of Nassau to retire to Bodegraven. Fullana did want to fight but some of his companies were taken over by other regiments. Major-General Königsmarck apologised to Fullana in his letter dated 10 November 1672 (written in Dutch and Italian!) about the order to retreat and ordered him to stay at the Uithoorn. Fullana then gave over command. Later, in Amsterdam, he openly adhered to Judaism, taking the name of Daniel Judah. According to Thomas de Pinedo's *litteris et astrologia eruditus*, Fullana was cosmographer of His Catholic Majesty in 1680 and had written excellent cosmographical works. He edited Blaew's *Atlas del Mundo* to which he also contributed. Thanks to Edwin Groot for details of this career.

52 Among the foreign states, in Italy, Venice enlisted Dutch officers, sailors and soldiers until 1645, and especially engineers during the Cretan War of 1645–71. See B. Mugnai, *The Cretan War, The Ottoman–Venetian Struggle in the Mediterranean* (Warwick: Helion & Company, 2018), p. 35.

53 Nimwegen, *The Dutch Army*, p. 435.

54 *Ibid.*, p. 309. In order to form an objective picture of the gravity of the situation, in early November 1657, the States General asked Major-General Frederick Magnus of Salm-Neufville (the Rhinegrave) to report on the condition of the army.

55 In the 17th century, all military personnel who laid a function (*officium*) were designated officers, including the sergeants, and even corporals, drummers, company clerk, surgeon and provost in infantry companies, and, in the cavalry, the quartermaster, trumpeters and furrier. These under-officers were known as the minor, common or lesser officers, the term 'non-commissioned officer' only being coined later. Command of each company was vested in the three 'chief officers': the captain, the lieutenant and the ensign in the infantry, and the *rittmaster* (cavalry captain), the lieutenant and the cornet in the cavalry.

bad effects on the conduction of the army. Because the officers had to relate exclusively with the province, during the First Anglo-Dutch War the Council of State was found to be unable to maintain oversight of the location of the troops, and considered that the States-Provincial were empowered to move the units within the province on their own authority. The lack of information worsened the situation even further, because the troops were sent to sea with the fleet, but nobody knew which, nor in which towns they had been garrisoned on their return.[56] Major problems occurred in the succession to ranks when a place became vacant. The Council of State was not always able to verify that the succession happened according to criteria of seniority and merit and networks of relations influenced the decisions much more than other factors.[57]

The government licensed reforms on this matter twice and only in 1668 was a new regulation for the officers finally achieved. In January 1668, the States General asked the Council of State to formulate an opinion on the ranks and their functions, in order to resolve the problem of status and precedence among them. The dispute about the precedence was finally resolved. Because the captain of the cavalry – the *rittmasters* – contended the title of colonel when the companies were assembled in regiment, they tended to outrank the infantry captain. This contention caused several problems and in wartime these quarrels could have serious consequences. In 1668, the Council of State expressed to be oriented to consider only the dignity of the functions without regard to the employment of the officer, whether he was a cavalry or infantry officer. For the officer of equal rank, the prerogative must be regulated according to the seniority of the commission, and lastly, no distinction was to be made between infantry or cavalry officers.[58]

Before 1672, the responsibilities and duties of the officers are described in detail in *The Principles of the Art Militaire, Practised in the Warres of the United Netherlands, under the command of His Highness the Prince of Orange, our Captain General*.[59] In general lines the Dutch officer were selected among the aristocracy but it took care of candidates who were predisposed to scientific matters, above all mathematics. Because the officers, especially German and French ones, endeavoured to use their diplomatic channels to obtain a rank, the preparation of several captains and even higher ranks resulted approximate. In 1661, three years late the introduction of a new regulation, there were still infantry companies where none of the three officers (captain, lieutenant and ensign) understood manoeuvring or firing.[60] The situation was no better in the following decade. In February 1673, Johan Maurits complained that 'the

56 Nimwegen, *The Dutch Army*, p. 306.

57 *Ibid.*, p. 313. In September 1661, the States of Holland assigned a company to Cornelis de Groot, county sheriff of Hertogenbosch, 'in order therewith to partly extinguish the pretension to Hugo de Groot's heirs by power of the sentence to their advantage pronounced by the Court of Holland against the town of Rotterdam'. Based on this same juridical pronouncement, Jean barton de Bret, viscount of Montbas, was 'given to expect the first French regiment that shall come to fall vacant.'

58 Ten Raa, *Het Staatsche Leger*, vol. V, p. 439.

59 Its author, Henry Hexham, was an English mercenary who for 42 years served as a quartermaster and captain in the Dutch Army.

60 Nimwegen, *The Dutch Army*, p. 312

negligence of all captains, lieutenants, and ensigns, as well as the abuse of their charge is so great that it is unbelievable and insupportable.'[61]

Colonels were the hub of the army and as occurred in the European armies they were selected for the promotion to the higher ranks. The Dutch colonels, however, had to perform their task under the strict control of the government, which probably was much more pronounced than in the rest of Europe. However, this does not mean that colonels were always prepared to follow orders from superiors and sometime they acted independently with alternate effect. A relevant case of impropriety happened in March 1666, when Colonel Otto of Limburg-Stirum, serving as commander of Groenlo, exacted a fire tax in the Bishopric of Münster, even though the Council of State had already issued safeguards.[62]

Alongside the colonels, the companies' commanders continued to play a leading role in administrative matter and in the relationship with the Council of State regarding the maintaining of the troops under them. This was a peculiar characteristic of the Dutch army, which remained unaltered until almost until the end of the century. As occurred in several European armies, the administration of the units was based on the principle that the colonels were responsible for the maintenance of their regiments. However, in the Dutch Republic the same obligation committed directly also the company's commanders. This is a direct legacy of the anachronistic structure of the States' army, as established in late 16th century. The original pattern viewed the captain as main actor for training, conducting, and recruiting the company under his command. This scheme did not change in the 17th century and practically continued to exist until 1688. The captains were obliged to maintain at their expense the strength of their units after they had been formed even when after 1650 the enlistment become exclusively a matter of the provinces. As usual, these obligations concerned not only the losses due to illnesses and desertion, or for discharge, and other physiological causes, but included also combat casualties. The major difference compared to other European armies concerned the financial aspect, namely the payment for the officer, who was reimbursed only after the accomplishment of the obligations, when this commitment usually involved only the owner colonel. The government stipulated the size and composition a regiment should have, and accordingly paid the colonels of foot and horse a monthly or a six-month lump sum for its upkeep. In the Dutch Republic, each colonel as well as each company commanders still acted as responsible for his own units. This involved a financial exposure that not all officers could afford without risk. There were never any exceptions to this rule, which in the government's view had to mitigate fraud and abuse. Unfortunately, it was the source of other problems and, above all, generated other irregularities affecting no less the military finances. Moreover, because the Dutch army

61 *Ibid.*, pp. 343–344. Johan Maurits remarked: 'They are so impertinent that they quit their posts at night and go to the lodgings to bed down two sheets. During the winter months many officers went as they themselves saw fit without asking the colonel's permission, in order to conduct their affairs.'

62 *Ibid.*, p. 316. The Council of State commented this fact with the peremptory words: 'We hereby want to announce to You our profoundly felt displeasure and indignation, with command and precise order to punctually respect our aforementioned safeguards and ensure they are respected.'

also recruited abroad, the financial basis of the foreign officers was often less solid than that of native-born company commanders. Consequently, Dutch captains were too valuable to ruin on purpose. The Dutch government had never given financial compensation for losses in men and equipment but the provinces at least tried to pay their troops regularly. They were aided in this endeavour by an institution peculiar to the Dutch army, namely that of the *solliciteurs-militair* (military solicitors). They were professional businessmen who concluded contracts with captains. In return for an agreed monthly sum, they advanced the pay to the company. Often the States-Provincial were not able to make payment in full and on time, but thanks to the intermediary role of military solicitors the soldiers were assured of their pay. This was of the utmost importance because the troops had to buy foodstuffs themselves when they were in garrison. The duties of a military solicitor were not limited to advancing money. He also looked after the captain's interests when, for example, there was a dispute with the Council of State over the 'closing' of the muster roll. Orders for payment were issued only after a muster sheet had been approved, namely closed. Muster were usually executed in spring and this did not chang even in wartime.[63] During the long Independence War, the system of the military solicitors had permitted to maintain the army's strength to an acceptable level and given an important advantage over Spain.[64] The system guaranteed the existence of the Dutch army at their basic level in the 1660s, but with the French invasion of 1672, the loss of four provinces caused an earthquake in the financing system for the army. Despite Holland assuming payment of the troops from the occupied provinces, the military solicitors were wary of serving those companies because their commanders were unable to stand any surety. By November 1672 the Colonel of Utrecht, Godard van Reede-Ginkel (the future Earl of Athlone), already owed his horsemen two months' pay, while in December Count Heinrich Trajectinus of Solms-Braunfels informed the Grand Pensionary that it was impossible for him to restore his Gelderland regiment to full strength.[65] In October, his unit had participated in the bloody fighting at Woerden, and now could deploy just 150 men in all. Restoring the regiment to its full complement would have required the recruitment of more than 800 men for sky-high bounties of eight *patagons* (20–25 guilders). Gelderland's officers could acquire credit nowhere, 'having lost all theirs', so there was not a single solicitor who wanted to do business with them, Solms-Braunfels explained.[66]

63 The execution of the muster in April caused some problem when the army was in campaign. In 1674, in response to the question from Brussels as to why William III had failed to march with his army to the relief of the besieged Argenteau and Navagne, Waldeck countered that the Dutch company commanders had not been required to have their companies complete before 1 May: 'If one had made them march sooner they would have had this pretext for not acquitting themselves of their duty.' *Ibid.*, p. 473.

64 *Ibid.*, p. 301: 'Heavy borrowing on the money market and the credit advanced by the military solicitors kept the military machine going, but after the conquest of Den Bosch in 1629 and Maastricht in 1632, the Regents of Holland became more and more alarmed about their province's financial position. At the same time, the military solicitors loudly complained about the enormous sums of money, they had already advanced to the troops and which continued to grow.'

65 The regiment becomes the *Gardes te voet* in 1674 (I-8).

66 Nimwegen, *The Dutch Army*, p. 33, letters dated 14 December 1672.

In 1643 the collapse of the army finances had been averted by a sharp reduction in the number of troops, but in the winter of 1672–73 a repetition of this was inconceivable, as all the soldiers were needed to withstand the French advance. In early 1673, Grand Pensionary Gaspar Fagel presented a plan intended to guarantee the payment of the troops. He divided all the companies of foot and of horse, numbering 505 and 123 at the time, into eight groups, respecting the regimental structure. Each group, formed in average by 63 companies of foot and 15 of horse, was assigned to an army pay ordinance only to the respective eight military solicitors. These 'directors' were obliged to pay the units assigned to them promptly 'not by companies but by whole regiment simultaneously, without favouring everyone therein in the least or making any provision to one company before the other.'[67] This meant they were not allowed to refuse less creditworthy captains and *rittmasters*. Holland deposited no less than one million guilders into a special fund, so that the directors could immediately issue a full month's pay. The money was obtained by a levying of extraordinary taxes to the substantial tune of more than 5.5 million guilders for the payment of the army and the military affairs affected. If necessary, however, the directions would also have to use their personal credit or that of their associates to appropriate funds for the army. Over this advance, they would receive a favourable interest and, in addition, they received a fixed monthly fee for each company they served: 28 guilders for a company of horse, 25 guilders for a company of dragoons, and 12 guilders for a company of foot. After the muster, the captains had two months to fill the vacancies. If a company was weaker, then the captain was subject to financial and disciplinary sanctions.

Dutch military scholars declare that it is unclear just how long this system functioned, but it is certain that in 1676 at least 33 military solicitors were employed to advance money to troops who were paid by Holland. Apparently, it had not been possible to limit their number to just eight, because of the enormous sums of money involved. The new situation was not disadvantageous to the troops, because the 33 military solicitors could not refuse a captain either. The States of Holland also helped the company commanders directly and in July 1673, two important measures were taken. Captains received reimbursement for expenses resulting from replacing troops killed in action. This was a very important development because, as already discussed, until that time the captains had had to compensate for losses out of their own resources. Troops who died of other causes than fighting (illness or accident) and deserters still had to be replaced by the captains out of their own pockets, but the States did not leave them to their fate in those cases either. The bonus system enabled the company commanders to create a fund out of which these replacements could be paid. Captains whose companies numbered fewer than 70 men, however, were not entitled to this bonus, and those whose companies mustered below 60 men were not only heavily fined, but were, moreover, dismissed if they were negligent in repairing their losses within a specified period of time.[68]

67 *Ibid.*, p. 332.

68 *Ibid.*, p. 312. The rank and file also benefited by the greater involvement of the government. Food and medical help were assured. The troops no longer had to receive the bread from local bakers,

Commanders of the 17th century considered the regularity of the payment of the troops' salaries as the better method to avoid desertion. In the dramatic period following the French invasion of June 1672, Johan Maurits warned William III about 'the erratic and incomplete payment of wages, [which] was also cause for serious disquiet among the Republics' soldiery'. How dangerous this situation could be was demonstrated already in the opening phase of the war. Johan Maurits, who was in command of the sector near Muiden and was therefore responsible for the defence of Amsterdam, wrote to William III in late June 1672:

> Many of our soldiers pass through here every day, their having been captured in the surrendered towns and having escaped. They have in many days seen no bread. ... Our soldiery, which is already weak enough, is deserting every day by reason of the taxing sentry, duties, the great deal of digging, and primarily those who have their wife and children in those towns that have been captured by the enemy.[69]

On 27 November 1672, when the French made an attack on the post near Ameide, a village on the River Lek. The Dutch troops stood their ground for half an hour, but then took to their heels. General Paulus Wirtz, who had the command in this sector, sent a report to the States General: 'If the soldiers of Bampfield's regiment [garrisoned in Ameide] had not been so long without pay, starved and exhausted, and if there had been more means to hand ... this misfortune would not have come about.' Colonel Joseph Bampfield had for weeks been complaining to the States of Holland about his regiment's pay arrears, and on 11 November he had confronted Grand Pensionary Fagel: 'The soldiers are performing a very unpleasant task ... without money or anything to eat or clothes on their backs or shoes on their feet. ... I do not even have wages for myself and am in serious arrears for my company.'[70]

Shortage of money could also cause mutinies, which were no less feared than desertion. In mid December 1672 all the soldiers of a company deployed to defend the redoubt near Woerdens Verlaat – a post on a strategic waterway at 110 km north-west to Utrecht – left the position and headed for Bodegraven to convey their grievances to Lieutenant-General Count von Königsmark. The officer in command at Woerdens Verlaat could sympathise with the soldiers, because 'for six or seven weeks they not had a *stiver* in money, and the captain has not yet returned, and the soldiers are suffering from great hunger and poverty, such that a person who sees it would have to lament.'[71] Further reports described more dramatic situation. Colonel Johan

---

but were provisioned by suppliers authorised by the States General. Wounded soldiers received first aid in field hospitals, and were not sent to the nearest city until after treatment, resulting in a decline of soldiers who died unnecessarily because of undressed wounds.

69 *Ibid.*, p. 442; letter dated 30 June 1672.

70 *Ibid.*, p. 457. Two weeks later, Bampfield complained that the company of the lieutenant-colonel counted just 18 effectives, another company 20, his own company 35, and the strongest not even 40 soldiers.

71 *Ibid.*, p. 331–332. Lieutenant-General Konrad Christoph von Königsmarck, Bodegraven, with a letter from Captain Jan de Roode van Heckeren, darted 12 December 1672: 'However, Königsmark was less sympathetic and had the mutinous troops immediately lodged with the military provost.'

13. View of a Dutch army's encampment, showing tents, supply waggons, sentinel with pike and other troops and officer; late 17th century. Unsigned ink and wash drawing, about 1680. (Author's archive)

During the 17th century, the Dutch Republic consolidated a highly professionalised army. It was the only way to fulfil the strategic aims of the Republic: defence and protection with forces that were often much smaller than those fielded by their opponents.

van Stockheim, in command at Weesp, a village south-east of Amsterdam, had received reports that referred to the soldiers of the Audignies infantry regiment, who were 'resolved to set their weapons before my house and go separate ways'.[72] The military solicitors were not keen on serving the company commanders of these units because they could not give any security, having lost all their property with the French invasion.

Government's control extended also in matter of recruitment, which took place on a national basis. In the infantry, regiments were divided by their ethnic composition, while in the cavalry, notwithstanding several Walloons, Germans, and others served as horsemen, there was any cavalry regiment classified as foreign. However, in several time the non-Dutch presence was probably equal to the half also in the indigenous regiments.[73] The German component was the most relevant, which included also some Swiss as well, and even Roman Catholics served in the Dutch army without restrictions.[74] The recruit's obligations were regulated by the *Articulbrief ofte Ordonnantie op de discipline militair* ('Letter of Articles or the Ordinance on military discipline') dated 1590, but still valid one century later and remained unchanged until 1795. The enlistment of foreigners, and Germans above all, was practised because it was believed that it reduced the risk of desertion. This conviction had been implemented by Maurits of Nassau

72 *Ibid.*, p. 332: 'Colonel Stockheim sent ten *dukatons* in cash, so that they could at last buy food, for already two men on watch at the Hinderdam, have died of hunger. However, such a sum of cash was insignificant. Jacob van Paffenrode, lieutenant-colonel of the regiment, informed the Bourgomaster of Amsterdam that he needed 1,400 guilders, because the whole regiment is to receive its pay in advance and it is to be feared that if we do not give them something then great calamities shall come about.' The officer added: 'I have given everything I had and last week I advanced eleven hundred guilders to the regiment, and I have therefore divested myself in one go. We have officers who have not eaten for two days.'

73 *Ibid.*, p. 334.

74 *Ibid.* Notwithstanding the access to the encampment was reserved only to Reformed preachers, the Catholic soldiers and officers could visit priests and attend Mass in nearby towns and villages.

and the trend never changed during the 17th century. In September 1665, when the war with Münster was in progress, the States concluded contracts for the raising of two cavalry regiments of 500 horse each, and after agreed that recruits should effectively be levied on the borders. Especially in the cavalry, recruitment of foreigners was favoured, paying higher prizes. For this reason, the *rittmasters* received 'riding money' of no less that 100 *gulden* per trooper. Compared with the travel allowance that was remunerated prior to 1648 – 3 to 5 guilders for a Dutch or German recruit and 10 to 14 guilders for a cuirassier – the States continued to grant company commanders a much higher fee. The war of 1665–66 compelled the Republic to reinforce the army quickly and this naturally worked to the advantage of the officers, whose negotiating position was strengthened. In 1668 the captains contracted to raise a new infantry regiment stipulated a recruitment fee of 15 *guilders* plus five *guilders* for marching money. In 1671, the Council of State fixed the recruitment fee at 20 *guilders* for a foot soldier and 100 *guilders* for a horseman.[75]

Like every army of this age, even the Dutch one, frauds, and peculation occurred in the management of the recruits. The Dutch army's discipline had been considered exemplary in all Europe, and the Dutch regents, and the military leadership did not see the need to improve the way companies were maintained. Muster commissioners checked whether the companies complied with regulations. They deducted the pay of missing troops from the specified sum. This may seem reasonable, but its effect was negative. Rather than encouraging the commanders to maintain their units at full strength, it forced them to defraud the government, the captains were obliged to replace any loss from their own pockets, regardless of how soldiers went missing, namely whether they were killed in action, died as a result of disease or accident or had simply deserted. It was only after they had made good their losses that the captains were once again entitled to full pay. However, it could take months before a new muster had taken place, and in the meantime the recruits had to be fed: 'The company commanders therefore adopted the habit of leading the muster commissioners by the nose in order to create a fund for the replacement of losses. They did this by hiring people who pretended to belong to the unit during the muster, so-called *passevolanten*.'[76] Expedients like this became physiological in the Dutch Republic as well as in the rest of Europe and also the Dutch muster commissioners were fully aware of this fraudulent practice, but they often looked the other way in order not to frustrate military operations. Even during the wars against England this kind of crime passed into the background, but with the stiffening of military discipline imposed by William III after 1672, frauds were unconditionally persecuted. Financial aid for officers and the improvement of living conditions for the rank and file justified the vigorous prosecution of this crime and the introduction of ruthless countermeasures. No one was exempt from harsh punishment any longer, not even colonels. If a colonel was caught guilty of fraudulent acts, the least form of punishment was disbanding the

75 *Ibid.*, p. 321.
76 *Ibid.*, p. 308.

regiment, and the refund of the money, as happened in 1673 with Colonels Hannibal von Degenfeld and Jan Albert Jorman. While Gaspar Fagel looked after financial matters, William III seconded by Waldeck and Johan Maurits concentrated on inculcating the Dutch troops with the proper fighting spirit. Officers were cashiered, heavily fined, and could even be beheaded, especially if they opposed poor resistance or abandoned a position without reason. After the execution of Colonel d'Ossory in 1672 for the surrender of Rheinberg, one year later Quartermaster-General Moïse Pan et Vin was sentenced to death for having abandoned the redoubt of Nieuwerbrug; the sentence was applied on direct orders of William III who overruled the first lighter verdict. The Prince also severely punished insubordination: officers lost their rank and obliged to serve as common soldiers in the Dutch Guards until they had learned to obey, as occurred in May 1673, when three captains and three lieutenants from the garrison of Blokzijl, who had refused to follow the order to dispatch troops to an advanced outpost, were not merely downgraded but also sentenced to carry the pike for the period of one year.

Officers were judged by the *Hoge Krijgsraad* (High Council of War), formed by the Commander-in-Chief alongside a small group of generals and the general provost to the army.

Private soldiers and NCOs were usually judged by the company's major staff, but more serious crimes required field deputies and senior officers. William III authorised the summary execution of troops who were caught in *flagranti delicto*, and units that disgraced themselves on the battlefield were collectively punished by executing one soldier out of each company. His ancestors always spoke of the Dutch troops as their children, and although William III was not indifferent to their plight, he was not as concerned for them as his forebears had been.[77] Soldiers' cowardice in the face of the enemy and looting of one's own population were considered offences punishable by death. However, for this latter crime, very few cases are recorded, because soldiers and civilians maintained relatively good relationships,[78] and within garrisons discipline was usually positive: an event not too common in this part of the century.

In peacetime, the most frequent crime after fraud was absence from duty. In the 1660s, captains, *rittmasters*, lieutenants, and ensigns or cornets were often absent from their companies for weeks, if not months. The Council of State addressed officers but this behaviour never ceased completely.

Supply and Logistics

Many of the problems afflicting the Dutch army were also common in those of other countries, among which the most worrying was certainly the maintenance of troops, namely supplies. Food, forage and other resources present in the war theatre were managed by a network of civil contractors who were responsible for supplying the troops in campaign after having awarded the contract. The

77 *Ibid.*, p. 376.

78 Marjolein't Hart, *The Dutch Wars of Independence*, p. 76.

14. Dutch infantry, *c.*1655, by Gerbrand van den Eeckhout (1621–1674)

Note the pikeman with pot helm and the standing officer wearing a blue sash. During the 17th century, officers maintained close contact with the Provincial States, and thereby safeguarding their interest and their family ties with the regents. After the Peace of Münster, the requirements based on professional competence were lost, while the links with the power remained steady, and in the following decades the Dutch army was filled with officers who had received assignments thanks to their clientele bonds.

States General paid the initial capital in the form of a loan, and the contractor was required to provide the food supply necessary for the maintenance of the troops. The contractor received the title of *Provediteur-Generaal van den Staat* and his business was under the control of the Council of State through the field deputies and their commissars. The abundance of resources of the Dutch countryside was not sufficient to cover the need for flour for the army, turning the contractors to buy grain in Poland. This market had its terminal in the Baltic state of Courland, ruled by a loyal ally of the Dutch Republic. The size of the army determined the engagement of more contractors, but in 1672 the monopoly of the army supply was held by the firm Machado & Pereira. Both families dominated this business until 1714, supplying not only food, but also material and other items and goods, included horses, wood, and wagons.[79]
The equipment of wagons for the regiments was taken care of by the companies through the officers, who usually retained a share from the soldiers' wages. There were no specific rules on these matter and normally every company had a wagon to transport the soldiery's property and naturally also tents, field beds, and other items. The officers could bring on campaign an indeterminate number of wagons as they pleased. Generally, this turned into a train of huge dimension that slowed the march of the army. This train constituted the coveted prize of every soldier after a victorious battle. At Seneffe in 1674, the Dutch army lost almost all the baggage estimated at about 200 wagons of various sizes. Before any further operations could be contemplated, the Dutch army needed to find shelter for more than 2,000 wounded and allow the troops the opportunity to procure new tents, field beds, and clothing. Brigadier-General Godard van Reede-Ginkel, for example, informed his father that he had 'not retained one single shirt, not even my slippers. ... Of my spare horses I have, thank God, lost no more than one. My chaplain, maid, valet, baker, and kitchen boy have been taken prisoner or are dead. My wagon master and two grooms aside, one does not know their whereabouts. All in all I have lost everything.'[80] Van Reede-Ginkel was a wealthy man, so he could recover from this setback, but for less well-heeled officers the loss of baggage, saddle horses, and personnel was a heavy financial blow, because the government did not compensate such losses. On 31 August 1673, a convoy of several hundred wagons with provisions and new equipment for the field army arrived in Mons, as well as a large sum of money for the advancement of one month's pay for a part of the army.

Even the care of the wounded was managed independently by the companies. Civilians under pay and the religious cared for the wounded and took charge of their transportation to the improvised field hospitals or loaded them on the cars. There is a good account on this task written by Agidius Van Couendael, minister of the *Gardes te voet*. He stated that the preachers actively

79 Jacob Pereira (1629–1699) was born in Madrid and eventually escaped the Spanish inquisition in 1646. In the Netherlands he became an extraordinary wealthy leader of the Amsterdam Jewish community and in 1656 joined Antonio Alvares Machado (?–1706) in trade affairs. This latter owned plantations in Surinam and financed the business ventures of Curaçaon settler Manuel Alvares Correa, which included slave trading. Both had a large trading connection with Poland, Caribbean and other markets. See in Yosef Kaplan (ed.), *The Dutch Intersection. The Jews and the Netherlands in Modern History* (Brill: Leiden-Boston, 2008), pp. 63–87.

80 Nimwegen, *The Dutch Army*, p. 479.

participated in battle, provided the guardsmen with water and helped carry their wounded to safety, besides supplying the soldiers with muskets, powder, lead, and matches.[81]

Infantry Organisation

In the first half of the 17th century, the Dutch infantry companies, no matter whether they were 89, 113, or 200 strong, had 12 or 13 officers and NCOs: one *kapiteyn* (captain, or captain-lieutenant, who served in absence of the captain), one *lieutenant*, one *vendrigh* (ensign), 2 *sergeanten* (sergeants), three *corporaels* (corporals), two *trommel flagers* (drummers), one *schriyver* (clerk) and one *chirurgijn* (surgeon). Since 1599, each company also had its own *provoost* (provost). Regiments could be formed by an indeterminate number of companies, and this characteristic did not cease even later. The first company belonged to the *kolonel*, followed by those assigned to the *lieutenant-kolonel* and *majoor*. Companies continued to be assembled in larger corps for tactical reason, and the peacetime delayed the need to form permanent regiment of equal size. The administrative function of the regiment and its benefit for the regular management of the army was prevented by the policy of decrease of the armed forces, resulting in infantry regiments of different sizes, which were assembled in field-battalions sometime formed by three or more regiments, because even the companies were of unequal strength. The senior commander considered this difference as a serious inconvenient for a war campaign. In 1658, during the first crisis of Münster, the States General suggested bringing the companies earmarked for this corps to their full complement by borrowing troops from garrisons that would not be participating in the expedition to Münster in order to have companies with equal strength. The Council of State rejected this plan, pointing out that it would wholly upset the company administration, because:

> ...such reinforced companies shall be commingling of two and three sorts of soldiers from diverse companies and garrisons, to whom the payment of the salary advances cannot be organised as well as for whole companies, besides it having to be kept in mind that the companies are so weakened, first by the sending of troops to Danzig and by the musketeers who are detailed to the fleet and are fighting at sea, that no soldiers can be missed from them.[82]

In January 1666, General Johan Maurits of Nassau-Siegen, commander of the Dutch army against Münster, tabled a raft of proposal to improve the infantry's fighter strength. He insisted that the battalions earmarked for field service should as far as possible be composed of companies, which belonged to the same regiment. Colonels, lieutenant-colonels and majors should have their own companies included under these, in order to be better able to lead,

81 *Ibid.*, p. 479. 'Van Couendael's bravery knew no bounds: he lay under the dead for half an hour and thus saved one of the regimental colours captured by the French, which he will be able to prove with the testimony of several officers should it be required.'

82 *Ibid.*, p. 409.

with discipline and affection, with their own soldiers.[83] Each regiment had to be provided with flags in a specific colour, so that soldiers on the march or in battle could easily relocate their company, 'having been learnt during the last campaign that the soldiers were unable to find their respective unit for three or more days, because they had forgotten the name of the captain and could not distinguish between the colours'.[84]

In the 1660s, the number of companies fluctuated from 10 to 12 and even more in some regiments, like the *Gardes te voet* (Foot Guards, the old regiment); while, as a result of the decrease of the army strength, the foreign regiments deployed fewer numbers. The number of companies remained undetermined and in 1665, Captain Caspar Richard Hundebeck was appointed as colonel of a newly raised regiment established with 10 companies. In 1667, after the insistence of Johan Maurits, the government established the number of companies for an infantry regiment as 14, resulting in 1,400 men in overall, excluding officers and major staff. Each company deployed 62 musketeers and 34 pikemen; NCOs and drummers completed this figure. In this count were also excluded the boys – *enfants de troupe* – who served inside the regiment. Nevertheless, this rule was not applied everywhere, because in early 1668, a newly raised regiment was established at 15 companies, for an overall force of 1,555 men included major staff and other personnel.[85]

The regiment's strength was usually reduced by half in peacetime. In 1665, the emergency of war persuaded the States-Provincial to increase the number of soldiers with 36 men for each company; then, four years later, the strength was increased again as effect of the French invasion of the Spanish Low Countries. Finally, in December 1670, the provinces consented to the advice of the Council of State to strengthen all the infantry companies to 100 men. This measure was partially accomplished and mostly of the infantry regiments entered the war with incomplete strength. The series of setbacks suffered by the Dutch army, with the continuous surrender of garrisons, involved the infantry more than cavalry or artillery, causing the loss of whole regiments. Before the end of 1672, five regiments had been dissolved or disbanded as consequence of the loss suffered in campaign; then a further 12 regiments had been disbanded the following year and two more reformed for disciplinary reasons. The emergency forced the commanders to merge soldiers of the disbanded regiments into the others, resulting in a wide range of different strengths. For instance, in December 1672, the company of Captain Snaerts, belonging to regiment *Königsmark* (I-77) numbered 140 rank and file; nevertheless, two days later it had only 40, because 100 soldiers had deserted in a single night.[86] The regiment had been raised at the beginning of 1672, and this could cause a physiological tendency to dissolve, but also veteran regiments led by experimented commanders claimed the loss of whole companies overwhelmed

83 *Ibid.*, p. 322.

84 *Ibid.*, text by anonymous and without date, but very probably drafted by Johan Maurits of Nassau-Siegen in 1667.

85 *Ibid.*, p. 321.

86 *Ibid.*, p. 344.

by the French offensive.[87] Desertion and easy surrender were not the norm for the decreasing and some regiments dissolved for different reason.

Before the war of 1672–78, four regiments were qualified as French and commanded by French colonels. The actual French composition of these regiments is disputable, but among the officers there were several French names. This is related in the casualties list of the 'French' regiment *Thouars* (I-84) after the battle of Seneffe in 1674. Among 21 officers killed, wounded, or missing there are some Dutch names, but at least eight are very probably French natives.[88] Also in the other 'French' regiment involved in the battle, *Villamair* (I-9), six of the eight fallen officers have French names.[89] It is quite surprising to find such a large number of French people in the Dutch army fighting against the Sun King. Apart from the famous Richelieu sentence 'there has never been a war fought by France without among her enemies there were some Frenchman', the presence of these 'exiled' officers constitutes a less investigated matter. The French presence was not only the direct consequence of the *Fronde*, or the religious hate that rose up after the revocation of the Edict of Nantes, which occurred later, in 1685, but also because of the strong links between aristocracy and commanders, with the latter who managed their client relationship with the noble cadets.[90] The French invasion closed many of these links, and in 1673 the original French regiments maintained only the ancient legacy: most of them were disbanded or completed with German or Dutch indigenous recruits, but in 1673 an attempt was made to raise a new French regiment enlisting the deserters from the enemy army.[91]

Similar events had involved the English regiments in 1665, when the regiment *Craven* (I-4) and *Sidney* (I-18) were licensed as the war against England began; while a third 'English' regiment – *Dolman* (I-16) – was converted to a 'national' one in the same year. However, the English colonel continued to serve until 1672.[92] The long tradition of the foreign regiments in the Dutch infantry was then represented by *Walen* (Walloon, I-11) and Scottish regiments, which were still in service in 1678.

Alongside the other foreign regiments, the Scottish too had suffered from the reduction of strength in the 1650s. However, in the 1660s their fighting strength had been restored at least partially. In 1665, regiment *Kirckpatrick*

87 This was the case of the regiment Bulkesteijn (I-20) raised in 1623.

88 *Kapiteyn* du Four, de l'Espée, la Primée; *Lieutenant* de l'Espée, Mirop, Vangelac, de Colombe, Corstel. Also the colonel, Marquis George le Vasseur de Huyle et Thouars, is registered among the wounded. See in P.J.E, de Smyttere, *La Bataille du Val-de-Cassel de 1677, ses preludes et ses suites* (Hazelbrouck, 1865), pp. 244–248.

89 *Ibid.*, *Majoor* Porteclaire, *Kapiteyn* la Sale, la Rocque, Taillafer; *Lieutenant* la Riviére and Colonel Maurice de Maurier-Villamair, who was killed in action. He was replaced by another French colonel and this tradition lasted until 1709 with the Huguenot *Brigadier* Maurice Pasque de Chavonnes, in charge until 1715.

90 On this topic, see also in Matthew Glozier and David Onnekink (eds.) *War, Religion and Service: Huguenot Soldiering, 1685–1713* (London: Routledge, 2017).

91 The Holland regiment of Colonel François de Courval (I-95).

92 Alongside Thomas Dolman, other Englismen continued to serve the Dutch Republic after 1665. They are the *Lieutenant-Kolonel* Humphrey Payton and *majoor* Edward Asteley. See in *Hoofdoficieren der Infanterie van 1568 tot 1813 door H. Ringoir in Bijdragen van de Sectie Militaire Geschiedenis* (BSMG) nr. 9 ('s-Gravenhage, 1981).

15. This is the only known picture depicting English infantry in Dutch service.

The image is included in the famous playing card series printed in 1685, illustrating the rebellion of 1685 led by the Duke of Monmouth. As the threat of rebellion increased, king James II had recalled the Anglo-Scots Brigade from the United Provinces. Note the musketeers are shown with baldric and bandolier in the distinctive cross belt appearance. (Author's archive)

(I-15) fielded 910 rank and files, divided into 16 companies.[93] During these years, the Scottish regiments were frequently divided between two provinces, and indeed in 1655 the States of Holland resolved, in view of the fact that of several regiments one portion had been allocated to them and another to that of other provinces, to bring all the apportioned forces together complete as the 'Holland regiments'; but it seems doubtful whether this was ever fully carried out, although the two Scots regiments in 1655, and the three in 1662, are described as regiments belonging to Holland.

Up to that time the regiments had remained thoroughly Scottish in character, and an army lists dated 1665 consist wholly of distinctive Scottish names. The war against England in 1672 modified the circumstances and gradually the composition of the regiments lost their actual Scottish origin. In 1673, in the regiment *Scott* (I-5), there can only be found the three field officers and three captains of Scottish surnames ; in *Kirkpatrick* (I-15) only three field officers and one captain; and in Erskine's (I-32) only the three field officers. *Scott* regiment had two or three English captains, and in the regiment *Erskine*, which became 'national' since 1665, two officer were certainly Englishmen, but all the rest of the captains of the Scottish regiments were not Scots.[94]

In 1678 the Scot Brigade had been fully established on its reorganised basis, the capitulation of that year expressly stipulated, that the pay of the soldiers was to be increased *d'un sous de plus par jour.*[95]

Before the end of the war, another Scottish regiment and three English regiments were raised, placing the Scots–English presence as the most relevant of the Dutch army in this period.

93 Ferguson, James I: *Papers Illustrating the History of the Scots Brigade in the Service of the United Netherlands*, Edinburgh, 1899; vol I, p. 496. The Colonel's, Lieutenant-Colonel's and Major's companies deployed 75 or 74 men, while the rest of the companies numbered 49.

94 *Ibid.*, p. 468. Ferguson added: 'In the following year Lieutenant-Colonel Allan Coutts is left as the sole representative of its original nationality in the third regiment, w'hose Scottish colonel, Louis Erskine, has been succeeded by Jacques de Fariaux, Heer van Maulde, a gallant officer, under whom it seems to have fought well at the siege of Maestricht, where in an important horn-work it faced the charge of the British troops that fought side by side wdth the French under the Duke of Monmouth.'

95 *Ibid.*, p. xii. According to Ferguson the Scottish presence in the Dutch army followed this path: 'From 1655 to 1660 the three were again converted into two, and between 1665 and 1672 the third regiment became completely Dutch, and its place was taken, in 1673 [actually in 1675], by a newly raised one.' The author outlines that 'the two older regiments had an unbroken existence from 1588, if not from 1572, and from 1603 respectively, while the third, dating from 1673 [namely 1675], substantially represented the one formed in 1628.'

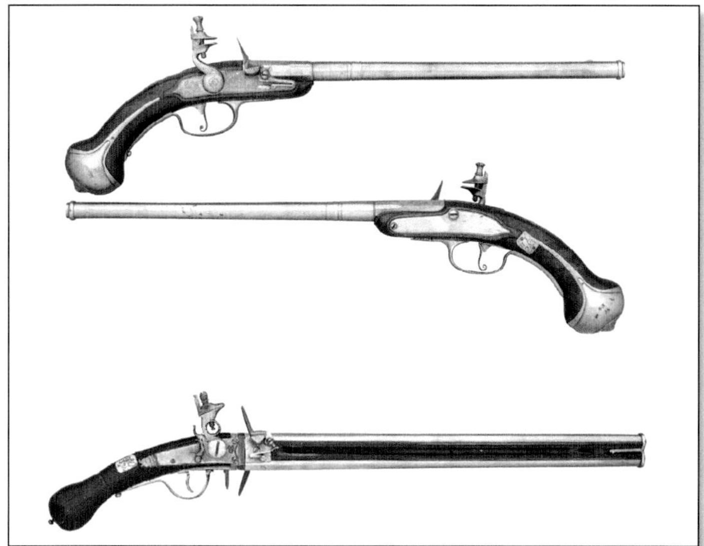

16 (left). The United Provinces were an interesting laboratory for producing new weapons or improved versions of common arms. Above, a pair of Dutch early flintlock holster pistols with pre-charged turn-off barrels, *c.*1665-70; below,a double barrel cavalry flintlock pistol, with turn-over barrels formed in two stages, probably Dutch 1660. (Private collection)

17 (right). Another unusual weapon, a flintlock holster pistol manufactured entirely of steel, Dutch or German *c.*1660. (Private collection).

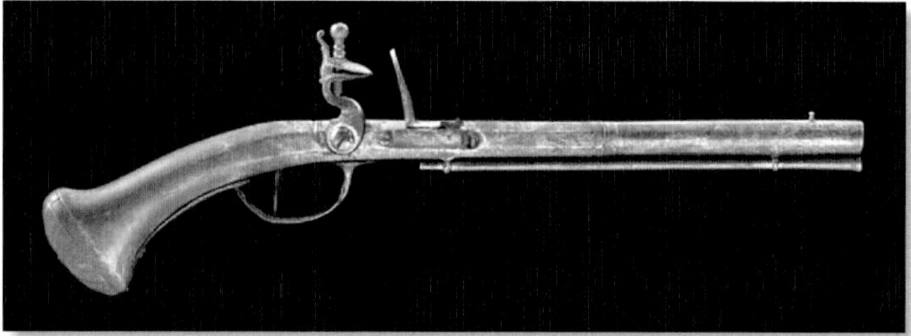

The need of foot soldiers forced the Dutch Republic to recruit mercenaries in all Europe. A very welcome help arrived thanks to Duke Friedrich Casimir of Courland, who in 1672 recruited for the Dutch Republic one infantry regiment alongside cavalrymen and dragoons. The infantry remained in Dutch service until 1678. Relationships abroad were exploited for searching for more troops. Thanks to the captain of the *Honders Suisse* (the hundred Swiss Guards of the Holland's Stadtholder), in 1672 one infantry regiment of 12 companies was raised in the canton of Zurich. The regiment had to move to the Spanish port of Finale in Italy before the end of the year to sail to Amsterdam, but delay and other difficulties forced it to delete the contract.[96]

The Dutch infantry supplied also the fleet as naval troops for the landing operations as well as in naval engagement. In the First Anglo-Dutch War, 5–6,000 musketeers served on the fleet and the growing need of naval infantry led to the formation of the first *marinier* (marine) regiment in 1664. The

96 In his authoritative work *Het Staatsche Leger*, F.J.G. ten Raa states that no Swiss troops were part of the Dutch Army before 1690. However, the assumption by other, non-Dutch, authors record that one Swiss regiment was recruited in 1672 by Colonel Bonstetten as a troop apportionment to Holland. The contract was later delayed, due to the difficulty of joining the Dutch army, but the companies had been formed and the payment for the engagement was authorised by Holland. This information was provided by Jean René Bory, an expert on Swiss mercenaries, but he died in 2009 and his research is still unpublished.

need of infantry grew again and about 2,600 other infantrymen were send to the ships in the Second Anglo-Dutch War. In 1669, a new marine regiment was raised and another regiment was converted in marine in the same year, but the employment of infantry on the fleet forced to assign further ordinary infantry for the naval campaigns of 1672–78, such the expedition against New York, Martinique, and the other French colonies in the Caribbean. Overseas commitments forced the government to dispatch a whole infantry regiment to Surinam, menaced by the English and French navies. In 1674, the regiment *Winkelman* (I-74) sailed to Fort Zeelandia, where remained until the end of the war without engaging in any fights. However, the regiment suffered greatly by diseases and the harsh living conditions in that remote region.

Grenadiers were introduced into the Dutch infantry in 1672 following the French example. Experiments with hand grenades had been already performed by the master 'fireworker' Johan van Haren.[97] In the frenetic weeks before the French invasion, he received the order to form a grenadiers company, followed by a second in 1673 for serving on the fleet, and attached to the marine regiment *Walenburg* (I-44). An army list dated 1673 mentions three companies of soldiers trained in the throwing of hand grenades, two of which are registered as separate units.[98] The third company with a full strength of 100 men was part of the Guards Regiment. Finally, in 1674, Prince William ordered that each company of infantry had to drill 20 men to throw hand grenades, extracting them from the pikemen. This order regulated a situation already existing, as related in the correspondence of Johan Maurits, who informed the Council of State that in the same year his infantry regiment (I-31) already had fully equipped grenadiers. Later in 1678, the number of grenadiers was reduced to six in each company. After the French invasion of 1672, and in order to re-establish the equal number of men in a company, the States of Holland proposed to reduce all the infantry companies to 70 men in rank and file. In fact already before the war, the number of 100 men on paper resolved more often in an average of 70 effective combatants. The States of Holland decided to go again further and in January 1673 all the companies were reduced to 89 men at all. Only the new Foot Guards – the regiment of the *Gardes te voet van Zijne Hoogheid* (I-8) – remained with their original strength. This regiment deployed the highest number of soldiers in the Dutch infantry, and in 1674 increased the number of company to 25; therefore it could field three battalions, while most of the regiments deployed two or just one. Strong differences in the strength between regiments remained a constant and the ordinary 14 companies for each regiment was largely unfulfilled. In early 1675, the Dutch army was in better condition compared to two years earlier, thanks to the economic support granted by the provinces. In December 1674, William III had ordered the Dutch captains to have their companies complete by 1 April 1675 at the latest. He had learned the lesson of May 1674, when the French had besieged Argenteau and Navagne without

97 Ten Raa, vol. V, p. 323.

98 *Staat van Oorlog*, 1673.

the least opposition from the allied side. However, after the inconclusive campaign of Maastricht, the infantry regiments numbered an average of just 428 men instead of an establishment strength of 700 to 800 men.[99] The reduction of the effective strength to 70 men continued to be not sufficient to facilitate the regiments in the deployment of the expected numbers. The muster of spring 1676 revealed that the regimenst *Birkenfeld* (I-59), *Uytenhove* (I-11), *Slangenburg* (I-32) and *Torsay* (I-21) could deploy for the incoming campaign an average of 62 or 66 men per company.[100] Differences between theoretic and effective strength was physiological, but in some regiments, the overall force had decreased to just 269 men. The regiments of Groningen and Friesland registered the major shortage of men and this problem persisted undiminished until 1678.

At the end of the war, the Dutch infantry numbered 51 regiments and two companies of life guards. In detail, Holland fielded 24 regiments (including five foreign regiments); Utrecht: six regiments; Friesland: six regiments and one life guard Company; Zealand: five regiments; Groningen: four regiments and one life guard company; Gelderland: four regiments (including one foreign regiment); Overjissel: two regiments; Drenthe: one regiment. Approximately, in the 1680s the overall peacetime strength was 50,180 men.

Since the beginning of the 17th century, the Dutch commanders experienced that hours of repeated drill made infantry more effective in battle. Drill also imparted a remarkable *esprit de corps* to the rank and file, even when the soldiers were recruited from the poor class of the society. A well-drilled army, responding to a clear and coherent chain of command capable to reach down to every corporal from a prince claiming to rule by divine right, constituted a more efficient instrument of policy than had ever been seen before.[101]

The trademark of the Dutch infantry was its firing system. It was in December 1594 that Stadtholder

18. Willem Frederik van Nassau-Dietz (1613–1664), painting by Pieter Nazon.

Williem was the second son of Ernst Casimir I, Count of Nassau-Dietz and Sophia Hedwig of Brunswick-Lüneburg. In 1640,Willem Frederikwas appointed as Statholder and Captain-General of Friesland. He played a key role in William II of Orange's coup by leading the attempt to seize the city of Amsterdam by force in August 1650. For a while, in the late 1650s, there seemed to be a chance of him becoming commander-in-chief, as part of a political compromise, brought together by Johan de Witt, but nothing came of it. In 1650 he held the statholderate of Groeningen and Drenthe too. On 1664, during the campaign against Münster in East Friesland, he was entrusted with the field command, and after the successful outcome of the Dijlerschans assault hoped for promotion to field marshal. However he was killed in October 1664, by a gunshot while cleaning his pistols.

99 Nimwegen, *The Dutch Army*, p. 469.

100 *Ibid.*, p. 339.

101 Moreover, in this period armies could establish a superior level of public peace within all the principal European states: 'this allowed agriculture, commerce and industry to flourish and, in turn, enhanced the taxable wealth that kept the armed forces in being.' W. McNeill, *The Pursuit of Power*, p. 137.

Willem Lodewijk van Nassau first informed his colleague Maurits van Nassau about the method he had devised to make it possible to fire a continuous volley. The Dutch captain explained what he had in mind with diagrams and footnotes. He subdivided the soldiers with firearms into groups numbering nine across by five ranks deep. After the musketeers had fired together by rank, they were to make an about-turn to the right and move to the rear between the files. It is true that the importance of infantry firepower became even further established in the second half of the 17th century. The successive improval restricted the rank of the musketeer wings to three in order to avoid the march to the rear, which resulted as the most critical phase. Now the musketeer would fire par platoon in order to maintain a non-stop volley.[102]

This system required great skilful and continued training, which after 1648 had been much diminished. Although some commanders continued to esteem the importance of infantry fire, the Dutch battalions performed the easier rank per rank fire. In 1672, the usual infantry formation still laid down the standard five ranks battalion with the pikes in the centre, although later many battalions formed only four deep – and eventually even three – due to the manpower shortages as the war continued. It is important to note how practical considerations often caused the officers and men to disregard the orders of higher authority. Although the new weapons with their superior reliability and speed of reloading were potent reasons for reducing the number of ranks in a battalion formed for battle in the interests of producing greater frontal fire output, no official attempt to implement such reforms was attempted for a considerable time. In 1672, battalions contained considerably more musketeers than formerly through the progressive replacement of the pike contingents deployed until 1648, but little effort was made to secure truly maximum fire output, although the initial discharge of these formations remained redoubtable. The ranks narrowed the distance between their front to the enemy, which made it impossible for more than the first three ranks to close up and fire in a concentrated volley. Thus, the front rank would kneel, the second crouch, and the third stand upright, while the others stood idly by. There were variations within this method, however the most commonly employed was the rank-by-rank discharge. This provided that the first rank would fire and then, lowered weapons, knelt to allow the second rank to discharge, who in turn would take to the ground to allow the third to fire, and so on. After five line volleys of this type, the whole formation would rise up and set about reloading, because the ram-rod could not be wielded properly in the kneeling position. However, it is not unlikely that some Dutch infantry regiment was still trained in the platoon system, or had reintroduced it after 1672, especially in the field army, as confirmed by the

102 It is almost impossible to trace the real origins of the platoon firing system with any certainty. According to David Chandler *The Art of Warfare in the Age of Marlborough* (Cambridge, MA: Da Capo Press, 1995), p. 116: 'French military writer Le Blond considered that fire by platoon ... has long been in use among the Dutch; there is some evidence that its invention is due to them, and that they furnished the model for the other nations of Europe which have copied it.' However the Dutch claim is not unchallenged, and there is a school that believes that firing by platoons dates back to the Swedish army of the Thirty Years' War.

French reports after the battles, which often emphasise 'the continuous fire' of the Dutch infantry.[103]

Cavalry and Dragoons Organisation

Because the nature of the warfare in the Low Countries turned to a defensive and stronghold based strategy, the Dutch cavalry fielded always a smaller force compared to the infantry. The usual average of three or four foot for each horse was even more unbalanced in the Dutch army, which in 1660s, fielded one horseman for every 10 infantrymen. This percentage lasted until 1665, when the States General voted for new recruitment and the cavalry had to be augmented to 3,500 troopers, and the infantry to 29,000 on paper. Dutch officers often complained about the shortage of cavalry, asking for an increase of the strength for the mounted force, but the cavalry-infantry ratio continued to remain one of the lowest in Europe, reaching just 1 to 6.5 in 1678.[104]

In 1660, a company of horse had eight officers: one *rithmeester* (captain of cavalry), one *lieutenant*, one *kornet* (cornet), one *quartier-meester* (quartermaster), two *trompetters* (trumpeters), one *schrijver* (clerk) and one *hoefsmid* (farrier). The ordinary strength was 42 troopers in peacetime, and this establishment lasted until 1668. In 1669, as occurred in the infantry, the provinces authorised the enlistment of further 31 troopers for each company. Therefore, the regiment deployed 480 horses, with six companies of 80 horses, obviously on paper. The effective strength of the cavalry regiment fluctuated considerably and some regiments remained at the original strength, as revealed by the musters executed in those years.

The reputation of the Dutch cavalry considerably decreased after 1648. In 1657, General Frederik Magnus *Rijngraaf* of Salm noted that most of the troopers were green and inexperienced people 'who had virtually bought their places from the officers by offering to serve for a few months without pay, were concerned only with farming and civilian trade' and did know nothing of their duties; even the horses were young and poorly trained.[105]

The *Rijngraaf* submit to the Council of State a regulation that invested in the provinces and the fortress commanders the responsibility for the training of the troops in the most necessary exercise. From April to September the troops had to exercise every two or three days, the company at least every month as a whole and the regiment every two or three months. Cavalry corporals were instructed to ensure that the trooper cared well for their comrades and that each of them knew how to bridle and saddle his horse. The training of cavalrymen was always a long and laborious process, although the majority of recruits knew at least the rudiments of horsemanship on joining the regiments. As the cavalry invariably fought in squadrons of two or more companies in strength, they exercised in this formation, being

103 Several quotes concerning the Dutch firepower are in M. de Quincy, *Histoire Militaire du Regne de Louis le Grand Roy de France* (Paris, 1726), vol. I.

104 In the 1680s, the peacetime ratio – including dragoons – was one horseman to every 11.4 infantrymen.

105 Nimwegen, *The Dutch Army*, p. 320.

drawn up in three ranks with their officers to the front. Every unit would first be made proficient in the ability to close up and open out the ranks and files. Cavalrymen and dragoons were also trained to perform the *postures* or exercise of arms. As occurred in several armies of this age, the Dutch cavalry – usually deployed on the flanks of the infantry and guns – still advanced at the trot to fire, in formation of three ranks at once. Following the discharge of pistol and carbine, the squadrons spurred through the smoke to engage in the melee, swords in hand, or repeated the manoeuvre as decided by the commander.

Reforms undertaken in 1658–60 improved the quality of officer and troopers. Moreover, cavalry suffered less compared to the infantry in decreasing the army's strength, maintaining a sufficient number of officers and later performing with proficiency. In 1664, During the campaign in East Friesland, the Dutch cavalry performed better than the infantry and the general commander Willem Frederik of Nassau-Dietz wrote to the States General that 'was a delight to see (this cavalry), consisting of very fine men and advantageously mounted and equipped, with such weapons that there a nothing to be improved or to be wished for therein'.[106]

Ten years later, the difference between the strength on the paper and the effective field strength was as great as for the most complete of the infantry companies. This forced the States to apply the reduction of strength as had happened in the infantry. The full organic size of a cavalry company was reduced to 69 men: eight officers, with 19 horses, and 61 troopers with one horse each. The muster rolls reveal an average field strength of 52 troopers, equal to 15 percent.

After the war of 1672–78, the regimental establishment totalled 22 cavalry regiments with three companies. Each province providing their cavalry regiments. Holland alone fielded 14 regiments, three regiments from Friesland, and one each the remaining provinces. The Stadtholder of Holland fielded his own Guard regiment with six companies and one *Garde du Corps* company. The Stadtholder of Friesland also fielded one Guard regiment with four companies (including his own company of life guards) and one *Gardes du Corps* company. This gave the Dutch cavalry a peacetime establishment of approximately 3,350 officers and troopers.

The dragoons represented a novelty in the United Provinces. The first regiments were raised in 1672, one of which provided by Duke Friedrich Casimir of Courland, who had relationship links with Hendrik Casimir of Nassau-Dietz, Stadtholder of Friesland, and Groningen-Drenthe. The regiment had been recruited in the Polish-Lithuanian Commonwealth for the province of Friesland. They travelled from Lithuania through northern Germany to the Frisian town of Stavoren and stayed in a winter camp there. In the following spring, they joined the field army and in 1676 became an elite regiment under Prince William III.

In 1672, both dragoon regiments comprising eight companies of 100 men. Each company of dragoons comprised 94 men and 100 horses for 14

106 *Ibid.*, p. 321.

officers, three boys, and 77 rank and file. The average field strength was 71 men in rank and file, no less than 92 percent of the paper strength.[107]

In addition, there were also for independent companies with 100 men each. Holland raised two independent companies for Prince William III, which in 1676 were added to the *Gardes Dragonders* regiment, established with 10 companies.[108] In 1678, all dragoon companies were reduced by two men, then on 6th January 1679 the *Nassau-Saarbrucken* dragoons companies were merged into the Holland regiment *Brandt* (D-2). This regiment was eventually assigned to dismounted duties, while the dragoon guards companies were reduced to 80 men. In 1680, the regiment still had 80 dragoons in each company; the other regiment reduced the strength to 52 men still dismounted. In 1684, the regiment was remounted by reducing one trumpeter and one trooper from 65 cavalry companies of Holland.[109]

Artillery Organisation

Like the majority of European armies, before the 1670s the United Provinces did not possess artillery organised as a tactical corps. In the Dutch army a special command rank was created in 1590, namely a senior artillery officer who was responsible for the direction of the artillery on campaign. Before 1677, the artillery personnel served in temporary units in the garrisons or assembled in a company for a campaign depending on the number of guns. An actual regiment of artillery was raised only in 1677, however in advance compared to other major powers. The first commander was Lieutenant-Colonel Johan de Bye van Albrandsweerd, in charge until 1686, and replaced by Charles de Coulon, a former Imperial officer.[110] In 1677, the regiment deployed six companies of 175 men each;[111] then, after the Peace of Nijmegen in 1678, two companies were disbanded, and the remainder reduced to 90 men. In 1677, the regiment included also 60 pioneers divided among the companies.

The regiment's major staff comprised one *kolonel*, one *lieutenant-kolonel*, and one *adjudant*. In detail, each company was formed by one *kapiteyn*, one *lieutenant*, two *adjudanten* (officers' servants), four *meesters van de vuurwerkers* (master fire workers), four *bombardiers*, three *under-luitenants*, 46 *konstabel* (gunners), one *korporaal timmerman* (corporal pioneer), nine *timmerlieden* (pioneers), 4 *corporaels knecht* (corporal servant), 100 *knechten* (gun servants or labourers). Bombardiers were also responsible for the civilian personnel enlisted for the artillery train.

The standardisation of the Dutch artillery had been established in 1590 by Prince Maurits of Nassau, and comprised only four calibres: the *carthoune* of 48 lb, the *half-carthoune* of 24 lb, the 12 lb, and the 6 lb guns. This latter was

107 *Ibid.*, p. 339.
108 Ten Raa, *Het Staatsche Leger*, vol. VI, Page 270.
109 *Ibid.*, p. 271.
110 *Afstammingen en Voortzettingen der Artillerie door H. Ringoir in Bijdragen van de Sectie Militaire Geschiedenis* (BSMG) nr. 4 ('s-Gravenhage, 1979).
111 Ten Raa, *Het Staatsche Leger*, vol. VI, p. 456.

the most employed in campaign, while both the heavy *carthounes* formed the siege artillery park. For this task there were also mortars of several calibres. The 12 lb gun provided the counter-battery fire during a siege as well as in field. In 1668 lighter colubrine of 3 lb of three sizes – short, medium, and long – were introduced as field guns following the Swedish pattern. Howitzers were also introduced in the 1670s. Civilian contractors supplied horses and wagons for guns and ammunition as well. Suppliers were required to meet specifications comprised in the contract, and in order to preserve the artillery and the gunpowder, the ammunition wagons had an oiled waterproof cover to protect the load from the rain. The artillery train represented always a significant economic concern. The heavy 24 lb gun required 17 or 19 horses; the 12 lb was usually drawn by 13 horses, and the 6 lb by seven or eight horses.[112] These figures included the horses required to draw the ammunition wagons, loaded with 100 projectiles, and 20 cartridges for each piece when in campaign; this number could rise 10 times for a siege. Because of its size, the siege artillery was more exposed to the lack of horses. This problem represented a source of drawbacks, as happened in November 1665 during the campaign against Münster, when two mortars had arrived, but without munitions, so these weapons were useless, as the field deputies complained.[113]

Provincial Militias

The Dutch 'Military' still retained many aspects of the medieval heritage and one of the most iconic feature was the provincial militia. Close to the States' permanent army, there were the *Schutterij*, or *het Uitschot*, an infantry reserve force descending from the ancient town's corps instituted in the 15th century. Service in the Dutch militia was originally on voluntary basis, but the States-Provincial could call to arms civilians in the case of an imminent danger. The Dutch militia gained a growing political role in the 17th century Netherlands. Usually enlistment into the militia granted special permission and tax exemption, and only the wealthy citizens could rise up the ranks until the position of officer. Moreover, the honour of belonging to a militia company is widely represented by the rich collection of paintings representing officers and sometimes even the private volunteers of these units, proud of their membership of them.

The primary role of these militiamen was the replacing of the regular troops in the ordinary duties, like the surveillance of the access to the towns, escorting for personalities and other tasks when the regular force was engaged in field operations. Big cities, like Amsterdam, The Hague, and Rotterdam, deployed up to 60 companies, usually grouped by the residence or even professional categories. The size could vary considerably and in many cases there were officers in excess, in order to gratify the most important families and attract other aspirants to serve in the ranks. Though each province had its own militia, the effectiveness of the companies was obviously different from one case to another. However, militiamen represented the first reliable force for the maintenance of public

112 Nimwegen, *Kanonnen en houwitzers*, in Armamentaria 32, 1988.

113 Nimwegen *The Dutch Army*, p. 423.

order in the towns as well as in the countryside. The companies had their own officers with an undetermined number of drummers and NCOs. The troops comprised musketeers and pikemen in proportion probably not much different compared to the regular infantry. Iconographic sources not always confirm the presence of pikes and often the musketeers are equipped with old weapons with fork. However, pikes were registered in the town's arsenals. In February 1671, the States of Groningen ordered to provide 3,000 muskets, plus bandoliers and forks, and 1,500 pikes inside the city, in order to distribute this weapons to the provincial militia.[114] Besides the militia, there were also the *waardgelders* (literally 'Waiting for Money'). These volunteer were originally enlisted as temporary troops, paid and hired by towns, after permission of the States General in order to supply recruits for the regular army.

The Peace of Westphalia drastically changed the position of the town militias, which immediately lost their military function. In some town the authorities reduced the formation half of the original strength. The willingness to support the cause of the Republic was obviously much reduced after 1648. The decreasing size of garrisons in the wake of the Peace negatively affected urban prosperity in all frontier areas. In 1648–50 the number of soldiers in most garrisons was reduced to a third. All male inhabitants were still formally required to participate, but many preferred to purchase exemption at a rate of five *guilders* a year. This changed early in 1672, when the threat of war prompted the sudden revival of the militia companies. The States-Provincial of Holland ordered their regular exercise in April. But numerous burghers were unwilling to take up arms. The companies experienced enormous difficulty in filling the full strength now required. Apparently, the community solidarity evident during the Eighty Years' War had faded away.

In that dramatic spring, everyone understood that Louis XIV's invasion army outnumbered the Dutch regular forces. In June 1672, in order to fill the gaps in the infantry regiments caused by the French invasion, all the available *waardgelders* had sent to the regular corps. The Dutch troops were qualitatively inferior, and dangerously dispersed in the garrisons and around the defensive ring. Emergency steps were taken already in May, when the States General ordered the raising of several thousand civic militiamen in Holland and Utrecht, and rushed them to stiffen the garrisons to the south and east. The States of Gelderland too tried to assemble 3,000 armed civilians, within their province, to bolster the frontier strongholds. But it was all too little too late: the province was occupied and the militiamen disarmed. The field deputies van Beverningk informed de Witt on the actual scenario, preparing The Hague for the worst. He did not expect the Rhine strongholds would hold back the French for long, 'because the burghers are not only fearful and discontented, but some of them are fleeing, others remain, and yet others threaten to cause harm, so those poor garrisons are in an awful situation, expecting an attack from without and obstruction from within.'[115] In

114 This information is provided by Edwin Groot, who thanks the Groningen's historian Hary Perton for sending a picture of a page from the great order book of the States of *Stad & Lande*, namely the province of Groningen.

115 Hieronymus van Beerningk and Samuel van Huls to the States General, 2 June 1672, in Nimwegen, *The Dutch Army*, p. 439.

19. Two portraits painted by Jacob Fransz van der Merck, representing the captains of two of the six companies of the civic guards of Leiden, dated 1657.

In the portrait of captain Nicolaes Hendriksz (left) there appear in background the militiamen of the 'orange company', indicated by the colour of the ensign and the sash worn by officer and troops. The other portrait represents Gerrit Leendertsz van Grootveld as captain of the 'blue company'. Usually the enlistment into the militia granted special permission and tax exemption, and only the wealthy citizens could rise up the ranks to the position of officer. Moreover, the honour of belonging to a militia company is widely represented by the rich collection of paintings representing officers and sometimes even private volunteers of these units, proud of their belonging to the corps.

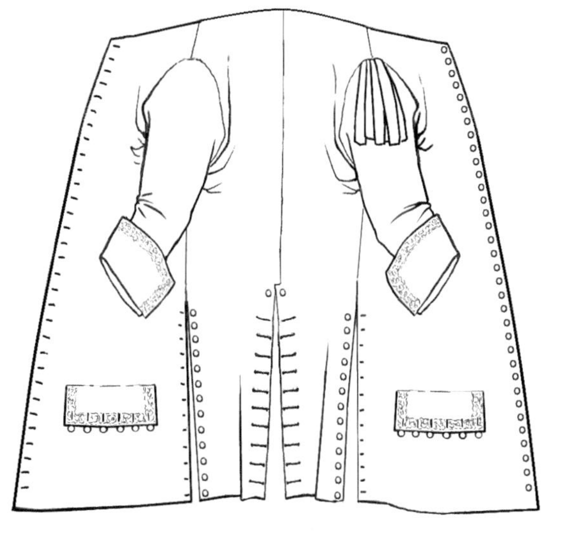

Anti-clockwise from top left:

20. Detail from the painting 'Playing Card' by Pieter de Hooch, dated 1672. Dark blue coat with red cuffs and ribbon, silver buttons and embroidery, suggest that this officer could belong to the Foot Guards company of Friesland or Groningen. Both these companies are documented wearing this uniform in 1680–90, but the same colours could have been adopted already in previous years.

21. Reconstruction of the officer's ***justaucorps*** after 'Playing Card' by Pieter de Hooch.

22. Infantry regiments comprised a variable number of boys and soldiers' sons – ***enfants de troupe*** – who served as junior adjutants or, the lucky ones, as apprentices to the senior officers. This fine portrait, made by the Dutch artist Johannes Verspronck in the early 1650s, shows one of the first examples of a ***justaucorps*** coat with flap cuffs. Note the pattern of buttons and buttonholes.

23. Cover illustration from the ***Nieuwe Jaars aan de Manhafte Schuttery van Nederland*** of 1672. The town militia of Amsterdam called to arms for the incoming war against France wear justaucors coat with flap cuffs. Note the flag with the Holland motto VIGILATE DEO CONFIDENTES.

June 1672, the near disintegration of the Dutch army and the loss of whole provinces caused a surge of emotion among the public, a form of national feeling which expressed itself through special church services for the safety and well-being of the state. Many cried betrayal, not only of the regular officers, but also by those of the militia and their soldiers.[116]

By January 1673, the States-Provincial of Holland decided to take firm action: more than 20,000 citizens were mobilised, and compensated when they were sent for service in another town. In moving militias between towns, the danger of local militias turning against their own urban authorities was reduced. For instance, the Gorinchem's militia departed for elsewhere and the town received 750 militiamen from Haarlem and 250 from Alkmaar.[117] These attempts to introduce some kind of compulsory military service proved short-lived, however, and disappeared when the direct war threat of the 1670s had subsided. This poor scenario weakened morale in the frontier towns and further undermined their defences. When the French army arrived in Doesburg in 1672, the town appeared sufficiently fortified, the fortifications having been repaired in time, with batteries in place and a reinforced garrison of 3,500, plus the urban militia. But the town surrendered remarkably quickly. At a certain point during the siege a number of burghers, farmers, and town soldiers planted a white flag on the ramparts. The governor ordered it to be taken down, but the urban authorities supported the inhabitants, and then the military command decided to surrender.[118]

The war against France marked a turning point in the history of the Dutch army, and also

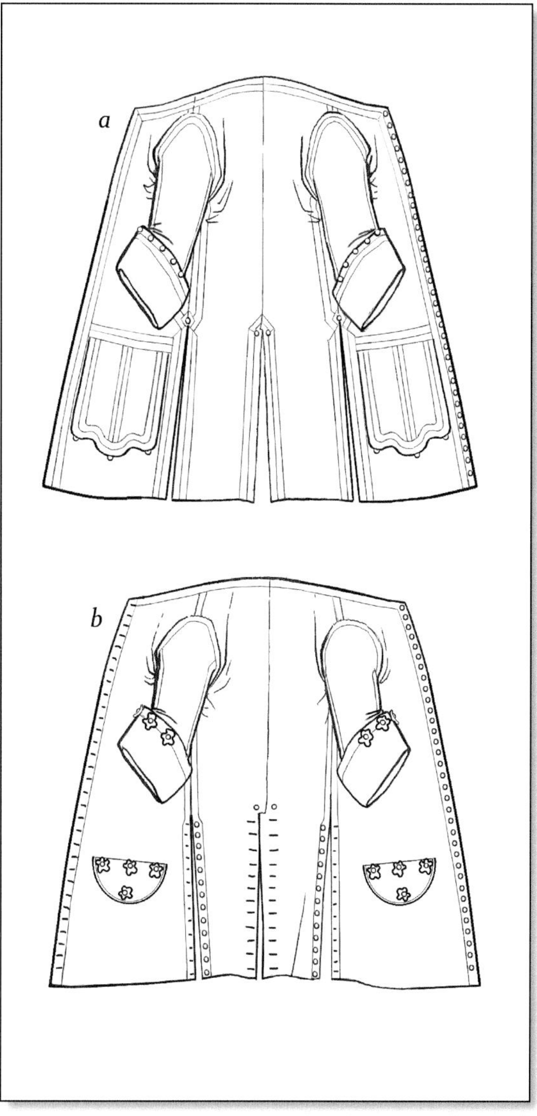

24. Coat patterns after the *Nieuwe Jaars Gift aan de Manhafte Schuttery van Nederland*, dated 1672 (opposite); a: ensign; b: drummer.

116 Israel, *The Dutch Republic*, p. 738: This emotional tide, on the one hand, fed anti-Catholic sentiment. Reformed resentment of Catholic behaviour, in 1672, was intense. The Catholics of Nijmegen, according to Brun, welcomed the French as they had the Münsterite, in 1666, with open arms, displaying a *rage furieuse contre ceux de la religion*, revering Louis XIV as a Messiah come to save the Catholic faith. But at the same time, it was noticed that other Churches were as stirred by the peril as the Reformed, and no less demonstrative of their commitment to the Republic. In one case, the Jews' patriotic conduct in 1672 was subsequently used as a justification for toleration. Stouppe laid special stress on Dutch toleration of Jews as part of his campaign of disparagement. Brun, in reply, cited the special services the Jews held in their synagogues in 1672, and their prayers *pour le salut du pais*, remarking that he wished that all native-born Christians had proved, *aussi bons patriots* as the Jews.

117 Hart, *The Dutch War of Independence*, p. 85.

118 *Ibid.*, p. 86: 'The consequences were disastrous; the French destroyed 33 houses and another 55 were set on fire; troops were forcibly billeted on the population: even the burgomaster had to house four cavalrymen. But most far-reaching was the destruction of the fortifications, which left the town an easy prey in the future.'

with regard to the militia institution, their relevance in society was greatly reduced. Even if the provincial militias continued to exist until the following century, it is certain that their usefulness against regular armies could be considered almost irrelevant. Provincial militias continued to perform their duty far from the front, entrusted with easier tasks like town policing and static duties at gates, roads, and government buildings.

A significant exception was represented by the Friesland militia, which supplied troops for guarding the strategic posts across the Frisian *waterlinie* alongside regular troops. This happened in September 1672, when Count Johan Maurits of Nassau-Siegen, in charge for the defence of Friesland, called to arms the *plattelandsschutterij* (peasant militia) and ordered them to march on Gorredijk. On 2 October, in order to secure the outposts of Legemeer and St. Nicolaasga, between the marsh of Tieukemeer and Langwarder on the northern sector of the *waterlinie*, the aged general dispatched the provincial militia to form a reserve corps. The militiamen were under the command of an infantry lieutenant-colonel of the regiment *Gardes Friesland* (I-20).[119] However, Johan Maurits was aware that the use of these troops should be limited only to the defence of the less threatened points.[120] Though these troops provided limited support, Johan Maurits was of the opinion that in the event of a French invasion of Friesland, the whole militia should be transferred to Coevorden, in the province of Groningen for protecting the next line of defence. For this it should be necessary to receive the permission of Friesland's States, because the militia, unlike the regular army, belonged exclusively to the respective province.

The provincial militia of Friesland continued to provide its men for the formation of reserve corps in the rear of the *waterlinie* until the end of 1673. With regard to the numerical consistency, the sources provide little indication, however in June 1672 it was estimated that at least half of the Friesland militia could replace the regular troops in the garrisons. Therefore, the general mobilisation could field 5–6,000 'volunteers'.

The other major war event that saw the active participation of the militia was the defence of Groningen in the summer of 1672. On 21 July the Bishops of Münster and Cologne started their siege of the town. Beside the regular troops, the garrison comprised town militiamen and even a company formed by the students of the University of Groningen. The civilians in arms performed well, thanks also to the enemy's difficulties in maintaining the siege, which lasted until 28 August.

Volunteers forming the Groningen town militia participated in the successful assault on Coevorden in December 1672. At least 150–200 volunteers marched alongside the regular troops, including several Jews, who possibly were the first to be involved in a military operation since the start of the early modern age in Europe.

119 Van Dam van Isselt, *De Verdediging van Friesland*, p. 214.

120 *Ibid.*, p. 219: 'well-suited militiamen for manning posts in the northern waterline may be employed for the defence of his own towns and villages, but it should be appropriated if these "militia" (volunteers) of the State, did not act for strategically offensive operations outside their posts.'

3

The Dutch Army on Campaign

Warfare in the Netherlands

The war-theatre in the Low Countries is delimited to the north by the Meuse estuary and the Rhine. The Rhine, with the River Ijssel, borders also the eastern territory with its lower course. The Ardennes with the Aisne and the Somme delimit the southern area, and the North Sea to the west. The territory has not changed in recent centuries, apart from the increase in urban areas, and then as today the plain was intersected by a great number of channels. The major rivers were navigable and widely used for the transport of goods. The Meuse could be crossed at Roermonde, Stevensweert, Maastricht, Liège, Huy, and Namur. The Sombre, a tributary of the Meuse, could be crossed at Namur, Charleroi, Marchienne au Point, and Mauberge. The Scheldt, after its conjunction with the Lys, had its main crossing places in Ghent and Dendermonde. The movement of the armies was therefore hampered by the rivers and by the network of channels that connected them to the smaller centres; however the road network of the the Dutch Republic was more developed compared to the one in the Spanish Low Countries and in the mid Rhine area. The heights of the Ardennes to south, and the Hohe Vee high ground to the east did not represent relevant obstacles. A large part of the territory was cultivated and large pastures favoured the breeding of livestock and especially horses. The abundance of resources made these regions an almost perfect theatre of war. For this reason almost all the towns were fortified, although not all of them staked their safety on modern curtains and bastions. The Dutch Republic had a good number of fortified cities, but only a couple could be considered truly up to date. The most significant strongholds were Maastricht and Bergen op Zoom, the latter located on the course of the Scheldt and defended by wide flooding. The powerful and robust Maastricht, straddling the Meuse, dominated the access to the territory of Liège and Limburg, and was defended by numerous external works with moats that could easily be flooded and overflow onto the surrounding terrain, thanks to the cataracts of the River Geer. Here the Dutch and Liège's domains intersected each other and borders often remained uncertain. Other strategically important towns, and therefore better fortified, were Hertogenbosch, defended by a large swamps, Nijmegen and Thiel, protected by the Waal, Grave and Gorinchem both on the

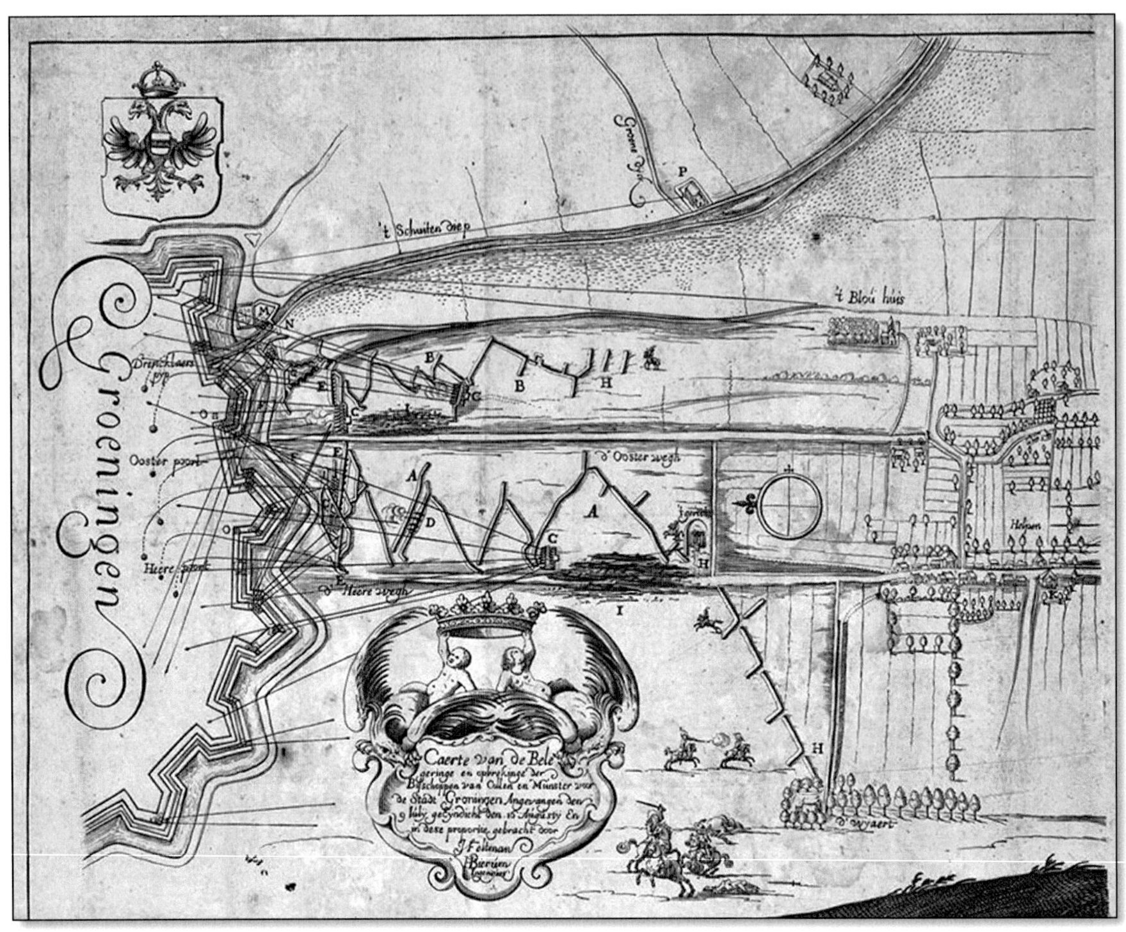

25. A map of the city of Groningen made after the siege in 1672, showing the Munster and Cologne trenches and approaches. Most of the troops assigned to Groningen – infantry regiments Clabt (I-6) and ***Broersma*** (I-30) and cavalry regiment prince ***Georg Frederik van Nassau*** (C11) – had been drafted into the field army in Holland, but at least four companies of the old regiments remained in Groningen. There also remained 10 foot companies raised in March 1671, nine new companies recruited in spring 1672, and a further five new companies raised just before the siege. The number of regular troops was increased by the presence of the infantry regiments ***Holstein-Plön*** (I-63), ***Königsmarck*** (I-77) and three companies of ***Coerland*** dragoons (D-1). The total strength might be around 3,000 regular troops and 1,500–2,000 militiamen and volunteers, including the University's company. These troops were divided between the town and the strongholds around it. Shortly before the siege, the garrison was augmented with the regiment ***Jorma***n (I-59) sent from Holland. After the siege, regiments Jorman and ***Holstein-Plön*** returned to Holland, while regiments ***Clabt*** and ***Broersma*** could be filled with returning troops from the ***waterlinie***. The siege began on July 19 1672 and ended on 27 August, but it was no more than a protracted bombardment that, incidentally, caused 100 casualties on the Dutch side, while the losses suffered by the besiegers amounted to no fewer than 11,000 men, including 5–6,000 deserters. Many thanks to Edwin Groot for this caption.

Meuse, Arnhem on the Rhine, Utrecht, and Naarden, this latter edified as the protection of Amsterdam. Most of the fortresses guarded the southern frontier, while in the north-east the largest fortresses were Groningen and Coevorden. The expenditure for fortifications represented a significant percentage of the Dutch economic balance until 1648. In the 1650s expenditure decreased to less than 20,000 *guilders*, but in 1664 the expense grew to 40,000 *guilders*. The years of peace before 1672 were marked again by a sharp decline in investment, which grew in a short time to over 52,000 until the Peace of Nijmegen.[1]

Moreover, the Republic had long been an extreme defensive resource, represented by the possibility of flooding the countryside and supporting a line of marshes to protect the provinces of Holland and Zealand to south-east and another, less extensive, in the province of Friesland to north-east.

Conflict in the Netherlands centred mainly in the sieges, an inevitable consequence of the nature of the terrain, with its many fortress and towns. Furthermore, marshes and the network of waterways severely hampered the movement and deployment of large armies. Indeed, Dutch strategy has depended so heavily on fortifications and siegecraft that it has been remarked that 'the spade was Prince Maurice's main weapon'.[2] Any military operation in this area was doomed to lose momentum before long; in a couple of months, the belligerents were able to regain their strength. Inevitably, it took both sides no time at all to recognise the importance of holding fortified positions, which as well as commanding major routes and limiting the territorial losses resulting from a field defeat, could at least prove a serious drain on the enemy's resources. That the terrain strongly conditioned strategy was shown on numerous occasions during the war against Spain, and this experience strongly influenced the Dutch approach in matter of military policy even in the following regional conflicts.

Wars Against Cologne and Münster (1660–1664)

The first serious engagement that involved the Republic after 1648 was the intervention in the Northern War. In the spring of 1656, the States General voted for the expedition of 42 warship with 1,400 foot soldiers to Danzig to break through the Swedish blockade. The soldiers who were assigned to this expeditionary corps were musketeers detailed to serve on the ships as marine infantry. The Dutch fleet appeared before the besieged city in late July 1656, whereupon the Dutch soldiers joined Danzig's garrison. The corps returned to the Republic in December 1657.

The war resolved in a positive outcome for the United Provinces, but the policy of decreasing of the Dutch army did not pass unnoticed in the neighbouring states. After 1658, except Maastricht, Dutch garrisons decreased their strength and a few places could be considered sufficiently manned.

The weakness contrasted with the Dutch role in the region. The Republic considered East Friesland, Bentheim, the Bishopric of Münster, and the area between the Rivers Meuse and Rhine to be within her strategic sphere of influence. However, the Prince-Bishop Elector of Cologne, and above all Christoph Bernard von Galen, Prince-Bishop of Münster since 1650, refused to resign themselves to this situation. Disagreements arose for the possession of some territories on the western border of Gelderland, claimed by von Galen as fiefs of the Bishopric of Münster. Tension between the Republic

1 Hart, *The Dutch Wars of Independence*, p. 78.

2 W. McNeill, *The Pursuit of Power* (Chicago: The University of Chicago Press, 1982), p. 128.

26. Johan Maurits Count of Nassau-Siegen (1604–1679), here portrayed during his mandate as Governor of Brazil from 1634 to 1644. Engraving by unknown artist. (Author's archive)

Johan Maurits was the most renowned Dutch commander before the arrival of William III and fought successfully against Spaniards and Portuguese in Africa and Brazil. After his return to Europe to participate in the campaigns against Spain in 1645 and 1646 as general of cavalry, in 1648 he accepted from the Elector of Brandenburg the post of governor of the Hohenzollern possession of Cleves in Westphalia, Mark and Ravensberg, and later also of Minden. His success as governor there was as great as it had been overseas, and he proved himself an able and wise administrator. In 1664 he came back to Holland when war broke out with England and the prince-bishopric of Münster. In 1665 he was appointed commander-in-chief of the Dutch States Army for the campaigns against Münster. In 1668, he was appointed field-marshal and in 1673 was charged by Statholder William III to direct the defence of Friesland and Groningen. Johan Maurits was later appointed commander in the southern sector of the waterlinie. In 1675, poor health forced him to give up active military service, and he spent his last years in his beloved Cleves, where he died in December 1679.

and the two German states mounted rapidly over the course of 1656. In March, Count Johan Maurits of Nassau-Siegen, Brandenburg's governor of Cleves, and Dutch commander of Wesel, had warned The Hague about the secret plans of Maximilian Heinrich of Wittelsbach, Prince-Bishop Elector of Cologne. Thanks to friendly agents in Germany, they received news that the Prince was preparing an assault against the Dutch garrison of Rheinberg. One month later, Johan Maurits informed the Grand Pensionary that the attack was imminent. With the assistance of the Prince-Bishop Electors of Mainz and Trier, Maximilian Heinrich had assembled troops near the border, and further troops were added by the Prince-Bishop of Münster. In late May, on learning that Rheinberg had been reinforced and brought into a state of defence, both the German princes had called off the operation at the last moment. The situation remained tense and concerns grew when Dutch spies informed about the coming to Cleves of Prince-Bishop Christoph Bernard disguised in bourgeois dress. For a few weeks the agents of Johan Maurits followed the movements of the Prince-Bishop, until the cold war between the United Provinces and the Münster threatened to finally break loose in the following years. Determined to find a definitive solution to crush the city's resistance to claim the status of a free Imperial city, von Galen laid siege to Münster in August 1657. Immediately, the city council appealed to the Dutch government for assistance against the Prince-Bishop. Interested in saving commercial links and Dutch property in Münster, the States General voted to assemble 3,200 men near Groenlo and relieve the city.

The States General eventually managed to assemble part of the intended corps, but discipline and skill of the troops was in a sorry state, and their equipment suffered from several shortcomings: 'Many weapons were so neglected and have become so dilapidated that times of urgency they would barely be serviceable.'[3]

3 Nimwegen, *The Dutch Army*, p. 409.

The Republic could count itself lucky that the Bishop did not yet dare enter into an open confrontation with the Dutch troops and therefore concluded an agreement with the Münster's Magistrates before the corps set out on their march to the beleaguered city. Negotiations were opened, while the city requested a Dutch garrison, which was refused. Emperor Leopold I of Habsburg sent an envoy offering his mediation, but the Prince-Bishop opposed any composition. In 1658, the States General agreed to maintain a military presence on the eastern border, sending troops just behind Emden, Leerort, Emmerich, Rees, Wesel, Büderich, Rheinberg, Orsoy, and Meurs.

Meanwhile, other threats were coming from the northern theatre. After the succours to Danzig in 1657, the Dutch fleet had faced the Swedish in the Baltic, and in November 1658 had prevailed in the battle of the Öresund. The army had contributed 2,000 soldiers on board the warships. In 1659 the States General increased their military presence in Denmark with a further 3,000 men, so in overall there were 5,000 infantrymen engaged in the conflict. In June 1660, after the Swedes had been driven from the island of Fyn, and the route to the Baltic Sea was free again, the Peace of Oliva closed the war.

However, the problems with von Galen were not finished. In 1661, the contentions between the Prince-Bishop and the city of Münster exploded again. Von Galen besieged the city and ordered it to be shelled without regard to the inhabitants. The States General sent troops who forced him to interrupt the siege. It was not long before the Prince-Bishop and the Republic came into a sharp conflict. In December 1663, a small corps of troops from Münster marched into East Friesland. The invasion was aimed at territorial claims and then forced collection of debts from Prince Georg Christian, but it was obvious to everyone that this operation was primarily aimed against the United Provinces. Von Galen's troops laid siege to Dijlerschans, a modest fort that overlooked the River Ems, and in doing so posed a direct threat to the Generality Land of Westerwolde, close to the eastern border of Groningen and Drenthe, and the Dutch garrisons of Leerort and Emden.

The few East Frisian defenders surrendered after the first cannon shots. The conquest of the Dijlerschans redoubts caused great clamour in the neighbouring provinces of Friesland and Groningen, which asked for a resolute reaction. On 26 December, the States General voted to form a field army 'to effect the dislodgement of the Münster troops from East Friesland without having to fear suffering any affront'.[4] On 30 December, the Council of State submitted a list of troops who could be deployed for the expedition in East Friesland: 20 cavalry companies in three regiments of horse and 76 infantry companies in seven regiments of foot. This force was assembled having taken care to collect companies from the garrisons closer to Dijlerschans, choosing moreover officers and soldiers who had been in Denmark, about 5,000 men with recent campaign experience. This force would have to march to Deventer in early May 1664. Theoretically, the

4 Letters of Epeus van Glinstra, delegate of Friesland to the States-General, addressed to Willem Frederik van Nassau-Dietz, in Nimwegen, *The Dutch Army*, p. 411. The States-General accorded to Prince Georg Christian a loan of 135,000 rix-dollars to pay the first instalment of his debt to von Galen.

27. Henri Charles de La Trémoille (1620–1672). Engraving by Jean de Baen. (Author's archive)

He was son of Henry de La Trémoille, Duc of Thouars and of La Trémoille, and his wife, Marie de La Tour d'Auvergne. Initially educated by his father in Catholicism, the mother convinced him to re-convert to Protestantism when he reached the age of majority. In 1638 he joined the army of his uncle, Frederick Henry, Prince of Orange. In October 1651, during the *Fronde*, he came out against Cardinal Mazarin and supported Condé openly. As a result, in 1656 he was imprisoned in Amiens. He obtained his release after several months. After a forced exile in Poitou, he turned to serve in Holland as a general of cavalry and in 1664 took part in the East Friesland campaign against Münster. In 1668 he returned from Holland to manage the affairs of the Duchy of Thouars, and again re-converted to Catholicism.

corps had to deploy 1,225 horsemen and 4,496 footmen, but the effective number was only half of its strength: 750 horse and approximately 2,100 foot, with the infantry regiments being on average just 300 strong. The corps was also supported by a siege artillery park with three 24 lb demi-cannon and three 12-pounder pieces. The command was assigned to Willem Frederik of Nassau-Dietz, Stadtholder, and Captain-General of Friesland, with Colonel Ernst van Ittersum van de Oosterhofas his lieutenant, and Prince Henri-Charles de la Trémoille Thouars-Talmont as commander of the cavalry. The campaign started on 6 May. Marching through the county of Bentheim, by the middle of May Willem Frederik arrived at the Ems River, along which the Dutch soldiers continued to advance into East Friesland.

Anxious to led the expedition to a successful conclusion, Willem Frederik maintained a strict discipline on the troops, forbidding any act of oppression against the population and averting the risk of looting, but the Dutch were not welcomed everywhere.[5] The expedition continued despite some setbacks, especially the depletion of bread rations, sufficient only for a few days. This inconvenience caused time to be lost, forcing the army to live from the land, before the arrival of new rations from Deventer. Fortunately, in order to deal with this emergency, the army commissioner decided on his own initiative to bake bread in Neuenhaus and Lingen, in the princedom of East Friesland, while waiting for the rations to come from Deventer.[6] The great distance between the army and Deventer caused the changing of the army's route. Moreover, supply problems continued to be a concern for the Dutch corps, because the bread wagons had been prepared for the roads

5 *Ibid.*, p. 412, 'At every place to which we come we find no people in the house, although I have by public drumbeat had the soldiers forbidden, on the threat of corporal punishment, besides cursing and swearing, that they shall not plunder, burn or do anyone any harm.' Letter of Willem Frederik to the States-General, dated 14 May 1664.

6 *Ibid.* Other problems resulted from the economically disadvantageous conditions that the German bakers had for baking bread, forcing van Ittersum to negotiate the best price.

in Germany, where the gauge of the tracks was different from that in the Republic.

On 20 May 1664 the Dutch troop finally arrived before the fort of Dijlerschans. This action was the first important field operation undertaken by the Dutch army since 1648. Willem Frederik divided the corps into two parts, the first under his personal command and the other under van Ittersum. The commanders esteemed the enemy garrison to be 400 men strong. On 25 May, the Dutch battery opened fire and the enemy replied, beginning a furious artillery duel which lasted three days. On 28 May two of von Galen's deputies were received in the Dutch encampment, claiming they had been sent by the Prince-Bishop to find a friendly settlement. Willem Frederik agreed for a three-day truce, but the negotiations led to nothing. The Stadtholder lifted the ceasefire and the Dutch artillery reopened fire on 1 June. After three days, the fortification had been transformed into a ruin and then the defenders asked to surrender. Willem Frederik granted the garrison a free withdrawal to Meppen and the exodus took place two days later. The garrison numbered more than 300 men, including 80 sick and wounded, but the casualties of Münster soldiers remained unknown, as well as the losses on the Dutch side. After hastily repairing the fortifications, Willem Frederik struck the encampment and marched to Deventer, leaving behind a garrison of 160 infantrymen.

The Second Anglo-Dutch War (1664–1667)

Compared to the first conflicts of 1652–54, the Second Anglo-Dutch War presented more geo-strategic implications, which, although involving mainly the fleet, required the ground forces to defend the extended Dutch overseas domains and the threat coming from the Continental allies of England. The lack of a trained military force was fatal to the Republic in the early stages of the war. The news of the capture of Nieuw Amsterdam in North America (the later New York) by the English on 7 September 1664, reached the States General in early October. The open war between the two maritime powers was now just question of time. Soon the government alarmed its domains in the Americas, Asia, and Africa too, all without a regular field force capable of countering an enemy attack.[7] The recruitment of troops in the Republic was tackled in great haste, while the news concerning the capture of the African ports in the Gold Coast arrived not unexpectedly. On the same day of the Dutch naval defeat at Lowestoft, in June 1664, Charles II and the Prince-Bishop of Münster had been forged an offensive alliance against the United Provinces. England officially declared war on the Republic on March 1665, when the States General had just voted to strengthen the army to 39,500 men on paper, 4,000 of which were marine infantrymen. Von Galen's war preparations did not go unnoticed in the Republic. The government esteemed

7 The forts of Cape Coast and Elmina in the African Gold Coast had garrisons of 200 regular soldiers at all with a few dozen bronze guns. This force was supported by 30 African warriors. D. Howarth, *The Dutch Warships* (New York: Time-Life Books, 1978), p. 112.

the Münster force to be 25,000 soldiers, but only the summer brought more clarity about the Prince-Bishop's strategic plans. Count Johan Maurits, the army commander in Friesland, had received news on the von Galen's secret intention to seize control of Greetsiel in the princedom of East Friesland and to join there an English corps landed by the fleet. To face this threat, the Dutch commanders could count on a few troops, approximately 1,700 cavalry and 9,500 infantry. The raising of new troops would naturally take time, but the government considered Münster's army very poor, and did not expect any negative consequences.

Following the agreements made in 1664 during the East Friesland's crisis, the Dutch government could always turn to hiring troops from the German princes, especially in Brunswick and Osnabrück. On late July 1665, the States General sent Colonel Arent Jurren van Haersolte to Brunswick to negotiate an agreement for hiring an auxiliary corps. The terms discussed with Duke Georg Wilhelm of Brunswick-Lüneburg Celle, agreed the hiring of 4,000 cavalry and 8,000 infantry from Brunswick and Osnabrück, where ruled the Duke's brother, the Protestant Prince-Bishop Ernst August. As an additional demonstration of goodwill, they proposed to provide another auxiliary corps formed by their third brother, Duke Johann Friedrich of Brunswick-Lüneburg Calembeg (Hannover), with 6,500 men. These troops had to join the main force to form a league of mutual defence under the command of Count Georg Friedrich of Waldeck, who had already a good relationship with the Dutch Republic. The first 6,000 soldiers were immediately available; the further 6,000 should become available months later when the States General would pay the first instalment. This would mean the Prince-Bishop of Münster having to face a considerable threat to his rear. The States General considered the timing of the agreement with Brunswick and Osnabrück too long and onerous, and while the actors discussed for new solutions, von Galen's plans for the invasion of Overijssel were made known.[8] De Witt had wanted to wait out Münster's invasion until the enlistment for the Dutch army was complete, the 6,000 French auxiliary troops had arrived, the Dutch fleet returned to port and more than 2,000 musketeers could then disembark and rejoin the field army. Obviously, after the arrival of these reinforcements, it would require little effort to face the Münster troops, and then could reduce the support from the German allies in the engagement of mercenaries. The Council of State prepared a detailed report on the strategic scenario. Until the arrival of the reinforcements, Johan Maurits would have to thwart any enemy action as best he could. Münster's imminent advance towards the River Ijssel represented a serious threat, and actually the Dutch commander could do little else. Johan Maurits was faced with two strategic choices. He could reinforce the garrisons of the endangered Ijssel towns, or he could assemble a field army. With the troops at his disposal he could not perform both these options.

8 Von Galen's 'Grand Design' entailed invading Overijssel with his main army and then attempting to cross the River Ijssel: 'in order to establish his winter quarters there, hoping to make some fortified town for his safety', in Nimwegen, *The Dutch Army*, p. 419.

The war with Münster had been not yet declared, and on 20 September a messenger sent by von Galen arrived in The Hague. The Prince-Bishop demanded the immediate restitution of Borculo in Gelderland. The day before, the Republic had entered into a league with Brunswick-Lüneburg Celle and Osnabrück and this made useless waiting for a formal answer to the ultimatum from the government. On 21 September the troops of Münster crossed the Dutch border and marched into Twente: they were about 20,000 men under *Generalmayor* Johann Georg Gorgas.

Johan Maurits established his headquarters in Zwolle. For the first time after 1648, the Dutch army participated in a campaign of war for the defence of the Republic's territory, but the majority of the troops had for almost 20 years performed nothing but sentry and garrison duties. From 19 to 21 September Johan Maurits mustered the garrisons along the eastern frontier. At his disposal, he had on paper 15,000 infantry in 191 companies and 1,470 cavalrymen in 24 companies spread across 31 strongholds and forts. Two more cavalry companies arrived in Deventer a few days later, increasing the mounted force to almost 1,600 troopers. Unfortunately, after discounting the sick men and other unavailable, the musters revealed that the actual force was only 12,800 men.

On 27 September 1665, Münster's troops appeared before Borculo. The Dutch garrison surrendered after just one day of fighting. The governor of Groenlo and lord of Borculo, Count Otto of Limburg-Stirum, informed Johan Maurits about this loss and the casualties sustained by the garrison: 100 dead and wounded. Both officers complained about the scarce resistance and the unfavourable terms of surrender, but after Borculo, also the towns of Oldenzaal, Almelo, Otmarsum, and Diepenheim opened their gates to the enemy. After reinforcing the main garrison, Johan Maurits could assemble only 1,500 cavalry and 1,250 infantry and with this small force he posted himself near Dieren. In this way, he hoped to achieve the most important objective, namely the defence of the towns along the River Ijssel. Meanwhile, Gorgas had wanted to take Doesburg and/or Arnehm by surprise, but with his presence, Johan Maurits prevented the design. A regular siege was equally impossible, because continued rain had turned the roads into a such miserable condition that Münster's troops had been forced to leave behind their redoubtable siege artillery. General Gorgas therefore continued the assault in a northerly direction. On 12 October 1665 some 8,000 Münster troops assaulted the Dutch defence by Rouveen. The 280 defenders abandoned the position almost immediately. Now, Hasselt, and Zwartluis could be invested, but Johan Maurits considered this action a feint to draw him away from Dieren, knowing that Gorgas had left 3,800 men in the area between Oldenzaal and Diepenheim, so that he would be able to quickly assemble 2–3,000 men along the Ijssel. The departure of the Dutch troops from Dieren it would be impossible to prevent the Prince-Bishop's troops establishing a bridgehead on the river between Doesburg and Zutphen. However, October marked the turning point in the war against Münster. Instead of laying siege to Hasselt or crossing the Ijssel line in another point, part of the Prince-Bishop's army marched onward into the province of Groningen. This decision revealed the enemy's shortage of funds and the difficulties of moving their siege artillery on the impractical roads of that region. There was no means for von Galen to receive the subsidy promised by King Charles II until he had established contact with the English fleet, so the Prince-Bishop ordered to his army to seize the port of Delfzijl. The long march of the Münster army gave to the Dutch army the time to prepare a counter-offensive. While new contracts were signed for the raising of four infantry and two cavalry regiments, by mid November some 760 cavalry and almost 2,900 foot soldiers had been recruited, and finally the arrival of the French auxiliary corps near Maastricht on 10 November permitted th designing of a plan to counter the enemy invasion. The French corps reached the River Ijssel in mid November 1665 and camped between Doesburg and Zutphen. As soon as the 6,000 French troops had joined the Dutch along the River Ijssel, Johan Maurits proposed to launch a campaign with the aim of driving away the Münster troops from Twente and the other occupied places. Then, in conjunction with Brunswick-Lüneburg Celle and Osnabrück's troops, to move the war into the Bishopric of Münster. Until then he endeavoured inflicting as much damage as possible on the enemy troops with small-scale actions. However, the preparatives for the counter-offensive were affected by several problems. Dutch units were always understrength and various officers informed the command that their soldiers were waiting for the pay of six, seven, and even nine months of pay in arrears. Furthermore, logistical problems and the serious shortage of siege artillery menaced the start of the campaign. These setbacks caused the weakening of Johan Maurits' enthusiasm for the campaign. Moreover, he was concerned about the discontent among the French troops over provisions.[9] The French commanders went so far as to advise the field deputies to abandon the campaign and send the troops to their garrisons in France as swiftly as possible. The utterances of the French officers further embittered Johan Maurits who informed the States General that he considered the campaign into the Bishopric of Münster to be out of question.

The government, with Johan de Witt at the head, refused to endorse suspension of the war against von Galen. The Dutch fleet had by then returned to port and the commissioner for the provisions had arrived in Zutphen at the start of December, where he had ordered the baking of bread for more than 20,000 men. With this assumption, the Grand Pensionary insisted that the campaign against Münster should be executed.

On 7 December 1665, the Allied army crossed the River Ijssel. The Dutch forces amounted to 88 companies of foot and 38 of horse for an overall total of 9,000 men.[10] The initial plan provided the conquest of Lochem and then Bocholt, in order to advance into the Bishopric of Münster with the communication lines safe. The town of Lochem surrendered after four days, but the siege of Bocholt had to be abandoned because the artillery train was reduced to speed the march and only six 6-pounder field guns, four 3-pounder, and one 24-pounder chamber-piece were brought along. This artillery was

9 The French intendant Etienne Carlier complained incessantly about the shortage of beer, food, and oats. According to him, the soldiers of the King were not accustomed to carrying loads other than their weapons and that the provisions must be delivered to them from day to day in the respective quarters. See in Quincy, *Histoire Militaire* vol. I, p, 343.

10 Nimwegen, *The Dutch Army*, p. 424.

inadequate for reducing modern defences like those of Bocholt and also the attempt to seize this town by surprise failed, because the 800-strong garrison remained in readiness. The campaign closed after Johan Maurits's order to retreat the army to Groningen.

In 1666, new designs were discussed to defeat von Galen definitely, including the plan proposed by Waldeck, in which he recommended launching an assault against the Münster towns on the River Ems with 9,000 Brunswick and Osnabrück troops and 6,000 Dutch troops. De Witt wanted to keep the war going, but preferred to involve in the campaign the Elector of Brandenburg as well. Because the government was keen to have its hands free for the next round against England, the war with Münster had to be decided before the Dutch fleet returned to sea. On 16 February 1666, the States General signed an alliance with Friedrich Wilhelm of Brandenburg, but before to begin the campaign, the Great Elector would first try to persuade the Prince-Bishop to agree a diplomatic solution. In early March 1666, a delegation from The Hague travelled to Cleves in the domains of Friedrich Wilhelm to meet von Galen's plenipotentiaries. The Prince-Bishop's acceptance of the Great Elector's mediation meant that there was no need for the Brandenburg troops to take action. On 18 April 1666, the United Provinces and Münster concluded the Peace of Cleves. The Prince-Bishop renounced his territorial right to Borculo and committed himself to reduce his army to a peacetime strength of only 3,000 men. The end of the war made useless the French presence, so in June the French auxiliary corps returned home.

The Republic could resume the war against England with highly favourable prospects. In the Four Days Battle, fought from 11 to 14 June 1666, de Ruyter inflicted a painful defeat on the English fleet, which reacted in early August in the Saint James' Day Battle and in the bitter raid against the island of Terschelling. This latter action suggested to de Witt the plan for retailing the enemy's exploits and directly hitting the English fleet while the crews were at rest. The plan for a direct raid against the dockyard on the Medway River estuary had been drawn up by Johan de Witt. Even Admiral Ruyter did not know this plan in detail when, in early June 1667, he received the order to assemble the fleet off the island of Texel. Only the mind of a man who did not know the sea could have conceived a plan like that. Even assuming that the entire English fleet was not in a position to fight and that the coastal defences could be overcome without serious damage, more difficulties remained to be overcome. Navigation in the River Thames was notoriously hampered by sandbanks and at low water for a large vessel it was almost impossible to avoid running aground. The fleet could only go up the river with winds between the north and south-east. Moreover, once the fleet entered the estuary, it would have to wait for the reverse wind to get out. The River Medway was even worse. Its estuary was a narrow channel that ran tortuously between huge expanses of mud which remained submerged during the high water, and to reach the dockyards of Chatham it was necessary to sail up that treacherous way for six and a half miles. Therefore, it was necessary a wind from the north-east to enter and one from south-west to exit the channel and the tidal currents were so strong that the fleet could enter only with the flow and exit with the ebb. The action seemed almost unachievable, but de Witt did not accept objections and sent his brother Cornelis as a government's deputy to the fleet. The Dutch fleet consisted of about 50 vessels with the usual following of fireships and light vessels for an overall total of almost 80 units, with 12,000 sailors and soldiers on board. On 17 June, de Ruyter anchored in the King's Channel, one of the main entrances to the Thames. The English admiralty regarded that presence as a demonstrative act, while peace talks were underway at Breda and no one believed an attack from that direction was possible. But de Ruyter was waiting for the right moment. On 18 June,[11] he knew from a Danish merchantman come out of the Thames that 20 English merchant ships were at anchor in the Hope, in the stretch of the river downstream from the town of Gravesend. Cornelis de Witt, impatient to get into action to avenge the burning of Terschelling, convinced the Admiral to go up the river to find a squadron looking for the merchant ships. The attempt failed because the wind stopped blowing in the ideal direction, and when the tide began to fall the Dutch had to anchor to avoid the sandbanks. Despite the failure, a Dutch squadron penetrated the Thames for 20 miles, pushing in further than any fleet since the Vikings. Furthermore, the action panicked the population of the region and the fear of an invasion spread to London, where the rumour ran that the Dutch had landed with an army of thousands of soldiers.[12] King Charles II sent the Duke of Albemarle to Gravesend to organise a defence, but he found a very critical situation there. The Duke was dismayed to learn that 20 Dutch warships were anchored just outside the mouth of the Medway, a place that the English ships used to stay in safety. The huge dockyard of Chatham was practically defenceless, after financial constraints had diverted economic resources in favour of the reconstruction of London, destroyed by the fire of the previous year. To make matters worse, the personnel had not been paid for months. A fort of the Elizabethan era, the castle of Upnor, and another built recently on the point of Sheerness, were the only military defences worthy of note. In fact, no one had considered it possible that an enemy fleet could go so far inside. Most of the dockyard's workers had fled and only 200 militiamen and artillerymen remained to defend the area. In Chatham there were 18 great warships under repair, included some of the most powerful vessels in the world, the pride of the English navy: the *Royal Charles*, flagship of the fleet, the *Royal Oak*, the *Royal James*, the *Loyal London*, the *Monmouth*, all above 1,000 tons with 60 or 90 cannons. The urgent requests for aid had some effect, and officers from the army and navy began arriving at Gravesend and issuing orders. Chaos increased and a series of conflicting orders caused serious setbacks. An infantry regiment marched from Kent, but after a wrong order was issued the regiment went back and only a company of 35 soldiers arrived in Sheerness. On the night of 20 and 21 June, two light vessels with 100 sailors were dispatched to join the garrison, but the ships ran aground, and when in the morning the sailors managed to get out, more than half of them had fled. At that moment, the Dutch attacked.

11 In 1667, the Dutch used the 'modern' Gregorian calendar instead of the Julian calendar. At that time there was a difference of 10 days between the calendars.

12 Howarth, *The Dutch Warships*, p 153.

In the afternoon of the previous day, thanks to the high water, six fireships, and 17 transports and frigates anchored not far from Sheerness. On 21 June, at sunrise, the Dutch fleet sailed behind the fort preparing for the action. Soon, the incomplete Sheerness fort was under bombardment from the Dutch ships, led by the frigate *Vrede*. The only British vessel present was the *Unity*, which soon withdrew under withering fire from the enemy ships and was finally captured. Meanwhile, 800 Dutch marines landed to assault the fort of Sheerness. They belonged to the Zealand regiment *Vrijbergen* (I-35), which acted the first actual marine engagement of the modern era. Under the ineffective fire of the defenders, the marines advanced in the muddy terrain armed only with *shnaphan* muskets and swords, led by an English 'colonel', Thomas Dolman, alongside Lieutenant-Colonel Jacob Campe de Bruhese. The English resistance was easily overwhelmed. Inside the fort the marines found only seven defenders, but a large quantity of the navy's materials and gunpowder worth four or five tons of gold.[13]

The assault continued with the warships, which headed to Chatham. An iron floating chain defending the access to the dockyard was quickly destroyed, with two fireships employed like rams. Here, notwithstanding the fire of the English battery deployed on the shore,[14] the Dutch sank three ships and fired in succession the *Royal Oak*, the *Royal James*, and the *Loyal London*, towed by English sailors outside the dockyard, in an extreme attempt to escape the enemy. *The Royal Charles* was eventually captured and exhibited in the Netherlands as a war trophy, alongside another warship. The winds also collaborated with the Dutch, starting to breathe in the opposite direction and facilitating the exit of the ships from the channel, completed after three days, despite some difficulties due to the shallow waters. Dutch losses had been minimal, while for the English fleet the Medway had been one of the most severe defeats in its history.

Guerre d'Hollande (1672–1678)

In 1668, to celebrate the Peace of Aix-la-Chapelle, a medal coined by the Republican government made the Sun King like the star which Joshua, portrayed like a Dutch regent, ordered to stop, but now, in the spring of 1672, nobody prevented Louis XIV from invading the United Provinces. On 12 June, the French army crossed the Rhine without difficulty at Elten, under the direct order of Louis XIV, assisted by his most talented generals. The enemy forces amounted to 118,000 infantry and 12,500 cavalry, without counting the troops of Münster and Cologne, deployed further north. One month later, an English pamphleteer had confidently asserted: 'In the eye of

13 Report of the 24–24 June 2017 Conference (Society Vrienden van De Witt & Naval Dockyards Society of Chatham, Amsterdam-Chatham, 2018).

14 The guns, hastily placed on the beach, sank in the mud after the first shots; at Upnor Castle the artillery could not fire, because in the chaos of the previous day the balls sent were of a calibre not suitable for the old cannons of the previous century. Howarth, *The Dutch Warships*, p. 155.

all human reason, they (the Dutch) are like to be a sinking state.'[15]

The disastrous campaign of 1672 provoked an authentic earthquake in the United Provinces. The murder of Johan de Witt and the end of his era opened the way to the irresistible rise of William III of Orange. All these factors changed completely the internal political scenario and with it the military policy of the Dutch Republic in the following 30 years. The year 1672 was the most traumatic of the Dutch Golden Age. It was a year of military collapse, of almost complete demoralisation, the moment when the overthrow of the Republic, if not in its entirety, then certainly as a major power, seemed at hand. It was also a year of sensational domestic political events and feverish ideological conflict. Finally, it was the year when the common populace and militias intervened in the political process, and ideological warfare, more extensively than at any time since the 1580s, with lasting consequences for political and social life. The full gravity of the threat to the prosperity, independence, and very existence of the Republic became clear only after William III's elevation to the captaincy-general. The Republic was on the point of being invaded and blockaded, its trade and industries ravaged, its territory dismembered.

During the weeks preceding the French invasion, uncertainty about where the main enemy attack would be directed left the Dutch political and military leaders with a strategic dilemma. There were serious doubts about the actual French strategic goal. The discussion was whether the French armies would have bypassed the most important stronghold on the southern border, namely Maastricht, or would have concentrated on the Rhine to lure the Dutch away from their fortress. For the Spanish General Governor of the Low Countries there were no doubts that a French advance between the Meuse and the Rhine served only to distract attention from the true operational goal: the conquest of the Spanish domains lost with the Peace of Aix-la-Chapelle. In early 1672, in accordance with the defensive alliance with Spain, the States General had sent six infantry regiments to Mechelen and seven others were assembled at Bergen op Zoom. In April, Maastricht had been reinforced with more troops that brought the garrison to 6,000 men. The governor of Maastricht, General Karel Florentijn *Rijngraaf* of Salm, demanded more reinforcements for 2–3,000 men, but the field deputies answered that this request could not be received.[16] The sector that most worried the Dutch commanders was the line of the River Ijssel. On that sector, the defences appeared in a very bad state, so that an attack on the eastern border could be repulsed only by sending as many forces as possible. Inspections executed in the area revealed a poor scenario. In the fortress of Büderich, only two of the 18 cannons available were in good condition, while in several other forts the moats were completely dry, and the curtains

15 Israel, *The Dutch Republic*, p. 768.

16 Hieronymus van Beverningk and a fellow who served as field deputy in Maastricht with him, sneered that for Salm: 'it would be disagreeable if all the Republic's force were to come and encamp before the gates, but we are of the opinion that 5,597 effective soldiers ... not counting the officers, is a sufficient corps of soldiers to defend a town.' Nimwegen, *The Dutch Army*, p. 437.

without palisades.[17] Several officers believed the chance was slight that the Dutch troops would be able to thwart the French on the River Ijssel, because the enemy was about to march with all his forces, overestimated at 200,000 men.[18] The government, with de Witt, was instead of another opinion and had full trust in a net of fortresses that had denied the pass to the Spaniards for 80 years, and more optimistically believed that militia could effectively support the regular troops in every enemy siege.

The field operations were anticipated by the first hostile acts of the English fleet against the Dutch sea trade. On 23 March, without warning, the English navy attacked the returning Dutch Levant convoy, off the Isle of Wight. France declared war, remarkably publishing the King's grievances, on 6 April. On 16 May Louis XIV led his army, the largest and best in Europe, across the Spanish Netherlands towards Maastricht. As the French advanced, the Prince-Bishop of Münster declared war on the Republic on 18 May, the Elector of Cologne shortly after. On 22 May, the French columns crossed the River Meuse north of Maastricht to invest the fortress.

The task that attended the Dutch army and its young leader was nearly impossible. With at most 22,000 field troops, Prince William III had to defend a line extending for 60 kilometres. De Witt complained bitterly to the army when he heard that the Dutch commanders had contemplated abandoning the Ijssel line without engaging the enemy.[19] The Grand Pensionary claimed that 8,000 men were on the march to the Ijssel as reinforcements, and that the French had first to capture Maastricht and the Rhine strongholds, giving to the Dutch army the opportunity to considerably strengthen the garrison along the river. Unfortunately, de Witt's strategic vision had not contemplated the real situation of the Dutch garrisons and the overwhelming offensive power of the French army; soon events opened the eyes of The Hague regents.

On 1 June, the French laid siege to four fortress simultaneously: Wesel, Büderich, Orsoy, and Rheinberg, while the troops from Münster and Cologne marched towards the eastern border of Gelderland and Overijssel. The Dutch garrisons, which mostly numbered on average just 150–200 men, capitulated in just four days, and soon also Rees and Emmerich surrendered to the French on 9 June. These towns were never to return to Dutch control, reverting subsequently to Brandenburg. Wesel and Rheinberg, two strongest fortified towns, were the exceptions, each manned by large garrisons of between 1,500 and 2,000 men. In Wesel, the defence appeared more promising, and the civic guard had acted to support the siege alongside the regular soldiers. Soon discouragement seized the civilians after the enemy

17 *Ibid.*, p. 437. Colonel Godard van Reede-Ginkel van Athlone took a grave view of things. 'I hear that Prince Johan Maurits is very busy along the Ijssel.' He wrote to his father, the Republic's envoy in Berlin, in early 1672: 'We may all of us hope that something good shall be made of the defences there, because the whole state depends on that post.'

18 Ten Raa, *Het Staatsche Leger*, vol. VI, p. 112.

19 Johan de Witt to field deputy Hieronymus van Beverningk, 4 June 1672. 'I would like to hope that if among the senior officers there should ever again be such narrow-minded thoughts and opinions, or that should be uttered, that Your Honour shall resolutely dismiss them with remonstrations of an exceptional seriousness, and shall not tolerate such proposals or views becoming known within the army among the lower officers and common soldiers.' Nimwegen, *The Dutch Army*, p. 464.

Map 2. (right) Holland's ***waterlinie*** was divided in four sectors, here represented by the commander's name in the autumn of 1672. The Dutch resilience during the fighting which followed was impressive, thanks not least to the territorial circumstances which permitted strategic use of flooding. This measure proved to be successful for arresting the French advance. During the Eighty Years' War against Spain, the Dutch Statholders used the flooding of land as a strategy against the enemy. In the 17th century, a defence project was realised with dikes, sluices, and fortifications to protect the province of Holland. After these works, polders could be easily inundated. The system was modernised and shifted eastward in the province of Utrecht during the 19th century and resulted in a new Dutch waterline. During the Second World War the Dutch started their defence even further eastward, but they were forced to surrender before they could use the new waterline.

Map 3. (overleaf) Besides Holland's waterline, another less extended waterline was formed by flooding the territory from the Lauwersmeer to the Zuyderzee, in order to defend Friesland and part of the province of Groningen.

had captured a redoubt and killed the guards who were inside. The execution occurred in sight of the townsmen and in a short time the inhabitants forced the governor to open the gate. In Rheinberg, despite the militia showing determination to resist, the Walloon colonel Daniel d'Ossory surrendered to the French without a single shot being fired.[20] Meanwhile the troops of Münster and Cologne conquered Lingen, and then penetrated Overijssel, where they joined the French corps under François-Henry de Montmorency, Duke of Luxembourg, in besieging Grol, which capitulated on 9 June.

The main French army crossed the Rhine at Lobith, south of Arnhem, on 12 June, engaging the Dutch in an open field battle, and closed with heavy casualties for both sides. With the French stably deployed on the bridgehead in the Betuwe area, the Ijssel line was effectively outflanked. The threat caused great agitation in The Hague. A quick choice had to be made between the two evils: abandon Gelderland, Overijssel and Utrecht to the enemy or risk that the French would cut off the field army's retreat to Holland. The States General appointed a war crisis committee to discuss the future plans and sent it to Arnehm, to meet William III and the field deputies. These latter supported the Prince when he declared that he considered the Ijssel indefensible, and the only realistic solution could be the voluntary evacuation of the line, waiting for the most favourable time to engage the enemy. While the council of war debated in Arnhem, the news of the siege of the Schenkenshans reached the Dutch headquarters. Here the line was held by 18 companies of foot, but the majority were understrength and four of them could not form a single company. The threat of communications with Holland being lost was always more concrete and without the field troops this province would be lost. The order to retreat from the Ijssel line was issued on 12 June in the evening by the States General after the insistence of the field deputies. In those dramatic hours, William III attended with the army and the decision was taken without consulting him but in any case, there were no alternatives.

Before the retreat, the Prince dispatched two infantry regiments to Friesland and Groningen, and reinforced the garrisons of Doersburg, Zutphen, Deventer and Zwolle with 7,000 infantry. With the remaining 4,000 infantry and the whole cavalry (5,000 men) William III marched to Utrecht overland, while the

20 D'Ossory was later sentenced for cowardice and betrayal, and his cavalry regiment was disbanded. He was accused of having relied on military assignments from a relative who was a herald in the French Army. See also in Reinders, *Printed Pandemonium*, p. 103.

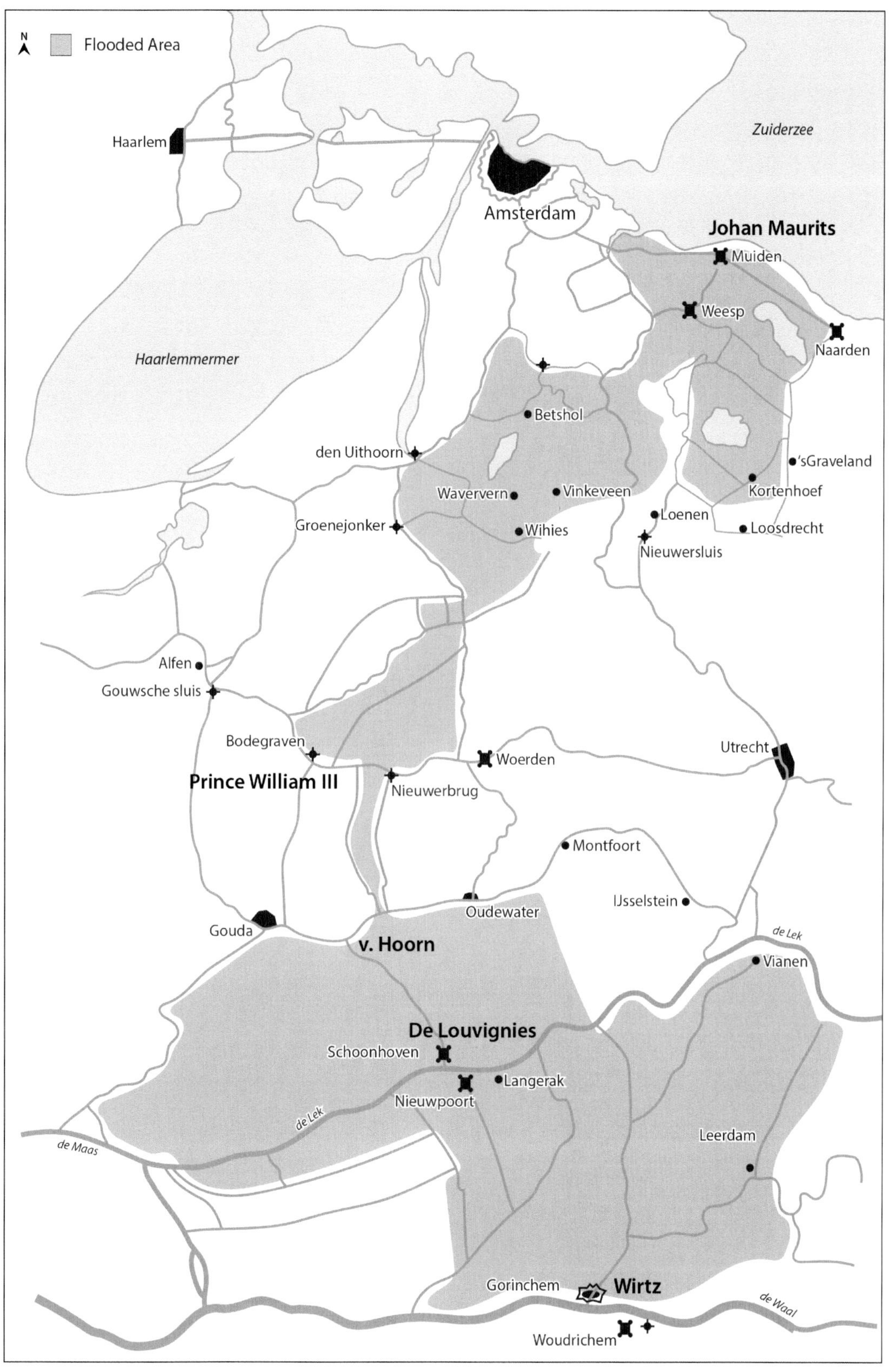
N
Flooded Area
Zuiderzee
Haarlem
Amsterdam
Johan Maurits
Muiden
Weesp
Naarden
Haarlemmermer
Betshol
den Uithoorn
'sGraveland
Kortenhoef
Waververn
Vinkeveen
Loenen
Groenejonker
Wihies
Loosdrecht
Nieuwersluis
Alfen
Gouwsche sluis
Bodegraven
Woerden
Utrecht
Prince William III
Nieuwerbrug
Montfoort
IJsselstein
Oudewater
Gouda
v. Hoorn
de Lek
Vianen
De Louvignies
Schoonhoven
Langerak
Nieuwpoort
de Lek
de Maas
Leerdam
Gorinchem
Wirtz
de Waal
Woudrichem

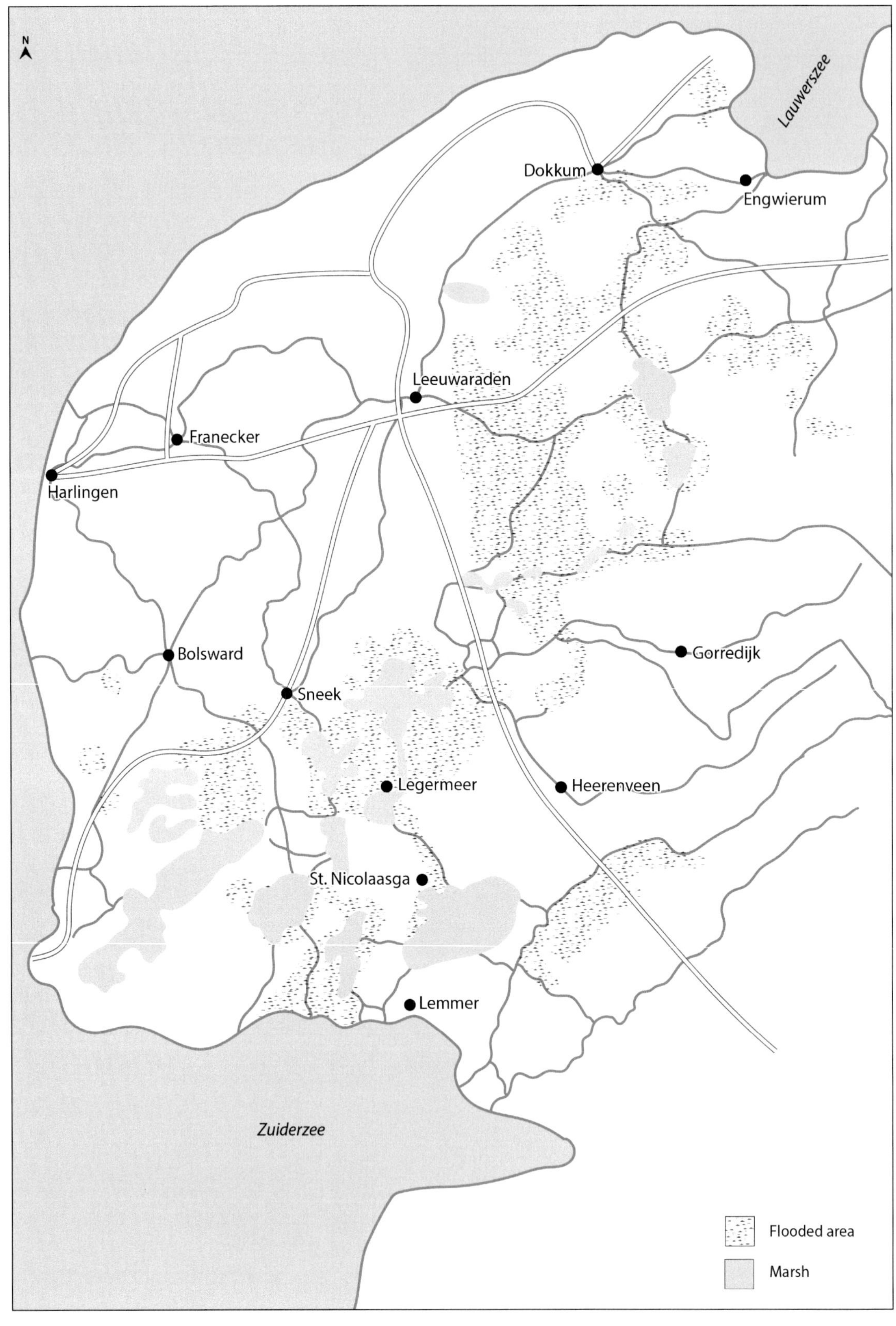
N
Lauwerszee
Dokkum
Engwierum
Leeuwaraden
Franecker
Harlingen
Bolsward
Sneek
Gorredijk
Legermeer
Heerenveen
St. Nicolaasga
Lemmer
Zuiderzee
Flooded area
Marsh

28. ***Het Rampjar***: 1672 was a true year of disaster (***rampjaar*** in Dutch), which seemed to provoke the bitter end of the Republic. The image of prince William inspecting the waterline and ready to face the imminent trial became iconic in the Netherlands as symbol of resistance and national pride. The famous painting of Hoynck van Papendrecht presents this epic scene. The Prince is escorted by the newly formed regiment of ***Gardes te Paard*** and the ***Coerland*** dragoons. They are reproduced correctly, however there are a couple of mistakes: first, the ***Gardes te Paard*** wear the ***casacque*** with the complete monogram W (William) and M (Mary), but in autumn 1672 the Prince was not yet married; second, the dragoons could not have escorted him because they had just arrived from Courland, and joined the field army only the next spring.

rest were shipped across the Zuider Zee. During the march, the Dutch troops joined 2,000 Spanish cavalry sent by Monterrey. Despite his small field army, Prince William wished to take an offensive action against the enemy, but on 16 June the States General ordered him to evacuate Utrecht and withdraw to Holland with all the troops for the final resistance.

The news coming from the front was very bad. Reports described the Dutch troops as terrorised and instead the French seemed more and more bold and daring. Even the civilians were dismayed by the news concerning the lootings and violence committed by the enemy soldiers. Large garrisons still manned the strategic strongholds along the frontier, but morale had disintegrated. The government accused the army, but the officers refused these claims rejecting the critics of the regents. Often the actual course of the events was disputed, but some episodes appear as emblematic of the faulty government's action and of the growing hate towards the politicians. As the French approached Arnhem the citizens rioted, refusing to support the defence. The city capitulated, without a fight, on 15 June. The French advanced rapidly behind the withdrawing

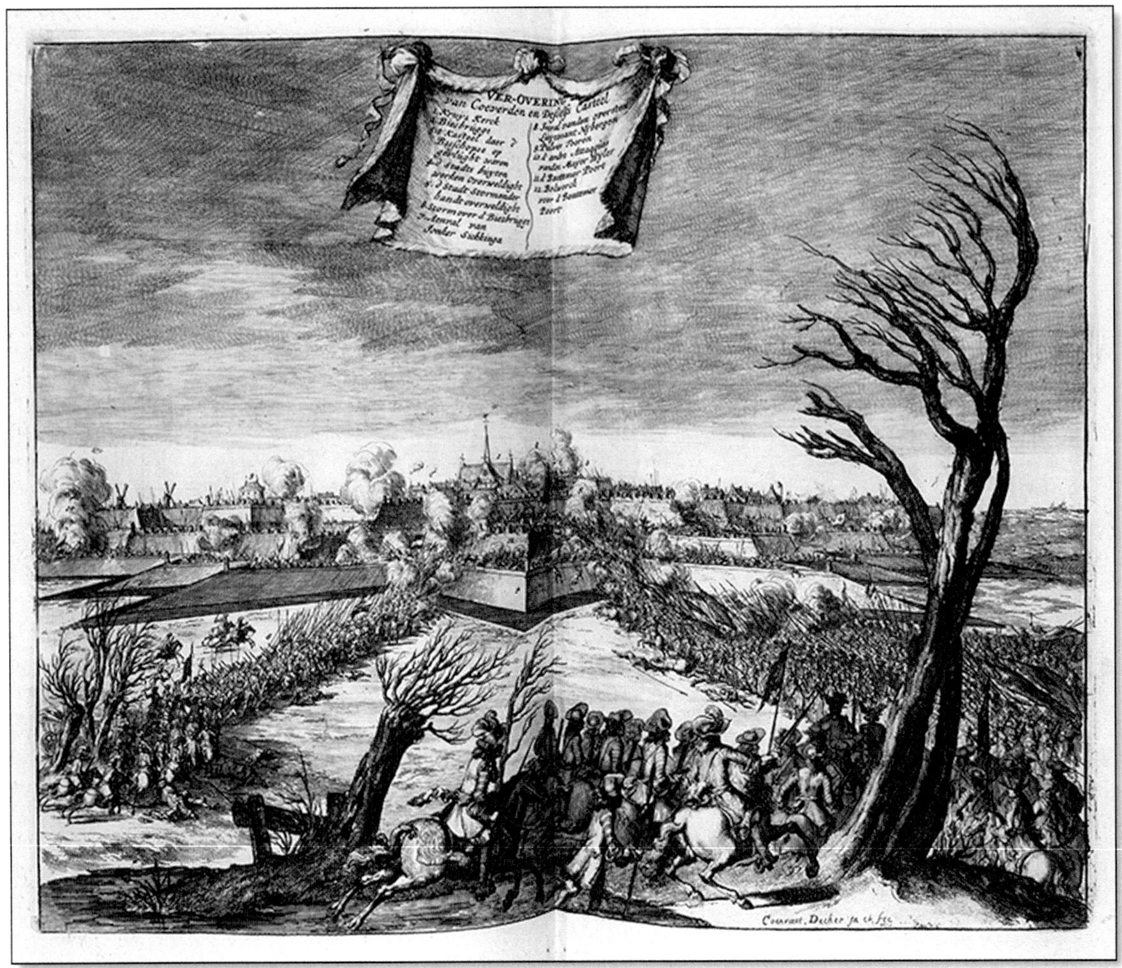

29. The attack on Coevorden, 1672. It involved about 1,000 men: 400 men on foot, five companies of cavalry and three companies of dragoons. The dragoons were led by ***overste*** Nellis van Bebber. There were also volunteers from the militia and students of the university. In addition there were present ***Polaks***, namely Jewish emigrants from Poland, armed with axes and employed as pioneers. The troops were commanded by Lieutenant Colonel Eybergen of the infantry regiment ***Königsmarck***. The guide and mastermind of the plan to attack the fortress was a certain van der Thijnen, a vicar and teacher who in the summer fled from Coevorden before the fall of the town. Approximately 250 of the 550 defenders died, while the rest fled into the church and surrendered themselves there. Casualties on the Dutch side ran to about 100.

Dutch troops, entering Amersfoort on 19 June. The collapse in civilian morale also seriously hampered defensive operations in Utrecht where the civic council refused to permit provision for a siege. Having unsuccessfully tried to succour the city, William III had no choice to deploy his troops towards the post selected as the pivot for the defence of Holland. The French army entered Utrecht on 23 June; the same day Münster and French troops captured Zwolle, Kampen, Deventer, and Steenwijk. The French continued to advance, and on 24 June the Holland town of Naarden was taken by surprise.

The retreat of William III saved the Republic: initially by sheer luck, and subsequently by effectively inundating the stretch of terrain, the *waterlinie*, an improvised line of redoubts linked by defensively inundated tracts of ground, running from Muiden, in front of Amsterdam, on the Zuider Zee, via Bodegraven, where the Prince established his headquarters, Schoonhoven and to Gorcum, on the Waal. At first, this line of defence was in a state of hopeless disarray, and presented no real obstacle to the French. The castle of Muiden, at the northern end, the last position before Amsterdam, was almost lost without a shot being fired, being completely empty just before the French vanguard arrived and without Muiden the entire *waterlinie* was useless, because the locks were located there. The aged Count Johan Maurits rushed troops in with two hours to spare. Over the next fortnight the French could still easily have crossed the *waterlinie*; for although the dikes and sluices were opened after some resistance, particularly around Gorcum, by armed peasants reluctant to see their land ruined by the water.[21]

The day after, Friesland and Groningen also opened the dikes. Here, another less extended waterline had been formed by flooding the territory from the Lauwersmeer to the Zuyderzee. The centre of gravity of the defence was in Friesland's capital – Lewardeen – where Johann Maurits, designated as commander of this sector, took residence. The Frisian *waterlinie* had in the sector between Terherne and Grou the most threatened point, since here it had not been possible to flood the ground. The troops were scattered in the garrisons, leaving just 1,000 cavalrymen and 2,000 infantrymen for the reserve army, moreover demoralised and short of resources.[22]

Finally the French advance had been arrested, but this did not lessen the dismay about the events of the last three weeks. A mixture of fear, pandemonium, and popular fury gripped the towns of Holland and Zealand. The people were incensed with both the army and the regents. There were accusations of scandalous neglect of duty and even blatant treason. The surrender of the strategic key fort of Schenckenschans on the Lower Rhine, which occurred on 21 June without a shot being fired, was ascribed to its having been placed in the charge of an inexperienced and drunken young officer: the son of a Nijmegen burgomaster who supported de Witt.[23] The regents were allegedly going through the motions of preparing the towns for defence, but were not doing so in earnest. At the same time, to provide men for the waterline, while simultaneously strengthening the watches on the town gates and walls, and carrying out last-minute repairs, large numbers of additional men were recruited into the civic militias, and hastily armed and drilled. The catastrophe of June 1672 was followed by further defeats. In July the French captured Nijmegen and part of north Brabant, while Münster and Cologne troops conquered Coevorden, and penetrated Drenthe and much of Groningen. By late summer, the greater part of the Republic was in enemy hands and the rest gripped by riots and political turmoil. The only province both unoccupied and untouched by rioting was Friesland, but even there, there was profound unease.

Prince William deployed his troops behind the Holland's *waterlinie*. This net of redoubts was not consistently strong. The sector near Bodegraven

21 Ten Raa, *Het Staatsche Leger*, vol. VI, p. 128.

22 W.E. van Dam van Isselt, *De Verdediging van Friesland, 1672- 1673* (s'Gravenhage, 1931), pp. 66–67.

23 Israel, *The Dutch Republic*, p. 789.

30. Prince William III of Orange by Caspar Netscher. (Rijksmuseum, Amsterdam)

After his appointment to the position of Statholder of Holland and Zealand, on 8 July 1672 William III was appointed Captain-General and Admiral-General of the United Provinces. Physically weak and of delicate health, the Prince retained a haughty aloofness, remaining cold and impenetrable, never uttering a false word while remaining perfectly courteous the whole time. As established in the 'Perpetual Edict', the Prince would be appointed as commander-in-chief as soon as he had reached the age of majority of 23 years, namely in November 1673, but the emergency forced the government to change the law. After the 1672 spring offensive France made unacceptable demands for peace, forcing the Dutch to fight on. Indeed, King Charles of England, his father-in-law, offered William the crown of the Netherlands to entice him but with such restricted authority that he would have been merely an instrument of the Stuart king. An English envoy tried to persuade William to accept the inevitable but was met with an indignant refusal. 'But don't you see that the Republic is lost,' he is said to have pleaded. 'I know of one sure means of not seeing her downfall,' William proudly replied, 'to die in defence of the last ditch.'

31. Carl Rabenhaupt (Lambert Visscher).

Veteran of the war against Spain, Carl Rabenhaupt. He was a Bohemian Protestant who went into exile for his religion in 1620, after the failure of the Bohemian Revolt. After short service in Saxony, by 1622 he had followed Ernst von Mansfeld into Dutch service. Rabenhaupt gained a strong reputation in trench warfare and participated in several successful major sieges. Notwithstanding, in 1630 he moved to Hessian service, maintained the rank of officer in the Dutch army and in 1671 he was appointed as colonel of an infantry regiment for the province of Groningen. He brilliantly performed the defence of Groningen in late 1672, and two years later participated in the campaign for the conquest of Grave.

was the weak point, then the main part of the field army established its base here, while the remaining troops positioned at Muiden, Goejanverwellesluis, Schoonhoven, and Gorinchem.[24] Every French attempt to cross the *waterlinie* had to be repulsed sending troops from these strongholds, but it was uncertain whether that would be effective. Hundreds of Dutch soldiers managed to escape from the French field prisons, but with just as many men deserting, on balance this was of little help. From the middle of July the situation improved gradually. The States of Holland and Zealand proclaimed a raft of emergency measures intended to preserve the Dutch army from total collapse, William III and his officers worked hard to return the Dutch troops' discipline, fighting strength and self-confidence, in order to be able to persevere with the war through the next winter. The circumstances under which this goal had to be achieved were very difficult. The summer and autumn allowed a few months of rest, but the French would certainly resumed their offensive in the winter, for the frozen inundation would no longer form an obstacle. The winter of 1672–73 would then have to be used to deal with the reform of the Dutch army more thoroughly, after which the war could be resumed the following spring with more evenly balanced odds. For yet it was necessary to gain time.

Three days after the fall of Utrecht, the States General voted to send a delegation with Pieter de Groot, former Dutch envoy in Paris, to the French headquarter in Zeist. De Groot was authorised to cede the Generality Lands to Louis XIV in exchange for peace. The King refused to settle for this, demanding Nijmegen, Grave, and Bommel, as well as the forts of Schenkenschans, Voorne, Sint-Andries, Crevecoeur, and Lowenstein. Possession of these strongholds and towns would give to France total control of the area between the Rivers Meuse and Waal. After these requests, there were also demands from the English, Münster, and Cologne, which claimed further territorial gains and strong economic refunds. Compliance with these demands would have been sacrificing the Republic's independence, because the enemy would henceforth be able to march into the United Provinces in a very short time. Therefore, negotiations had to be interrupted immediately. William III was of the same opinion. Johan de Witt was also against a peace at any cost, but since being seriously injured in an attempted murder on 21 June, he no longer held any political weight. The Dutch navy's successful actions supported the government in itss determination to continue the resistance. The victory gained at Solebay by de Ruyter had averted a possible English landing on Holland coast and this success permitted the release of many Dutch troops, who otherwise would have been needed to guard the shore, for duties along the *waterlinie*. Moreover, Dutch diplomacy was working to solicit the formation of a league against Louis XIV together with Spain and the Empire. The Spanish governor of the Low Countries sent an additional 6–7,000 men in support to the Republic. Later, this auxiliary force grew to between 9,000 and 10,000 men after more of Holland's subsidies. The Spaniards replaced the Dutch garrisons in Hertogenbosch, Breda, and Bergen op Zoom, releasing the units assigned there for the

24 W.J. Knoop, *Krijgs- en geschiedkundige beschouwingen over Willem den derde, 1672–1697* (Schiedam, 1895), part one, p. 245.

defence of Holland. On 25 July, the States General and Emperor Leopold I of Habsburg entered into a pact with the object of ensuring observance of the Peace of Cleves and preventing any future actions contrasting the agreement signed with the Peace of Westphalia. Vienna promised to raise 16,000 men in exchange for a subsidy of 30,000 rix-dollars a month, and as soon as these troops were ready to march, they would be deployed under the *generalissimo* Raimondo Montecuccoli against the enemies of the Republic in conjunction with an army of 20,000 men from the Elector of Brandenburg. In May 1672, before the launch of the French offensive, the States General and the Great Elector had entered into a defensive alliance, but the speed with which the French had trampled over the Dutch strongholds had thus far prevented him from meeting his obligations.

William III merged the ransomed Dutch prisoners of war into the regiments quartered in Holland and Zealand. Before the end of summer, Münster and Cologne troops besieged Groningen. The States-Provincial pressed the Prince of Orange and Grand Pensionary Gaspar Fagel to send some troops to the north as well, in order to lend a hand in their province's defence, but Holland's States in accordance with William III did not send a relief force as expected. They were of the opinion that the preservation of the city of Groningen could by no means outweigh the integrity of Holland. So long as enemies were kept outside this province, there was still a chance to recapture the lost towns. The Prince believed that soldiers and militia in Groningen would be sufficient to withstand the siege. Moreover, it was still doubtful whether the Münster and Cologne army would be able to besiege Groningen successfully. The Dutch garrison was under the command of the experienced Bohemian General Carl von Rabenhaupt. On 19 July, first day of the siege, he could deploy about 3,000 regular soldiers dispatched from four infantry regiments and three companies of dragoons. This force was strengthened by another infantry regiment arrived in Groningen during the siege. There were also 1,500 militiamen and volunteers, included a company formed by the University's students.[25] On paper, the enemy totalled about 24,000 men, but their strength was evaporating because of financial difficulties and lack of food supplies. Under Rabenhaupt the garrison performed very well and Groningen resisted the siege, inflicting heavy losses on the enemy, who left the area on 27 August 1672. The successful outcome of the siege of Groningen was the first actual success of the Dutch army. This

25 Van Dam van Isselt, *De Verdediging van Friesland*, pp. 261–263. Most of the troops repartitioned on Groningen – regiments *Clabt* and Broersma infantry and the regiment cavalry prince Georg Frederik van Nassau – had been drafted into the field army in Holland, but at least four companies of the old regiments remained in Groningen. Also there remained 10 companies raised in March 1671, nine new companies recruited in spring 1672, and a further five new companies raised just before the siege. The number of regular troops was raised by the presence of the infantry regiments Holstein-Plön, Königsmarck and three companies of Courland dragoons. The total strength might be around 3,000 regular troops and 1,500–2,000 militiamen and volunteers, including the University's battalion. These troops were divided between the town and the strongholds around it. During the siege, these troops were augmented with the regiment Jorman sent from Holland. After the siege, regiments Jorman and Holstein-marched to Holland, while regiments Clabt and Broersma could be filled with returning troops from those regiments. Special thanks to Edwin Groot for this data.

event and the news about the war preparations of the Austrian Emperor and Brandenburg were an important boost for the Republic in the darkest hours.

In late August, the Dutch commanders maintained their position on both the water lines, controlling the French vanguards that continued to appear on all sides. Johan Maurits sustained there was no longer any danger that the French would launch a surprise attack before the winter.[26] On 25 August 1672, Saint Louis' day, it was expected that the French marshals would try some daring enterprise, as was customary for celebrating the monarch's onomastic. Concerned by the assembling forces from Brandenburg and Austria, Louis XIV had dispatched Prince Louis II of Bourbon-Condé (the *Grand Condé*) with 18,000 men in Alsace, while Henry de la Tour d'Auvergne, Viscount of Turenne, with 20,000 men, occupied the bridgeheads on the Rhine. To the control of the occupied Dutch territory remained a force of 50,000 men, included a mounted corps of 7,000 troopers entrusted to the blockade of Maastricht. The task of facing the Dutch army behind the *waterlinie* was assigned to the Duke of Luxembourg, who was military commander in the province of Utrecht. The Dutch war council, which sat at the end of August, had full knowledge of the distribution of the enemy and also knew that a considerable part of the French troops who had invaded the country in June were now marching to France for the winter quarters. The weakening of the enemy seemed to William III the propitious condition for a counter-offensive to demonstrate to Europe that the United Provinces were not beaten yet. The Prince was aware that he lacked the experience to launch the campaign alone and therefore agreed to Waldeck accompanying him as his lieutenant.

On 26 September, the Imperial and Brandenburg troops were finally quartered in Hildesheim, ready to march in the direction of the Bishopric of Münster. The plan that could reasonably be immediately executed was that of ousting von Galen and the Elector of Cologne from the conflict and recovering the provinces of Gelderland and Overjissel conquered by the enemy in the spring-summer campaign. Alongside their allies, the Dutch commanders could assemble 36,000 field troops for this task. However, Emperor Leopold of Habsburg was not ready to openly engage the French and the secret instructions for his general commander Montecuccoli did not contemplate a direct military engagement. Therefore, the Imperial troops prepared to perform just a 'demonstration' along the Lower Rhine. However, even this action came to nothing, because *Maréchal* Turenne quickly moved his troops and prevented Montecuccoli's march to the west, occupying both side of the Rhine at Wesel and Koblenz. Lack of forage and shortage of supplies, moreover menaced by the Turenne's cavalry, forcing Montecuccoli to withdraw to Frankfurt-am-Main, soon followed by Brandenburg's troops. William III and his generals understood that any operation against the enemy would have to be undertaken without the direct help of the Allies. Field marshal Johan Maurits proposed a surprise attack on Naarden. He pointed out to William III that the way would then be clear to thrust ahead to Amersfoort and Harderwijk.

26 On 24 August 1672, Nassau-Siegen wrote from Muiden to the Amsterdam burgomaster: 'The enemy continues to sniff at us on all side, but rest assured that by letting in the meadows with this fine wind, he shall change his mind.' In Nimwegen, *The Dutch Army*, p. 449.

The capture of the first fortress would make the conveyance of supplies to the city of Utrecht very difficult and would probably force Luxembourg to retreat back to the Ijssel. The capture of Harderwijk would make it possible to launch an assault on the Ijssel towns in conjunction with the troops quartered in Friesland and Groningen. Anxious to perform an offensive action worthy of the name, the Prince accepted the plan and planned the assault on Naarden for the early hours of 28 September 1672. The attackers did not expect great resistance from the French garrison, estimated in about 1,000 men. Moreover, the moats were almost dry and the curtains, high and without a covered road, were not reinforced by ravelins. For the assault, four infantry regiments were mobilised, including those of the Guards, which were transported from Amsterdam to Naarden by river, while the others marched overland. Despite the favourable predictions, the operation ended in a failure. Johan Maurits and William III, with only one infantry regiment, stopped before Naarden at the time convened. Instead, the arrival of the *Oude Gardes*, commanded by Colonel Karl Florentijn *Wald-en-Rhinegrave* of Salm, son of the governor of Maastricht, was late. Having waited in vain for two hours, the Prince was informed that a lack of wind had prevented the Guards sailing any further than Muiden, while the position of the other two regiments remained unknown. After calling off the assault, the Dutch commanders learned that the other two infantry regiments had lost the way marching in the dark.[27]

The failure of Naarden did not discourage the Prince, who soon after took into consideration the conquest of Woerden. Here the French garrison was more numerous, about 2,000 men, but the control of that small town, would gave him two major advantages. In Woerden the defenders were not on the alert, as now in Naarden, and Luxembourg had sent reinforcements there to secure him against a possible attack on Utrecht. In the second place the conquest of this outlying post would at least consented the access to ground free of marshy ground, and consequently permitted the employment of the Dutch cavalry to disturb the French lines of supply. The assault on Woerden would have resulted in more losses than expected in Naarden, however the positive outcome seemed certain, because as all veteran captains claimed, when the troops did not perform well and they are conducted before the enemy for a second time, they have accomplished the task with double courage. William III assembled 8,500 men, included some of the best experienced troops, like the *mariniers* of the Palm regiment. The plan of assault established that William III had to enclose the western side of the town with 2,400 men, while the eastern side had to be secured by Waldeck with the 3,000 infantry, supported by Count Willem Adriaan van Hornes, general of the artillery, with 1,600 infantrymen as tactical reserve. William III and Waldeck would have moved simultaneously, storming the towns from both sides. The Dutch commanders knew that the defenders would call on Luxembourg for help using signal fires, and the French general would send a relief force from Utrecht, which was just

27 The failure of the assault on Naarden sparked a furore in Holland. To mollify the popular outrage, on 29 September Nassau-Siegen insisted that the burgomaster of Amsterdam should publish the written report of the operation that he had submitted to them. He was prepared to pay for the printing of several hundred copies himself. See Nimwegen, *The Dutch Army*, p. 449.

a few hours march from Woerden. To engage the French troops who could come to help the besieged garrison, William III dispatched General Count Frederik of Nassau-Zuylenstein, with about 1,500 men, to block the road from Utrecht to Woerden. This choice would have proved unfortunate, because the general did not have battle experience since 1648 and owed his appointment to friendship with the Prince, of whom he had been a tutor. Nassau-Zuylenstein and his men marched past Woerden and took position near Grovenbrugge, on the road to Utrecht, facing the possible arrival of the French from there. He had received notice from local peasants that there was no other passable route in the area, whereby it would be impossible to be attacked from behind: an assertion that turned out wrong.

The operation against Woerden started on the evening of 10 October, with the arrival of Hornes who placed a battery of 12 cannons, followed by William III and Waldeck in the respective positions. The Dutch deployment required more time than expected and provoked some drawbacks. In the first hours of 11 October the French discovered the presence of the enemy before Woerden, and warned Luxembourg with fire-signals and cannon shots. The French marshal assembled immediately 8–9,000 men and marched to the town's relief. The French columns sighted the corps of Nassau-Zuylenstein between two and three o'clock and promptly assaulted the enemies, barring the road, but they were repulsed by the well-aimed Dutch fire. Luxembourg gave orders to outflank the position and sent 2–3,000 infantrymen through the flooded countryside. Marching with water up to their knees, the French succeeded in less than an hour to stand behind Nassau-Zuylenstein and his men. The Dutch general fought bravely but lost more than three-quarters of his infantry.[28] There was no hope of receiving help; eventually Nassau-Zuylenstein was killed and his troops routed. The arrival of Luxembourg before

32. Willem Frederik van Nassau-Zuylenstein (1624–1672). (Portrait by Peter Lely, Private Collection)

Willem Frederik van Nassau-Zuylenstein (1624-1672)was a natural son of count Frederik Hendrik, and he had been charged with the Prince of Orange's upbringing from 1659 to 1666. For this, William III had become deeply attached to him. As military leader, he had received a command position in the army primarily owning to his personal ties with the Orange family. The count had been promoted to Lieutenant-Colonel in 1645, but he had seen no action after 1648 and had not been promoted to General until April 1670. On the night of 10–11 October, he was the unfortunate officer entrusted with the difficult task of watching the road from Utrecht during the storm on Woerden. He and his 1,500 soldiers were assaulted by 9,000 French troops led by Duke of Luxembourg to relieve the besieged town. The Dutch soldiers fought bravely and repulsed the first assault, but finally the enemies were able to outflank their position. Like the Spartan king Leonidas at Thermopylae, Nassau-Zuylenstein died a hero in the midst of his troops. His body bore no fewer than 36 wounds.

28 After the encounter, the regiment *Solms* (I-8) counted just 150 soldiers survived. See Nimwegen, *The Dutch Army*, p. 452.

Woerden triggered the battle. Hornes targeted furiously the advancing French infantry with his battery, while the marines of the Palm regiment, after a general volley, assaulted the enemy at swordpoint, as they were used to while performing the boarding of a ship. Notwithstanding the fierce resistance of the besiegers, Luxembourg succeeded to dispatch 1,500 men inside Woerden. Now the opportunity to take the town by storm had been dissolved and William III ordered the retreat.

After the battle, William III expressed his satisfaction for the behaviour of the troops. Finally, the troops of the Republic had held up the feared French soldiers, and despite the sacrifice of Nassau-Zuylenstein's corps they had inflicted twice their losses. The French lamented 2,100 dead and wounded, and Luxembourg confirmed in the battle report that the Dutch troops had fought admirably.[29]

The expedition to Woerden had the effect of convincing the French commanders that this was the only significant military action that the enemies were able to perform, and were convinced that there would not be another offensive. Therefore, the subsequent assault on Charleroi was completely unexpected. The risk undertaking in this action was high, but if it succeeded, the strategic effect would be commensurately great for the Dutch side. The capture of this key stronghold in the 'French' Low Countries would menace the communications between the enemy army and France, forcing Luxembourg to evacuate Utrecht and Gelderland. Furthermore, William III hoped that the successful outcome could interrupt the blockade of Maastricht too. The Dutch army had to march through the Spanish Low Countries – and this was an easy task thanks to the good relations with Monterrey – and then penetrate into the territory conquered by France in the recent War of Devolution. However, William III could not undertake this action only with the troops at his disposal. Waldeck reported to the Prince that 37,000 men were needed for a regular siege of the town: 12,000 men as siege corps and 25,000 as an observation army.[30]

William III's design depended therefore on external aid, namely the Spanish governor Monterrey. The Spanish troops in the Low Countries had to join the Dutch army for the storm on Charleroi. However, the state of war between France and Spain had not yet been declared, and the direct participation of King Charles II's troops would have offered Louis XIV an easy excuse to resume the war against Madrid. Monterrey was prepared to deal with the French ambassador, but he was not mistaken in regarding an open rupture with France as a foregone conclusion. As yet, the Spanish aid would go no further than adding 10–11,000 men in total.

Therefore, the more optimistic prevision put at 30–32,000 men the overall strength of the new constituted Allied Army of the Flanders. William III could assemble 20,000 men in total as field troops, because at least 18,000 men were deployed to secure the Holland *waterlinie*, and a further 23,000 were

29 *Bertrand Fonck Le Maréchal de Luxembourg et le commandement des armées sous Louis XIV* (Seyssel: Champ Vallon, 2014), p. 323.

30 Notes by Georg Friedrich von Waldeck about the number of troops needed for a siege of Charleroi, in Nimwegen, *The Dutch Army*, p. 453

required for the guarding of the other paces in Zealand, Friesland, Groningen, and Maastricht. Furthermore, mostly Dutch regiments were formed by inexperienced troops, recruited just before the incoming French invasion and unreliable to perform a regular campaign. The success of the expedition to Charleroi depended therefore on the offensive that Montecuccoli could undertake. If the Imperial *generalissimo* were to cross the Rhine and join his troops with the Dutch–Spaniards, then it would certainly be possible to achieve successfully the siege.

Preparations for the campaign were begun in early November 1672. Nearly half of the Dutch field corps was formed by cavalry, which have sailed by ship from Rotterdam to Bergen op Zoom, where they would have waited for the infantry, embarked a second time. On 7 November William III and Waldeck mustered the allied army, which numbered 10,000 infantry, 18,000 cavalry and 2,000 dragoons.[31] The two commanders moved to Maastricht the following day with 11,000 horse and 5,000 foot; the remaining troops stayed behind Bergen op Zoom, to secure the rear and join the main corps later. Depending on the circumstances, they would quickly return to Holland to support Johan Maurits for an assault on Utrecht. The Dutch–Spanish army marched unnoticed via Herentals, Peer and Lanaken, and on 12 November halted not far from Maastricht. As guessed by the Dutch generals, the enemy cavalry engaged in the blockade of the town hastily raised the encampment, while Luxembourg called for the bulk of his troops from the garrisons in the vicinity. In the first moment, the alarm seemed to involve also the French garrisons in the province of Utrecht. As soon as William III was informed about this news he sent 5,000 infantry back to Bergen op Zoom, in order to join Johan Maurits to drive out the French from Utrecht. William III wrote to his general to act the assault quickly, because the new resulting scenario could permit the recapture of several important strongholds such as Kampen, Zwartluis, Naarden, Amersfoort, and Woerden. Despite this favourable promise, Johan Maurits realised that Luxembourg had not evacuated Utrecht, disappointing the Prince of Orange's hopes. The diversion could yet produce a success for the Allies, but now it depended on the Imperial–Brandenburg army, which was marching to cross the Rhine. William III transferred to his army the infantry from Bergen op Zoom, in order to assemble all the troops available for the decisive operation against Charleroi. On 18 November, the Spanish governor Monterrey sent further troops to William III: 4,500 men in all including several battalions taken from Maastricht, now the Dutch–Spanish army grew to 24,000 men. However, the news on the arrival of Montecuccoli was unfavourable and related the difficult encountered by the Imperialist–Brandenburg in their approaching march to Charleroi. William III intended to move from Maastricht until he was certain that Montecuccoli would cross the Rhine. The success of the expedition to Charleroi ultimately hinged on the action that Montecuccoli undertook. If the Imperial general were to cross the Rhine with the Imperial–Brandenburg army and join forces with the Dutch–Spanish army then it would certainly be possible to

31 Ten Raa, *Het Staatsche Leger*, vol. VI, p. 285.

33. The Looting of Zwammerdam. Between 3th and 4th of January 1673, the French under-*maréchal* Luxembourg crossed the frozen waterline and seized control of Bodegraven and Zwammerdam, going on a horrendous rampage of murder, rape and pillage. Nothing could extenuate the behaviour of the French, a fact that pamphleteers in Holland seized upon with rapacity. Fortunately for the Dutch side, the heavy rain turned the ice to marsh, forcing Luxembourg to retreat. Both places were small but strong fortresses which had been taken by storm only after a long and bloody siege in the war against Spain.

expect a successful conclusion of the siege. Against his better judgement, the Prince remained hopeful until mid December, while the Count of Waldeck had already given up hope by the end of November.[32] However, it was not an option to call off the operation while Montecuccoli was still in the field, because the Emperor would then be able to place the blame for the joint operations on the Dutch–Spaniards. However Prince William, Waldeck, and the other generals considered that there was no choice but to continue to advance on Charleroi, considering it a favourable occasion for the morale of the army and of the whole nation.

The incoming winter season was not cold, but heavy rain tormented the troops. Moreover, the continue marches had weakened the infantry, while the cavalry suffered from the bad climate and a shortage of food.[33] Finally,

32 In a letter to Grand Pensionary Fagel, Waldeck stated that he considered the campaign to have been a failure: 'The tardiness of the allies has ruined our measures for the great coup (against Charleroi).', *Ibid.*, p. 454.

33 'It would be desirable to begin something quickly, because in the fourteen days that they have stood still (since 15 November), our cavalry has been more badly affected than from the preceding march, for we have had quarters where the French had eaten up everything within a radius of about six hours.' Letter of Colonel van Reede-Ginckel to his father, Dutch ambassador in Berlin, dated 29 November 1672, in Nimwegen, *The Dutch Army*, p. 455.

Plate A

Infantry, 1660–69

1. Private of Marine Regiment *Vrijbergen* (I-35), 1667; 2. Musketeer, *Gardes te voet van de Staten van Holland* (Holland's Foot Guards, I-28), 1662–68; 3. Senior Officer, *Gardes te voet van de Staten van Holland* (Holland's Foot Guards, I-28), 1662–68

(Illustration by Bruno Mugnai, © Helion & Company)

See Colour Plate Commentaries for further information.

Infantry, 1672–79
1. Musketeer, Regiment *Königsmark* (I-77), 1672
2. Ensign, Regiment *Aylva* (I-2), 1674
3. Pikeman, Regiment *Reede* (I-86), 1675
(Illustration by Bruno Mugnai, © Helion & Company)
See Colour Plate Commentaries for further information.

Plate C

Infantry, 1680–87
1. Grenadier, *Gardes te voet* regiment (I-8), 1680–85
2. Musketeer, Regiment *Nassau-Ottweiler* (I-11), 1686
3. Drummer, Regiment *Nassau-Ottweiler* (I-11), 1686

(Illustration by Bruno Mugnai, © Helion & Company)

See Colour Plate Commentaries for further information.

Plate D

Cavalry, 1660–67
1. Trooper with greatcoat, 1665–69
2. Senior officer, unknown cavalry unit, 1664–68
(Illustration by Bruno Mugnai, © Helion & Company)
See Colour Plate Commentaries for further information.

Plate E

Cavalry, 1672–74
1. Trooper, Regiment *Kingma* (C-24), 1672
2. Trumpeter, unknown regiment, 1673
(Illustration by Bruno Mugnai, © Helion & Company)
See Colour Plate Commentaries for further information.

Plate F

Cavalry and artillery, 1680s
1. Trooper, *Gardes te Paard* regiment (C-25), 1687
2. Officer, Regiment *Ginkel* (C-10), 1686
3. NCO, Artillery Regiment, 1680

(Illustration by Bruno Mugnai, © Helion & Company)

See Colour Plate Commentaries for further information.

Militia
1. Officer, 1660–65
2. Militiaman, Blue Company of the Leyden Town Militia, 1660
3. Militiaman, The Hague Town Militia, 1672
(Illustration by Bruno Mugnai, © Helion & Company)
See Colour Plate Commentaries for further information.

Above: the coats of arms of the Dutch Provinces: Gelderland, Holland, Zealand, Utrecht

Below: Infantry Regiment *Ingen-Nielant* (I-19), 1672

(Illustration by Bruno Mugnai, © Helion & Company)

See Colour Plate Commentaries for further information

Plate I

Above: the coats of arms of the Dutch Provinces:
Overijssel, Friesland, Groningen, Drenthe

Below: Marine Regiment *Vrijbergen* (I-35), 1672

(Illustration by Bruno Mugnai, © Helion & Company)

See Colour Plate Commentaries for further information

Infantry Regiment *Kirckpatrick* (I-15), 1672

(Illustration by Bruno Mugnai, © Helion & Company)

See Colour Plate Commentaries for further information

Above: Utrecht Militia company ensigns
Below, left: Regiment *Garde te Paard* (C-25), 1674-87
Below, right: Cavalry Regiment *Obdam* (C-12), 1686
(Illustrations by Bruno Mugnai, © Helion & Company)
See Colour Plate Commentaries for further information

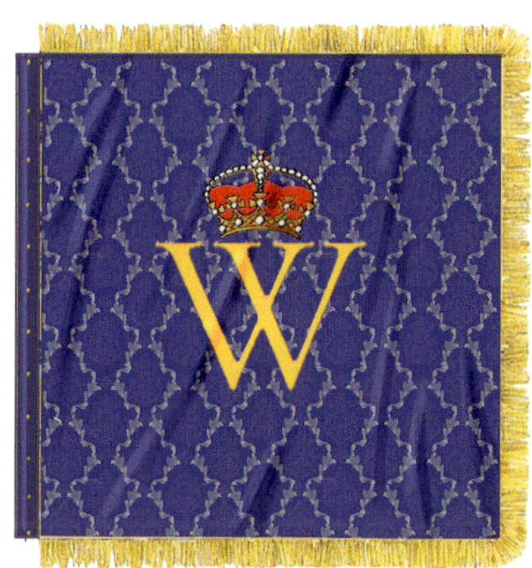

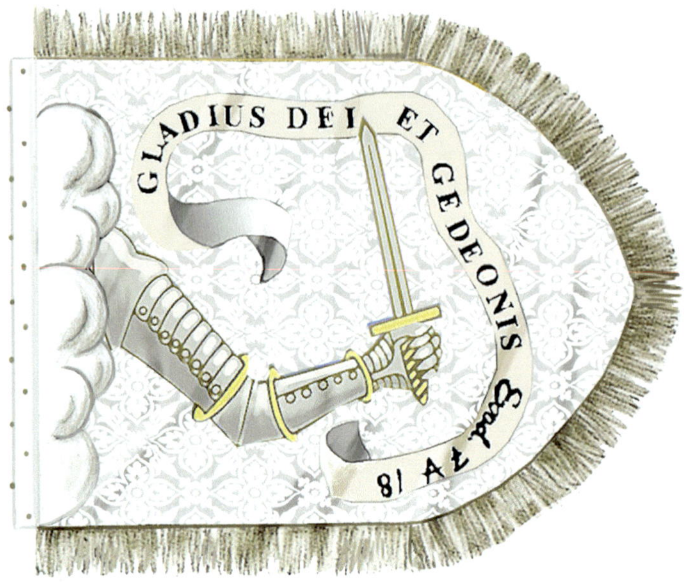

Above: Cavalry Regiment *Heyden* (C-16), 1690
Below, left: Cavalry Regiment *Oyen* (C-8), 1686
Below, right: artillery flags, 1690

(Illustrations by Bruno Mugnai, © Helion & Company)

See Colour Plate Commentaries for further information

Plate M

Above: Infantry Regiment *Aylva* (I-2), lost at Seneffe, 1674
Below, left: Infantry Regiment *Schwartsenberg* (I-24), lost at Seneffe, 1674
Below, right: Infantry Regiment *Gardes te voet* (I-8), lost at Seneffe, 1674

Plate N

Above: Infantry Regiment *Brandenburg* (I-89), lost at Seneffe, 1674
Below, left: Infantry Regiment *Beaumont* (I-28), lost at Fleurus, 1690
Below, right: Infantry Regiment *Aylva* (I-2), lost at Fleurus, 1690

Plate O

Above: Infantry Regiment *Lymburg-Styrum* (I-33), lost at Fleurus, 1690
Below, left: Infantry Regiment *Nassau-Friesland* (I-24), lost at Fleurus, 1690
Below, right: Cavalry Regiment *Montpouillon* (C-26), lost at Fleurus, 1690

Note: the small ensigns on plates K–O are copied from ***Les Triomphes de Louis XIV représentés par les Drapeaux pris sur les Ennemis***, 18th century, preserved in Paris (Bibliothèque Nationale de France)

Plate P

The storming of Coevorden in December 1672, by Pieter Wouwerman (1623–1682)

on 15 December 1672, William III invested Charleroi. The operation was announced to be easy, because the town was defended by a garrison of just 7–800 men devoid of the governor, and supplies were assured by Spaniards and Dutch providers, but these favourable circumstances vanished for several reasons. Though the Spaniards were to provide the siege artillery it took three to four days to arrive. The French governor had in the meantime managed to rejoin his garrison and to make matters worse the freeze set in, forcing William III to leave the siege. In addition, engagements along the *waterlinie* demanded his fast return to Holland.

While William III and Waldeck were in the Spanish Netherlands, Johan Maurits was in command of the troops in Holland together with Field Marshal Paulus Wirtz. Several times Johan Maurits complained about the bad condition of defences and the lack of soldiers to reinforce the garrisons.[34] He and Wirtz had 14,000 men at their disposal for the defence of the Holland *waterlinie*.

In the middle of November the 5,000 men who William III had sent back from the field arrived, but this made the task of the two field marshals no easier. Now their force attained an effective strength of 19,000 men, just 1,000 more than the strength that was called for as an absolute minimum. Luxembourg could then carry out surprise attacks anywhere and this threat was greatest if the terrain began to freeze. Johan Maurits and Wirtz calculated that of the 18,200 infantry and 800 cavalry under their command, at least 13,250 foot and 480 horse were the minimum indispensable for securing the posts along the *waterlinie*. This measure left fewer than 5,000 men to face a French assault, and these troops were weakened by diseases, discomforts, and other inconveniences. Johan Maurits warned William III that Luxembourg could assemble two to three times as many soldiers. The French winter offensive seemed to become reality on 27 November 1672, with the storming to the village of Ameide. Fortunately, the assault had no serious consequences and the French withdrew after plundering the village and setting it ablaze.

In the middle of December 1672, as frost set in and the situation threatened to turn critical, Johan Maurits received reports from every quarter that Luxembourg was assembling 12,000 to 13,000 men for a surprise attack on Gouda or Leiden and would then attempt to advance to The Hague. It was therefore of the utmost importance to render Bodegraven and the other posts in the area as strong as possible. Here the troops were under the command of the experienced Lieutenant-General Königsmarck, who received the order from Prince William not to abandon Bodegraven except in the utmost extremity. The situation appears even more desperate to Grand Pensionary Fagel, when he read the report of the deputies sent by him to Bodegraven to know the actual situation. The government had urged the sending of all the available troops between Bodegraven and Zwammerdam, but it was the opinion of the deputies that Königsmarck was ready to withdraw to Leiden.

34 Johan Maurits wrote to Wirtz on 28 November 1672: 'We are standing together as if positioned in a counterscarp (covered road), but the most important fortress and town that we have to defend, namely the whole of Holland, is denuded of soldiers, so it presents no small danger if the enemy should break through, because of the great length of that counterscarp, if I might describe our posts thus.' *Ibid.*, p. 456.

34. The Dutch seizure of New York in 1673, anonymous engraving.

The French-Dutch war of 1672–78 was not only a great European war, but involved also the overseas colonies. The most famous episode that occurred in North America was the conquest of New York, an act that occurred after a series unexpected events. New York (formerly Nieuw Amsterdam) had been occupied by the English in 1664 and remained in their possession even after the peace of Breda. Cornelis Evertsen the Younger (1642–1706) was vice-admiral of the Republic's fleet in the Atlantic when in early 1673 he received the order to seize Saint Helena. This island in the southern Atlantic Ocean belonged to England, but when Evertsen arrived, ships belonging to the Dutch East India Company had already conquered the island. Evertsen therefore decided to sail on to the Caribbean, heading to Cayenne, which was part of French Guyana. This destination was mentioned in his assignment as an alternative to his primary objective of Saint Helena. The Dutch vice-admiral, however, deemed his fleet too weak to be able to attack Cayenne and decided to join the Dutch squadron in the Caribbean. These ships were under the command of Jacob Benckes, who was on his way to Virginia.

The ships reached the Hudson River in August 1673. The Dutch fleet consisted of 23 ships carrying nearly 600 men. After passing Chesapeake Bay, where it had chased some trading ships from Virginia, it had cast anchor two days before at Sandy Hook, a stone's throw from New York. Eleven ships were overpowered and claimed as a trophy while still in the river. Evertsen received information from Dutch farmers about fort Jems (James), located on the island of Manhattan, which was apparently badly defended. Moreover, in New York lived many Dutch and they were impatient to overturn English rule. The Dutch commander decided to move against the fort the following day. The defence was made by Captain John Manning, an experienced soldier who was the sheriff of New York since 1667. He had a company of 80 men at his disposal. On the morning of 9 August 1673, a trumpeter was sent to the fort demanding their surrender. After a first negotition occurred in the afternoon, 600 soldiers landed on the west side of Manhattan under Anthony Colve's command and walked to Fort St James supported by a militia of about 400 armed people of Dutch origin. Captain Manning decided to surrender four hours later. New York returned to English rule in 1674 after the peace of Westminster.

Of no less concern to the deputies was the lack of discipline among the Dutch soldiers.[35]

In the final days of December, it seemed the most pessimistic predictions would become reality. Luxembourg marched from Woerden into Holland across the frozen water with 12,000, perhaps even 15,000 men. However, the ice proved to be too thin to withstand the passage of artillery, wagons, and horses. The French commander modified his plans and ordered the continuation of the march to Zwammerdam with approximately 3,000 men, aiming to cut off Königsmarck together with the troops who were quartered in the area between Bodegraven and Zwammerdam. He did not succeed in his scheme, because Königsmarck fell back towards Gouda with his troops in time. This move saved the small Dutch army corps, but left unopposed Bodegraven and Zwammerdam. The French seized control of both strongholds, going on a terrible rampage of murder, rape, and pillage.[36] The climate came to the rescue of the Dutch again, leaving Luxembourg in an awkward position, because the rain turned the ice to marsh and the only road to Woerden was blocked by the redoubt at Nieuwerbrug, which was manned by 1,000 Dutch infantrymen under the command of the Colonel and Quartermaster-General Moïse Pain et Vin. He was stricken with panic and ordered the evacuation of the redoubt, a decision for which he would pay with his life on 23 January 1673. The untoward act gave Luxembourg the opportunity to lead his men to safety.

Before the end of the year, the Republic managed to close the winter campaign with an important military success. In the early morning of 30 December 1672, Lieutenant-Colonel Frederik Eybergen managed to recapture Coevorden by surprise. He assembled a storming party of 400 Dutch foot soldiers and militiamen from Groningen, escorted by 400 horsemen in five companies and 200 dragoons.[37] The Münster garrison had failed to keep the moats clear of ice, so the Dutch could penetrate the renowned stronghold without much difficulty.

The conquest of Coevorden was achieved notwithstanding the weakness of the Dutch forces engaged in the war. However, the failed expeditions to Naarden, Woerden and Charleroi, and Luxembourg's incursion to Zwammerdam had highlighted how the Dutch army's strength was inadequate to operate far beyond its own borders. In addition, the war would eventually be extended on other fronts, to begin with by the Spanish Low Countries. In fact, the Spaniards were gravely concerned that Louis XIV would no longer leave the Spanish Netherlands unmolested. Monterrey received news from all quarters that French troops were being assembled near Courtrai and large stock of siege tools like shovels, spades, and pickaxes amassed at Oudenarde.

35 'Furthermore we must state that the farmers hereabouts are being seriously mistreated by our troops ... and it is barely possible to bring the food to the posts without already being plundered by the soldiers.' *Ibid.*, p. 457.

36 On the atrocities committed at Zwammerdam see in Valkenier, *'t Verwerd Europa*, p. 841, as well as the famous series of engravings by Romeyn de Hooghe which appeared in 1673 under the title *Spiegel der France tirannye* (The Mirror of French Tyranny).

37 Van Dam van Isselt, *De Verdediging van Friesland*, p. 283.

Information had also been obtained about the state of all the ovens, and a calculation had been made of what quantity of bread it should be possible to bake each day for the French troops both in Oudenarde and in the vicinity. The Spaniards used this intelligence to estimate the French force build-up at between 20,000 to 22,000 men. Monterrey suspected that the French would open the campaign by laying siege to Brussels. This new threat could be positive for the Republic, but at the same time could turn to an unfavourable outcome. A large-scale French commitment in the Spanish Low Countries would almost certainly have saved the Republic from a new enemy assault, but extended the war on a larger front, turning the Dutch strategy at serious risk, because more states' troops would be needed to return the help to the threatened Spanish ally on his territory. It was directly Louis XIV who removed the Allies' doubts, ordering the conquest of Maastricht as the first action of the new campaign.[38]

The siege of the greatest fortress still in Dutch hands on the Meuse was meant to regain the strategic initiative and show the France's military might. Furthermore, Spanish intelligence estimates turned out to be wrong, because the French assembled a force double the size of that expected. Louis XIV would command the army in person. Maastricht had a garrison of 5,000 to 6,000 regular troops under Major-General Jacques de Fariaux.[39] The possibility that the siege could be resolved in a success for the defenders became even smaller after the separate peace between the Elector of Brandenburg and France, signed at Vossen in early April. Without the support of their ally and the neutrality of Hohenzollern's possession in Westphalia, the Dutch Republic, and Spain – with a barely 18,000-strong field army – could only with difficulty engage the enemy with some prospect of success.

In early June, the naval victories gained by de Ruyter over the enemy fleets on the Schoneveld dispersed the threat of English landings in Zealand and Holland, but the good news was counterbalanced by the bad one concerning the investment of Maastricht, begun on the night of 17–18 June 1673. The fortress' garrison was formed by companies from several regiments just formed and only 400 soldiers from the regiment *Prins Maurits* (I-45) and *Beaumont* (I-28) could be considered as veteran.[40] The defenders enacted a vigorous defence, but the great French engineer Vauban performed his masterwork and the town surrendered after just 13 days. During the siege, the defenders lost 1,500 men. The surviving garrison obtained free evacuation and marched to Hertogenbosch. However, the French advance did not materialise again. On 1 July the Emperor had signed the alliance with Spain and the exiled Duke of Lorraine, assembling an army of 30,000 men in West Bohemia. The French war

38 According to the American historian Paul Sonnino, the Sun King wanted to have his hands free for the showdown with Spain and he hoped that the loss of Maastricht would at last compel the Dutch to acquiesce and opt for peace, and in the process sell-out the Spanish Low Countries. See *Louis XIV and the Origin of the Dutch War* (Cambridge: Cambridge University Press, 2003), p. 160.

39 Jacques de Fariaux, viscount of Maulde (1627–1695), was a Walloon officer who had served the Spanish army until 1672. The States Generals appointed him as commander in Maastricht after the death of the *Rijngraaf* in January 1673.

40 Knoop, *Krijgs- en*, p. 262.

cabinet expected the Imperialist offensive on the Moselle for invading France and therefore modified the plans against the Dutch Republic and the Spanish Low Countries. To secure the possession in Lorraine, Louis XIV ordered the seizing of Trier, but this decision had a counterproductive effect, because the German princes asked the House of Austria for protection against French aggression and Leopold I took this opportunity to profile himself as protector of the Holy Roman Empire, replacing in this role Louis XIV.

On 9 August, after leaving the Caribbean ports, Vice-Admiral Cornelis Evertsen landed with 600 marines at New York and occupied the former Dutch colony. The enterprise had a resounding echo, but the best news arrived shortly after. On 21 August 1673, the Dutch fleet clashed with the English and French for the third time that year. This victory gained the Republic a major political prize, because Leopold I and the Empire turned to openly support the Republic. On 30 August 1673 the 'Triple Alliance' was concluded by the Habsburg Emperor, Spain, and the Dutch Republic. In exchange for large subsidies,[41] Leopold I agreed to send the army to the Rhine and to continue the war until the States General and Spain had recaptured from France all the fortresses and towns they have already lost or might lose in the future.

Within a few weeks, the war had changed the strategic situation, allowing William III to design an offensive plan. Before the end of August, the Prince sent 11,000 Dutch troops to Hertogenbosch, then, on 6 September 1673, William III appeared before Naarden with 25,000 men. Despite the French commander being in command of a considerable garrison of 3,000 men and the engineers having extended the defensive works with a covered road, he timidly kept his troops within the fortifications and even the artillery fire was minimal. This feeble defence favoured the besiegers' work and the digging of the trenches progressed so swiftly that the Dutch infantry was soon able to prepare for the storming of the covered road. The morale of the troops was excellent and not even the news that Luxembourg had assembled a relief corps and was marching to Naarden caused their fighting spirit to decrease.[42]

The storming of the covered road took place at night on 11 September 1673. Colonel Palm's marines opened the action and confirmed their reputation gained at Woerden of being hardened soldiers. Coeval reports related that the marines fought uncommonly well and effectively penetrated the town. The following day the French garrison surrendered after negotiating the free evacuation that took place on 13 September.[43] During the three-day siege, approximately 300 dead and wounded had fallen on each side.[44]

41 Spain promised to transfer 50,000 rix-dollars per month to Vienna, while the Republic promised 45,000 rix-dollars. See Wilson, *Dutch Armies*, pp. 47–49.

42 Field deputy Adriaan van Bosvelt wrote with satisfaction to Gaspar Fagel that Luxembourg's approach 'has not ended up causing the least agitation here; on the contrary, one observes a great courage among the officers as well as the soldiers, who are full of self-assurance about combating the approaching enemy.' Nimwegen, *The Dutch Army*, p. 463.

43 The faint-hearted defence of Naarden was a disgrace for the French army, and Van Reede-Ginkel was jubilant: 'The French have hereby squandered much of their reputation, having defended this place much more poorly than any of ours (the Dutch garrisons) last year. … They undertook no sortie nor anything else, but surrendered as soon as our troops were on the counterscarp!', *ibid.*

44 Knoop, *Krijgs- en*, p. 284.

The conquest of Naarden represented an actual turning point for the Dutch army. It would be difficult to imagine a contrast more stark than that between this self-confidence and the great terror which had seized all the Dutch troops in 1672. William III contributed to this outcome with his personal valour. The disregard for death which the Prince demonstrated by appearing twice or thrice a day in person in the forwardmost trenches stirred the fighting spirit of the soldiers even further.

The war worked out equally unfavourably for Louis XIV within the Holy Roman Empire. In September 1673 his troops had indeed captured Trier, but the Imperial forces set out on their march to the Rhine that same month.

Now there was at last a real chance of a conjunction of the Dutch–Spanish army and the Imperialists. William III, Monterrey, and Montecuccoli agreed that they would jointly lay siege to Bonn, capital of the Electorate of Cologne. The conquest of this fortified town would force Bishop-Prince Elector Maximilian Heinrich to switch allegiances, laying the Bishopric of Münster open to invasion. The defeat of both the German allies of France would sever the lifeline between the French army in the Republic and Charleroi and from there to its bases in France. For the siege of Bonn, William III assembled 5–6,000 cavalry, 1,500 dragoons and 2,000 infantry for mid October. Monterrey added 1,000 horsemen and 2,000 foot soldiers, so the whole Dutch–Spanish army numbered between 11,500 and 12,500 men.[45] On 23 October, the Dutch and Spanish troops crossed the Meuse and entered the Duchy of Julich and Cologne. The campaign promised a favourable result but the task was not easy, because it was very probable that the march of troops into enemy territory should pass unnoticed, despite the Allies trying to keep highly secret their advance and the French could react in a short time to face the threat. This quickly became evident when, more or less simultaneously, the French war cabinet realised that William III had set his sights on Bonn. Luxembourg received orders to evacuate Utrecht and the Veluwe area and move to Maastricht with all the troops under his command, estimated at 18–19,000 men. If possible, the King and Turenne were to hamper the investment of Bonn.

Since the retaking of Naarden the clearance of the French conquests to the north of the major rivers in the Republic had been but a question of time, but the expedition to Bonn made the immediate implementation of this decision ineluctable. The 10,000 to 12,000 Dutch field troops who had been left behind near Naarden under the command of Waldeck posed a constant threat to the French occupation of Woerden, Utrecht, Amersfoort, Harderwijk, and other places. If the French were to delay the evacuation of these towns until Bonn had been captured and William III had returned to the Republic with his army, then the withdrawal of their garrisons would be cut off and Waldeck would then have been able to take them prisoner one by one. *Maréchal* de Bellefonds, commander in the Gelderland quarters of Zutphen and Nijmegen, had in the meantime concentrated all his troops, 26,000 men in all, in Zutphen, Arnhem, Nijmegen, and Grave for this purpose. If Luxembourg and Turenne managed

45 Nimwegen, *The Dutch Army*, p. 465.

to prevent the investment of Bonn then these four bridgeheads on the Ijssel, Rhine, Waal, and Meuse would make it possible to penetrate into the heart of the Republic anew. Instead, if they failed in their plan, the French could quickly retreat to France along the Meuse. In this latter instance, the three towns to the north of the Meuse would be abandoned, but a garrison of 4–5,000 men would be left behind in Grave. This fortified town was the key to the strategic scenario. The possession of Grave denied the Republic the use of the Meuse, it also served as a collection point for artillery, munitions, and supplies from the provinces of Utrecht and Gelderland, as well as for the Dutch hostages who served as collateral for payment of the contributions imposed. Besides retaining a garrison in Grave, Maastricht would be left with a stronger French garrison. Luxembourg's attempt to catch up with the Dutch–Spanish army failed, their having too great a head start. Dutch and Spaniards acted very hard in the Electorate. The plundering had been terrible leaving the country no less ruined than the Dutch provinces the previous year.[46] A low point was the massacre of armed civilians carried out by the Dutch troops after their storming of the small town of Rheinbach.[47]

On 6 November, the Dutch–Spanish army was approaching Bonn. Montecuccoli was already there with the Imperial troops, so the siege could start immediately. The Dutch–Spanish opened the trenches on the north-west side of Bonn and the Imperialists on the south side. The siege proceeded propitiously. The garrison of troops from France and Cologne had a strength of about 2,000 men but opposed a little resistance. On 11 November, the besiegers began the undermining of the main rampart, forcing the enemy to turn his thoughts to a reasonable capitulation: the parley about the town's surrender began the following day, and the agreement was reached in the evening. The 1,200 defenders remaining were granted a free withdrawal to Neuss, but only a small portion actually arrived there, because a great many of them, namely Cologne's troops, had entered into the Imperial army. After the damage to Bonn's fortifications had been repaired, Montecuccoli and William III cleared away the remaining garrisons of troops from Cologne and France within the Electorate. In Linnich and Kerpen there were garrisons of a mere 200 men, who surrendered after offering a very feeble resistance. Dutch–Spaniards then headed for Herentals, arriving there in early December 1673. Waldeck had in the meantime marched to meet William III with the troops under his command. Monterrey had sent a further 6,000 Spanish troops, so the allied forces grew to 27,000 men. William III hoped to defeat Luxembourg with these amassed forces, but the French commander managed to evade a battle and reached Charleroi in safety.

---

46 General Van Reede-Ginkel wrote to his father on 29 October 1673: 'Your High Honour is invited to imagine what astonishment this has caused in these parts, where very few (inhabitants) had taken flight, and the people could not have imagined that our army would come so far (from the Republics borders)'. *Ibid.* p. 466.

47 Further acts of violence occurred days later, when the Dutch troops hanged the major of Bonn at the town gate, and brutally killed numerous inhabitants as reprisal of the Cologne Electorate troops' plunders in 1672. See Marjolein't Hart, *The Dutch Wars of Independence*, p. 76.

The strategic scenario offered now better prospects to the Allies, who finally could gain the initiative after two years of continuous French predominance. This affected also the political balance that turned to the Triple Alliance. After Münster and Cologne were defeated, England seemed close to leaving the French alliance. The failure of the naval war and the rumour that Charles II was cooperating with Louis XIV in order to establish absolutism and popery in England and to bring about the establishment of a French 'universal monarchy' in Europe became widespread in the arena of English public opinion. Parliament consequently refused to continue providing money for the struggle against the Republic, compelling Charles II to discontinue the war. In the second Peace of Westminster, signed on 19 February 1674, King Charles II waived the demand of garrisoning the Dutch towns of Sluis, Vlissingen and Den Brie, and the Republic was to pay him an indemnification of just two million guilders instead of the 10 million initially requested. On 22 April 1674 the Bishop of Münster also left the French camp. Without the protection of the French army, he could not safeguard his bishopric against the Imperial troops. Von Galen had to be satisfied that he was not required to pay any damages to the Republic and that his land was spared the devastations which had befallen Cologne. Soon thereafter, the Elector of Cologne also made peace on 11 May 1674. In exchange for the retrocession of all the places captured by Münster and Cologne troops in the Republic, the States General waived its right to a garrison in Rheinberg. Before the end of May, the French army evacuated the Gelderland towns of Zutphen, Arnhem, and Nijmegen. After the news on the French retreat, William III trusted in a general withdrawn from the occupied provinces, but the loss of three allies would not prevent the Sun King from continuing the war. According to a plan designed by the war cabinet, strong French garrisons of between 4–5,000 men and more than 7,000 men remained behind in Grave and Maastricht, respectively. The Republic's *Existenzkampf* might have been over by early 1674, but the struggle to preserve the European balance of power had only just begun.

On 31 March 1674 the German princes declared 'Imperial War' against Louis XIV; the Holy Roman Empire was now formally supporting the Republic in the war against France. William III hoped that it would hereby be possible to counterbalance the numerical superiority of France. In early 1674, on the basis of reports about French troop concentrations and movements, he and the Dutch generals assumed that Louis XIV would bring a further 65,000 men into the field, divided across four theatres of war: the Low Countries, Alsace, Franche-Comté, and Roussillon. On paper the Allies could muster sufficient troops. Diplomatic deliberations involving The Hague, Madrid, Brussels and Vienna led to the determination of the main thrust of an operational plan that covered all fronts. France's war preparations left no shadow of a doubt that Louis XIV would no longer hold his troops with regard to the Spanish Low Countries. In February 1674, the French under Navailles had invaded Franche-Comté, seizing the whole province in a single campaign. Now *Maréchal* Condé would in all probability invade the Low Countries at the head of 30,000 men, but Monterrey could for the time being assemble no more than 10,000 men for the defence of the Spanish Netherlands. The new French threat forced the Spanish governor to call back the majority of the

35. The siege of Grave. Anonymous engraving. (Author's archive)

The campaign of 1674 concluded with the Dutch success at Grave, which was reconquered in October after a three-month siege. The possession of Grave granted the Republic the use of the Meuse, and deprived the French of the major collection point for suppies from the provinces of Utrecht and Gelderland. The capure of Grave definitively moved the war from the Dutch Republic to the Spanish Low Countries.

Spanish troops involved with the Dutch under William III. Monterrey's plan was to remain behind in the garrisons until there was greater clarity about France's plan of attack, and this meant that at least 20,000 extra men were needed to stand up to the French in the Spanish Low Countries. However, Spanish expectations were positive because in Brussels Monterrey was certain to set up enough forces, turning to the German princes to permit William III to begin the campaign with 24,000 men. Emperor Leopold and the Imperial Diet promised to mobilise two armies, one along the Upper Rhine and the other on the Moselle. The Imperial army's field marshal-general Alexandre Hippolyte Balthasar de Hennin, Prince de Bournonville, with 40,000 men, was given the task of preventing Louis XIV from dispatching his army from Franche-Comté to the Spanish Low Countries. The Allied objective could best be achieved conquering Philippsburg, the main French stronghold on the Rhine. The capture of Philippsburg would provide the Imperial forces with a strong bridgehead for operations in Alsace.

The expectation was that an Imperial advance into Alsace would compel Louis XIV to deploy his army in Franche-Comté for the defence of France's eastern border, The second German army – 31,000 strong including, 9,000 from Münster and 2,000 from Cologne – was commanded by the 66-year-old Imperial Field Marshal Louis Raduit, Count de Souches (1608–1683), son of a French nobleman from La Rochelle, with the task of operating along the Moselle, and ensuring that the army always remained ahead and was able to join with Bournonville or the Allies in the Low Countries, as needs required. Lastly, 16,000 Spanish troops in Catalonia were to threaten Roussillon, where an estimated 6,000 Frenchmen were dispersed across garrisons.

In early May 1674, Waldeck travelled to Brussels for further deliberations with Monterrey and the other Spanish commanders. Here he found the Spaniards very concerned about the Imperial troops. As the greatest interest of the Spanish governor-general was the preservation of the country and that the Imperial army should act offensively outside it. News on the poor pay and deficient logistical organisation of the Imperial forces meant they were highly undesirable guests. The Spanish governor-general informed Waldeck that if Condé should receive reinforcements then he would ask the Emperor to send Souches to the Low Countries for staying on the same side of the Meuse, but not before; and that so long as there was not an extreme and ultimate necessity.

Two weeks after this meeting, Louis XIV and Condé's son, the Duke of Enghien, captured Besançon, followed a few later by the surrender of Dole. The reduction of the main cities of Franche-Comté meant the campaign there was effectively at an end, and the bulk of the invading army was therefore available for operations elsewhere. Louis XIV sent reinforcements to Turenne's army, but directed the majority of his troops, estimated by the allies at between 8,000 and 10,000 men, to the Spanish Netherlands. In anticipation of the arrival of these reinforcements, Condé captured Argenteau on 17 May and Navagne five days later: two castles on the Meuse between Liège and Maastricht. The capture of Argenteau and Navagne was of great strategic importance for the French, making them master of the Meuse corridor to the north and south of Maastricht. They therefore no longer had to be wary of an unexpected investment of this stronghold. The Allies were still unprepared to counter Condé's offensive and this provoked Spanish complaints. After this drawback, the Dutch troops were immediately sent to the rendezvous at Roosendaal and headed for Mechelen-Malines in mid May. Further inconveniences occurred days later, because the Spaniards had failed to establish any forage magazines, so the Dutch cavalry, which had already suffered greatly from the expedition to Bonn the previous winter, would have been utterly ruined, and William III would still have been unable to assemble the Dutch troops any sooner. Moreover, the Dutch as well as the Spanish siege artillery would now have to be transported overland; Condé could then begin preparations for a large-scale offensive operation against Namur and Mons. The capture of Namur was important with a view to the safety of Charleroi and would at the same time block an important route of access into France via the River Meuse for the allies, while the capture of Mons would consent to a complete control of communications between Flanders and Spanish Brabant. Allied general staff discussed the option to carry out a direct assault against Condé, but not all agreed to the idea of engaging the French army in the open field. Uncertainty about the enemy's actual strength deterred the Dutch commanders from an assault, but the enterprises could be tried by joining the forces in the field. William III was intent on seeking out the French and giving battle as soon as the Imperial troops had crossed the Meuse at Namur and joined with the Dutch–Spanish army. De Souches replied that he would head to the River Meuse but not with the promised 31,000 men, because the Emperor was afraid that Louis XIV would further reinforce Turenne's army and that this corps would subsequently launch an invasion into Breisgau or the Swabian Circle. The army of the Moselle, under Bournonville, was still far from complete and de Souches was thus compelled to send part of the Münster contingent to the Upper Rhine, then his own force decreased to 25,000 men. William III employed all his talents as a negotiator to develop a common plan, but all these problems and divergences of view among the allies caused considerable mishaps and delayed the beginning of operations. The weakening of de Souches' army and the increasing of activity that was simultaneously noticed in Condé's army, which in Le Quesnoy and Ath was amassing a large food supply. The news gave Monterrey cause for graver concern about the safety of Mons, but he also had to bear in mind the peril of the French who were preparing a surprise attack on Ghent. He therefore urged de Souches to come to the Spanish Low Countries as quickly as possible and lay siege to Charleroi. De Souches had to disappoint him, however, as he also had no forage magazines at his disposal and the grain was not yet ripe enough for the horses to be able to live from the land. It was therefore the end of June 1674 before the Imperial troops arrived near Namur. On 2 July, a meeting happened between the allied commanders. William III, Waldeck, and Monterrey noted that the Imperial *Feldmarschall* displayed a very great repugnance to crossing the Meuse.[48] This notwithstanding they tried to persuade him to do so and to conjoin himself with them, in order jointly to go and defeat the Prince of Condé, who lay close by Ath. However, de Souches stood by his standpoint that the Dutch–Spanish army, which had by then swelled to 45,000 men, was strong enough to attack the French successfully even without Imperial support.[49]

Meanwhile, nothing was left unturned. On 27 June 1674, Admiral Cornelis Tromp with the fleet and a corps of marines headed to Bretagne. Here he landed siege equipment and menaced Poiteu, plundering the suburbs of Dieppe and Bayonne.[50] The attempt to seize Harfleur with the complicity of the commander failed when news of the arrival of French troops forced Tromp to withdraw on the ships.[51] Further bad news came from other fronts. De Ruyter's attempt to seize Martinique had failed with heavy casualties; in Germany Turenne had crossed to the right bank of the Rhine at Philippsburg in the middle of June 1674 and had defeated Bournonvilles at Sinzheim. After this failure, Emperor Leopold I had firmly ordered de Souches to remain on the east bank of the Meuse. This order frustrated the Dutch–Spanish plan, nevertheless, the Imperial commander submitted an alternative plan. He proposed to advance to Dinant, a small stronghold within the Prince-Bishopric of Liège, with the Imperial army and part of the Dutch–Spanish force. William III and Monterrey were not in the least enthusiastic about this proposal. The occupation of Dinant would have no effect on the strategic situation in the Spanish Netherlands whatsoever. They therefore resorted to a ruse in order to persuade de Souches to cross the Meuse after all. William III informed the

48 Nimwegen, *The Dutch Army*, p. 475.

49 *Ibid.* Waldeck rebutted this argument by pointing out that Condé was expecting substantial reinforcements from Franche-Comté and that his army would therefore be 50,000 strong. The Allies would then be unable to risk giving battle or laying siege to Charleroi, unless Souches conflated his troops with those of the Republic and Spain. However, the Imperial Field Marshal categorically refused to cross the Meuse, and when Waldeck asked him the reason for this he replied, 'Because Bournonville does not have a force sufficient to oppose Turenne.'

50 Gaetien de Courtilz, *Histoire de la Guerre d'Hollande* (The Hague, 1689), vol. I, p. 359.

51 Lynn, *The Wars of Louis XIV*, p. 160.

36. The Battle of Seneffe, fought on 11 August 1674 between the French and the Dutch–Imperial–Spanish army, was the major engagement of the war of 1672–1678, resulting in an indecisive outcome with heavy casulaties for both sides. In the French army no fewer than 36 field officers, 163 captains, and 260 lieutenants and lower-ranking officers lost their lives. The allies lost hundreds of officers as well. General van Reede-Ginkel, wounded in the opening phase of the battle, wrote to his father the day after that 'One sees hardly any officers among the infantry either (they) are dead or injured.' The total casualties were 10–11,000 for the French, and 14–15,000 for the Allies: this figure is proof enough that the General's words were no exaggeration. In France as well as in the Dutch Republic, people proclaimed that there had never been such a bloody battle. Years later, Voltaire wrote that Seneffe had been a terrible massacre. Some Dutch accounts related that the Prince of Condé refused to allow ransom for the officers taken prisoner – giving as a reason that neither Dutch troops nor the Imperial ones lent any quarter to his – and shot them all dead.
(Many thanks to Edwin Groot for image and information)

37. The Battle of Seneffe. Note the baggage wagons in the foreground. In the battle were lost several Dutch ensigns, collected by the French in the series ***Les Triomphes de Louis XIV représentés par les Drapeaux pris sur les Ennemis de S. M.,*** preserved in the Bibliothèque National de France. This document represents the best source of knowledge on the Dutch ensigns of the period 1672–87.
(Collection of print of the University of Leyden, NL)

Imperial Field Marshal that he would in person join the Imperial army with 17,000 to 18,000 Dutch troops and would lend assistance to the siege of Rocroi. This stronghold's reduction would clear the way to attack Charleville-Mezières, a fortress on either side of the Meuse on which de Souches had set his sights. In exchange for this offer, William III expected that de Souches would have his cavalry cross the Meuse in order to ensure the conjunction. At the same time, the French army camped near Charleroi and William III therefore had no doubt that Condé would attempt to block the passage of the Dutch corps marching in three days to Namur. This was what William was actually hoping for, because if Condé abandoned his positions by Charleroi then de Souches would be forced to come to the aid of the Dutch corps. It was a real game of chess conducted on a chessboard in which the pieces of one side did not cooperate willingly to share a common victory. Considering the debate as inconclusive, William III ordered Lieutenant-General Rabenhaupt to proceed to the siege of Grave with the troops in Groningen and Friesland. The town was blocked on late July by 3,000 infantry and 600 cavalry.[52]

On 18 July 1674, some 1,800 Imperial troops marched into Dinant, and 10 days later de Souches arrived with his cavalry at Perwez, a village 18 kilometres north of Namur, where the Dutch-Spaniards had their encampments. After further discussion about a common plan to pursue, the Imperial infantry crossed the left bank of the Meuse as well, so no fewer than 70,000 allied troops were assembled there: 30,000 Dutch, 15,000 Spanish and 25,000 Imperial. Now the allied army was stronger than the French one, but Condé avoided the engagement, displaying his troops near Charleroi, where he could easily reject any direct assault thanks to the favourable terrain.[53] The Allied manoeuvre had as a result to force Condé to no longer hold under threat Namur and Mons, but it was a very small success, considering the numerical superiority achieved by the Allies. On 10 August, the Allied war council discussed the plan to besiege Ath, for securing Brussels from any French assault, as proposed by Monterrey. Rather than laying siege to Ath, William III and de Souches advised heading to Hainaut in order to attack if possible a place on the frontier of France, such as Le Quesnoy, Douai, or Saint-Quentin. With one of these towns as an operational base, the allies would be able to exact contributions from France. This plan implied a serious risk, because the allied army would pass within a short distance from the French army. The hilly terrain, criss-crossed by morasses and ditches, provided some protection against a flank attack, but Condé would still be able to attack the Allies while they were marching and would then be in a position to defeat the fragmented main corps. Reconnaissance and skirmish had revealed that the French army was deployed along the road to Charleroi–Brussels, south of the small town of Seneffe, 15 kilometres north-east of Charleroi.

The allied commanders were well aware of this danger, but they underestimated its gravity, because this latter proposal obtained the majority's consensus, and the following day the allied army moved south divided into

52 Nimwegen, *The Dutch Army*, p. 476.

53 Lynn, *The Wars of Louis XIV*, p. 161.

three columns. Near Seneffe, the Allies positioned a corps of 3,500 Dutch and Spanish cavalry and dragoons with five Dutch infantry battalions in order to secure the passage of the main army. These troops – 5–6,000 in all – were under the command of the able Spanish commander Charles Henri of Lorraine, Prince of Vaudemont. The battle of Seneffe (11 August 1674) began at about 10 o'clock in the morning with a sudden French assault on the village itself. Condé sent four cavalry squadrons to ,make contact with the enemy rearguard. After a brief exchange of fire, the Dutch infantry sought cover amidst the cavalry. Brigadier-General Godard van Reede-Ginkel commanded the Dutch cavalry in two successive charges, leading the *Obdam* (C-12) regiment's squadrons in person.[54] Soon the French main corps arrived and as easily predictable, Vaudemont's corps was unable to face the whole enemy army. Under the continuous French assaults, the allied cavalry began to lose ground and eventually fled. The Dutch battalions were abandoned to their fate and just about annihilated. The noise of the fighting was also heard by William III, who ordered the inversion of march, and led the troops again to the north. The allied army was deployed on two lines, with the cavalry at the wings, proceeding in column through the irregular terrain that made the approach to the enemy particularly insidious. Condé too did not have exact knowledge of the position of the enemies, but he saw the possibility of inflicting a decisive defeat on William III, and then the two armies faced each other in a continuous series of clashes at a short distance, outflanking each other and inflicting heavy losses with deadly volleys. There was no question of coordinated attacks. The battle proceeded with varying success without one side prevailing. The French and Allied generals led one unit after another into combat and several times the troops routed. The battle continued in the afternoon until 11 o'clock, when the darkness made further fighting impossible and Condé ordered the retreat to Charleroi. Casualties were huge on both sides. The total losses of the Allies amounted to 14–15,000, of whom 6,000 were Dutch troops. Some regiments had lost entire companies and many of the officers. The *Gardes te voet* (Foot Guards) regiment claimed the loss of one major, four lieutenants killed, a further 16 officers wounded and 24 captured.[55] The marine regiment *Walenburgh*, involved in the task of covering the withdrawing troops after one of the first Dutch assaults, lost 24 officers who remained surrounded together with their companies, a further two officers were killed and 12 wounded. In overall, 10 colonels died in action, including the valiant marine commander François Palm.[56]

The French had suffered 8,000 or 10,000 dead and wounded. Condé could show off a great many colours and standards captured from the Allies and his troops had also seized most of the Dutch army's baggage wagons. If

---

54 In the large correspondence with his father, van Reede-Ginkel described this action: 'It came about that, for me personally, I penetrated a little too far into the enemy force, when the said squadron (Obdams) loosed a salvo, in which I was shot through and through by a pistol ball just under my left shoulder, which because of the unusually profuse bleeding made me slightly faint and forced me to retreat.' Nimwegen, *The Dutch Army*, p. 477.

55 J.M.G. Leune, *Staatse infanteristen die gedood werden, gewond raakten en gevangen werden genomen tijdens de Slag bij Seneffe op 11 augustus 1674*. See also in the appendices for more details.

56 *Ibid.*

Condé had limited his action to the annihilation of the enemy rearguard, the French victory would have been certain,[57] though modest, but now it was clear that the battle had ended without a winner and his intention of inflicting a crushing defeat on the Allies had failed.

The Allied columns reached Mons on 13 August 1674. Here the army spent some days recovering the nearly 2,000 wounded and allowing the troops the opportunity to procure new tents, clothing, and field beds. Despite the many casualties suffered, William III decided to take advantage of the situation, presuming that Condé was facing no less difficulty. The Prince examined the possibility of laying siege to Ath again, which in his view had a good chance of success now, because Condé had reduced the garrison to 3,000 men. De Souches agreed to this proposal, but a couple of days later he suddenly changed his mind; he was only prepared to lend assistance for the besieging of Oudenarde.

On 16 September 1674 the Allied army arrived before Oudenarde and the opening of the trenches followed a day later. Oudenarde had a garrison of approximately 2,500 men under the aged but always capable Rochepère. Moreover, he was assisted in this task by Vauban, who had moved himself to this stronghold when it became apparent that the allies no longer had designs on Ath. The Dutch and Spanish troops approached the covered road energetically, while the Imperial troops performed very badly. On 19 September, there was news that Condé had crossed to the left bank of the River Scheldt at Tournai and was advancing to the relief of the town. For William III this was an extra incentive to capture Oudenarde as quickly as possible, and the Dutch and Spanish trenches reached the curtain that same night. Success seemed close, but suddenly de Souches ordered to his troops to leave the trenches; then the following night he dispatched his entire field artillery and all the munitions to Ghent. Obviously the Dutch-Spaniards were forced to retreat, scuppering the possibility of besieging Oudenarde. Without their field artillery and munitions the Imperial troops could not take part in a battle and with only the Dutch and Spanish troops William III and his Spanish allies could not hazard a battle against Condé.

The unprecedented actions of de Souches caused a storm of indignation in The Hague. Grand Pensionary Gaspar Fagel ordered the States General's envoy in Vienna to lodge an official protest with the Emperor.[58] William III no longer wanted to serve in the same army with de Souches.

On 8 October 1674, the Prince moved to Grave, which Rabenhaupt maintained under siege. The French had headed for their winter quarters, making the conquest of the town an easy task. Grave had a garrison of 4–5,000 men under the 38-year-old Chamilly, a highly capable and aggressive officer. Chamilly used this town as a base for his marauding forays into the

57 Lynn, *The Wars of Louis XIV*, p. 173.

58 'He (the diplomat) was instructed to underscore that the Republic's war effort had amounted to more than 30 million guilders for the year, and that this sum was raised by extraordinary taxes from the [Republic's] inhabitants. … That the said inhabitants … would become reluctant to contribute if they were to learn that the outlays were poorly spent due to such poor conduct.' Nimwegen, *The Dutch Army*, p. 482.

Nijmegen suburbs. Inside Grave there were the hostages whom Luxembourg had carried off from Utrecht in late 1673. However, Rabenhaupt could just perform a blockade, because his troops were insufficient to wholly invest the town, allowing Chamilly to have the hostages transferred to Maastricht. Grave was well defended thanks to the strong garrison and the huge supply of artillery and munitions in the stronghold. Rabenhaupt's force was not strong enough to begin the formal siege until 11 August, when the Brandenburg troops arrived at the Dutch camp, swelling Rabenhaupt's army to approximately 16,000 men. After the Holy Roman Empire had declared war on France, with the Emperor mobilising two armies and the Republic fighting together with Spain against France in the Spanish Low Countries, the Great Elector felt the time was ripe to participate in the struggle again. He thought the renewal of the pact with the Dutch Republic was desirable, primarily in view of the threat of war with Sweden.[59]

William III arrived in the camp of the besiegers on 9 October 1674. The troops that he brought with him were a welcome reinforcement which turned the siege in favour of the Dutch.[60] After consuming all the supplies, the French commander openened negotiations for surrender on 27 October. [61] Casualties were high for both sides. The defenders had suffered more than 2,000 dead and wounded, while the besiegers had lost between 7,000 and 8,000 men killed or wounded. After the recapture of Grave William III dispersed the Dutch troops across the garrisons, but in the Holy Roman Empire there was no question of an end to the campaign. In fact, Turenne exploited the winter months to begin an offensive along the Rhine, while Bournonville's troops were scattered in small corps too distant from each other. The French offensive demonstrated once again that logistics were the major problem of the Imperial forces. While the Dutch Republic and Spain had adopted the French magazine system, at least with respect to the bread supplies, the Emperor was still trying to provision his troops as happened during the Thirty Years' War, namely by requisitioning supplies. This method was effective with small armies, but it forced the larger ones to spread themselves far from the front.

59 Charles XI (1655–1697), King of Sweden from 1660, was an ally of Louis XIV. In accordance with an alliance concluded with France in 1672, the Swedish king was obliged to help discourage the German princes from assisting the Dutch Republic by assembling an intervention force of 16,000 men, but he was for a long time hesitant to meet this commitment. In 1674, he was nevertheless forced to keep his word, because otherwise Louis XIV threatened to make overtures to Denmark. Charles XI therefore augmented his army in Swedish Pomerania from 15,000 to 22,000 men and ordered preparations to be made for a campaign in northern Germany.

60 At the siege of Grave participated with the rank of infantry captain the future specialist of fortification and siege Menno van Coehorn. See in J. Bosscha, *Neërlands Heldendaden te land* (Breda, 1872), vol. II, p. 188.

61 Nimwegen, *The Dutch Army*, p. 483. Colonel Gaspar Richard Hundebeck wrote to Waldeck on 22 October: 'This siege … is currently not proceeding as desired. We are losing many soldiers. The enemy is very well equipped in his positions, with all the advantages and mines, which do us great damage. Yet I believe the enemy shall run into a shortage of flour and other necessities, and will therefore have to surrender in eight to ten days, otherwise they are pretty much immune to the siege assault as it is now being carried out. Our regiments have become very weak. I have no more healthy captains, never mind a senior officer. They are all injured and have fallen sick, thus I shall once again have to think about raising recruits.'

After the bitter experiences of 1674, William III was convinced that the French could be successfully challenged in the Spanish Low Counties only if the Allies would decide to join the armies operating in this area, to be commanded by a single commander.[62] However, the Prince realised it was unlikely that Vienna and Brussels–Madrid would consent to this. As an alternative, he therefore proposed 'with authority to concert the military operations with those who will be in command of the separate armies (and) to come to a decision by plurality of votes'. William assumed that this would obviate the objection that the Imperial and Spanish generals might harbour against his appointment as Allied commander-in-chief in the Low Countries. For William it was a foregone conclusion that the rank of supreme commander would fall to him. The Prince could count on the support of the States General committee for secret affairs for his plan. The behaviour of de Souches during the siege of Oudenarde had, after all, caused great commotion and annoyance, among the regents as well. William entrusted Waldeck and the Amsterdam regent Coenraad van Heemskerck with the difficult task of raising this delicate matter in Vienna and Brussels, respectively. Waldeck was partly successful in his diplomacy: Leopold I suspended de Souches and assigned command on the Rhine to Montecuccoli, but at the same time the Emperor explained that he was in no position to dispatch an army to the Low Countries again. The remaining Imperial troops were necessary to support Brandenburg against the Swedes, or destined for a campaign along the Moselle. The Emperor's response came as an extremely unpleasant surprise, for the Republic's relations between The Hague and Vienna become tenser, conditioning the cohesion of the Triple Alliance.

For the campaign of 1675, William III could assemble a field army of '30,000 fine and well-disposed soldiers',[63] but the Spanish forces were in poor condition. Carlos de Aragón de Gurrea y Borja, Duke of Villahermosa, replaced Monterrey in January 1675 was facing a hard financial shortage, which caused bitter consequences for the Spanish army.[64] The only Spanish contribution to the field army materialised in just 5,000 horsemen. Reciprocal suspicions poisoned relations between the Dutch Republic and the Spanish Crown, especially after the recapture of Grave, which virtually closed the struggle for survival of the United Provinces, leaving the Spanish Low Countries as the major battlefield of foreign armies. Moreover, Madrid

62 *Ibid.* p. 484. In a discussion about this with Grand Pensionary Fagel, William III expressed the view that this commander-in-chief should preferably be authorised, having heard the counsel of the commanders of the separate armies, to decide (upon the course of action) as he judges will best serve the common cause.

63 *Ibid.* p. 485.

64 On paper, the Spanish army in the Southern Netherlands numbered 49,000 men, but the companies fell far short of their establishment strengths and Villahermosa had distributed all the infantry among the threatened forts. Mutual distrust between Brussels and The Hague was an important factor in this decision.

accused the allies of disinterest in supporting the Spanish claim to restore her possessions in the Low Countries as in 1659.[65]

The 1674 campaign had demonstrated that the Dutch Republic, Spain, and the Emperor could jointly assemble in the Low Countries forces numerically superior to the French army. Internal discord had prevented the Allies being able to take advantage of this, but there was no assurance that this would also be the case in 1675. Louis XIV therefore ordered Condé to seize control of Dinant, Huy, and Limbourg before laying siege to Namur. Liège had been occupied by French troops since 31 March 1675 and after capturing these three towns, all the fortified crossing places upstream of Maastricht on the River Meuse would be under French control, and it was highly unlikely that the Emperor would once again dispatch troops to the Spanish Low Countries when his lines of communication would have to run via Roermonde. Condé was assigned more than 40,000 men for his offensive, augmented later to between 50,000 and 60,000 men in all. Condé charged his lieutenant Créquy to besiege Dinant and he appeared before the town on 19 May. The Imperial garrison of this small fortress, just 250 strong at the time, capitulated on 29 May.[66] Next in line was Huy, where the 550 defenders surrendered on 6 June. Four days later the French invested Limbourg, where the garrison of 1,000 men kept up the defence until 21 June. The French offensive caused great consternation in Brussels. William III and Villahermosa advanced with the Dutch and Spanish troops on Louvain, but the French superiority was too great to hazard a battle, they therefore agreed to go to Roermonde and await the arrival of a corps of cavalry from Brunswick and Lorraine before launching a counter-offensive. However, this plan soon had to be abandoned, because Condé led the French army to Ath, stoking fears about the safety of Brussels, Mons, and Ghent. William III and Villahermosa struck camp and, travelling via Malines, at the end of July 1675 they reached the environs of Halle, a small town to the south-west of Brussels, with forced marches. From there they could soon reach Ghent. Troops were sent to Brussels as reinforcement. The allied army was now decreased from 35,000 to 29,000 men in all.[67]

---

65 Spanish suspicions of secret negotiations between The Hague and Louis XIV for a compromise peace was no longer unthinkable. 'A precondition for this was that the King of France consented to the Spanish Netherlands serving as a rampart between the Republic and France, Otherwise the Republic would have to be prepared for the possibility of a French invasion at all times, even in peacetime, and thus be forced to keep her army at wartime strength and permanently maintain the forts in a state of defence, Establishing the Spanish Netherlands as a buffer zone required Frances retrocession of Veurne (Furnes), Courtrai, Oudenarde, Ath and Charleroi. Louis XIV would have to be indemnified for this and the Spanish therefore harboured suspicions that the Dutch would accept France pursuing conquests in Artois and Cambrai and not make any troops available for the defence of these provinces.' Nimwegen, *The Dutch Army*, p. 485.

66 Lynn, *Wars of Louis XIV*, p. 187.

67 Field deputy Coenraad van Heemskerck reported to the States-General on 27 July: 'Excepting the units left behind (namely one regiment in Brussels, two in Malines, one in Dendermonde, some soldiers in Roermonde, Venlo, Louvain, etc.), the States' army probably still consists, by estimation, of 25,000 combatants, and the Spaniards in the field have 4,000 men in all, both cavalry and dragoons.' He did, however, expect that the allied army would soon be reinforced again, because besides the various regiments which had been ordered to leave their garrisons and join the field army, there were also hundreds of soldiers who had fallen behind en route

On 27 July 1675, there was an event on the Rhine that would also have major repercussions in the Low Countries: the brave Turenne was killed by a cannonball, during a reconnaissance of the Imperial positions near the small town of Salzbach. Without their valiant commander, the French were no match for Montecuccoli and they beat a swift retreat to Alsace. To prevent the Imperial forces crossing the Rhine, Louis XIV ordered Condé to head immediately to Alsace with part of his army and to assume command over the Rhine army. Fifteen days later, on 11 August, another French army under Maréchal François, Marquis de Créquy suffered a defeat at the Battle of Konzer Brücke, after which Duke Charles IV of Lorraine laid siege to Trier. This city fell on 6 September 1675, after the French garrison rose in mutiny.[68]

After Condés departure, Luxembourg assumed command over the French army in the Spanish Low Countries. He considered his forces as insufficient to besiege Namur or to seek battle with the Dutch–Spanish army. Luxembourg was therefore ordered to limit himself to the defensive for the rest of the campaign. For William III and Villahermosa it was difficult to gain any advantage from Turenne's death, because they had too few troops at their disposal. As a consequence, the Dutch, Spanish, and French troops remained in the field until early November 1675 carrying out only defensive tasks, but there were no more significant operations that year.

The war registered important events on other fronts, especially in Pomerania, where at Fehrbellin the Great Elector of Brandenburg defeated the Swedish army on 28 June 1675. After this outcome Denmark involved herself in the struggle as well, capturing the Swedish provinces of Wismar and Bremen. In the Republic and Spain, however, there was growing disappointment about military successes failing to materialise. In December 1674 Amsterdam's deputies to the States of Holland had still consented to the States assembly approving the 'state of war' army overview without referring it to the town councils, but now they were no longer prepared to do this. The regents had no intention of supporting Spain again and were of the opinion that Brussels–Madrid had to make a much greater contribution to the defence of their domains in the Low Countries.[69] The States General estimated that at least 20–25,000 Spanish soldiers could be assembled for the field army. These troops, together with 30,000 men from the Republic, would then make it possible to put together a siege corps and an army of observation. An offensive was out of the question if this precondition was not accomplished. Besides this demand for more Spanish troops, the States General had to insist that the Republic be relieved of payment of all the subsidies to the Emperor and the German princes in 1676.

during the long march from Roermond to Halle and would trickle into the allied camp over the coming days, *Ibid.* pp. 485-486.

68 De Courtilz, *Histoire de la Guerre d'Hollande*, vol. I, p. 378.

69 In December 1675, Van Heemskerck left for Madrid to elucidate the Republic's standpoint. He was instructed to impress upon the King of Spain that the war in the Spanish Netherlands could be decided to the advantage of Spain and the Republic only if Villahermosa likewise 'may be strong and capable of bringing into the field an army of 25,000 or at least 20,000 men over and above the requisite garrisons of the forts.' Nimwegen, *The Dutch Army*, p. 487.

However, the Dutch forecasts were soon disappointed. As related in early January 1676 by the Dutch diplomat in Madrid, the Spanish treasury was in a precarious situation. The King's minister looked forward to the arrival of the galleons from the Americas with the contributions from the colonies, without which every government action was paralysed. The possibility that Spain could deploy a sufficient field force therefore seemed very far away. William III had to give up high expectations because even if the treasure fleet were to put into port soon, he could still not count on many Spanish troops being sent to the Low Countries, because the Sicilian revolt and the French treaty in Catalonia would certainly have absorbed most of the forces collected.

The war's costs were exhausting the Allies as well as France. Though Liège, Huy, Dinant, and Limburg had been captured, none of the main goals such Namur, Ghent, and Brussels had fallen. The death of Turenne and the retirement of Condé, tormented by gout, had serious consequences for the French *Stratégie de Cabinet*. From 1676 the French war effort was focused on establishing buffer zones along France's frontiers. The strongest line of fortifications had to be established along the border with the Spanish Low Countries. This led to the realisation of the *pré carré* (the fortified zone covering France's northern frontier), as devised by Louvois and, over all, Vauban. Louis XIV approved the plan, whereupon he began preparations to seize Condé, Bouchain, Valenciennes, and Cambrai in the 1676 campaign.[70] For this large-scale offensive Louis XIV reserved an army of 60,000 men, over which he and his brother Philippe, Duc d'Orléans, would assume personal command, assisted by no fewer than five French *maréchals*. On 17 April 1676 the French invested Condé and four days later the trenches were opened in the presence of the King. The Spanish garrison numbered just 1,500 men. William III immediately gathered all the available Dutch troops, about 28,000 men, while Villahermosa assembled approximately 13,000 Spanish troops. The allied army reached Mons on 26 April, but Condé fell into French hands that same day. The French then marched to Bouchain, and invested the town on 2 May. After Villahermosa's insistence, William III agreed, despite the imbalance of strength, to relieve Bouchain to deliver a battle.[71] This decision was a daring challenge, because a defeat would have opened the way to the French conquest of the whole Low Countries, creating the threat of a new invasion of the Dutch Republic.

On 10 May 1676, the allies had approached the French siege camp within a cannon shot. The battle seemed inevitable. That day represented an extraordinary moment in the history of the 17th century. Two men, who would fight each other still for many years and embodied two diametrically opposed concepts of politics, were a short distance from each other, ready to

70 Cénat, *Le Roi Stratège*, p. 228.

71 Waldeck informed Grand Pensionary Fagel about this daring decision: 'The decision has been taken to attempt to cross by force the defile that the Most Christian King of France has before him in order to endeavour to relieve Bouchain or at least to save Valenciennes, and it is a plan that, if it succeeds, has never been equalled, as His Highness (William III) will have without doubt written to You. … We are marching tomorrow, the 7th *Nous serons au mains*.' Cited by Nimwegen, *The Dutch Army*, p. 491.

engage a battle that would resound with the tone of the medieval epic. Louis XIV was keen to throw down the gauntlet, but Louvois and a majority of the marshals and generals advised him most strongly against giving battle. They pointed out that the allies could easily find refuge under the guns of Valenciennes, but the actual reason was that they did not want to imperil Louis XIV's life. In the meantime Waldeck was trying to persuade an equally determined William III not to pursue an aggressive course of action. The Dutch army could not be imperilled, he impressed upon the Captain-General of the Union, and the key objective of preventing the loss of Valenciennes had been achieved. Both the Sun King and William III allowed themselves to be dissuaded, albeit with great reluctance, from joining battle. Bouchains capitulated the following day. This was followed by a lull in hostilities which lasted more than a month, On 27 May the French established a position on the River Dender between Geraardsbergen and Ninove. From this position they could threaten Brussels, Aalst, and Ghent, but even more important was that the French horses could recuperate there at the expense of the Spanish Low Countries. The horses of the Allies were in an even worse state than those of the French, because no forage magazines had been established for the Dutch and Spanish troops, leaving them dependent on stores that farmers had amassed for their livestock. William III and Villahermosa took up positions between Aalst and Dendermonde with their army. In the latter half of June 1676, the French shifted their position. They set up a new camp between Mons and Valenciennes, but they made no moves to attack these towns, because the Imperial army had been besieging Philippsburg since 24 June and Louis XIV wanted to be free to direct reinforcements from the Spanish Low Countries to Alsace. On 4 July, the Sun King returned to France after having sent several detachments to the French army in Alsace.

As soon as William III became aware of this plan, he began preparations for a counter-offensive. Maastricht seemed to be a conquerable objective; furthermore, having provided the majority of the troops for the defence of the Spanish Low Countries for two and a half years, William III thought it only right that the Spaniards should lend their assistance to the recapture of Maastricht. The States General had clearly indicated this objective as the necessary fulfilment of the liberation war engaged by the Republic against France since 1672.[72]

72 The most zealous advocate of this undertaking was Johan Pesters, the town's former Pensionary. He acknowledged that the 'liberation' of Maastricht would be an extremely difficult task, but this would be more than compensated by the glory and 'splendour' this operation would garner for the Republic. At this regard, Pesters wrote to the Grand Pensionary Gaspar Fagel: 'I need neither to remind nor to mention to Your Honourable Worship how much value was attached to Maastricht at the time of the Spanish War [the Eighty Years' War] whence one did not merely extend the contributions across four or five provinces, prevented the enemy occupying the winter quarters outside his own bosom, disrupted and made impossible all the (Spanish) recruitment drives, and made difficult the communications between (the Spanish Low Countries) and the German Empire; but moreover one had at the same time also been able to extend her (the Republic's) influence over the lands of Liège, Jülich, Cologne, Trier and other adjoining territories, and what damage and mockery the Republic has for some years endured from the said town and still experiences daily, running to millions in cash, and being inestimable in its derision.' *Ibid.* p. 494.

William III assigned 16,500 Dutch troops for the siege of Maastricht. Alongside 2,200 troops from Brandenburg, 4,000 from Pfalz-Neuburg, and 7,500 from Brunswick this amounted to an army of 30,000 men.[73] William allocated 20,000 Dutch troops for the army of observation, to which Villahermosa contributed a further 6,000 Spanish cavalry. With these 26,000 men, Waldeck and the Spanish governor-general had to cover the siege of Maastricht and at the same time watch over Spanish Brabant and Flanders. Waldeck doubted whether this two-pronged task was feasible, considering that the French could deploy 40,000 to 45,000 men. He therefore advised William to make the line of circumvallation extremely strong, because 'if the lines [around Maastricht] are not safe from assaults then things could go badly, for this army would not be able to prevent some corps from reaching the besieged town as well as watch over Flanders.'[74]

William III appeared before Maastricht on 8 July 1676, but it was eight days before the siege artillery arrived, because the water level in the River Meuse was extremely low. The opening of the trenches eventually took place on 18 July, and four days later the siege artillery began to shoot from 30 cannon of great calibre. Two weeks passed before the siege of Maastricht really began, a loss of time that the allies could ill afford. French seized the opportunity to besiege Aire, being of the opinion that the relief of Maastricht could wait a few more weeks. The French commander of Maastricht, Jean-Sauveur de Calvo, had assured that he would defend the stronghold to the bitter end, ready to scarify the whole garrison of 7,000 men. Moreover, Aire's garrison counted just 1,200 men, so it was unlikely that the capitulation of this town would take long. Schomberg and d'Humières, who had replaced the King as army commanders, were therefore satisfied that there was sufficient time to capture Aire first and only then to relieve Maastricht. D'Humières assumed responsibility for the siege with approximately 15,000 men, while Schomberg surveyed the troops of Waldeck and Villahermosa with the remaining 25–30,000 men. On 19 July 1676, the French invested Aire. Three days later, on the same day that the Dutch siege artillery opened fire at Maastricht, d'Humières ordered the opening of the approach trenches.

The chess game could resolve in favour of the French side, because with the loss of Aire, Schomberg was at liberty to advance to the Meuse. Waldeck allowed Villahermosa's request to relieve Aire, despite the German field marshal fearing that otherwise the siege of Maastricht would never be brought to a successful conclusion. So long as d'Humières was besieging Aire, the allies were almost as strong as Schomberg's army of observation, so giving battle, or at least threatening to do so, was the better option.. It did not come to a fight, because when Waldeck and Villahermosa reached Deinze on 2 August 1676, they received news that Aire had capitulated on 31 July. The news stunned William III too: he now had to choose between two evils, and the lesser of these was that Villahermosa and Waldeck should garrison as best they could the towns in Artois and Flanders still in Spanish possession, and that Waldeck

73 Gaetien de Courtilz, *Histoire de la Guerre d'Hollande*', vol. I, p. 413.

74 Nimwegen, *The Dutch Army*, p. 494.

with the rest of the army should return to Spanish Brabant to cover the siege of Maastricht. Villahermosa proposed a different plan. He suspected that the army under d'Humières would invade Flanders as soon as the Allies had left for Brabant, and he therefore considered it necessary to furnish the most threatened Flemish towns with strong garrisons. There was therefore no other option but to split the allied force: Villa Hermosa posted six battalions in Ypres, three in Dixmude and as many in Nieuwpoort, and with the remaining Spanish troops and 5,000 Dutch foot he established a position near Ghent. Waldeck departed with the majority of the Dutch troops for Brussels, where he would remain until there was clarity about the enemy's plans. If Schomberg marched on Maastricht, then Waldeck would immediately follow him and Villahermosa promised that the Spanish cavalry would then join the Dutch corps. If d'Humières besieged a Flemish town, then Waldeck would in turn place the Dutch cavalry at the disposal of Villahermosa. On 18 August 1676, Waldeck's reconnaissance spotted Schomberg marching to Charleroi: the French had decided to relieve Maastricht. Villahermosa and the Spanish cavalry joined up with Waldeck, but they could not prevent the French commander establishing a position that made it possible for him to throw troop reinforcements into Maastricht from the Wijk side, namely from the east via the stone bridge. The allied war council was of unanimous opinion that the troops engaged in the siege were not sufficient for closing the ring without risk of a defeat in the case of an enemy sortie. The commanders no longer saw any means of continuing with the siege operation. Therefore, in the night of 26–27 August the besiegers lifted the siege of Maastricht.

The news caused great dismay and rage in the United Provinces. Everyone expected a success or at least it was believed that the allied army would fight a battle instead of retreating.[75] William III did not intend to resign himself to this failure. In the following weeks he tried to force Schomberg to give battle in every way imaginable, but without result.[76] On 9 September the French established a position near Waremme to the west of Liège. Having the town of Liège under their control, the French could subsist there better than the Allies.

Psychological stress and fatigue became too much for William III. He suffered a fever and therefore felt he had no choice but to retire in order to recover his health. Waldeck assumed command of the Dutch army in his place.

The failed siege of Maastricht was the last episode of the 1676 campaign in the Low Countries. The allied and French troops remained in the field for several weeks. The Dutch army was too severely weakened by the siege of Maastricht for performing any action. On the other front, setbacks in the Holy Roman Empire once again concerned the French war cabinet. On 8 September 1676, the Imperialists captured Philippsburg, leaving Alsace threatened again

---

75 *Ibid.*, p. 496. 'This event surprises and disconcerts the whole World', a correspondent of Van Reede-Amerongen wrote from The Hague. And later: 'The people of Amsterdam and Rotterdam are spitting fire and flame, but it cannot thereby be remedied.'

76 *Ibid.* According to the field deputy Van Weede-Dijkveld, 'Schomberg has always tried to evade the enounter, either by changing his route slightly and moving aside, or by taking up advantageous positions, or by giving the impression that he was about to march with his army and then remaining standing still.'

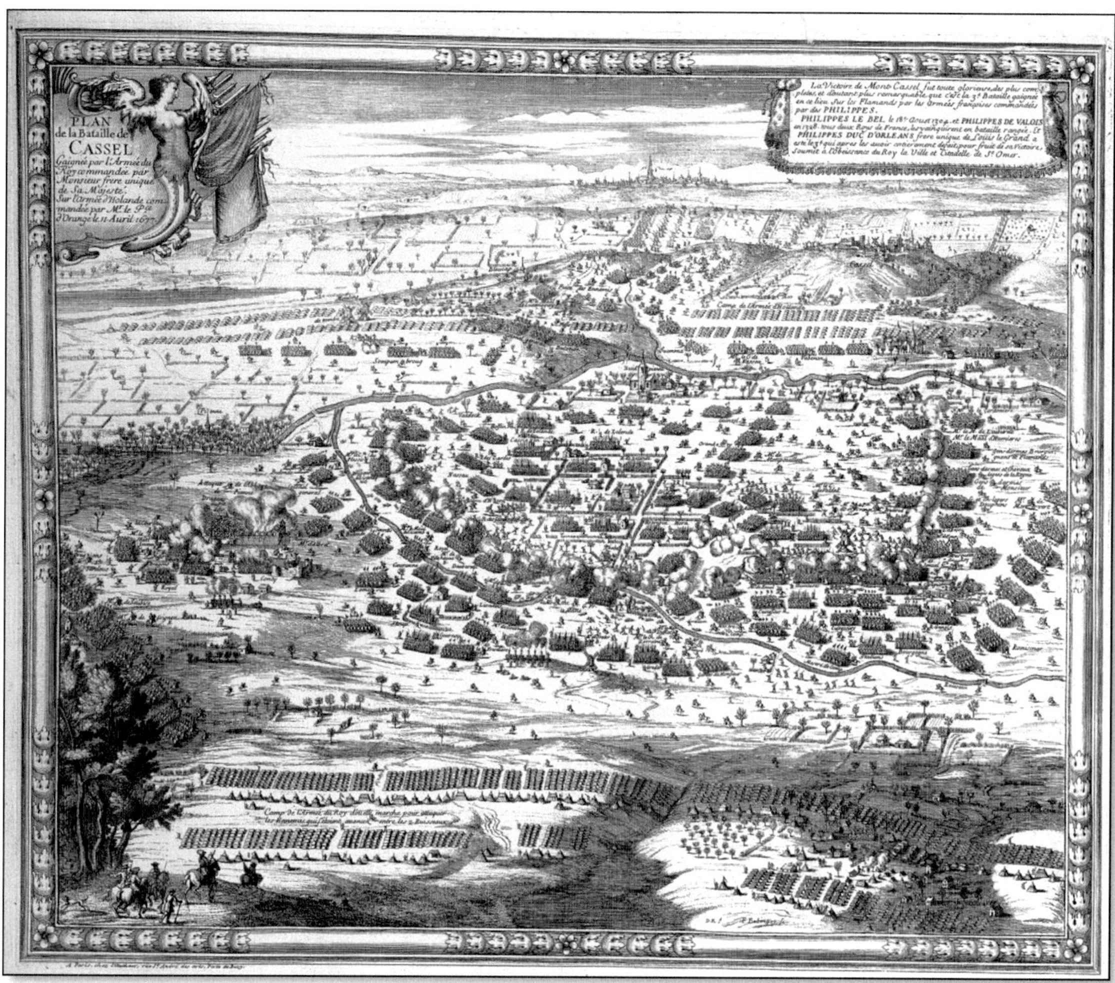

38. The Battle of Mont Cassel, fought on 11 April 1677, in a contemporary Dutch print.

Despite the many problems that afflicted the allies in maintaining a field army in the Spanish Low Countries, Prince William never stopped acting offensively to hinder French progress in the theatre of war. These factors, combined with imprudent conduct, provoked the defeat of Mont Cassel.

with an invasion. This important success could turn into a favourable outcome for the Republic. The scenario permitted negotiation with the enemy in a stronger position than months ago. The States General examined the proposal for a peace with Louis XIV, who would have subordinated his interest in the Low Countries with the ones to the Rhine. The Dutch government was equally balanced between the continuation of the war or with peace. However, after the failure of the siege of Maastricht the Amsterdam regents were of the opinion that the opening of peace negotiations could be delayed no longer. For two years they had been patient, but now that was at an end. As long as Madrid made no serious contribution to the defence of the Spanish Low Countries and tried to mislead the Republic with empty promises, Amsterdam's regents saw no point in continuing the war.[77] A separate peace was going a step too far, but it could do no harm to try to negotiate a general peace plan with France, since the belligerents had already agreed to join a peace congress in Nijmegen.

77 *Ibid.*

39. Brunswick-Lüneburg born, Count Georg Friedrich of Waldeck-Pyrmont (1620–1692). Copper Engraving of unknown artist, dated 1682. (Author's archive)

Waldeck entered the Dutch service for the first time in 1641 as colonel of a German infantry regiment. Eventually, he served under Sweden, Brandenburg, the Habsburg Emperor and Bavaria. On the eve of the French invasion of 1672, Waldeck was one of the most skilled officer in the staff of William III, who often left him in command of the army as the main lieutenant. In late 1672, Waldeck took advantage of the interim to restructure the Dutch army. He carried out a major reformation among the troops by disbanding companies and redistributing the soldiers. Waldeck considered training and discipline as fundamental for every army, rather than huge numbers, which required a considerable economic effort. Major powers, such as Habsburg Spain and France could always, if they wished, field major armies. However, these same states had significant difficulty in maintaining the troops, feeding, arming, and paying them, and avoiding mutinies: time and again the military threat faded because enemy troops deserted or were short of provisions. The solution proposed by Waldeck was simple: the Dutch army must be regularly provisioned and more professional than their opponents'.

Despite the truce signals, Louis XIV and his minister Louvois wanted to try the conquest of the Spanish Low Countries, given that this opportunity could not reoccur again. During the winter of 1676-77 Louvois ordered the accumulation of enormous forage magazines along the border with the Spanish Low Countries. The plan was to bring the French troops into the field as early as March 1677, a month earlier than in the previous year.[78] The expectation was that the French would thus be in a position to lay siege to Valenciennes and Cambrai, the two strongholds that Louis XIV had already wanted to capture in 1676. Besides these two towns, the French would lay siege to Saint-Omer, an operation for which the capture of Aire had provided a good base. The *frontière de fer* would then be largely complete and Louis XIV expected that this would deprive the Republic of her determination to continue the war. In order to fan the will for peace among the regents even further, the Sun King assigned the command over the 60,000 French troops in the Spanish Low Countries to Luxembourg. Along the Rhine the French would conduct a defensive war. The preparations of the French offensive did not remain unnoticed to The Hague and Brussels, but the taking of countermeasures was no simple matter. In December 1676, Waldeck drew up memorandums about the strategic situation and the military resources that the allies in general and the Republic in particular could mobilise for the defence of the Spanish Low Countries. Waldeck pointed out that the fortunes of war would never turn in favour of the Allies unless they were in a position to counter that which the enemy might undertake, and to enter France with a considerable corps. In 1677 no fewer than seven towns in the southern Low Countries were in serious danger of being besieged by the French: Saint-Ghislain, Valenciennes, Cambrai, Charlemont, Ypres, Diksmuide, and Saint-Omer. These towns could not be covered with two single armies. The French could lure the allies away from their true target with feints. That is

78 Lynn, *The Wars of Louis XIV*, p. 186.

why there was a need for two armies: the one to observe Hainault and the Meuse, the other to act in Flanders. Waldeck did not believe that the allies would be able to assemble two armies that would both be equal to the French deployment. He continued his reflection, declaring, '...but it seems to be feasible to assemble one that is considerable and strong enough to resist the enemy, and the other will be capable of taking up a position that covers the forts and sufficiently reinforces the garrisons when required.'[79] With a view to provisioning, it was preferable to have the main army operate from Flanders, but this advantage was wholly negated because in that region the French could establish very strong defensive positions. An invasion into France would therefore had to be directed via Hainault, even if finding forage there presented problems. The next question broached by Waldeck concerned where to find the necessary armies. He computed that more than 70,000 men had to be found: 60,000 men, included Münster, Brunswick and Osnabrück troops, from which to assemble the aforementioned armies and 10,000 to 12,000 men to cover the Dutch provinces against the raids from Maastricht. Waldeck proposed laying siege to Charleroi with 35,000 men. In the meantime, Villahermosa would have to observe the main French army with 26,000 men, and protect Flanders against an enemy counter attack. The Dutch Republic could supply 4–5,000 men for the blockade of Maastricht.[80] The Electors of Brandenburg and Cologne and the Duke of Pfalz-Neuburg would have to provide a further 5–6,000 men to render the blockade effective.

William III and the States General's committee for secret military affairs adopted Waldeck's operational plan. Discussions continued for ensuring the cooperation of Madrid and Brussels, because the States General wanted to shoulder to Spain the cost of the troops hired in Germany. In a resolution promulgated on 21 December 1676, William III and the committee for secret military

40. Hendrik Casimir II of Nassau-Dietz (1657–1696) was the second Dutch Statholder in charge of the province of Friesland and Groningen. He was appointed as Statholder in 1664, but for his young age he took on any task. This fact, similar to the case of the young William III, he left the Republic without a Statholder. Before the age of majority, both the Princes acted under the supervision of regents, which for Hendrik Casimir was his mother Albertine Agnes of Orange. Unlike William III, Hendrik Casimir's mother played a decisive role in his education and demonstrated a great energy even in the most dramatic moments, as occurred on 19 July 1672, when the princess visited the forts and exhorted the residual forces in Groningen, Drenthe and Friesland to extreme resistance.

79 Nimwegen, *The Dutch Army*, p. 498.

80 De Courtilz, *Histoire de la Guerre d'Hollande*, vol. I, p. 448.

41. *Veldmaarschalk* Pauls Wirtz (also Würz or Würtz, 1612–1676), German-born freelance officer who at various times was in Swedish, Brandenburg, Danish, and Dutch service. He joined the States' Army in 1664 and eventually served as commander in Groningen from the first stage of the French invasion of 1672. He was another capable commander in William III's staff.

affairs issued a warning to Madrid, pointing out the Dutch plan for the defence of the Spanish Low Countries.[81]

William III had no intention of being forced to stand idly by for the third year in succession while the French captured one town after another The weakness of the Allied army depended primarily on the poor condition of the Spanish finances. The letter made a great impression in Madrid, forcing King Charles II to enact serious change in the government.[82] The new Prime Minister, Don Juan of Austria, was a champion of a plucky war policy and promised that Spain would deploy 25,000 men for the incoming campaign in Flanders.[83]

However, good intentions did not correspond with the reality of the facts. Waldeck informed The Hague that Villahermosa was cooperating but he was far from accomplishing Madrid's orders in respect of finding troops for the Allied army. Shortage of resources and difficult in the hiring of German auxiliary troops made it clear that William III should not have any high expectations of the coming campaign, because even if the German auxiliary troops were to arrive in the Spanish Low Countries soon it would not be possible to begin the offensive into Hainault directly; without considering the lack of forage and supply for sustaining the army.

The French offensive began on 1 March 1677, when the army appeared before Valenciennes, where there was a garrison numbering just 1,150 men. William III assembled the Dutch troops near Roosendaal in all haste. The levying of new recruits was by then largely complete, so he had 30,000 men at his disposal, including 3,800 Spaniards. However, the delivery of forage constituted a major problem, because no hay or oat magazines had been established. This forced William III to remain near Antwerp until early April. In the meantime, on 17 March, the French had captured Valenciennes. Louis XIV then ordered the simultaneous besieging of Cambrai and Saint-Omer. On 22

81 In his letter, prince William III declared: 'without two armies … nothing in the world can be accomplished or any harm done to the enemy. 'That they [the States General] would be pleased to help with the formation of one of the said armies … but that his Majesty may rest assured that the army of this State shall not enter into the campaign if his Majesty has not also arranged that another army is assembled there (in the Spanish Low Countries) in due time.' Cited in Nimwegen, *The Dutch Army*, p. 499.

82 The Republic's unequivocal tone made a forceful impression in Madrid, at the very moment the power struggle at the Spanish court was reaching a climax. In early January 1677, Don Juan marched on Madrid together with 18 Castilian *grandes*, the majority of Aragon's nobility, and with an army of 15,000 men. He made his entry on 23 January, whereupon Charles II consigned the charge of government to him and banished the queen dowager to Toledo. See also in J.H. Elliot, *Imperial Spain, 1496–1716* (London: Penguin Books, 1990), p. 402.

83 Nimwegen, *The Dutch Army*, p. 500.

42. *Colonel* Hans Willem van Aylva (1633–1691). (Engraving by Lambert van den Bos and Lieuwe van Aitzema, Fries Museum, Leeuwarden, NL)

Frisian-born, in 1667 Aylva participated as a volunteer in the Raid on the Medway. In 1668 he was appointed a major-general and was promoted to lieutenant-general four years later. Aylva was also Lieutenant-Admiral of Friesland. He saw a great deal of service in the war against France, and in 1672 he was appointed as commander of the most exposed sector of the Frisian waterline, a task that he accomplished with success. He fought and was badly wounded at the Battle of Seneffe in 1674.

March the main French army under the personal command of the King invested Cambrai, and the opening of the trenches followed six days later. On 4 April, Louis XIV's brother Philippe did the same before Saint-Omer. William III reached Bruges that same day. The Prince considered Cambrai to be lost, but he was determined to relieve Saint-Omer. In the rush, he neglected to have the battleground thoroughly reconnoitred: an omission that Luxembourg and d'Humières, the two marshals who were assisting *Monsieur*, would exploit to the full. On receiving news of the approach of the Dutch–Spanish army, the Duke of Orléans had established a forward position near Mont Cassel, about 15 kilometres west of Saint-Omer.

William III was intending to surprise the French in their positions on 10 April, but was hampered by the passage of a stream that ran between him and the enemy. Early on 11 April, the Dutch–Spanish army crossed the Peene Becque stream, but another obstacle was found. Unexpectedly, there was a second arm of the stream between them and the enemy. Thanks to this delay, the French commanders had the opportunity to deploy their troops in battle order; moreover, in the course of the night reinforcements of nine infantry battalions had arrived from the main army, so the French had now more or less the same strength of the Allies.[84] Luxembourg and d'Humières commanded a mixed force of infantry and cavalry on the left and right respectively, with the bulk of the infantry and artillery under Orléans in the centre. Honouring his reputation as an aggressive soldier, d'Humières attacked with his cavalry, but he was stopped by the squares of the Dutch infantry. A charge led by the Prince Maurits Lodewijk of Nassau-La Leck then threw the French back across the river in disorder before running into heavy fire from the French artillery; the Dutch cavalry now retreated to the far side of Mont Cassel and played no further part in the battle. The French reorganised and launched a coordinated attack around 12 o'clock, with Luxembourg's infantry engaging the Dutch in a bloody struggle centred on some farm buildings; these were eventually taken, with a cavalry

84 Lynn, *The Wars of Louis XIV*, p. 203. The question about the actual number of troops engaged in the battle had been debated until today. Nimwegen says that the French deployed at least 5,000 soldiers more than the Dutch–Spaniards.

43. Saint-Denis, 1678. The treaty between France and the Allies was not yet signed in Nijmegen, and it was the intention of the French to make further pretexts for delay, in the hope that the town of Mons would fall meanwhile. Some authors relate that the report of the conclusion of peace reached William III on 13 August, but unofficially. On the morning of 14 August, the news reached Marshal Luxemborg, and the French commander was on the point of forwarding the message to the Dutch camp, when he heard that the enemy was advancing to attack him, forcing him to accept the challenge. The bloody fight took place close to the abbey of Saint-Denis, a short distance from Mons, and cost thousands of casualties for both sides.

charge then scattering the remainder. D'Humières was also successful on the right but the French centre was overrun by infantry under Count Waldeck and the line only re-established after a counter-charge led by Orléans himself. After further four hours of fighting, and with his flanks giving way, William disengaged and ordered a general retreat towards Ypres; Nassau's cavalry had by now recovered sufficiently to cover the retreat of the infantry. The French did not pursuit the Dutch–Spaniards, but baggage, munitions, and artillery had to be abandoned on the battlefield.[85] According to French estimates the Dutch army suffered 3,000 dead,[86] and 4,000 to 5,000 wounded.[87] As to their

85 The following day, the field deputy Nicolaas Witsen informed Grand Pensionary Fagel about the defeat: 'The spilling of blood that took place there was terrible on both sides … I had to leave all my baggage and managed to rescue myself from many perils, and at the same time saved the Land's money, which I threw in all haste into the oat sacks, cut free the horses from the waggons and flung it onto their backs.' Cited by Nimwegen, *The Dutch Army*, p. 501.

86 Lynn, *The Wars of Louis XIV*, p. 203.

87 Quincy, in 'Histoire Militaire', vol. I, p. 573, relates also 4,000 prisoners, who probably have to be considered as included with the casualties.

casualties, the French claimed 1,200 dead and 2,000 wounded. The Spanish garrison of Saint-Omer resisted until 22 April, but then had no choice but to capitulate. Cambrai had fallen five days earlier. The defeat at Mont Cassel caused but little controversy in the Republic and there was no hint of panic, rather a mood of resignation. There was criticism of the inaccurate manner in which the Dutch troops had approached the French position and the rout of the infantry on the left wing, but to counterbalance this the bulk of the Dutch army had fought courageously. Special mentions were made to the regiment of the *Gardes te Paard*, Dragoon Guards, the cavalry regiments Waldeck, Brederode, Ginckel, Croonenburg, Eppe, Flodorff and Hoornberg, and most of the infantry, including the *Gardes te voet*, the regiments Prins Maurits, Holstein, Brandenburg, Courland, Rijngraaf, Kirckpatrick and the three regiments of Zealand, included the marine regiment *Vrijbergen*.[88]

After the fall of Saint-Omer and Cambrai the French troops then returned to the garrisons and Louis XIV returned to France. The Dutch government felt confident about the rest of the campaign especially because Villahermosa was at last making haste with the hiring of the German troops. The total number of subsidy troops increased to 24,000 men to which number the Spanish should add 5,000 to 6,000 men. Villahermosa assured the States General that within two or three weeks 30,000 men would be ready to march. At the end of May or by early June at the latest, the allies would at last have two considerable armies, both capable of facing the enemy, at their disposal in the Spanish Low Countries. William III hoped to revenge the defeat of Mont Cassel in the second round by taking Charleroi, and if the Imperialists were to lay siege to Thionville simultaneously, then France would be threatened with invasions from two sides. In June, the preparations for the allied counter-attack were in full swing. The blockading force of 12,000 men destined for Maastricht was assembled in Maaseik; the 24,000 troops from Münster and Brunswick were marching to Spanish Brabant to join Villahermosa and the Spanish troops, and in mid July, William III was close by Dendermonde with the Dutch army, which numbered an effective strength of 26,900 men.[89] William III and Villahermosa were in command of a combined total of 60,000 men and soon advanced to meet the enemy. Louis XIV had ordered Luxembourg to enact a defensive strategy during the summer. Besides a military argument – now that the Allies were in the field at full strength, it would be much more difficult to achieve new conquests – there was also a political argument that weighed heavily in this decision. France could not wage war too successfully, because new conquests in the Spanish Low Countries would force the King of England to intervene in favour of the Triple Alliance.

On 6 August 1677, William III appeared with the Dutch army before Charleroi. Meanwhile Villahermosa surveyed the main French army encamped near Ath. William prepared The Hague for a protracted and costly siege operation. The town was well protected and the discipline the effectiveness of the

88 P.J.E. de Smyttere, *La Bataille de Val-de-Cassel* (Hazebroeck, 1865), p. 140.

89 Ten Raa, *Het Staatsche Leger*, vol. V, p. 345 and Nimwegen, *The Dutch Army*, p. 502.

Spanish auxiliary force left a lot to be desired. The Prince estimated the garrison at about 5,000 men. On 8 August a convoy arrived in the allied camp with 24 demi-cannon and a second convoy was expected two days later. It was, however, doubtful whether the artillery could be brought to bear, because Luxembourg had left his quarters by Ath and was approaching Charleroi. On the night of 8–9 August the French crossed the River Sambre, placing them about 20 kilometres south-west of Charleroi. William III considered as probable an encounter in the days ahead and asked to Villahermosa to move his army in the night in order to cover the besiegers and to observe the enemy. Villahermosa failed to catch up with Luxembourg, who had deployed his troops on a favourable terrain, allowing to him to close the way for the forage from the Sambre and the Meuse for the besieging army. Meanwhile, d'Humierés closed the supply road from Brussels. The Allies' war council estimated that within three days the supply would be terminated. On 14 August, for a further time, William was therefore forced to leave the siege of Charleroi. The failed siege was a bitter disappointment for William. He now also understood that the restoration of the 1659 situation was unachievable, but at the same time, he realised that the war could not be ended unless the Republic had the guarantee that the Spanish Low Countries could serve as an effective buffer against France. As noted, this required the conquest of several towns on the southern border that had been captured by France, and English assistance was needed to achieve this goal. But the position of the English king was ambiguous. Charles II Stuart was still receiving funds from Louis XIV. To gain greater insight into the relations between Parliament and the Crown, William III sent his confidant Hans Willem Bentinck to London. Bentinck was to sound out the King concerning his readiness to arbitrate a general peace settlement between the allies and France, Seeing in this an opportunity to profile himself as an arbiter, the English king agreed to this proposal and he also granted his consent to a marriage between his 15-year-old niece Mary Stuart and William III of Orange.[90] The marriage was solemnised on November 1677. Charles II then exerted pressure on Louis XIV to break off his assault on the Spanish Low Countries and to reach a peace agreement. The King of France would be allowed to keep Franche-Comté and various strongholds captured in the Spanish Low Countries, but in accordance with The Hague's demands, he would be obliged to return Tournai, Courtrai, Oudenarde, Ath, Charleroi and Condé to Spain, and to cede Maastricht to the Republic. The King of England's request was received very badly in France. As response, Louis XIV ordered a limited winter offensive in Hainault; d'Humières received the task of seizing Saint-Ghislain, the possession of this small fortified town being important with a view to a future siege of Mons. The French plan was intuited by Waldeck, who alerted Villahermosa. The Allied armies were dispersed in a wide area from Brussels and Malines, but the Spanish General Governor remained inactive, because his main concern remained the protection of Brussels. However, when the French actually invested Saint-

90 James, the Duke of York, firmly opposed this, but Lord Treasurer Thomas Osborne, Earl of Danby, had convinced Charles II that a union of the Protestant champion with James' eldest daughter was a suitable means of appeasing the mistrust that Duke of York's second marriage with the Catholic Maria d'Este had provoked in Parliament. See also in J. Miller, *James II* (Yale, CT: Yale University Press, 2004), pp. 204–209.

Ghislain on 1 December, Villa Hermosa changed his ideas. He now exhorted Waldeck to move there immediately with a relief force, fearing that if this town were lost, Mons would also certainly follow. Waldeck moved from his base with poor supply and his troops received poor assistance during the march. Meanwhile Saint-Ghislain surrendered on 11 December. The defeat of Mont Cassel and the failed siege of Charleroi caused the fading of support for the war in the Provinces. Nobody in the Republic doubted the courage, discipline, and proficiency of commanders and troops, but the struggle against France was too unbalanced. It would only be possible to reverse the course of war in the Spanish Netherlands if Spain could be able to supply 30,000 men, year in year out, for the operations there and, moreover, shoulder responsibility for building up substantial forage magazines, but Spanish finances did not allow this and the States General was neither willing nor able to assume extra expenditures.[91] In other words, the Dutch Republic was ready to make peace independently from the Allies. Concluding a peace before the new campaign was opened presented a solution, but the disadvantage was that the odium of treason would beset the Republic, because Spain and the Emperor continued to insist on the restoration of the geopolitical situation as it was in 1659, which had been agreed in the alliance of 1673.

For William III this was out of the question; he still hoped to be able to broker a general peace settlement. However, poor expectations waiting for the Prince in the incoming 1678 campaign. Alongside 30,000 Dutch troops, Villahermosa could add to the field army only 16,000 men. An army of this strength was not only too small for an offensive war but would also be unable to obstruct the French continuing their campaign of conquest in the Spanish Low Countries. The aftermath was the French conquests of Ghent on 5 March and Ypres on 26 March. In the wake of these two conquests, on 15 April Louis XIV let it be known that he would suspend hostilities until 10 May 1678, in order to give the allied diplomats in Nijmegen the opportunity to agree to the French peace terms.[92] At the end of June 1678, while the diplomats were meeting, a French cavalry corps of between 6,000 and 7,000 men surrounded Mons. Luxembourg took up a position with the main French army of about 50,000 men near the abbey of Saint-Denis, about seven kilometres north-east of Mons. The threat led to an acceleration of the negotiations, with the Dutch diplomats trying to convince the Spaniards to accept the French peace terms.

---

91 Dutch diplomat van Weede-Dijkveld, who in the winter of 1677–78 held discussions with Villahermosa in Brussels about the coming years campaign, complained in a letter to the *griffier* of the States-General: 'I must admit to Your Honour that the finances here are so depleted and the income so minimal that if the king of Spain does not send significant sums the result shall be utter chaos. Van Weede-Dijkveld warned that as a consequence not only the German subsidy troops but also the Spanish army remained unpaid and instead of being augmented with recruits it is every day subject to incredible diminution and desertion.' Cited in Nimwegen, *The Dutch Army*, pp. 506–507.

92 The three most important articles were: 1. In exchange for the return to Spain of Ghent, Courtrai, Oudenarde, Ath and Charleroi, the King of Spain must cede Franche-Comté, Ypres, Saint-Omer, Aire, Cambrai, Bouchain, Valenciennes and Condé to France; 2. Maastricht will be returned to the Republic; 3. All the Swedish territories which Brandenburg and Denmark had conquered since 1675 had to be restored to Sweden. Louis XIV expected that these conditions would be acceptable to the States-General, because the Spanish Low Countries would then be able to fulfil its role as a buffer zone between the Republic and France. De Courtilz, *Histoire de la Guerre d'Hollande*, vol. II, p. 187.

Luxembourg's headquarters were also involved with the arrival of the Dutch envoys to find out about the actual French intentions to invest Mons, and know the substantial existence of a truce as agreed between the Allies and France. At the peace conference in Nijmegen the French negotiators were by now behaving just as intractably. They categorically refused to evacuate the places to be restored. The ambiguity of French diplomacy persuaded William III that Louis XIV did not truly desire peace. The French stance had repercussions in England, too. On 26 July 1678 the States General and the King of England entered into an alliance. On 10 August, an ultimatum was sent to Louis XIV, declaring that England and the Dutch Republic would jointly attack France if the King had not accepted their terms of peace. William III had in the meantime arrived in the vicinity of Mons with the Dutch troops. Including 15,000 troops from Brunswick, Brandenburg, and Münster, about 200 English troopers, and some Spanish cavalry, he had an army of approximately 45,000 men at his disposal. At the very last moment the French negotiators in Nijmegen accepted the Dutch terms and at midnight on 10 August 1678, the Republic and France made peace. Surprisingly, nothing was reported to William III, who on 14 August ordered a storm assault against the French positions near Saint-Denis.[93]

There are several reports on the battle and in many cases, there are contradictions between one version and another. The Dutch attack was directed to the sector between the abbey of Saint-Denis and the castle, where the headquarters of Luxembourg were located. A furious fight would have happened here with both the commanders exposing their lives freely. The battle involved the best units of both armies, and continued until the afternoon. After six hours of bitter fighting, finally the Allied pressure succeeded in breaking the French resistance, forcing Luxembourg to order the retreat.

The battle was bloody and almost inconclusive but the Allies claimed the victory, because Luxembourg withdrew, and ordered the raising of the blockade of Mons.[94] The Battle of Saint-Denis definitively closed the war, also because it was fought when the peace had now been signed. Finally, on 17 September 1678 France and Spain also made peace, and the Emperor followed on 26 January 1679.

93 William III later contended that he was unaware that the peace had by then been concluded. It is impossible to ascertain whether he was speaking the truth. Further reading: Stephan B. Baxter, *William III* (London: Longmans, 1966), and W. Troost, *William III, the Stadtholder-King, A Political Biography* (Abingdon on Thames: Routledge, 2005). The authors debate this question, embracing two different opinions.

94 Quincy claimed 4,000 dead and wounded for the allies, while the Dutch admitted just 5–600 casualties: the battle of Saint-Denis is a mystery in many respects. See on this topic the fine essay of F. Samsoen, *La bataille de Saint-Denis le 14 août 1678. L'abbaye dans la tourmente!* (Mons: Belgian Bavarian Society, 2011).

4

Uniforms, Equipment, and Ensigns

In the mid 17th century, the development of standing armies and the improvement of manufacturing technology coincided in increased uniformity of the troops. Uniform identified the soldier from the rest of the population and made it more difficult for deserters to hide themselves among civilians. Even if he threw away his uniform, the deserter had to get another suit, but remaining only in his shirt certainly turned the suspicion of the authorities to him. Uniforms were also useful to avoid fraud during the musters, presenting *passevolanten* or civilians in the ranks. Even on occasions when actual soldiers were secretly transferred from one regiment to another to defraud the government during the muster, the differences in their dress served to unmask the deception. The economic aspects were probably decisive for the establishment of uniforms in the Dutch army too. This trend appeared, more or less at the same time throughout Europe. However, some countries experienced this process more effectively, and in introducing actual 'uniforms' they created a model for other European armies to copy. In the mid 17th century, the Dutch army seems to be one of the more trusted in the establishment of military uniforms in the modern sense, and many of the features introduced here had become a reference for several foreign armies. In this regard, the United Provinces appears to be an interesting laboratory in the phase of separation between civil and military clothing.

Some important scholars, such as Frans Gerard de Wilde, doubted that one could speak of actual uniforms before the 1680s.[1] He maintained that in 1688 the concept of 'uniform' was still relatively new in the army:

> Until around 1670, the troops were usually recruited only for a single campaign. The 'mercenary soldiers' – here in the most literal sense of the word – brought along their own clothing, weapons and equipment. Only when in the last quarter of the 17th century, the so-called standing army had been established, permanently in the service of the state, the situation changed. Then, the commanders of the

1 De Wilde, 'De Mannen van 1688' (The Men of 1688), *Armamentaria* 23, 1988.

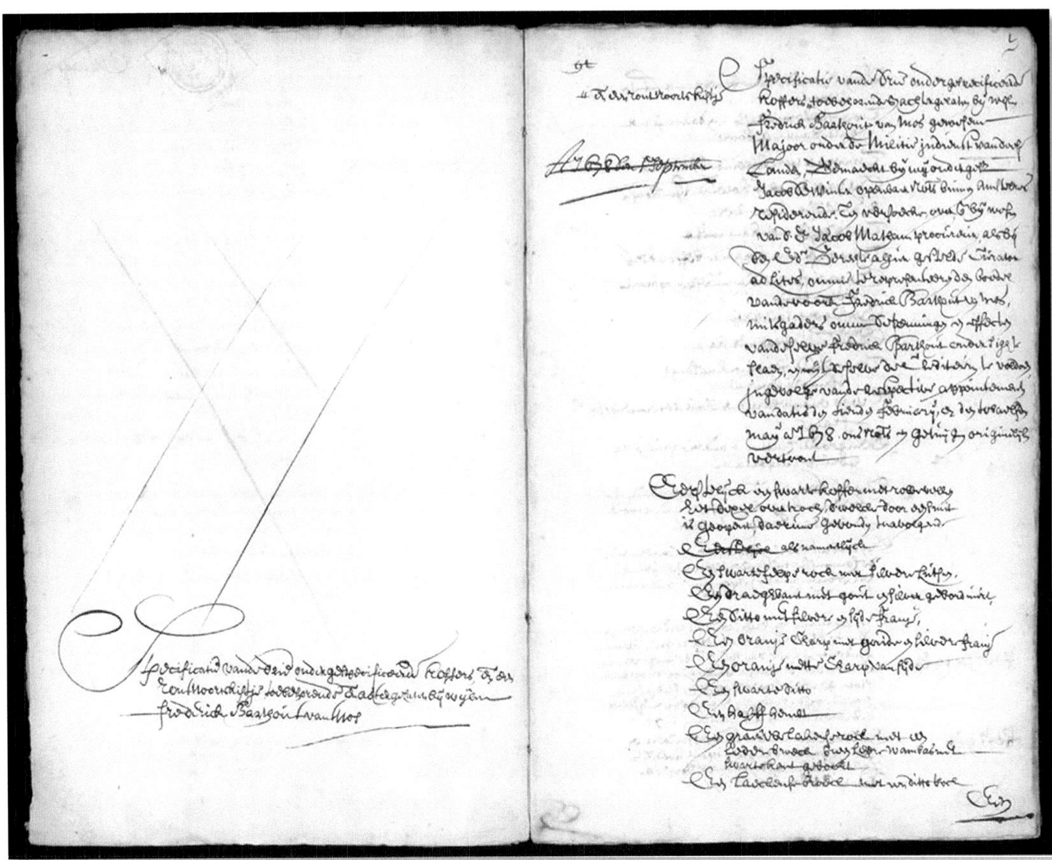

44. In the United Provinces, as well as in mostly European states, senior officers had to respect very few limitations on their dress and could tailor the uniform at their own expense. This makes it difficult to establish a common pattern, but fortunately, some sources come to light in various forms: such as an act from the Amsterdam Notary Archives dated 1678, with a list of the belongings of a former Major of the army, in three suitcases, including his clothing and a flag. The text notices that he had a grey uniform coat. Notary acts are a useful source for the knowledge of the troops' uniform too, because the officers and merchants signed contracts in the presence of a notary who kept a copy of the contract. (Thanks to Edwin Groot for this notice).

companies and squadrons were required to purchase the necessary clothing, weapons, and further equipment for their recruits.

This statement is not completely valid, and today we can actually discuss of military uniforms even in previous decades, however de Wilde focuses on a very important point, namely the reduction of strength that affected the establishment of an identical dress for all. Moreover, dispersion and consumption altered the clothing and probably before the 1680s the main item issued to the recruit was only the coat. This is one of the possible explanations for the approximate and multicolour appearance of the soldiers in the 1660s and 1670s.

On one point de Wilde is fully agreed, when he complains that the knowledge about clothing, equipment, and armament of the Dutch army before 1680 is rather minimal.[2] There are many causes for this. First of all, the lack of rules, and regulations in modern sense. Furthermore, several documents were lost with the destruction that occurred in the World War Two.[3] Scholars depend on summary period descriptions, pictures, or later descriptions and if information fails, it is only the tedious and difficult archive research.

Despite the lack of information, the Dutch army represents an interesting case study and methodological approach in the field of military uniforms. The investigation on 17th century Dutch military uniforms had started already at the beginning of the 20th century thanks to the efforts of Frederik Jan Gustaaf ten Raa and Jan Hoynck van Papendrecht,[4] but the first 'scientific' contributions appeared in the 1970s with Jean Belaubre and the aforementioned de Wilde, who executed a fruitful campaign of research on uniforms and ensigns for the period 1680–1714. They analysed the acquirement contracts of cloth and 'Passports' registered by the Council of State for supplies crossing the Dutch borders,[5] in order to reconstruct the regimental uniform and calculate – as they knew how much cloth and what type of cloth was used for a single uniform – how many uniforms were made and what colours they were. Their researches brought light to a matter full of flourishing speculative reconstruction in the early 20th century, but which had been produced without any indication regarding the original sources.[6]

2 The research of the de Wilde was implemented by J.G. Kerkoven in the article entitled 'Het Nederlandse lager tijdens de stadhouder-konig Willem III (1672–1702)', published in the magazine *Armamentaria*, n. 23 – 1988. In the article, the artist F. Smits reproduced some Dutch infantry, cavalry and artillery uniforms of the 1680s.

3 In the heavy fighting around Arnhem in the autumn of 1944, the National Military Museum was destroyed completely with the loss of 15,000 texts. Louis Ph. Sloos, *Warfare and the Age of Printing* (Brill: Leiden-Boston, 2008), vol. I, pp. 43–44.

4 Lieutenant-Colonel Frederik Jan Gustaaf ten Raa (1851–1926), better known as a historian and author, was particularly active in the research of uniforms and weapons, and assembled an important collection of documents and iconography concerning the Dutch army. In 1908, he was assigned as lieutenant-colonel (retired) to the Military History Archive of the Dutch Army General Staff. He beneficed the collaboration of the artist Jan Hoynck van Papendrecht (1858–1933), for executing an extensive campaign of research on Dutch military uniforms especially through paintings, prints and engravings and finally published the results in the book entitled *De uniformen van de Nederlandsche zee- en landmacht, hier te lande en in de koloniën*, printed in the Hague in 1900.

5 De Wilde made an accurate study of the documents filed by the Council of State and found many passports. Further investigations through the minutes confirmed this findings and also found a few more for which the passports apparently no longer exist, only the mention in the minutes. Here it would seem that the Council of State later passed the job of signing passports on to a lower level, because there are relatively few documents after 1697.

6 The reference concerns the famous series of Dutch uniforms for the period 1672–75 commissioned by Gustav de Rydder to the Austrian military illustrator Norbert Robitschek in the 1920s. The original artworks are preserved in the *Österreichische Nationalbibliothek* in Vienna, but there are several copies in other European libraries, such as the *Bibliothèque Nationale de France* in Paris, and an incomplete series is preserved in the Dutch National Military Museum too. In the late 19th century there started a wave of nationalism and militarism that invested every country, and this produced a large quantity of uniforms books to celebrate the glorious national past, just as de Rydder's intended. The series contains 83 colour plates representing mostly infantry regiments. The style is more or less coherent with the 1670s, but there are many evidences that Robitschek performed a lot of arbitrary reconstructions. Moreover – unfortunately – Robitscheck and de Rydder did not mention their sources.

More light concerning the colours worn by Dutch regiments comes from two coeval documents, today preserved in the Hessian state archive of Marburg. They are the coloured plans of the camp rosters executed after the army review held by Prince William III near the Moor of Mook dated 1686, and one that occurred at Dieren a year later. The regiments are schematically identified by the ensigns and the colour of the coat, which evidently summarise *justaucorps* and facings. Though uniforms were recycled, it is not certain that items issued in 1686 or 1687 were used already in 1672 or before. Usually, only the household troops tended to maintain the same colours for their uniforms, like the *Gardes te voet* regiment (I-8), which was always dressed in blue and yellow-orange (mustard) since 1672.

Belaubre and de Wilde were able to reconstruct the uniforms of several regiments after 1681 and 1686, because in those years Prince William III had issued the first two *ordre* (ordinances) concerning military clothing for the infantry. Both the documents prescribed that uniforms had to be made of 'good and satisfactory *carsaay* [kersey], and the *surtout* and upper garments should be made of good *baai* [a coarse wool textile]'. The ordinance stated though that 'not to burden the common soldier, all unnecessary costs and rich accessories should be avoided, though within the rules and regulations that are stipulated here [in the ordinance], especially regarding the costs.'[7] The colonels chose the colours, and every two years new clothing had to be issued in the month of May. In order to register the condition of the soldier's dress, the muster rolls began to record the colours of the uniforms of each regiment mustered.

Because the distribution of the uniform occurred at the time of the arrival of the recruits to the regiment, the replacement every 24 months of the old items would have involved an expenditure in excess for the soldiers who had arrived a few months before. This obvious precaution regarding economic savings suggests that the colours of the uniforms remained the same over the years, but unfortunately, this seems to be happened in very few cases in the Dutch army. After the Guards, the most detailed records about the uniforms regard the *mariniers*. Observing the succession of uniforms documented between 1660 and 1680, it is possible to ascertain that the colour of the coat changed at least six times. Although not completely uniformed, in 1667 the marine regiment *Vrijbergen* appears dressed in grey or butternut; then in 1671, the coat is now dark blue with crimson facing.[8] In 1673, the coat is recorded as 'blue-grey',[9] and then changed to grey with dark blue cuffs some years later.[10] These colours seem to be unchanged until 1680, when all the marine regiments were uniformed in dark blue. In 1687, the private soldiers' coat is always dark blue with some minor changes.[11]

7 *Nadere Ordre ende Reglement op het stuck van de Kledinge der Infanterie*, chapter I–V, 1686.

8 After Ludolf Backhuysen's painting illustrating the boarding of the marine infantry at Texel.

9 This colour is recorded in the diary of captain Droste and referred to regiment *Weede van Walenburg* (I-44); cited by C.B. Nicolas, in *De Mariniersbrigade te kiek* (Amsterdam: Omegaboek, 1986), pp. 30–31.

10 *Ibid.*

11 Hessische Landesarchiv Marburg (HLM), Wilhelmshöher Kartensammlung, Karten WHK 42/17; *Feldlager bei Dieren1687.*

Dutch *mariniers*

45. Right; Dutch ***marinier***, 1665–67. Moses Ter-Borch, younger brother of the famous Dutch painter Gerhard, served as a volunteer in the navy and like his brother was a talented artist. During his service on the fleet in the Second Anglo-Dutch War, he portrayed several sailors and marine soldiers. This drawing is possibly the more accurate iconographic source concerning the ***mariniers*** in the early stage of their history. The coat is probably worn over a jacket and short breeches, as suggested by the long tail on the side. The short sleeves are completed with buttons in a less common pattern. (Metropolitan Museum of Art, New York)

46. Left: Marine soldier, regiment ***Vrijbergen*** (I-35), 1678–80, after de Wilde and Nicolas. Black hat piped yellow, dark blue coat with white collar and lining, yellow-piped buttonholes, sleeves and pockets, blue breeches, yellow stockings, brass buttons. Dutch marines was the leading landing force in the 17th century and constituted a model for several armies. Brandenburg regiment of marines Bolsey, raised in 1674, followed the Dutch experience and the soldiers were recruited, equipped and trained in the Netherlands. (Author's illustration)

47. The Austrian illustrator Norbert Robitschek performed many arbitrary reconstructions in the series on Dutch uniforms commissioned by Gustav de Rydder in the 1920s. However, at least one subject might be less fancy than the other drawings of the collection. In fact, If we turn to Ludolf Bakhuysen's painting, illustrating the marine regiment embarking at Texel in 1671, is possible to find some interesting details. A group of soldiers wearing blue coat with pot helm appear in background. This is a very interesting coincidence with the Robitschek's pikeman of the regiment Vrijbergen, which had been the first marine regiment since 1667. Moreover, Bakhuysen should confirm that marines were obviously equipped only with firearms when they served on the fleet. Note the Officer in dark blue coat, with orange sash and grey broad-brimmed hat.

There are very few cases of units that maintained the same colours throughout the years, like the household cavalry and infantry or the foreign regiments, especially Scottish and English regiments. The earliest uniforms had to be as simple as possible, but there were just a few demands regarding quality and colours of the materials. Undyed coarse broadcloth was largely used, as confirmed by contemporary images. The medium grey kersey was the more common, and only the lining appeared coloured with *baai*, and sometimes the cuffs were coloured as well. Only some regimental commanders could or would afford the expense for better uniforms, by using the more expensive broadcloth or other materials. If they did, it was usually limited to commanders, officers, NCOs and musicians. In most cases is extremely unusual that the colour of the fabric was explicitly mentioned in the most ancient documents. In fact, these sources are often just administrative receipts reporting the amount of items or the total expense, while they were silent about the style, cut, materials, trimmings, or other specific relevant information useful to reconstruct the uniforms in detail. De Wilde sustained that natural colours were the most used. To make the identification of supply contracts even more difficult, the fact remains that before the 1680s the acquirement was matter of colonels or captains, and much of the information concerning the uniforms should be looked for in family archives, where they still exist.

On 20 January 1675, in order to rationalise the supply for his army, Prince William III required troops on campaign to be dressed in grey coats. The infantry regiment – probably the Dutch regiments of the field army under his command – should be equipped with broad leather belts and hats with black trimming. Musicians' headdress had a broader trimming, and bandoleers as for the private soldiers, and sergeants wore cuffs in blue.[12]

Nevertheless, it seems that this order has not been entirely followed, because for multiple reasons, regiments continued to be dressed in red or in blue depending on their colonels. Therefore, 'the States' Army offered for several years a colourful sight during the *Guerre d'Hollande*.'[13]

The reconstruction of Dutch uniforms before 1680s comes also from indirect evidence and deductions. De Wilde gives a description of the uniforms of the infantry regiment *Oranje-Friesland* (I-27), also known as *Nassau-Friesland*. He describes an ensign and a non-commissioned officer in 1672.[14] The ensign wears a red *justaucorps* with light blue cuffs, which are again lined in white and with small gold laces. A light blue-yellow sash is worn at the waist. The NCO, a *Veldtwaibel* (related to the German word *Feldwebel*) is described as having a red coat, blue cuffs, blue waistcoat, and breeches. According to de Wilde, this does not mean that the whole regiment was dressed in red as well, on the contrary a contract signed in 1678 and a 1692 inventory list[15] register shipments of blue cloth to this regiment. Probably the same difference in colour between the ranks was adopted also in the other *Oranje* regiments. De Wilde added further information in an article of the magazine *Armamentaria* (the magazine of the Dutch National Military Museum). He remarked that there were still a few written sources from which it was possible draw something about the colours of the uniforms. He notes a description of the uniform of the Foot Guards in an order of Prince William III dated 30 January 1675. Then the article lists the commissions for the shipment of items for manufacturing the uniform of the infantry regiment *Brandenburg* (I-89) between 1685 and 1687: 'In 1685 there was grey and blue *carsaay*, blue *baai*, red *baai* and red *rat* [ratiné], together with 30 pairs of blue stockings and 30 orange sashes. The private soldiers were dressed in grey with blue facings. NCOs wore an orange sash around the waist and had blue stockings, while the soldiers probably wore

12 Ten Raa, *Het Staatsche Leger*, vol. VI, p. 266.

13 F.G. de Wilde, 'De ontwikkeling van de Infanterie-uniformen in het Staatse Leger gedurende de 18e eeuw', in *Armamentaria* 17.

14 De Wilde examined the drawings collected by F.J.G. ten Raa, who commissioned to Jan Hoynck van Papendrecht the copy of a part of the de Rydder-Robitschek series. Notwithstanding the unreliability of this source, ten Raa at last considered three subjects as likely.

15 Koninklijk Huisarchief (Royal Archives) The Hague, A 26-343; contract signed at Leewarden in March 1678, in Nimwegen, *The Dutch Army*, p. 354.

undyed wool stockings. Consequently, the drummer wore a red coat and the armament for the NCO consisted of a sword with brass hilt and halberd.'[16]

Some information comes from unexpected episodes too. During the operations against Münster in 1673, a case of friendly fire is reported between the Dutch infantry and the mounted company of Friesland Life Guards (c-ii). The latter rode grey horses and were dressed anew in mid July. After a few days, they were shot at by their own troops, who had mistaken them for the Prince-Bishop of Münster's Guards, who rode grey horses too, and red coats and *casaques* with white crosses.[17] Belaubre relates regarding the Friesland Horse Guards, that later in 1696 the uniform was blue with red lining and waistcoat. Therefore, again, uniforms changed over time.

Further quotations come from contemporary printed sources, like the journal of the siege of Groningen of 1672. The anonymous chronicler relates that on 10 August in the later afternoon, troops of the *Königsmarck* infantry regiment (I-77) arrived in the town, all dressed in blue, who were stationed in tents on the *Nieuwe Kerkhof* square: 'also that evening the reinforcements as promised by his Highness, the Prince of Orange, arrived, in the form of 14 companies of the Jorman Regiment [I-59].' The same source relates that since 1 July troops of the *Königsmarck* regiment were already encamped in Groningen, 'armed with sharp curved axes, which they used instead of the swords.'[18]

In the United Provinces existed a developed network of journals that published useful information, such as the *Haarlemmer Courant* and the *Amsterdamsche Courant*, which both represent very fine and interesting sources. The latter relates that on 6 November 1674 two merchants of Amsterdam offered '400 blue soldier coats with red cuffs' for an infantry regiment of Holland. Other news referred to particular clothing, such as the *barakan* [goat wool] brown coat belonging to a horseman, and found in a village near Utrecht on 27 November 1677, 'without lining, with hanging sleeves, and two holes to put ones arms through'. On 1 October 1684 in Amsterdam some money had been stolen, 'the thief being named Carel Manuel, with a brown face, black curled hair, with many warts on his hands, wears a spotted brown-grey coat, a light grey hat with golden lining. Being a soldier of Amsterdam, he speaks very high-German.' From the Haarlem newspaper *De Oprechte Haarlemmer Courant*:

> A certain Captain Bernard Herman Rutgert van Solingen, born in Silesia in the Lauwsnitz, serving in the regiment of Baron van Horn, last known residence in Leyden, on 7 March between 10:00 and 10:30 in the evening, has killed Aerlof Gustaef Wolfzhagen, Captain-Lieutenant of the same regiment, and he has fled afterwards. Therefore, the Lords-Magistrates of the city of Leyden, promise those

---

16 De Wilde, 'En nu de uniform reconstructies van 1688', in *Armamentaria* 23.

17 Ten Raa, *Het Staasche Leger*, vol. VI. p. 134 and T. Verspohl, *Das Heerwesen des Münsterischen Fürstbischofs Christoph Bernard von Galen 1650 –1678* (Hildesheim, 1909), pp. 22–23. Thanks to Edwin Groot for this notice.

18 *Wytlopiger Journael* (Groningen, 1672). On 10 August, the Dutch troops came on 33 ships 'easy to be seen by the enemy, and of course that must have been a shock to him. It was quiet the following night.' Another very useful notice discovered by Edwin Groot.

> who can bring to justice the aforementioned van Solingen: a small and rather fat person, with pocks, of yellowish complexion, sometimes wearing a blond wig, short grey and greyish hair, blue eyes and thick lips, usually dressed in a grey coat, lined with fur, with a leather shirt under it, and a pant and grey socks, speaking high-German, having a servant [a musician?] wearing a red jacket lined white and hanging cuffs, so that he can be arrested, for a reward of 100 silver *ducatons*, and his name will be kept secret.

Possibly these two gentlemen were duelling and it ended fatally for one of them. The regiment is that of Carel Christoffel van Horn (I-96).[19] Information such as these is very useful for forming a framework of cases; however, the researcher is often forced to move between many doubts. Another source of complication derives from contemporary descriptions apparently without explication.[20]

Moving backwards through the years, direct information on uniforms becomes increasingly rare. Before 1670 is very difficult to find description about coat or other clothing. Fortunately, the abundance of military-themed paintings from the Dutch golden age helps us to form a more accurate scenario, although it is often problematic to identify which regiments are represented. The paintings by famous authors, such as Gerard ter Borch Pieter de Hooch, Romeyn de Hooghe, and many others represent an inestimable and accurate source of documentation. From this point of view, the Dutch army can certainly boast an iconographic repertoire of very high artistic level.

Infantry

Some early uniforms of the Dutch infantry appear in the regulation entitled *Vertoogh van de Kryghs-Oeffeninge* by Johan Boxel, published in 1673. The text deals with the drill of the infantry of the states of Holland and Friesland, and is fully illustrated with figures representing ranks and files. Although the year of publication is 1673, the matter can be backdated at least 10 years. The author of the text was a captain-lieutenant in the *Garde te Voet* regiment (I-28) and commissioned the illustrations of musketeers and pikemen portrayed in

19 Edwin Groot investigated also the works of Bix Schipper-van Lottum, a historian who wrote several works on cloth and clothing. She published several books using news, ads, and missing person reports from the *Amsterdamse Courant*. Unfortunately, the years 1672–1680 are difficult to find in the archives and are probably not there any more.

20 Another add from the *Opregte Haarlemmer Courant* of the year 1673, noticed by Edwin Groot: 'It is made known to all high and low ranking officers, that a certain Karel, who took service with the company of Captain Mum in Haarlem on 13 January, and who claimed to be a horseman of Esweyler, from the county of Gulick, named Jan Adams (?), a long man with long black hair, dressed in a grey overcoat, with red cuffs, and a red shirt, that has some wear on it, a yellow leather band, white woollen socks, who after committing the terrible crime of stealing has run off.' The description of Karel's dress is interesting; it looks like a uniform but of which regiment? Thanks to Mr Joop van Campen, it is possible to have a candidate: Captain Mum could be Mumm van Schwarzenstein, an officer of the Horse Guards Regiment. The problem is that they had blue uniforms, not grey ones.

the different motions of their training. These figures are well detailed and show dress and full equipment of the private soldiers. The musketeer wears a cloth cassock with open sleeves over a jacket with arm cuffs. The metal helm is the headdress for musketeers as well as for pikeman, and these latter are protected with three-quarter protective armour for the back, worn over a coat sometimes with short cuffs over the elbow. Wide breeches and socks are the same for all. Some illustrations show groups of soldiers alongside officers dressed with *justaucorps* coat with short sleeves and a plumed round hat. In some cases, NCOs and musicians are also represented.

Concerning the items issued to a musketeer, Boxel lists 12 objects, including musket, rest, coat (or cassock), doublet, a pair of breeches, headdress, bandolier for ammunition, sword with belt, shirt, cravat, socks, and shoes. Pikeman received two items less, excluding doublet, ammunitions, musket, and rest, but taking a 450 centimetre-long pike, and armour. Boxel's text represents the *Oude Garde* regiment in the 1660s in its actual dress and equipment, but there is any notice about the colours. Fortunately, we may turn to the rich gallery of painting, where we find a work of Jacob Ochtervelt (1634–1682), dateable to 1665, where a young Dutch ensign is portrayed with his white flag: reasonable evidence of a Guards regiment. In the background appears a group of soldiers with muskets who are wearing grey cassocks and helms, very similar to the musketeer figures depicted in the Boxel regulation. They are represented in grey cassocks and medium-blue coat and breeches.

The cassock was the principal coat of the Dutch infantry in late 1660s. Nevertheless, early *justaucorps* are represented already in 1667, especially for the *mariniers*. There are several sources that relate this. The engraving of Romeyn de Hooghe illustrating the raid on the Medway is one of the most detailed. The infantry wear a coat of variable length and some have a short jacket or doublet, all with long sleeves with or without cuffs with some exceptions. Officers also wear indifferently *justaucorps* or doublet with *Rhingraeve* style breeches; the broad-brimmed hat is the common headdress. A light musket (flintlock) is the firing weapons for all the soldiers, and just one soldier carries a bandolier with cartridges. Officers are leading their men only with the sword; pikemen are absent, evidently of poor utility in an amphibious action, and some men, possibly sailors, bear spontoons. In another illustration celebrating the victorious landing of 1667, the Dutch infantrymen are dressed as in the de Hooghe artwork, but this time the figures are coloured. The author is Abraham Beerstraten, and compared to de Hooghe he was a less able artist, considering the naive appearance of the figures. Officers and private soldiers wear grey or butternut coats and jackets; plumes appear on the officer's hat and on some soldiers' headgear too. Finally, another painting shows the naval infantrymen with coats and other kind of clothing. The author is a renowned artist, Jan van Leyden, who executed the painting after the order of Cornelis de Witt. Here soldiers and sailors are dressed also in red and dark blue. All these variants would indicate that full uniformity in the marine regiment had not yet been reached, but it could also allude to the fact that fleet sailors also participated in the action. Possibly the best illustrations regarding the Dutch marines are the drawings of Moses ter Borch, who volunteered in the *marinier* regiment until his death in 1667, during the storming of Fort Landguard, near Felixstowe in England. Like his brother Gerard, he mastered drawing, and left a very precious series of portraits of soldiers and sailors of late 1660s. In one of this drawing appears a marine soldier wearing a long coat with short sleeves tailored in an unusual form, the same represented for some figures also in the de Hooghe engraving.

The scenario of the Dutch infantry uniform in the late 1660s becomes increasingly complex when we turn to pictures coming from smaller military environments. This is the case of the figures drawn by Hendrick van Buren in the *Dril Konst* printed in Utrecht in 1668 for the manual of training of the province's infantry.[21] Here the pikeman has received a long coat apparently without sleeves, probably of leather, worn over a cloth doublet with cuffs, and wide breeches. Armour and helm seems of poorer quality compared to the pikeman depicted in the Boxel's work. Instead, the musketeer wears a doublet with open cuffs and *Rhingraeve* breeches; the musket is apparently of the same model depicted in the Boxel's manual, and a sword hangs from a waist belt. This is a very obsolete dress for 1668, but it can be believed that it was still in use in a period when savings on army spending was the main concern of all the States-Provincial. The illustrations suggest that the musketeer could be better protected in winter with the cassock. This remained a typical item of military clothing in the United Provinces, and in England it was also known as a 'Dutch coat'. An infantry cassock still appears in a print dated 1672,[22] where a Dutch private musketeer with broad-brimmed hat is represented alongside a pikeman and a drummer. It is reasonable to believe that the cassock was widespread as a winter overcoat for the infantry until the early 1670s, and replaced by the *justaucorps* in a short time in early 1670s, as confirmed in several contemporary pictures. In these sources, the aspect of the infantrymen is strongly different compared to Boxel's soldiers and other illustrations, confirming that the new fashion has been fully affirmed in the United Provinces. The series of drawings made by Josua de Grave in 1675, depicting the Dutch infantry in campaign, shows soldiers and officers in their less attractive appearance all wearing *justaucorps*. Unfortunately, the drawings are in black and white, but the dusty and worn-out aspect of the soldiers is effectively represented while they are moving or resting in the midst of tents, palisades, and improvised camp kitchens. Pikemen and musketeers wear the same clothing and headdress, and only the equipment distinguishes their role.

21 *Dril Konst of Dienende,zo voor de Bevelhebbberen, om een Bende bekwaamin order te brengen; en om te konnen zien of haar onderhorigezoldaten behoorlijk geoeffend zijn: als ook voor deSoldaten, om onderwezen te worden, op wat anier'tligste tot alle nodige Wapen-oeffeningen konne vorderen. Gesteld, en met nodige afbeeldingen voorzien DoorHenderik van Buren; aan De Edele Mogende Heeren, Mijn Heeren de Staten's Lands van Utregt.* (Utrecht, 1668)

22 See the cover illustration of the *Ordres Van Batailjen, Gepractiseert in de Legers der Vereenighde Nederlanden. Onder het Beleydt van Syn Excellentie Mauritius, En Syn Hoogheydt, Frederick Henrick, Princen van Oranjen, Graven van Nassau, & c. Hooghloflijcker Memorie. Als Capiteynen Generaels van de selve Krijghsmachten. Geobserveert, beschreven, en vertoont, door wijlen Johan Le Hon, in sijn Leven Ingenieur, gebleven in den dienst deser Nederlanden, voor Maestricht. Nu breeder verklaert, door C. Le Hon, Ingenieur, en Regiments-Quartiermeester. Met verscheyden Figuren, (tot het selve Werk dienstigh) daer by gevoeght. Noyt voor desen gedruckt,* printed in Amsterdam in 1672.

48. ***Veldtwaibels*** (NCOs) of the regiment Holstein-Norburg (I-88) and Nassau-Friesland (I-27), dated 1672–75, copies by Hoynck van Papendrecht after de Rydder-Robitschek. This famous series of Dutch uniforms was commissioned by Gustav de Rydder to the Austrian illustrator Norbert Robitschek in the 1920s. The series contains 83 colour plates representing mostly infantry regiments. The style is more or less coherent with the 1670s, but there are many evidences that Robitschek performed a lot of arbitrary reconstructions and he and de-Rydder did not mention the sources. Nevertheless, retired lieutenant-colonel Frederik Jan Gustaaf ten Raa and van Papendrecht copied some drawings from the series, evidently deemed to be more reliable. In 1928, the Dutch Military Museum acquired the collection belonged to ten Raa. This series was added to a large data of old editions preserved in the museum collection. Ten Raa was active in the areas of uniforms and military history. In 1908 he was assigned as lieutenant-colonel (retired) to the Military History Archive of the General Staff, founded in 1891. Here, alongside with van Papendrecht, he produced an interesting series of reconstructions of the early Dutch uniforms.

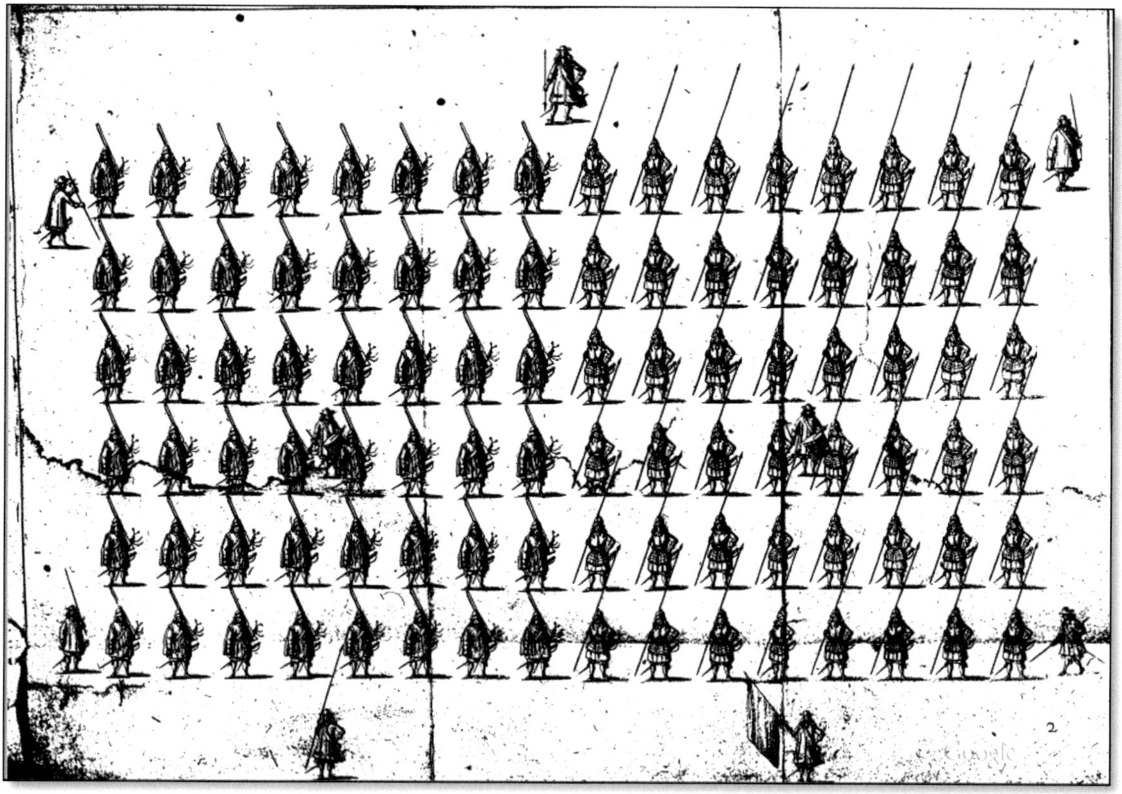

49. Above: musketeers and pikeman in training, from the V***ertoogh van de krijghs-oeffeninge*** by Johan Boxel, published in 1672, but datable in the previous decade. The musketeers are deployed in six ranks and ready to perform the manoeuvre of the conversion, a tactic developed in the beginning of the century and trademark of the Dutch infantry till 1648. Note the officer with spontoon and the NCO with pole weapons or double handed swords.

50. Overleaf: Dutch musketeers and pikemen from the ***Vertoogh van de Kryghs-Oeffeninge*** by Johan Boxel. The text deals with the drill of the infantry of the states of Holland and Friesland and represents the Foot Guards in the different motion of their drill. Although the year of publication is 1673, the soldiers can be backdated at least ten years.

51. Right: Armour and pot helm, Dutch manufacture, mid 17th century. This is the typical composite armour issued to Dutch pikemen until the early 1670s, very close to the items illustrated in the Boxel manual. (Private collection)

22

28

19

18

52. Musketeers and pikemen by Hendrick Cornelissen van Buren (1736–1703), from the ***Dril Konst*** printed in Utrecht in 1672 for the manual of training of the province's infantry.

53. Right: Dutch infantrymen of the late 1660s, from the ***Ordres van Batailljen***, published in 1672. Musketeer and drummer wear open-sleeve cassocks, while the pikeman has armour and buff coat.

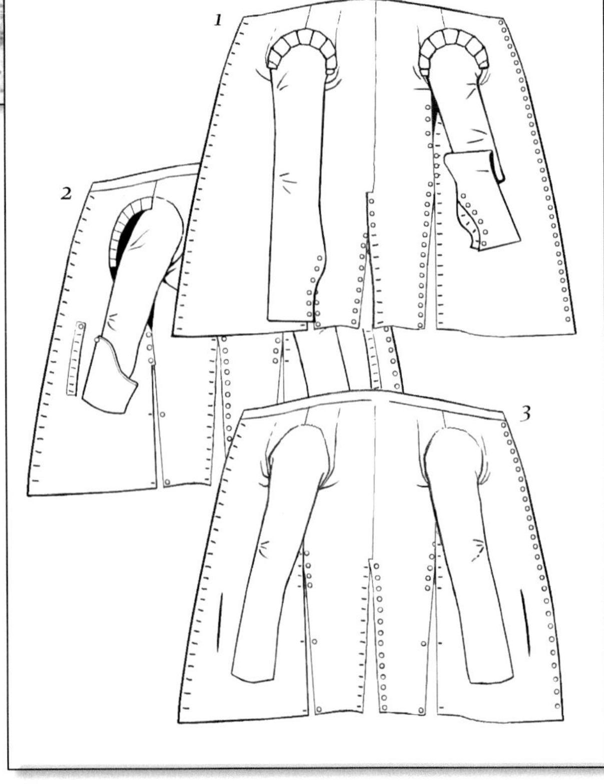

The cassock

54. Above: Dutch soldier wearing cassock, 1665–68, by Gerard ter Borch. (Collection of prints of the Libreria Reale of Turin)

55. Top right: another fine detailed cassock is represented in this painting by Jacob Duck, entitled 'The Distraint', 1658–60. The cassock was widely issued in the Dutch Army and become very popular in the mid 17th century, but disappeared quickly after 1672, replaced by the simpler and less expansive *justaucorps* coat.

56. Right: Dutch cassock patterns, 1: after Boxel's manual, 1663-69; 2: after Jacob Duck, 1658–60; 3: after Gerhard ter Borch, 1665–68. (Author's illustration)

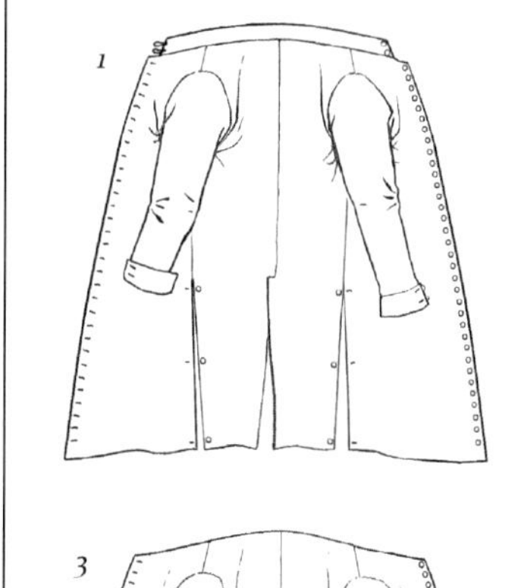

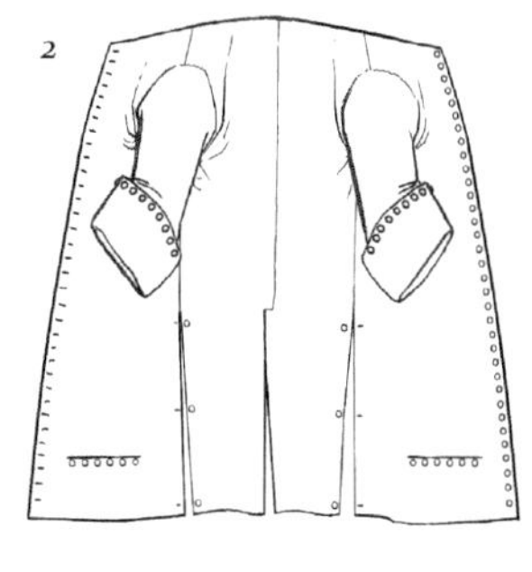

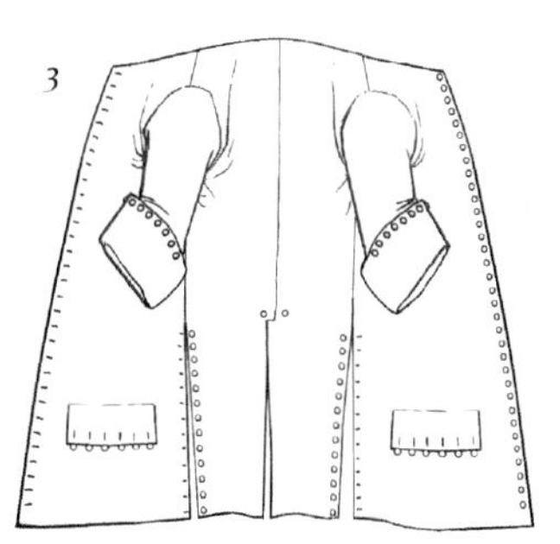

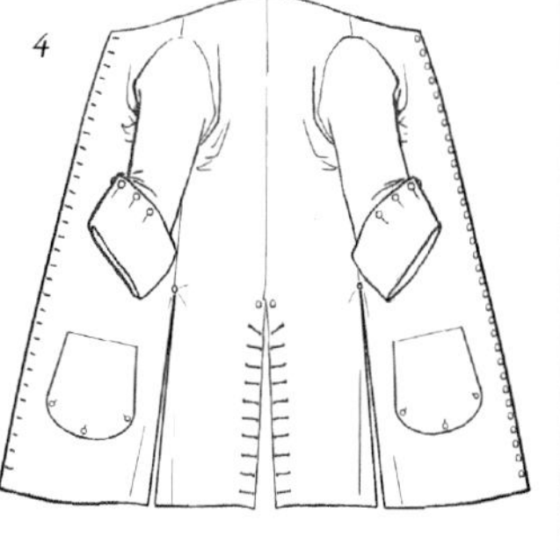

The *justaucorps*

Clockwise from top left:

57. A very good detailed image representing an early ***justaucorps*** worn by this smoking Dutch soldier, by Jacob Duck, dated 1660–65. Note the pattern of flap cuffs and the straight collar.

58. The reading man in the painting by Pieter de Hooch, executed after 1672, well shows the evolution of the ***justaucorps***, which complete sleeves and large flap cuffs.

59. Early ***justaucorps***; 1: after Jacob Duck, 1660–65; 2: after Gerard ter Borch; early 1670s; 3: after Jan Verkolje 1670; 4: after anonymous, 1672. (Author's illustration)

Buff coats

60. Dutch cavalry officers, 1662–65, by Gerard ter Borch and Pieter de Hooch. They wear the same kind of buff leather coat with sleeves piped with silver or gold lace. Note the officer above with Rhingraeve breeches with golden pendants. Close to the door is also depicted a red-coated pikeman with burgonet helm and breast armour.

61. Left: the officer portrayed by Jan Verkoljein the early 1670s wears a fashionable buff ***kolder*** with dark blue cloth cuffs and red fringes. Under the buff coat are visible a pair of ***Rhingraeve*** style breeches. The military origin of the ***justaucorps*** appears here outlined by the pattern close to the contemporary leather ***kolder***.

62. Right; Dutch buff coat, 1660–70, Collection of the *Centraal Museum* in Utrecht.

As discussed before, prior to 1681 the infantry uniforms followed no regulation regarding colour and pattern and this resulted in a wide range of style. Only the equipment appeared more homogeneous, because after 1665 the officers were not required to arm and equip new units themselves; the Council of State took care of this. For a company of 100 men, the provincial arsenals provided 62 muskets with rests and bandoliers for the musketeers, 34 pikes, sets of armour, and helms for the pikemen, two halberds for sergeants, and two drums.[23]

In 1681 and 1686, William III signed orders for regulating the acquirement of clothing. In 1686, the matter included precise instructions to avoid waste and loss.[24] To achieve a good quality and economise the available money the colonels had the uniforms made as simply as possible with the most convenient textile. Uncoloured kersey was preferred, being cheaper than uniformly coloured fabric.[25] This is the same material recorded in the deliveries as grey, light grey, or ash grey *carsaay*: today it would be called natural or undyed fabric. For manufacturing coats and *justaucorps* the tailor used baize, bay or *plets* (from English 'plaid', a thin woollen fabric). Breeches and waistcoats were usually lined with linen. The cut was similar to that of the simple civilian clothing, but ribbon and laces could be added to avoid similarity with civilian dress.

The contracts of acquirement specify coat and breeches, made of good and sufficient kersey in three sizes, while the waistcoat begins to be mentioned in the 1680s. The earlier descriptions relate of 'coats and surtouts' and *justaucorps* are mentioned later. Note that the words 'coat and surtout' of the early orders could indicate that at least some regiments received greatcoats typical in the German and Danish regiments of the period. Regarding this latter item, a contemporary reference stated that already in 1672 Dutch troops were equipped with greatcoats and additional wool socks as winter clothing.[26]

It is interesting to note that regiments with red uniforms had to recoup the major cost in the *retentiegeld* (deduction) from the salary of the private soldiers. This occurred with the English and Scottish regiments, which were subjected to a specific regulation introduced in July 1687. It was the *Nader Ordre en Reglement voor de Engelsche en Schotse Regimenten, zynde in dienst*

23 The overall cost totalled about 1,100 guilders, and as usual was deducted from the recruit's pay. Nimwegen, *The Dutch Army*, p. 246.

24 'When the colonel judges it necessary that the regiment should be clothed, he is to make a muster of the cloth and other necessities available to the officers whereupon the officers are to delegate two or three of their number to seek the cloth and other necessities that they think are required according to the muster and at the best conditions they can find. This being done they are to report back to the colonel who, if in agreement, is to make a contract with the merchants in the presence of the officers who as deputies are to sign the above mentioned contract in the name of all the officers, obliging them to punctually follow the agreement.' *Ibid.*, p. 247.

25 The colonel and the officers were to agree with the merchants that the required clothing was to be paid in instalments and that the captains were to retain enough funds in the hands of their military solicitors as due at each instalment. The military solicitors were instructed to withhold such amounts from the captain's funds as needed for each instalment and hand them over to the merchants according to the terms of the contract; the solicitors being held to this by a separate obligation.

26 F. Wagenaar's *Vaderlandsche Historien*, (Amsterdam, 1754–59), vol. 10, p 335. Thanks to Edwin Groot for this notice.

van den Staat, which followed the similar regulations for the Dutch infantry, *Nader ordre ende Reglement op het stuck von de Kleedinge der Infanterie*, containing the administrative norms and price of uniforms and equipment, and the relative deduction of the soldier's salary. The deductions also paid the salaries of the chaplain, the adjutant, the surgeon-major, and the drum-major along with the uniforms of the drummers.[27] New light on the colour of the uniforms is scarce in both these regulations, however we discover that the Scots regiments received leather breeches.

In several reconstructions of later period, Dutch pikemen are often represented with armour and helm also after 1672, and effectively metal protections are mentioned in the arsenal's inventory again in 1680s. Metal defensive weapons were useful in siege warfare, but represented a considerable limitation in field engagement. In 1670s, siege warfare became a matter of geometry and approaches, every man less exposed to the enemy fire, limiting the need of metal protection only for trench heads. Thus, the employment of armourers seems to be strongly reduced during the war of 1672–78, as occurred on the French side too. The pikeman was essentially requested to form the framework of the square into which the musketeers could pull back, saving them from the cavalry charges. Despite the increase in speed of fire brought by the new muskets, infantry were still vulnerable to the fast-moving cavalry and pikemen were thus still needed. The Dutch pikeman of the 1670s had small differences compared to the coeval musketeer. He carried a single bandolier over the right shoulder to hold the sword. In the following decade, the pikeman wore a waist belt which gradually replaced the bandolier, as for the musketeers.

Grenadiers also wore the same uniform of the musketeers, and only their equipment qualified their role. The first sources regarding Dutch grenadiers in 1670s mention them equipped with flintlock musket and hand grenade pouch, but nothing about clothing and headdress.[28] Surely, when the grenadier lit the grenade, he had to hang his flintlock over his shoulder, and this action required headgear more suitable than the broad-brimmed hat. Only in a commission to raise a grenadier company for the Guards Regiment dated 1673, are mentioned bearskin caps issued with the black leather grenade pouch.[29] There are no certain images depicting Dutch grenadier's cap before the 1680s, until an anonymous artist portrayed them in a print of the Battle of the Boyne. Some grenadiers wear headdresses with plumes, and the troops surrounding them are Dutch Horse Guards and Foot Guards, the first troops to cross the River Boyne on 1 July 1690. In the picture, uniforms and equipment are depicted with good detail and certainly these grenadiers belong to the Foot Guards, but there are some contradictions regarding the equipment. The grenadiers carry bandoliers for grenade pouch and sword, but there is no ammunition pouch or waist belt for hanging it. It should also

27 Each man paid 35 *stuivers* for the headdress and 20 *stuivers* for a pair of stockings. In the second year each soldier received a pie-coat or overcoat, called *overjas* for fivre *florijn*.

28 De Wilde, 'Grenadiersmutsen in het Staatse Leger 1672–1795', in *Armamentaria* 15, 1980.

29 Commission to Captain Herman Schrevet, dated May 1673, to raise a company of grenadiers of 100 men, in *Nationaal Militair Museum*, de Wilde Legacy.

63. The Battle of the Boyne, anonymous artist, 1690. Note the Foot Guards grenadiers on the left side (emphasised) with plumed fur cap, and the ***Gardes te Paard*** in the centre wearing cassocks. Quite strange for an elite units, the grenadiers (emphasised, right) appear here equipped with outdated bandolier and baldric instead the more modern items documented in contemporary sources. This suggests that the anonymous engraver turned to a generic model, probably from an earlier period compared to the event illustrated.

be noted that none of the grenadiers hold the musket, but this could have been an obstacle in crossing the river. In another print dated 1689, Romeyn de Hooghe represents the Foot Guards' grenadiers with a different headdress. Some details on the headdress's front plate suggests that the grenadier is wearing the classical mitre cap typical in the armies of the Protestant states.

As occurred also in many European armies, Dutch officers took advantage of great autonomy regarding their dress. The iconography produced before 1670s seems to confirm that also in the State's Army, infantry officers wore preferably leather *kolder* or cloth *justaucorps* without reference to the regiment's uniform. According to F.J.G. ten Raa, in the 1670s junior officers wore a coat of reversed colour compared to their soldiers, and similar dress was issued to NCOs and musicians. These latter wore coats with elaborated livery, usually sewn-on arms, cuffs, and edges.

Officers' coats were also decorated with rather more lace on the cuffs, pockets, and seams and all wore orange sashes after 1672, except the officers of the Walloon regiment, who wore red. Infantry officers wore also gorgets to differentiate their rank, as occurred for the Guards Regiment in the 1680s. In the same period, a captain carried a spontoon 335 centimetres long, and a lieutenant a partisan of 164 centimetres. A halberd marked the rank of sergeant. Some contemporary pictures show NCOs with ribbon on the coat's sleeves, a sash around the waist and a plumed broad-brimmed hat.

Regarding firing weapons, the Dutch army had already introduced regulations about calibre and size of muskets before 1665. The Boxel regulation shows the musketeer still equipped with the heavy musket with a rest. This was a relatively obsolete weapon requiring 36 different movements, untrustworthy over 60 metres from the target and nearly useless in rainy weather. In 1670, the Council of State proposed the adoption of a lighter calibre with barrel of 10 balls instead 12 of the previous model. The minor weight rendered the musket rest unnecessary: Now handling required fewer movements, increasing rate of fire from one shot per minute to one and a half, and the ranks could be reduced to six or five. However, the Dutch musket was always a matchlock and only marines had received the modern *snaphan* or flintlock by the 1660s, when they successfully used these weapons in the raid against the English fleet in 1665. This weapon changed the appearance of the infantryman; the cartridges which came with the flintlock were kept in a cartridge pouch on a leather belt over the left shoulder alongside the powder horn. In 1672–73, the first companies of grenadiers were armed with flintlock and after 1675 the whole Guards Regiment received the new weapons. Though flintlocks were in use since 1600, mostly as a hunting weapon, financial reasons delayed the introduction of the flintlock into the army, also because commanders preferred the major power of the matchlock, which had a greater calibre. A different calibre also means different bullets and bullet moulds, so a new supply chain had to be set up.[30] After 1680 more and more matchlocks were converted into flintlocks, changing the batteries, but the general introduction of modern firearms was resisted because of the cost of the flints and their limited availability. In 1680, the

30 Thanks to Edwin Groot for this clarification.

Council of State ordered that every company was to have 20 flintlock batteries available to be put on muskets when possible,[31] but matchlocks remained the most common infantry fire weapons until the 1690s.[32]

Early bayonets were introduced during the war of 1672–78. They were of the 'plug' type, where the bayonet was fitted directly into the barrel of the musket. This naturally prevented the gun from being fired. The lack of alternative against the cavalry left the Dutch infantry depending on the pike until the 1690s, when a socket bayonet, manufactured after Vauban's French models, became available in large quantities.

Cavalry

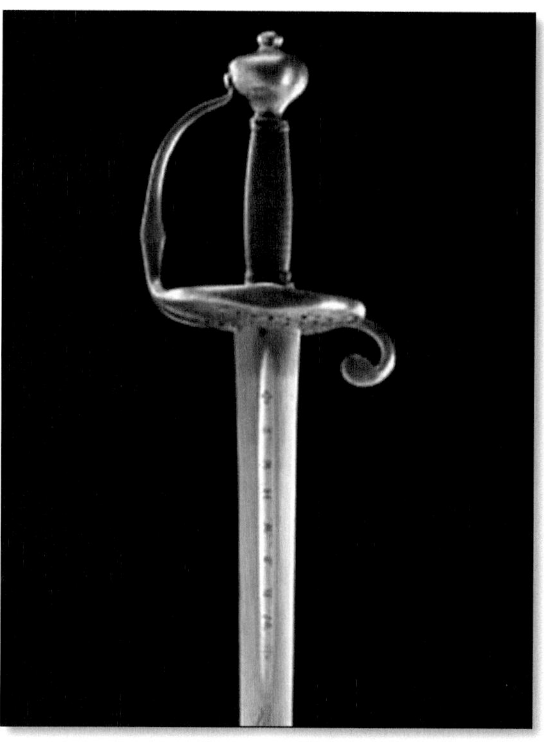

64. A Dutch cavalry sword, second half of the 17th century. Double-edged blade stamped 'SAHAGAM' within a short fuller and cut with a running wolf mark on each side, stamped with the bladesmith's mark and Amsterdam Town mark. (Private collection)

Dutch cavalrymen are widely represented in paintings and prints before 1670, a direct consequence of the major wealth of the customers. Compared to the infantry, cavalry dress appears less variable and shows the wide use of a leather coat or *kolder* until the beginning of the 1670s. Unlike the infantry, in 1665 Dutch cavalry officers were required to provide their men with clothing and also weapons. The armament consisted of a fine steel, a sword, a carbine, a pair of pistols, a thick leather coat, a cloak, a cuirass protecting front and back, and a lobster helm.[33] A leather coat was formed of eight pieces; the sleeves were usually manufactured with thinner leather or in cloth reinforced by silver or golden laces: a typical pattern of the Dutch officer in this age and a legacy of the original sleeves worn under the metal protection of the complete armour. Until the 1670s, the sleeves finished with little flap cuffs without distinctive colours. The boots were especially long and heavy, with squared tips at the toes and with wide and stiff tops to better protect the knees. This model of jacked riding boot changed little throughout the years, but before the 1670s the length appears more variable and wide-coloured double pairs of stockings are common for both

31 De Wilde, 'De Mannen van 1688', *Armamentaria* 23, 1988.

32 A notary's act of June 1682 relates that the regiment *Ossery* (I-101), ordered 144 flintlocks and 204 matchlocks, indicating that at that time the regiment was still armed with both kind of musket. The proportion of modern fire weapons and matchlocks was about of 50 percent each, which would match the contemporary scenario of the major states. The infantry flintlock had to be the same used by the Dutch guards and cost seven *guilders*, while the muskets cost six *guilders* and 15 *stuivers*. In 1687, the Dutch infantry was completing the conversion from the musket to flintlock but it was only by the beginning of the War of the Spanish Succession that matchlocks were completely replaced. See also in Mark Geerdink-Schaftenaar, *For Orange and the States. The Army of the Dutch Republic, 1713–1772. Part 1, The Infantry* (Wawrwick: Helion & Company, 2018).

33 Nimwegen, *The Dutch Army*, p. 246.

Dutch cavalry

65. Top left: a very fine engraving by Jan van Troyen, after Gerbrand van den Eeckhout, representing a Dutch cavalry officer of 1660–64. (Author's archive)

66. Above: Dutch cavalrymen, 1672–78, after de Hooghe and Belagering der Stad Grave (1674) by anonymous. (Author's illustration)

67. Below: Dutch cavalry trooper, 1665–68, reconstruction after Philips Wouverman. Buff leather coat with white metal armour; orange sash and grey-brown headgear. (Author's illustration)

officers and troopers, ostentatiously in sight over the folded top. Breeches remained often hidden, but the iconographic sources show the common wide breeches of cloth or, less usual, in leather.

The sash was part of the normal equipment of the Dutch horseman in this age. Before 1672 officers often wore sashes of the province's colours, then they were not always orange, while the junior officers and troops usually used sashes of the latter colour. The coeval iconography shows cavalry troops and officers with the typical broad-brimmed hat of grey, straw yellow, or light-brown felt in several nuances, while helms are rare. Headgear of black felt seems to be less common before 1680, but occasionally the high 'Puritan cap' is worn by some officers and troopers, as represented in some paintings of Pieter de Hooch, dating from the early 1660s. Occasionally plumes are fastened on the headgear, usually for the officers and NCOs as well as for the troopers. The wide iconographic sources concerning this period and the substantial identity of cavalry dress before 1672, facilitate the task for reconstructing the uniform of the Dutch horse regiments, which appeared with few exceptions in leather *kolder* and high boots. The only distinctive sign was the regimental standards and the musicians' uniforms, usually tailored with the colonel's livery.

However, also for the next decade, direct information on the uniforms of the cavalry is rare, and our fragmentary knowledge on this matter comes from the analysis of archival documentation.

The most interesting pictures illustrating the Dutch cavalry in the early phase of the war of 1672–78 are a painting and an engraving both relating the storming of Coevorden, which occurred in December 1672. In the painting by Pieter Wouwerman, today preserved in the Rijksmuseum in Amsterdam, are portrayed some mounted officers and troopers who could belong to the *Kingma* cavalry regiment (C-24), the only mounted unit to participate in the action. At a first examination, the horsemen are dressed with coats of different colours: butternut, light brown, medium grey, and dark blue; a trooper seems to wear a leather coat of buff. Some figures are wearing light-yellow sashes; equipment and weapons appear almost incomplete and heterogeneous. The yellow sash could identify troops of Groningen, considering that the order of William III to adopt orange for all the troops may not have been yet assumed in those dramatic weeks. The *Kingma* regiment belonged to Friesland, and in that case the mounted figures depicted could be not horsemen of this cavalry regiment, but officers of infantry or militia, and even volunteers. Despite the uncertainties arising from this painting, the variety of uniforms depicted shows that in late 1672 uniformity was probably still far from being achieved in the infantry as well as in the cavalry. The second source, an engraving made by Lambert van den Bos, surely represents regular cavalrymen, who forms the rearguard of the advancing infantry columns engaged in the storming of Coevorden. Here the colours are absent, but equipment and weaponry appears more regular and coherent for a horse regiment. Some troopers seem to wear a leather coat while others appear dressed with something more close to a cloth *justaucorps*. This could be the result of the delivering of new items that involved one company at a time, and that it may not have been completed for various reasons. Therefore, it is very likely that in the first months of the war the uniforms of the Dutch cavalry were different within the same regiment, both due to the emergency caused by the

Gardes te Paard **(Horse Guards)**

68. Above: a: cassocks, after the 'Battle of the Boyne' by anonymous; b: waistcoat (For more details see colour plate F). (Author's illustration)

69. Right: private guard in ***casaque***, after de Hooghe. (Author's illustration)

70. Portrait of Jacob de Graeff (1642–1690), by Gerard ter Borch, Rijksmuseum collection, Amsterdam. The de Graeff family sided with de Witt faction and lost its political influence in 1672. Jacob became an officer in the ***Gardes te Paard***, taking part in the occupation of Bonn in 1673, and in the battle of Seneffe in 1674. The portrait is datable to early 1670s. Here de Graeff wears a fashionable ***justaucorps*** with short sleeves and cuffs. Note the elaborate waistcoat in silver brocade with the sleeves that cover the coat's cuffs, typical of the Dutch dress of that age and represented in several other male portraits. His status of officer is outlined by the silk sword baldric, and the very posh orange sash around his waist.

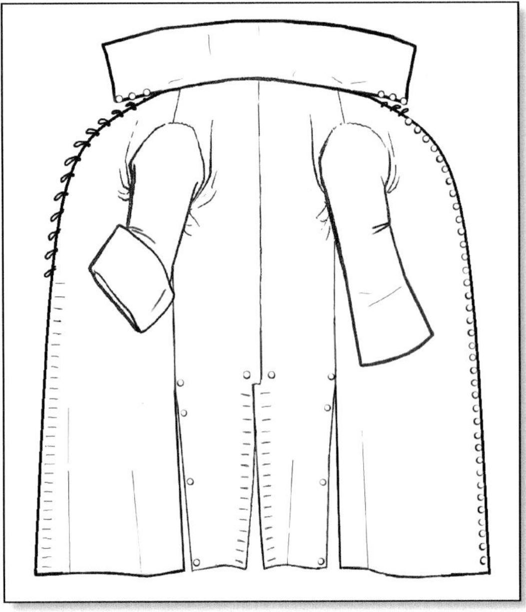

71. Above: cavalry ***surtout*** or greatcoat, after the painting by Pieter de Hooch (immediate right). (Author's illustration)

72. Right, and opposite page: Four interesting and well-detailed Dutch cavalrymen by Pieter de Hooch, all datable to the 1660s. They wear breast armour with back over buff coat of various pattern. Note the first figure with the greatcoat often mentioned in the source, issued to the cavalry troopers in winter and certainly useful in the rainy Dutch weather. This item is confirmed in the following decade also.

73. Dutch cavalrymen with girl outside tent, from a collection of copper-engravings after Philips Wouwerman (1619–68), dated approximately 1660. Leather coat and broad brimmed hat are the typical clothing of the Dutch cuirassiers in the early 1660s. All the figures wear a sash around the waist, except the one who seems to be a junior officer, who carries it on the left shoulder. The trumper wears a plain coat with long false sleeves, and ny lacing or livery appear on it.

invasion and to the critical situation of the army. The sources relating the cavalry uniforms during the war of 1672–78 confirm the general trend in the adoption of a grey coat. Obviously, the cavalry officers also could be dressed in a different colour compared to the troopers. However, there is an exception, even dated 1686, regarding a cavalry regiment still dressed with buff *kolder*, as it appears in the plan of the review in the moor of Mook. This exception regards the *Oyen* regiment (I-8), which possibly retained the buff leather coat as well as other units before 1678, especially the former cuirassier regiments.

Also the life guard units preserved the original blue or red uniforms to distinguish their status. The most represented corps of life guards is the *Gardes te Paard* regiment. De Wilde and Belaupre gave a version of the uniforms worn by this prestigious units after the research of F.J.G. ten Raa and Jan Hoynck van Papendrecht. These latter reconstructed the uniform after the engraving of Romeyn de Hooghe representing the siege of Naarden in 1673. The *Gardes te Paard* wear a dark blue *casaque* with false sleeves, inspired by that of the French *Maison du Roi*'s *Mousquetaires*. A yellow mustard waistcoat, large brimmed hat with feathers and huge cavalry boots complete the clothing. This uniform is confirmed in other pictures except one. This is an engraving by an anonymous artist illustrating the Battle of the Boyne in 1690. Here appears the horse guards wearing the same feathered headgear but not the *casaque*, replaced by a cassock with large cuffs. This suggests that the courtly uniform with the *casaque* was worn for ordinary duty, and that in a war campaign the warmer and more comfortable cassock was preferred.

The first complete regulation of the Dutch cavalry appeared in January 1687, when *the Ordre en Reglement op het stuk van de Monteeringe en Kleedinge der Cavalerie* was published in The Hague. From that year the cavalry uniform consisted of a coat or *justaucorps* of grey *carsaay*, a broad-brimmed hat, a pouch, a pair of gloves issued every two years, and a cloak, along with a saddle cover and a pair of holster covers substituted every four years.[34] The ordinance prescribed an orange sash too, to distinguish the Dutch cavalrymen from their enemies. The colours and other details of the uniform were decided by the colonel,[35] but the more common was the light grey cloth employed also for the infantry. However, the pattern of the coat was little different from that of the foot soldiers. Buttons appeared only on the breast, and in dismounted service the back skirts were often buttoned up. For the sword, waist belts had substituted the baldric earlier compared to the infantry. A black neck cloth of cotton or silk is repeatedly mentioned in the lists of items delivered to the troops after 1687. Leather coats are almost completely replaced, but some senior cavalry officers and colonels continue to wear the *kolder* as distinctive

34 F.J.G. ten Raa gives an overview of the item issued to a trooper in 1687–90: saddle, a pair of holsters, stirrups, bridle and belt for the horse, bit, reins, buckles, carbine belt with hook, sword belt with clasp and tassel, saddle cover and holster covers, carbine, a pair of pistols, sword, a pair of boots, coat, cloak with accessories, a pair of deer-leather gloves, a black pouch, a sash, a tent each four troopers; *Het Staatsche Leger*, vol. VII, p. 253.

35 Ten Raa, *Het Staatsche Leger*, vol. VII, p. 252.

74. Above: Four Dutch infantrymen dateable to c.1688, in this anonymous print preserved in the Royal Library in Windsor Castle. These subjects were copied also by Cecil C.P. Lawson for his authoritative work on the British Army, and some scholars suggest that they are actually English soldiers. Notwithstanding this uncertainty, the print gives an excellent idea of the appearance of grenadiers and musketeers in the late 1680s.

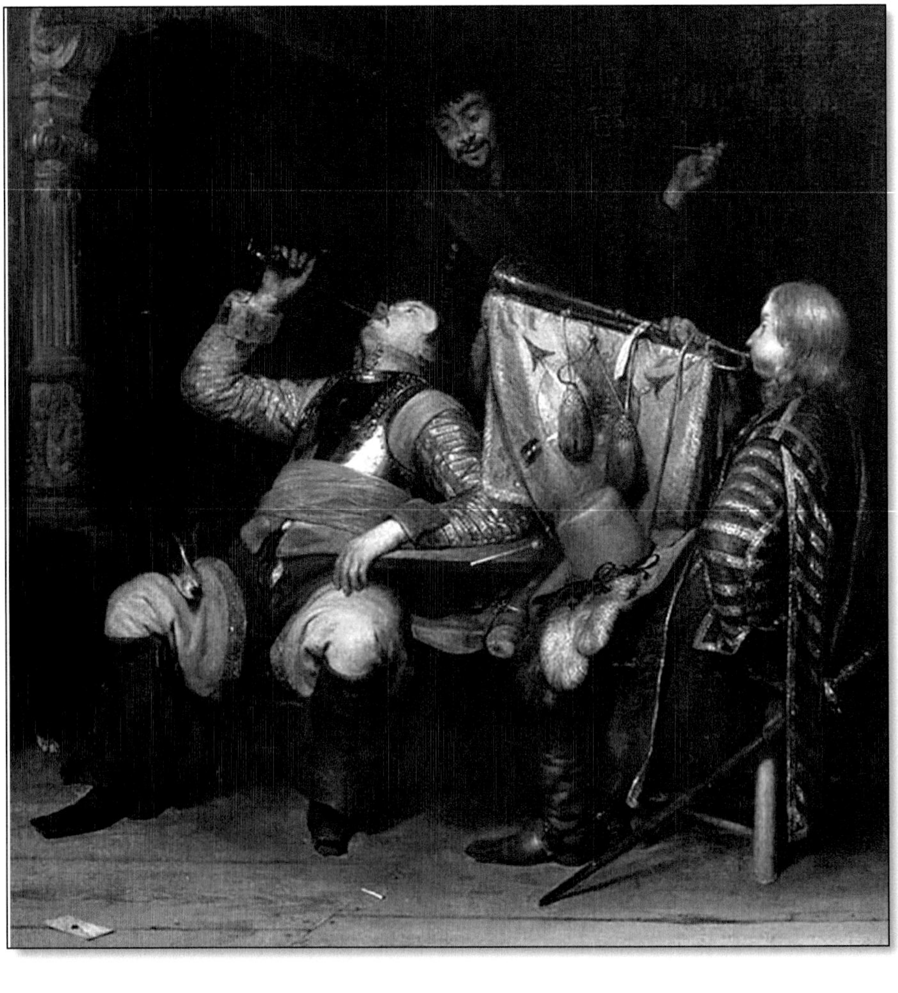

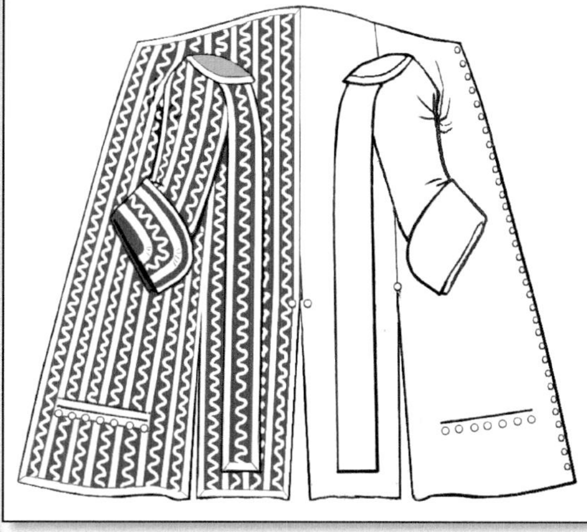

Cavalry trumpeters

75. Left: Cavalryman and trumpeter, 1660. The trumpeter, often portrayed as a message holder, was a favourite subject of Gerard ter Borch. It is difficult to identify the regiments from which they come, except the trumpeter in this painting, who, according to the heraldry on the trumpet, could behold to the regiment of ***Gardes te Paard van de Staten van Holland*** (C-1).

76. The trumpeter as main subject in the painting appears again in the works of Jan Verkolje (above, dated 1674; right, 1673). Note the elaborate gallon of the livery and the coat with false sleeves.

77. Top right: pattern of the coat of the 1674 trumpeter. (Author's illustration. For more details see colour plate E)

of their rank. Now the leather coat has size and form similar to the *justaucorps* and the cuffs are applied on the sleeves with buttons.[36]

The introduction of the flintlock followed the scheme of the infantry. In April 1675 the *Gardes du Corps* received flintlock carbines and the others regiments gradually followed in the next decade. However, wheellock carbine and pistols remained in use until the last years of the century. In the ordinance of 1687, the cavalry still retained the cuirass, but there is no evidence about the use of armour in the 1670s. Possibly, on some occasions, they wore cuirasses under the *justaucorps* as did their French enemies. Thereafter the cuirass gradually fell into disuse.

The first known uniform of the Dutch dragoons is quite similar to the French one. The coat is identical to the infantry's and the forage cap, trimmed with fur or not, is very close to the French dragoons' *bonnet*. This headdress is recorded by General F.J.G. ten Raa in his authoritative work, and it also appears in the iconographic sources as the headgear of the first dragoon regiments raised in 1672.

The more recent origin of the Dutch dragoons allowed a less problematic survival of the sources, and with the exception of the Friesland dragoon company, the uniforms of both regiments are well known, as well as the changes that occurred throughout the years. Iconographic sources, such as the engraving of the siege of Naarden of 1674 by Romeyn de Hooghe, shows the *Courland* dragoons (D-1) wearing a cloth cap.[37] A printed caption confirms that they belong only to this regiment. Their pattern seems more Polish than French and it could be obvious for a regiment recruited by the Duke of Courland. Portrayed from the back, there is a mounted dragoon with a cloth cap trimmed with fur and armed with a war hammer, a typical weapon of the eastern cavalry, while another dragoon is playing a wind instrument, more similar to a recorder than a hautboy. Moreover, a senior officer dressed Polish-style is portrayed together with the Dutch major staff; unfortunately, he is the only one unmentioned in the captions. Thus, the Polish-Latvian origin of this regiment should be confirmed also by the most important Dutch engraver of the age. However, the dragoons are equipped with cross bandoliers for sword and fire weapons typical of the western horsemen.[38]

The iconographic sources are absent for the other regiment recruited in 1672, but fortunately there exists an accurate description of the cloth purchased some years later for manufacturing the uniform.[39] After the green

36 A fine example of a later leather coat with applied cuffs trimmed with metal buttons is preserved in the Kent University Museum in England. Although this coat belonged to an Englishman, the manufacture is very probably Dutch.

37 In another engraving by Romeyn de Hooghe, relating the battle of Seneffe in 1674, the *Courland* dragoons appear identical to the ones at Naarden.

38 For his painting of the *waterlinie* preserved in the Dutch National Military Museum, Hoynk van Papendrecht was inspired by de Hooghe's engraving, depicting *Courland*'s dragons with a strong 'Polish' appearance.

39 Ten Raa, *Het Staatsche Leger*, vol. VI, p. 203. On 2 January 1676, Abraham Eppinger captain of a dragoon company under Colonel Brandt signed a contract with Artus Le Breton for the supplying of '72 coats for soldiers of his company, of green cloth, lined of red and with copper buttons, of such cloth, and buttons, as long and as broad as those Le Breton had already made'.

uniform of 1676, the regiment adopted in 1685 a red coat with pale blue cuffs, which turned to red lined with white in 1687.

The Dutch dragoons showed their infantry origin in the weaponry, which included the musket rather than carbines. Some documents relate that the matchlock remained the firearm of the dragoons until the 1690s.[40]

Artillery

If the formulation of a coherent framework concerning the uniforms of the Dutch infantry or cavalry before the 1690s is a difficult subject, for the artillery it is even more so. Artillerymen belonged to a close guild of professional elites, jealous of their status, and who guarded the secrets of their craft. Iconography sources relating to the 1660s or earlier reflect this cultural tendency and show the artillerymen dressed more like civilian artisans than professional soldiers. Concerning the first artillery uniforms there are very few original drawings and records useful to form the general lines. In some pictures artillerymen appear with doublet or jacket and broad-brimmed hat, some wear a sash around the waist, usually the NCOs who are carrying the linstock. The Dutch National Military Museum preserves the drawings collected by *Generaal-Majoor* Imbyze van Batenburg, who served in the artillery after 1769 and copied by F.J.G. ten Raa and Frans Gerard de Wilde. This is the most ancient source relating the 'actual' uniform of the Dutch artillery; nevertheless, some particulars seem to be old fashioned in the period to which they refer.[41] The 1680 artilleryman wears a dark blue *justaucorps* with red 'Swedish' cuffs, brass or copper buttons, dark blue breeches and stockings, white neck cloth and black broad-brimmed hat, with the brims turned up, and white plume. Major suspects turn to officers and other crewmen, who wear also in dark blue with red facings. Officers' coats have no decoration, apart from the hat with a white plume and they hold walking sticks. All the figures are armed with swords with a brass hilt. The officers carry the sword with a bandolier of natural leather over the right shoulder while others wear them on a waist belt with a frog of buff leather. All wear a broad-brimmed black hat, someone wears a white neck cloth,

Further, 72 *coddebeck hoeden* bordered with orange lace and a green cord of linen wool, 20 sword bandoliers of buff leather and 20 *Port de musquetons* as for the bandoliers.

40 In 1693 dragoon regiment *Mattha* should have received *snaphanen* (flintlocks) in substitution for their matchlock muskets. See in F.J.G. ten Raa, *Het Staatische Leger*, vol. VII, p. 272.

41 Dutch National Military Museum, Soesterberg, de Wilde Legacy MT 052-01. De Wilde took these drawings from the *Collectie van verschillende illustraties of artilleristen sinds de invoering van uniforme kleding in het Nederlandse leger tot heden 1821* (*Collection of different illustrations of artillerymen since the introduction of uniform clothing in the Dutch army up until the present times 1821*) by Jonkh J.W. Imbyze van Batenburg. This collection belonged to the military history archive of the Dutch Major Staff in The Hague and was lost in the fire of 1944. The collection survived the fire thanks to the copies made by F.J.G. ten Raa. Imbyze van Batenburg did not mention sources, but asserted that he had recorded information given him by his father and grandfather, also artillerymen. Then he introduced the development of the uniforms of the Dutch artillery from 1684. Richard Knötel also turned to the Imbyze van Batenburg collection for preparing his plates on the Dutch Artillery included in *Die Grosse Uniformenkunde*.

78. Dutch Artillery, 1668–80; illustration by Richard Knötel from ***Die Grosse Uniformenkunde***. The German artist reproduced these figures after the drawings by Jonkh J.W. Imbyze van Batenburg. The author did not mention sources, but asserted that he had recorded information given him by his father and grandfather, they also being artillerymen. The series of drawings belonged to the military history archive of the Dutch Major Staff in The Hague and was lost in the fire of 1944. The collection has miraculously survived thanks to the copies made by F.J.G. ten Raa.

79. The arrest of the de Witt brothers by The Hague militia in 1672, by Pieter Frits (1627–1708).

except the gunner, who has an old-fashioned white collar – blue breeches and black shoes. The stockings are red for officers and blue for the lower ranks. Officers' sashes are red, white, blue, or orange. Possibly some particulars are speculative, but they could be quite adherent to reality.

Another interesting source concerning the early uniform of the Dutch artillery is preserved in the Royal Dutch Artillery Museum. The curator of the museum has produced also some tri-dimensional reconstructions of artillerymen of the late 1670s. They wear red-brown and grey coats without cuffs over clothing of probable civilian provenance, black broad-brimmed hat, white neck cloth, and orange sashes around the waist.

Further sources are preserved in the Dutch National Military Museum, such as the picture of the Battle of the Boyne (1690). The source shows an artillery crew dressed with a dark blue coat lined red, blue breeches, and grey-blue stockings. According to de Wilde, before 1701 workers and pioneers wore blue coats and grey stockings.[42] Private artillerymen carried flintlock muskets from 1672.[43]

42 Dutch National Military Museum, Soesterberg, De Wilde Legacy.

43 Ten Raa, *Het Staatsche Leger*, vol. VI, p. 456.

80. The Hague Town Militia by Martinus Lengele, dated early 1660s. Grey doublets and hose breeches or ***Rhingreave*** breeches, in various nuances, dressed the members of this corps, and only the artilleryman or constable portrayed on the right wears an old-fashioned black coat. Large rabat collars outline this period of male fashion and qualify these personages as wealthy and proud ***schutterij***.

Militia

Before the 1670s, Dutch militiamen continued to distinguish their role through the traditional fashionable dress of the earlier, golden, decades. Despite the relative shortage of pictures depicting civic guards of the later period, there is enough information for establishing the general lines of their equipment and clothing.

The painting of The Hague Town Militia by Martinus Lengele represents a fine example of the appearance of civic guards in the early 1660s. Grey doublets and hose breeches or *Rhingreave* breeches, in various nuances, are adopted by the members of this corps, and only the artilleryman or constable portrayed on the right wears an old fashionable black coat. Large *rabat* collars outline this period of passage of the male fashion and qualify these personages as wealthy and proud *schutterij*. As a common sign, all the figures have a large orange sash, gold laced for officers. Further pictures show the companies of militia were identified by a distinctive colour. A two-page print dated October 1672 registers the 60 companies of the Amsterdam militia. Here the companies are divided in a group of 12, identified in couples by a colour, alternating orange blue, white, green, yellow, purple.[44] However, it does not refer to their clothes, but was just a distinctive sign. This is well exemplified in the portraits painted by Jacob Fransz van der Merck representing the captains of two of the six companies of the civic guards of Leiden.[45] In the portrait of Captain Nicolaes Hendriksz appears in the background the militiamen of the 'orange company', because of the colour of the ensign and the sash worn by officer and troops. The other portrait that has survived represents Gerrit Leendertsz van Grootveld as captain of the 'blue company'. In both paintings, the officers are wearing a black or dark blue coat, while their men are mostly dressed in grey or butternut. Grey in several nuances seems to be the favourite colour for militia, and this is partially confirmed in the painting representing the arrest of the de Witt brothers in 1672, by Pieter Frits. The action was carried out by The Hague town militia. The painting depicts several militiamen with their officers, recognisable by their polearms. Alongside the grey dressed figures, there are also red, green, buff, and even pink militiamen. One wears a coat or *justaucorps* with cuffs, while other figures appear in doublet or short coat; headdress varies from morion helm to broad-brimmed hat of several colours. On the roof of a house, three militiamen in grey coats with muskets are depicted wearing red breeches and different coloured stockings; one of them wears an orange sash on his left shoulder. In this case, the uniformity is much more approximate compared to the two earlier pictures, but this could have been a choice of the artist. However, some figures, both officers and NCOs, as well as one of the aforementioned figures on the roof, wear an orange sash. Another peculiar aspect of this painting is that all the militiamen have muskets.

44 *Ordre voor de 60 Compagnie Burgeren, op wat daghdie hebben te waken ...* Dutch Royal Library, The Hague, kn. 10570.

45 These portraits were commissioned as a set of four, each portrait depicting a captain of one of the civic guard companies of Leiden in 1657. Unfortunately, two portraits have been lost.

The limited commitment required of the militiamen is reflected in their equipment and weaponry, which usually consisted of old muskets with a rest and ordinary pikes, but officers often displayed rich and finely designed individual weapons to emphasise their status. This is fully represented in an engraving printed in 1672, as a cover for the New Year almanac. In the picture are depicted militia officers, soldiers and drummers of the province of Holland: possibly just assembled for the war against France.[46] They are wearing French-style *justaucorps* with large cuffs and broad-brimmed hat. In the centre, an ensign bears a large infantry flag with Holland's motto, VIGILARE DEO CONFIDENTES (Confident in God's Vigilance). He wears a fashionable fully laced *justaucorps* and waistcoat; the same as worn by another officer with a partisan standing on the right; while a third person carries a cassock on his shoulders. Sashes are knotted around the waist, and plumes are fastened on their laced headgear, in sharp contrast with the 'Puritan' hats worn by two civil officials close to the ensign. In the background, pikes and spontoons are collected on the wall, while musketeers and pikemen are deployed in more ranks, all wearing *justaucorps*. This source is already quite eloquent with regard to military clothing, now fully distinct from civil clothing, and also reserves other surprising details. On the left, two drummers are depicted engaged with their instruments. The first is beating the drum and shows the interesting detail of his coat's pockets. A large flap is tailored between the waist and knee. The size of the pocket is quite unusual for the early 1670s, and the buttons are sewn in a very bizarre pattern, enriched with laces or ribbons. Curiously, the second drummer wears a coat without pockets.

Ensigns

The Dutch military ensigns are well known thanks to many iconographic sources preserved both in the Netherlands and outside. Many of our knowledge on Dutch flags[47] comes from the collection *Les triomphes de Louis XIV*. This is a renowned series of plates illustrating the war trophies captured during the reign of King Louis XIV. The collection contains several Dutch flags, of which at least a dozen belong to the period 1660–87.[48] Further flags are depicted on plans of the reviews of Ath, dated 1696, although they appear barely reproduced in their main colours.

Further studies on the Dutch military vexillology involved specialists since the beginning of the 20th century and their research produced a wide literature. French historian Jean Belaubre identified many of the ensigns

46 Engraving by anonymous from the *Nieuwe Jaars Gift aan de Manhafte Schuttery van Nederland*, Amsterdam, 1673.

47 In Dutch vexillology there is a difference between a *vlag*, a term being only used for the national flag, while *vaandel* is applied to 'regimental, ship's or religious colour'.

48 *Les Triomphes de Louis XIV dit le Grand, roy de France et de Navarre représentés par les Drapeaux, Guidons er Etendarts qui ont été pris sur les Ennemis de Sa Majesté*, Bibliothèque Nationale de France. Also the Dutch National Military Museum has a copy of the illustrations made by military painter Hoynck van Papendrecht.

81. Courland's cavalry standard, probably the life colour, with the motto vigilanter et constanter, today preserved in the Military Museum of Stockholm. Some scholars paid attention at the lion with a sword and proposed that it is the Friesland's lion (the province of Friesland hired the Courland troops). The pattern suggests that the standard belonged to the cavalry regiment (C-30), which consisted of four companies. The regiment was eventually disbanded in 1702, and the ensign would be back in Courland.

82 1 – Colonel's ensign, infantry regiment ***Reede*** (I-86), 1673. This colour is described by Colonel Adriaan van Reede van Amerongen. After the burning of the family castle by the French, he wanted a banner with a picture of a burning castle and a rather revengeful motto. Van Reede talked his father out of this and the banner is described with 'orange flames in the corner', and as a motto NON IN ULTI FINUS. On the pole's corner is carried Holland's coat of arms.

2 and 3 – Scots infantry ensigns are described in 1686 in red or blue with the white St. Andrew cross. In 1686 there were three Scottish regiments in Dutch service, the red ensign is attributed to regiment ***Mackay*** (I-5), the blue one to regiment ***Wanchope*** (I-100).

83. 1 – Company ensign, infantry regiment ***Rabenhaupt*** (I-6) 1672: above yellow with emerald green band; below green with sky blue band, both carried with the Groningen's coat of arms (after Pieter Wouverman's painting of the storming on Coevorden).

2 – Colonel's ensign, infantry regiment ***Wijnbergen*** (I-99), 1690: white with orange branches in green and orange: musket and fork at natural. (After ***Les Triomphes de Louis XIV***)

84. 1: Company standard, cavalry regiment ***Nassau-Saarbrücken*** (C-22), 1690: red with gold tree, black ball and green ground; golden monogram and crown; black script on white scroll; red-gold fringes. (After ***Les Triomphes de Louis XIV***)

2: Company standard, cavalry regiment ***Berlo*** (C-28): light green with clouds, arm, sword and scroll in silver; sword hilt in gold; black script; silver fringes. (After Belaupre-de Wilde)

85. Company standards, regiment ***Waldeck*** (C-9), 1690: above black with gold-red grenade and flames, orange branches in green and orange, gold script; below, as above with white clouds, natural hand and red hearts: white scroll with black script; both with silver fringes. (After ***Les Triomphes de Louis XIV***)

illustrated and re-issued them with his commentaries: this study continue to be one of the most important sources for this period. Several interesting contributions appeared in recent years and later research has extended our knowledge on this matter.[49]

According to these authors, in the Dutch infantry or cavalry ensigns the design is more important than the colours. The range of figures used in the period 1660–87 is wide, but there are symbols never adopted on the Dutch ensigns. Because the Spaniards used the Saint Andrew cross on their flags and standards, this symbol never appeared in the United Provinces and also the white cross appeared only with the Swiss mercenary regiments in the late 17th century. The usual pattern of the Dutch infantry ensigns presents the lion as a major symbol. The lion embodies the Republican virtues, and his courage well matches the troops on the battlefield. The lion is represented standing on his rear paws and often holds a sword and the seven arrows representing the United Provinces. Some flags show allegorical figures too, such as the all-seeing-eye, the phoenix, the seven arrows, or the armoured right arm with a sword. Captions or mottoes of religious and political origin appear frequently during this age, usually in Latin. Golden laurel leaves are common in this period as an ornamental pattern. Since the beginning of the century, all infantry flags carried the coat of arms of the province they were paid by. Some ensigns used also the colonel's cipher. The shape was square, but the dimensions could be different from case to case, and normally the sides exceeded two metres.[50]

In all regiments, white was the colour of the colonel's company, later that of the colonel's flag. Usually, the ordinary companies had an ensign of the same design, but of a different colour. Between them, regiments further distinguished themselves by the colour of their flags, but there are several clues that flags of the ordinary companies in the same regiment were of different colours.

Generally, Dutch infantry ensigns modified little in the period under examination. The major change concerned the adoption of the orange colour only for the Guards after 1672. Specialists on Dutch vexillology do not mention specific colours for the infantry, and the ensigns appear mostly in yellow, red, and blue in various combinations. Nevertheless, the use of specific colours had interested the Dutch infantry in 1668. During his long proposal of training campaigns for the troops, Count Johan Maurits of Nassau-Siegen ordered 96 infantry regimental flags in eight different colours: orange, *bleu morant* (pale blue), grass green, yellow, red, white, sea green and Isabella (pink-brown). The Count established also the size: seven feet square (213 centimetres) and pikes were used as poles.[51] Unfortunately, it is not known whether this order was entirely executed and probably the use of these flags was required only to better identify the regiments in the training sessions.

49 In the Dutch National Military Museum, Military History section and in the infantry regiments with their own museum there are still a lot of ensigns to be explored, which can offer a useful contribution to the knowledge of this matter. Thanks to Edwin Groot for noticing this.

50 De Wilde states in 7 feet – 3.04 metres – the length of the pole for the Dutch infantry ensign; see in 'De Mannen van 1688', in *Armamentaria* 23.

51 Nimwegen, *The Dutch Army*, p. 324.

Another less investigated source is contained in the aforementioned Boxel's *Vertoogh* printed in 1673. The text reports a short description of infantry flags, like the one of the Scottish regiment *Kirckpatrick* (I-15): 'yellow and blue divided in four' and more flags of 17 different regiments.[52] It was also possible that some figures were placed on the flag, like the provinces' coats of arms and the Saint Andrew cross, as appeared on the ensigns of the Scottish regiments in Dutch service in more recent periods.

When Prince William III reserved the orange colour for his guard regiments exclusively, the States of Friesland ordered that their regiments should carry blue ensigns,[53] but the other provinces seem to have chosen any distinctive colours, and the order was not received universally, because in 1674 at Seneffe, the Friesland's regiments *Aylva* (I-2) and *Schwartsenberg* (1-24) carried red-white and black-red flags respectively.[54] Usually the infantry flags present just one colour, but in some cases there are flags with 'flames' or geometrical partitions of two colours. The pattern could vary in the extreme.. An infantry ensign dated 1680s consists of 17 horizontal stripes, alternately blue and yellow,[55] while the flag of the regiment *Beaumont* (I-28) in 1690 is documented as white with large red-blue flames, and of yellow with smaller flames of the same colours. Usually the flames are disposed like a wheel in eight parts, but in several later ensigns there appear just four flames turning to the flag's corners.

The Dutch ensigns follow the traditional heraldic rules and often display the history of the owner's family. This is well represented in the flag of the Foot Guards. The regiment assumed this title in 1672, when William III was appointed as captain-general. This regiment is the founding regiment of the present day Dutch *Garde-Grenadiers* and can date their lineage to 1572, the year in which the States General offered the regiment to the Prince of Orange. Originally, the flag was yellow, then the ensigns became orange in 1672. Decoration and figures remained possibly the same. The original sources depict the flag decorated with laurel, grenades, and lightning; other notable emblems are the crowned 'W' and the orange apples. In the centre, there is a blue ribbon with the motto of the Order of the Garter. Inside the ribbon, there is the red cross on a white field.

Similar heraldic quotes appear on the flag of the infantry regiment of Hendrik Casimir of Nassau (I-27), a regiment of Friesland, which was always led by the Frisian Stadtholders. On this flag, the decorations are in

52 Boxel, *Vertoogh van de Kryghs-Oeffeninge*, pp. 27–28.

53 However, for the regiment Aylva yellow and blue ensigns are known in 1690.

54 J.K.M. Bottema, in his article *Vaandels van het Staatsche Leger*, describes for regiment Aylva, a different flag: 'Regiment Aylva, a descendant of the regiment Rennenberg of 1577, and predecessor of the present day regiment Johan Willem Friso (1st Regiment of Infantry), flew a blue flag, covered with twisting rays from the centre in white. The white centrepiece was set within a silver laurel, with a silver monogram within the laurel. In the left upper corner the Frisian weapon in blue and yellow.' 'Nederlandse Vereniging ter Beoefening van de Militaire Historie', in *Mars et Historia*, October 1972 (4).

55 *Ibid.*, Colonel Bottema (1913–1997) performed a distinguished military career as teacher of the Dutch Royal Military Academy. His article was published when Jean Belaubre and Frans Gerarrd de Wilde were working on their books. Thanks to Edwin Groot for this and the previous notice.

86. Reconstruction of the ensign belonging to the Civic Guard of Kampen, Overijssel, dated 1672.

gold, except for the lining of the crown, which is light red, the sunrays are yellow with red flames and the crosses are lined in black. The monogram of the Prince, Hendrik Casimir of Nassau appears on the flag as well.

Again, the coeval iconography contributes to forming a more detailed scenario. Several flags and standards are reproduced in the paintings of military scenes. Although it is not always possible to establish with certainty to which unit some ensigns belong, a deep investigation may reserve significant results. The painting of Pieter Wouwerman representing the storming of Coevorden, which occurred in December 1672, shows five infantry flags, and one cavalry standard. On the right, there are two flags, a yellow one and a green one, big enough to be examined. The first flag is similar to the 1690 flag of *Stad en Lande* infantry regiment, captured by the French in 1690.[56] In 1620, this regiment was known as *Oranje-Stad*, but from 1625 to 1633 became *Nassau-Stad en Lande*. The regiment is obviously recorded with the name of the colonel, except for the period 1680–1696, when it was called again *Nassau-Stad en Lande*. This clue leads to the regiment *Rabenhaupt* (I-6), which was composed mostly of the storming force at Coevorden.[57] The flags carry Groeningen's coat of arms in the upper corner close to the pole, and traces of golden decorations appear on the green flags, while the yellow one has a sea-green strip in the middle. This is a strong evidence that ordinary companies' ensigns could be of different colours, at least until December 1672.

Regarding the cavalry standards, most appear reproduced in the plan of the review of Ath and just a small group come from the collection of war trophies. As for the infantry, the white ensigns identified the colonel's company, while the coloured ones belonged to the ordinary companies. Illustrations of cavalry standards captured in 1690 show that the colonel's ensign was in the form of a guidon with either two or one single tail.[58] The size was approximately 65x65 centimetres and the edge was fringed in gold or alternated with the standard's colour. The coat of arms of the province was usually the main symbol, and as with the infantry ensigns, further figures were reproduced on one side; the most common are the armoured right arm, arrows, animals, allegorical symbols, and even landscapes. Cavalry standards are quite rare in the contemporary paintings, and a red one appears in the aforementioned Pieter Wouverman's painting of the storming of Coevorden, unfortunately it is undecipherable. As far as we know, dragoons guidons were slightly larger than the cavalry standards, longer in the fly, and swallow-tailed; the tips were usually rounded.

Flags are often reproduced in the portraits of the civic guards, but a few belong to the period 1660–87. It remains difficult to form a general overview

56 *Les Triomphes de Louis XIV*, plates 3d and 6d.

57 The analysis of the painting had been executed by Edwin Groot and posted on his website 'Anno Domini 1672' on 24 May 2009.

58 *Les Triomphes de Louis XIV*, plates 191 and 192, regiment *Nassau-Saarbrücken* (C 22) and *Heyden* (C-16).

for these ensigns, which almost never followed a pre-established rule and usually reproduced coats of arms or emblems of the city. However, in one case, an actual militia flag of 1675 is known thanks to the record preserved in the Municipal Museum of Kampen. The museum owns a flag presented by Stadholder William V to the city's Cadet Corps in 1769. When Prince William visited the town in 1766, he did not bring a fitting flag, so he handed the Corps an old flag, given to the Kampen Free Company by William III in 1675. The promised new flag was delivered only in 1769. This episode represents a very special event, because the reverse side of this new flag shows an officer of the Corps who bears the 1675 flag. It is white, with the Kampen crowned municipal coat of arms and the motto PRAEMIUM VIGILANTAE (Reward for Vigilance). The Free Company was disbanded after William III's death, but William V's gift offers us a unique and rare source for a 1670s early flag.[59]

59 Thanks to Mats Eltzinga for this notice.

Appendix I

Orders of Battle and Army Lists

Seneffe, 11 August 1674

Kapitein-Generaal Prince William of Orange

Gardes van Zijne Hoogheid (c-i)	1 sqn
Gardes du Corps (c-ii)	1
Nassau Dragonders (d-i)	1
Gardes te Paard (C-25)	3
Coerland Dragonders (D-1)	3

Right wing

Veld-Marschalk Count Johan Maurits van Nassau-Siegen

Cavalry commander: *Generaal van Cavalerie* Georg Frederik van Nassau

Cavalry Brigade *Luitenant-Generaal van Cavalerie* Reede van Ginkel van Athlone

Nassau (C11)	3 sqn
Ginkel (C-10)	3
Langerack (C-21)	3
Obdam (C-12)	3
Coerland (C-30)	3
Flodorff (C-29)	3

Cavalry Brigade *Luitenant-Generaal van Cavalerie* Maurits Lodewijk I van Nassau-La Leck

Mountpouillon (C-26)	3 sqn
La Leck (C-3)	3
's Gravemoer (C-1)	3
Hoorenbergh (C-31)	3
Cronenburg (C-15)	3

Infantry commander: *Luitenant-Generaal van de Infanterie* Baron Hans Willem van Aylva

Infantry Brigade *Majoor General* Hendrik Trajectinus van Solms-Braunfels

Gardes te voet (I-8)	3 bat
Prins Maurits (I-45)	1
Limburg-Bronkhorst (I-13)	1
Salm (I-43)	1
Villamair (I-9)	1
Graaf Maurits (I-31)	1
Stockeijm (I-61)	1
Birkenfeld (I-59)	1
Torck (I-38)	1

Infantry Brigade *Majoor General* George Johan de Weede van Walenburg

Aylva (I-2)	2 bat
Fariaux (I-32)	1
Weede (mariniers) (I-44)	1
Thouars (I-84)	1
Amama (I-33)	1
Schwartsembergh (I-24)	2
Marnout (?)	1
Cassiopijn (I-42)	2

Left wing

Veld-Marschalk Georg Friedrich von Waldeck-Pyrmont

Cavalry commander: *Luitenant-Generaal van Cavalerie* Ludolf van Steenhuyzen van Heumen

Cavalry Brigade *Majoor General* Johan Theodor Metzger van Weybnom

Waldeck (C-9)	3 sqn
Steenhuysen (C-8)	3
Weybnum (C-33)	3
Well (C-32)	3
Emminghuysen (C-27)	3
Brederode (C-33)	3

Cavalry Brigade *Majoor General* Ludwig Christian von Wittgenstein

Nassau-Friesland (C-20)	3 sqn
Wittgenstein (C-28)	3
Nassau (*Lippe*) (C-22)	3
Kingma (C-24)	3
Schellart (C-16)	2

Infantry Brigade *Majoor General* Mathijs Asperen van Heeswijk

Waldeck (I-3)	2 bat
Heeswijk (I-1)	2
Sedlenitsky (I-40)	1
Marion (I-16)	1
Brantswart (I-37)	1
Burmania (I-58)	1
Holstein (I-88)	1
Palm (I-39)	1
Polents (I-62)	1

Infantry Brigade *Majoor General* Georg von Erbach

Erbach (I-49)	1 bat
Hockinga (I-48)	2
Eybergen (I-77)	2
Veersen (I-60)	1
Velpet (*Lüneburg*) (I-87)	1
Leendorp (I-89)	1
Amerongen (I-86)	1
Cotwal (I-95)	1

Source: J. Bosscha, *Neĕrlands Heldendaden te land*, vol. 2; pp. 664–668, after *Van Battaille van't Leger van sijn Hoogh. D'Heer Prince van Orange*, Koninklijke Bibliotheek, The Hague.

Infantry officer and NCO casualties

	Regiment	Dead	Wounded	Prisoners
I-8	*Gardes te Voet*	5	16	24
I-31	*Prins Maurits*	2	6	13
I-45	*Graaf Maurits*	-	5	18
I-33	*Amama*	4	7	1
I-39	*Palm*	11	2	4
I-44	*Walenburgh*	2	12	30
I-61	*Stockheim*	2	11	18
I-84	*Thouars*	1	5	18
I-9	*Villaumaire*	3	5	1
I-42	*Cassiopijn*	1	1	9
I-38	*Torck*	3	1	2
I-59	*Birkenfeld*	4	2	-
I-62	*Polentz*	7	5	5
I-32	*Fariaux*	5	8	15

I-89	*Lehndorf*	-	5	5
I-87	*Ulfsparre*	2	14	-
I-60	*Veerssen*	1	1	3
I-48	*Gockinga*	1	-	-
I-88	*Holstein*	1	-	-
I-49	*Erbach*	1	2	-
I-77	*Eybergen*	1	8	-
I-43	*Rijngrave*	3	9	3
I-40	*Sedlnitzky*	2	12	-
I-24	*Schwartzenberg*	1	6	17
I-2	*Aylva*	-	2	13
I-24	*Burmania*	-	-	1

Source: J.M.G. Leune, *Staatse infanteristen die gedood werden, gewond raakten en gevangen werden genomen tijdens de Slag bij Seneffe op 11 augustus 1674.*

Siege of Grave (29 July–27 October 1674)

In mid-August there were the following cavalry regiments: *Schwartsenburg* (C-17), *Amama*(?), *Wittgenstein* (C-28), *Burum*(?), two companies of *Wrangel*(?) regiment, 2 Groningen companies, 6 Spaniards and 12 companies of Brandenburg.

The foot regiments are described as follows:

Rabenhaupt (I-6)	12 coy
Golstein (I-52)	12 coy
Beaumont (I-28)	12 coy
Nieulant (I-19)	12 coy
Dutil (I-56)	6 coy
Klooster (I-23)	12 coy
Uilenburg (I-9)	11 coy
Lutzow (I-92)	12 coy
Lange (I-98)	11 coy
Hoorn (I-12)	6 coy
Verken (?)	5 coy
Hundebeek (I-67)	11 coy
Stek (?)	6 coy
Wagenheim (I-97)	12 coy
Wijnbergen (I-99)	9 coy
Hendrik Casimir (I-27)	10 coy
Coerland (I-93)	12 coy
Holstein (I-88)	5 coy
Frits of Nassau (I-54)	12 coy

2 companies from the town of Bommel and two from St-Andries.

Total 192 companies for an estimated strength of 16.000 men, 15 guns and 3 mortars.

Source: W.J. Knoop, *Krijgs- en geschiedkundige beschouwingen over Willem den derde, 1672–1697* (Schiedam, 1895).

Order of Battle at Mont Cassel, 11 April 1677

Right Wing

Sompembrough (C1)
Waldeck (C9)
Nassau (C-3)
Holstein (I-88)
Gardes te voet (I-8)
Hoorn (C-31)
Gardes du Prince (C25)
Lippe (C-22)
Grim (I-5)
Regiment de Zelande (I-36)
Cassiopijn (I-42)
Klooster (I-23)
Uyttenhove (I-11)

Centre

Alua (I-2)
Vanep (I-93?)
Lavergne (I-86)
Zobel (I-50)
Toursay (I-21)
Cronenbourg (C-15)
Zelande (C-29)
Grickel (C-10)
Oremberg (C-31)
Slangenburg (I-32)
Howege/Hoorn (I-26)
Jemma (I-45?)
Guinzel (I-89)

Left Wing

Kirchpatrick (I-15)
Albransvart (I-37)
Brederode (C-4)
Gardes de M. le Prince (C-20)
Vabenon (C-27)
Dragons de Prince d'Orange (D1)

Other regiments not included in the order of battle: *Waldeck* (I-3); *Brandenburg* (I-89); *Birkenfeld* (I-59); *Rijngraaf* (I-43) *Vrijbergen* (I-35), *Maregnault* (I-34) and *Thouars* (I-84).

Source: reconstruction after P.J.E. de Smyttere, 'La Bataille de Val-de-Cassel', Hazebroeck, 1865, and J.M.G. Leune, *Omgekomen, gewonde en gevangengenomen Staatse officieren tijdens de Slag bij Mont-Cassel (1677).*

Officer casualties

	Regiment	Dead	Wounded	Prisoners
C-25	*Gardes te Paard*	2	2	-
D-1	*Garde Dragonders*	1	-	
C-9	*Waldeck*	-	1	1
C-4	*Brederode*	3	-	-
C-31	*Hoornberg*	1	4	3
C-10	*Ginckel*	-	2	1
C-27	*Eppe*	-	1	-
C-22	*Van der Lippe*	1	1	2
C-29	*Flodorf*	1	-	-
I-8	*Gardes te voet*	6	19	1
I-45	*Prins Maurits*	2	1	3
I-88	*Holstein*	8	5	7
I-86	*La Vergnie*	1	2	5
I-15	*Kirckpatrick*	4	2	1
I-11	*Uyttenhove*	1	-	4
I-44	*Walenburgh*	1	4	3
I-21	*Torsay*	2	1	-
I-89	*Brandenburg*	9	5	1
I-59	*Birkenfeld*	3	2	1
I-3	*Waldeck*	1	-	-
I-23	*Klooster*	1	-	-
I-5	*Graham*	5	1	-
I-26	*Hofwegen*	2	2	-
I-50	*Zobel*	2	-	1
I-37	*Albrandsweerd*	1	-	-
I-32	*Slangenburgh*	1	1	-
I-84	*Thouars*	1	3	1
I-43	*Rijngraaf*	1	1	2
-	*Other officers*	4	1	2

Source: J.M.G. Leune, *Omgekomen, gewonde en gevangengenomen Staatse officieren tijdens de Slag bij Mont-Cassel (1677)* after P.J.E. de Smyttere, 'La Bataille de Val-de-Cassel', Hazebroeck, 1865.

Infantry regiments mustered between January and August 1676

	Regiment	Companies	Effective strength in rank and file	Officers	Sick
I-8	*Gardes the Voet*	25	1,648		
I-31	*Maurits van Nassau-Siegen*	13	799		
I-3	*Waldeck*	12	762		
I-2	*Aylva*	12	608		22
I-43	*Rijngraaf*	12	762		
I-12	*Willem Horne*	13	662		114
I-15	*Kirkpatrik*	12	636		
I-33	*Limburg-Stirum*	12	570		
I-49	*Erbach*	12	690		60
I-1	*Asperen*	10	418		
I-77	*Watteville*	12	674		
I-44	*Weede*	20	980		
I-59	*Birkenfeld*	12	561	114 incl. boys	
I-39	*Johan Horne*	20	1,252		
I-42	*Cassiopijn*	10	567		
I-28	*Beaumont*	10	649		
I-50	*Zobel*	10	550	117	
I-11	*Utenhove*	12	796		
I-100	*Colyear*	12	643		
I-26	*Manmacker*	10	554		
I-9	*de la Grandiere*	13	671		
I-101	*Widdrington*	12	281		
I-102	*Fenwick*	12	476		
I-103	*Lillington*	12	489		
I-60	*Ter Bruggen*	10	488		
I-86	*Lavergne*	12	567		
I-23	*Clooster*	11	489		
I-32	*Slangemburg*	9	573	64	
I-19	*Ingen-Nielant*	8	371		

	Regiment	Companies	Effective strength in rank and file	Officers	Sick
I-67	*Hundebeck*	8	456		
I-77	*Eybergen*	12	622	78	
I-16	*Marion*	10	571		
I-45	*Willem van Nassau-Siegen*	12	710	67	
I-30	*Tamminga*	15	890		
I-48	*Gockinga*	15	876		
I-58	*Burmania*	12	418		
?	*Reish*	9	385		
I-89	*Lehndorf*	12	674		
I-92	*Reuss*	12	400		
I-87	*Osnabrück*	10	415		
I-91	*Eylenburg*	8	297		
I-62	*Brumszen*	10	449		
I-56	*Baye du Theill*	8	384		
I-96	*Horn*	11	515		
I-99	*Wijnbergen*	10	544		
I-52	*Frederik van Nassau-Siegen*	10	521		
I-5	*Graham*	12	443		
I-84	*Thouars*	12	609		
I-54	*Coeverden*	10	458		
I-37	*Albrandsweerd*	10	455		
I-21	*Torsay*	13	674		
I-51	*Stecke*	12	454		
I-69	*Frentz*	12	701		
I-40	*Sedlnitzky*	12	618		
I-36	*Schotte*	12	762		
I-34	*Mauregnault*	13	821		
I-35	*Vrijbergen*	12	742		

Source: O. Nimwegen, *The Dutch Army*, pp. 530–531.

Infantry and Cavalry Regiments mustered 9 July 1677

	Infantry	Companies	Total (rank and file)
I-8	*Gardes te voet*	25	1,899
I-3	*Waldeck*	12	775
I-49	*Erbach*	12	743
I-77	*Watteville*	12	674
I-39	*Johan Horne*	20	1,430
I-101	*Mc Dowell*	12	654
I-103	*Bellasyse*	12	493
I-102	*Westley*	12	604
I-100	*Colyear*	12	786
I-37	*Albrandsweerd*	10	655
I-59	*Birkenfeld*	12	785
I-62	*Brumszen*	10	483
I-44	*Weede*	12	753
I-52	*Nassau-Ottweiler*	12	764
I-43	*Rijngraaf*	12	772
I-91	*Heemstra*	11	699
I-16	*Marion*	10	616
I-9	*de la Grandiere*	13	910
I-23	*Clooster*	11	661
I-40	*Sedlnitzky*	12	751
I-42	*Cassiopijn*	10	673
I-2	*Aylva*	12	634
I-28	*Beaumont*	10	600
	Cavalry & dragoons	**Companies**	**Total (rank and file)**
D-1	*Gardes Dragonders*	10	707
d-i	*Nassau Dragonders*	1	142
D-2	*Brandt Dragonders*	8	579
c-i	*Gardes du Corps*	1	140
C-24	*Gardes te Paard*	6	327
C-12	*Nassau*	6	230
C-1	*'s Gravenmoer*	6	340
C-29	*Flodroff*	6	279
C-4	*Brederode*	6	301
d-i	*Truchsess*	6	299

:-31	*Holtzappel*	6	322
:-30	*Coerland*	6	334
:-20	*Prins van Nassau*	6	277
:-27	*Emminghuysen*	6	339
:-26	*Mountpouillon*	6	336
:-33	*Weybnom*	6	349
:-24	*Kingma*	6	304
:-15	*Croonenburg*	6	333
:-17	*Burum*	6	293
:-32	*Quadt*	6	339
:-11	*Borch*	9	333
:-8	*Sommelsdijk*	7	371
:-28	*Berlo*	3	171
:-16	*Schellart*	6	339

Source: O. Nimwegen, *The Dutch Army*, pp. 532–533.

trength of the Dutch Army 1650–1687

igures estimated before the opening of the campaign)

ear	Infantry	Cavalry & dragoons	Artillery
650	26,415	3,000	-
660	22,000	2,000	-
664	15,000	1,470	-
665	29,000	3,500	-
670	34,000	3,200	-
672	69,000	11,300	-
673	52,000	10,500	-
674	58,000	10,000	-
675	59,400	9,800	
676	60,000	10,200	1,050
678	59,000	9,050	1,110
681	38,000	3,350	540
687	40,000	3,400	540
687	40,000	3,400	540

Source: *Ibidem*, pp. 532–533.

Appendix II

Companies, Squadrons and Regiments, 1660–1687

Infantry Companies

	Raised	Denomination	Province	Nat.	Engagements	Uniforms	History
i-i	1631	*Gardes Friesland*	Friesland	-	Dijlerschans (1664)	(1680s)[1] Private: indigo blue coat with red cuffs and lining, red waistcoat, bearskin cap with red bag piped silver. Officer: as above with silver buttons and lace on buttonholes.	Disbanded 1801
i-ii	1640	*Gardes Groningen*	Groningen	-		(1690)[2] Private: indigo blue coat with red cuffs and lining.	Disbanded 1801

Infantry Regiments

	Raised	Colonel or Denomination	Province	Nat.	Engagements	Uniforms	History
I-1	1572	**1654** Adriaan van der Mijll van Alblasserdam, Dubbeldam en Bleskensgraaf **1664** Mathijs Asperen van Heeswijk	Holland	-		-	Disbanded 1678
I-2	1577	**1659** Hans Willem van Aylva	Friesland	-	Dijlerschans (1664) Tolhuis (1672) Seneffe (1674)	(1686)[3] Private: light grey coat, dark blue facings. Musician, NCO and Officer: dark blue coat.	*Nationale Regt. 17* in 1772
I-3	1586	**1658** Frederik Nassau-Zuylenstein **1672** Georg Friedrich von Waldeck-Pyrmont Culemborg	Gelderland, later Holland	-	Dijlerschans (1664)	(1686)[4] Private: madder red coat.	Reformed in 1752 as 2nd battalion of Regt. *Kinschot*
I-4	1593	**1640** William Craven	Holland	English		-	Licensed 1665

	Raised	Colonel or Denomination	Province	Nat.	Engagements	Uniforms	History
I-5	1595	**1639** James Erskine **1665** Walter Scott of Balwaery **1673** Henry Graham **1677** Hugh Mackay	Gelderland	Scottish	Mont Cassel (1677)	(1686)[5] Private: madder red coat with pale blue facings. (1687)[6] Private: madder red coat with pale blue facings, pale blue waistcoat and breeches. Musician: pale blue coat. Officer: carmine coat.	*Nationale Regt. 22* in 1772
I-6	1595	**1646** Wigbolt van Isselmuden **1663** Andolf Clabt **1673** Carl von Rabenhaupt-Sucha **1680** Prins Hendrik Casimir II van Nassau	Groningen	-	Groningen (1672) Grave (1674)	(1687)[7] Private: blue coat with red facings, natural leather waistcoat and breeches, red stockings.	Also known as *Nassau-Stad en Lande* (1680) Disbanded 1752
I-7	1598	**1641** Anthoni van Haersolte	Utrecht	-		-	Disbanded 1668
I-8	1599	**1646** Hendrik Trajectinus van Solms **1674** *Gardes te voet van Zijne Hoogheid Prins Willem III* (Garde Oranjen)	Gelderland, then Holland	-	Dijlerschans (1664) Woerden (1672) Seneffe (1674) Mont Cassel (1676) Saint Denis (1678)	(1674-75)[8] Private: black hat with black silk piping, dark blue coat with ochre yellow (mustard) cuffs and lining, ochre yellow waistcoat, breeches and stockings, brass buttons. (1686)[9] Private: dark blue coat with yellow (mustard) cuffs Cadet: light grey coat with medium blue cuffs.	3 bat. in 1674. 1702 *Hollandsche Gardes*
I-9	1599	**1665** Pierre Durfort d'Autiège **1668** Maximilien de Beringen Arminvilliers **1672** Maurice de Maurier-Villamair **1674** Nicolas de la Grandiere **1674** Guillaume de Rocque-Cervière **1678** Daniel de Tassin de Torsay	Holland and Zealand	French then national	Seneffe (1674) Mont Cassel (1677)	(1686)[10] Private: blue coat with yellow facings. NCO and officer: grey coat with blue facings.	*Nationale Regt.* 5 in 1772

	Raised	Colonel or Denomination	Province	Nat.	Engagements	Uniforms	History
I-10	1599	**1647** William Killingrew	Holland	English		-	Licensed 1665
I-11	1600	**1644** Johan van Beveren **1673** Gerrit van Uytenhove **1679** Frederik Lodewijk van Nassau-Ottweiler	Holland	Walloon	(1674) Martinique	(1674)[11] Ensign: black feathered grey hat with red strap and lace, indigo blue coat with carmine cuffs laced white, carmine waistcoat and breeches, tin buttons, white cravat. (1686)[12] Private: light grey coat with dark red facings; brass buttons; Musician, NCO and officer: crimson coat; red sash for officers.	Also known as *Walen* Reformed 1795
I-12	1602	**1641** Johan Graaf van Horne 1663 Matthijs Drost 1667 Willem Adriaan Graaf Horne	Holland	-	Grave (1674)	-	*Nationale Regt.* 8 in 1772
I-13	1602	**1659** Otto Graaf van Limburg-Bronkhorst 1679 Willem van Bulow	Gelderland	-	Dijlerschans (1664)	(1686)[13] Private: light grey coat, azure-blue facings, tin buttons. (1687)[14] Private: dark blue coat, cuffs linings and breeches, brass buttons. Officer: buff coat lined crimson.	Also known as *Oranje-Geldern* Reformed 1795
I-14	1602	**1649** Maurice de Hallart **1661** Jean Barton de Bret de Montbas **1668** George le Vasseur Seigneur de Huyle et Thouars	Holland	French		-	Disbanded 1675
I-15	1603	**1639** John Kirckpatrick 1684 Barthold Balfour	Holland	Scottish	Grave (1674) Mont Cassel (1677) Saint Denis (1678)	(1686)[15] Private: madder red coat and cuff.	*Nationale Regt.* 23 in 1772

	Raised	Colonel or Denomination	Province	Nat.	Engagements	Uniforms	History
I-16	1605	**1642** John Cromwell **1663** Thomas Dolman **1672** Ferdinand Cary **1673** Johan Hendrik van Marion (Mario) **1678** Otto van Gent van Meynderswijk	Holland, later Gelderland	English until 1665	Maastricht (1673) Seneffe (1674)	(1660s)[16] Private: red coat.	Disbanded 1678
I-17	1615	**1639** François de Laubespine de Hauterive-Châteauneuf	Holland	French		-	Disbanded 1674
I-18	1616	**1654** Robert Sidney	Holland	English		-	Licensed 1665
I-19	1622	**1668** Johan Ingen-Nielant **1678** Joachim Gent van Meynderswijk **1682** Filips van Essen van Vanenburg	Gelderland	-	Dijlerschans (1664) Grave (1674)	(1689)[17] Private: grey-white coat, yellow lining and facings, tin buttons.	*Nationale Regt.* 6 in 1772
I-20	1623	**1657** Hendrik van Tuyll van Bulkesteijn	Holland	-		-	Disbanded 1672
I-21	1625	**1641** Louis Godefroy d'Estrades **1668** Daniel de Tassin de Torsay	Holland	French	Mont Cassel (1677)	-	Disbanded 1678
I-22	1626	**1641** Wigbold van der Does van Noordwijk	Holland	-		-	Colonel van der Does was also *Meester-Generaal* of the artillery. Disbanded 1672

	Raised	Colonel or Denomination	Province	Nat.	Engagements	Uniforms	History
I-23	1632	**1659** Arent van Haersolte **1662** Arent Jurrien van Haersolte **1673** Christoffer van Voorst tot Averberghe **1674** Hendrik van den Clooster **1678** Filips Otto van Coeverden	Overijssel	-	Grave (1674) Mont Cassel (1677) Saint Denis (1678)	(1686)[18] Private: light grey coats with madder red facings, brass buttons. Musicians: crimson coat.	*Nationale Regt. 20* in 1772
I-24	1633	**1660** George Wolfgang van Schwartsenberg en Hohenlansberg **1674** Watzo van Burmania	Friesland	-	Dijlerschans (1664) Bentheim (1674) Seneffe (1674)		Disbanded 1752
I-25	1634	**1658** Louis Taillefer de Moriac	Holland?	French		-	Disbanded 1674
I-26	1635	Lodewijk van Nassau van Beverweerd **1665** Filips van Steelandt **1668** Manmacker van Hofvegen	Holland	-	Mont Cassel (1677)	(1686)[19] Private: dark blue coats and breeches, blue cuff, brass buttons. Officers: red coat.	Disbanded 1717
I-27	1639	**1649** Ernst van Aylva **1666** Hendrik Casimir II van Nassau-Friesland	Friesland	-	Seneffe (1674) Grave (1674)	(1678)[20] Private: blue coat, red cuffs and breeches. (1689)[21] Private: blue coat, red cuffs and linings.	1702 *Oranje-Friesland*, *Nationale Regt. 14* in 1772
I-28	1643	*Gardes te voet van de Staten van Holland* **1674** Johan van Beaumont	Holland	-	Naarden (1672) Maastricht (1673)	(1680)[22] Private: grey coat, dark blue cuffs, lining, waistcoat and breeches; tin buttons. (1689)[23] Private: red coat with black facings.	Also known as *Oude Gardes* Disbanded 1748
I-29	1647	Ernst van Ittersum van de Oosterhof	Overijssel	-	Dijllerschans (1664)	-	Disbanded 1672

	Raised	Colonel or Denomination	Province	Nat.	Engagements	Uniforms	History
I-30	1647	**1658** Eppo Gockinga **1667** Wigbolt Broersma **1672** Sweer van Tamminga **1681** Hendrik Losecaat	Groningen	-	Groningen (1672) Grave (1674) Maastricht (1676)	-	1752 *Regiment Oranje Stad en Lande en Drenthe*
I-31	1655	Adriaan Cuyck van Meteren **1673** Johan Maurits van Nassau-Siegen (*Graaf Maurits*) **1679** Samuel de Lannoy	Holland	-	Seneffe (1674)	(1686)[24] Private: light grey coat and facings, brass buttons. Musician: blue coat with light grey facings.	Disbanded 1723
I-32	1660	Lewis Erskine **1673** Jacques de Fariaux **1675** Frederik Johan van Baer van de Slangenburg	Holland	Scottish until 1665	Maastricht (1673) Seneffe (1674) Mont Cassel (1677)	(1686)[25] Private: light grey coat and facings.	Disbanded 1723
I-33	1664	Duco van Hemmema **1667** Gerrit Amama **1678** Allart Polman **1679** Frederik Willem Albert van Limburg-Stirum en Bronkhorst **1683** George Albert van Limburg-Stirum en Bronkhorst	Friesland, Groningen and Drenthe later Friesland	-	Seneffe (1674)	(1686)[26] Private: light grey with blue facings, tin buttons.	Disbanded 1752
I-34	1664	Gaspard de Mauregnault **1680** Jaques Louis de Noyelles	Zealand	-	Seneffe (1674) Mont Cassel (1677) Saint Denis (1678)	(1686)[27] Private: light grey coat and facings, brass buttons. Musician: blue coats with light grey facings.	*Nationale Regt. 10* in 1772

	Raised	Colonel or Denomination	Province	Nat.	Engagements	Uniforms	History
I-35	1664	Theodorus van Vrijbergen **1681** Walrad van Nassau-Saarbrücken	Zealand	-	Chatham (1667) New York (1673) Martinique (1674) Mont Cassel (1677) Saint Denis (1678)	(1667)[28] Some private musketeers wear dark grey hat with red lace and ribbon, ash grey coat and breeches, red stockings, white cravat. Officer: black hat with white plumes, dark grey coat and breeches, black stockings. (1671)[29] Private: dark blue coat with crimson cuffs and stockings, dark blue breeches, white cravat, buff leather equipment. (1674-79)[30] Private: grey coat, dark blue cuffs, grey waistcoat, breeches and stockings. (1680)[31] Private: black hat piped yellow, dark blue coat with white collar and lining, yellow-piped buttonholes, sleeves and pockets, blue breeches, yellow stockings, brass buttons. (1687)[32] Private: as above but dark blue cuffs, natural leather breeches, blue stockings, red cravat.	*Mariniers regiment* Disbanded 1752
I-36	1664	Simon Schotte	Zealand	-	Brugge (1676) Mont Cassel (1677)	(1686)[33] Private: light grey coat with medium blue facings, tin buttons. NCO and musician: medium blue coat with light grey facings. (1687)[34] Private: light grey coat with dark blue facings. Musician: medium blue coat with light grey facings.	Become *mariniers regiment* 1698. Disbanded 1748
I-37	1665	Hartman Godfried van Stein-Callenfels **1672** Johan de Bije van Albrandsweerd **1680** Hendrik van Uytenhove van Amelisweerd	Holland	-	Seneffe (1674)	(1687)[35] Private: light grey coat with dark red facings.	Disbanded 1752

	Raised	Colonel or Denomination	Province	Nat.	Engagements	Uniforms	History
I-38	1665	Louis De Aquila **1673** Hendrik Torck **1674** Gerrad Plos van Amstel **1680** François de Ram van Hagedoorn	Utrecht	-	Seneffe (1674)	(1686)[36] Private: light grey coat with pink facings.	Disbanded 1752
I-39	1665	Willem Joseph van Ghent **1672** François Palm **1674** Johan Belgicus van Horne van Boxel	Holland	-	Woerden (1672) Naarden (1673) Seneffe (1674)	(1674-79)[37] Private: grey coat, dark blue cuffs, grey waistcoat, breeches and stockings. (1686)[38] Private: light grey coat and breeches, dark red cuffs, brass buttons. Musician: crimson coat with white facings.	Became *mariniers regiment* in 1669. *Nationale Regt. 4* in 1772
I-40	1665	Ferdinand de Perchoncher-Sedlnitzky **1687** Filips Carel van Wylich tot Lottum	Zealand	-	Seneffe (1674)	(1691)[39] Private: light grey coat and facings.	Disbanded 1748
I-41	1665	Caspar Richard Hundebeck	Holland	-		-	Disbanded 1668
I-42	1666	Robart van Ittersum **1669** Thomas van Cassiopijn **1682** Meynard de Perceval	Holland	-	Seneffe (1674) Mont Cassel (1677)	(1670s)[40] Private: dark grey coat, blue cuffs and lining, blue breeches and waistcoat.	Become *mariniers regiment* in 1698. Disbanded 1748
I-43	1668	Paulus Wirtz van Orneholm **1674** Karel Florentijn Rijngraaf van Salm **1676** Willem Florentijn Rijngraaf van Salm	Holland	-	Seneffe (1674)	(1686)[41] Private: light grey coat and facings, brass buttons.	Disbanded 1752

	Raised	Colonel or Denomination	Province	Nat.	Engagements	Uniforms	History
I-44	1669	George Johan van Weede van Walenburg	Holland	-	New York (1673) Seneffe (1674) Mont Cassel (1677)	(1673)[42] private: blue-grey coat (1674-79)[43] Private: grey coat, dark blue cuffs, grey waistcoat, breeches and stockings.	*Mariniers regiment*, disbanded 1678
I-45	1671	Unico Ripperda tot Hengelo **1673** Willem Maurits van Nassau-Siegen (Prins Maurits) **1684** Rutger van Haersolte	Utrecht	-	Maastricht (1673) Seneffe (1674) Mont Cassel (1677)	(1686)[44] Private: red coat with light grey facings, tin buttons. Musicians: yellow coat.	Disbanded 1717
I-46	1671	Otto van Gent van Oyen	Holland?	-		-	Disbanded 1672
I-47	1671	Joseph Bampfield	Holland?	-	Gorcum (1672)	-	Disbanded 1673
I-48	1671	Carl von Rabenhaupt-Sucha **1673** Arend Ludolf Gockinga **1686** Barend Johan van Prott	Groningen	-	Coevorden (1672) Bentheim (1674) Seneffe (1674)	-	*Nationale Regt. 2* in 1772
I-49	1671	Johan Nicolaas van Smitsburg **1672** Frederik Hendrik Backum **1673** Georg von Erbach **1678** Hendrik van Delwick	Holland	-	Seneffe (1674) Saint Denis (1678)	(1686)[45] Private: scarlet coat with dark blue facings. NCO: dark blue coat with white cuffs.	Disbanded 1748
I-50	1671	Moïse Pain et Vin **1672** Nicolaas Frederik Zobel	Holland	-	Nieuwerbrug (1672) Mont Cassel (1677)	(1689)[46] Private: ash grey coat.	Disbanded 1748
I-51	1671	Diederick Stecke 1686 Cornelis van Scheltinga	Friesland	-		(1690)[47] Private: red coat with grey cuffs and lining, grey waistcoat, tin buttons	*Nationale Regt. 13* in 1772

	Raised	Colonel or Denomination	Province	Nat.	Engagements	Uniforms	History
I-52	1671	Jacob van Golstein **1674** Frederik Hendrik van Nassau-Siegen **1676** Frederik Lodewijk van Nassau-Ottweiler	Holland and Utrecht	-	Grave (1674)	-	Disbanded 1678
I-53	1671	Filips Jakob van Brempt **1672** Frans Willwm van Nulandt **1672** Filips Remerhuysen van Essen	Utrecht	-		-	Disbanded 1673
I-54	1671	Willem van Brempt **1674** Frederik Hendrik von Nassau-Siegen **1675** Filips Otto van Coeverden	Holland, later Zealand and Utrecht	-	Maastricht (1673) Grave (1674) Saint Denis (1678)	-	Disbanded in 1678
I-55	1672	Hannibal von Degenfeld	Holland	-		-	Disbanded 1673, merged with *Birkenfeld* (I-59)
I-56	1672	Paul de Baye du Theill	Utrecht	-	Grave (1674) Maastricht (1676)	(1686)[48] Private: light grey coat, blue facings.	*Nationale Regt. 11* in 1772
I-57	1672	Karel Florentijn Rijngraaf van Salm	Holland	-	Woerden(1672) Seneffe (1674)	-	Disbanded 1674, become the second bat. of the *Garde Oranjen* (I-8)
I-58	1672	Watzo van Burmania (**1674–1685** vacant) 1686 Julius Beyma	Friesland	-	Bentheim (1674)	(1690)[49] Private: scarlet coat and cuffs, white stockings, tin buttons.	*Nationale Regt. 1* in 1772

	Raised	Colonel or Denomination	Province	Nat.	Engagements	Uniforms	History
I-59	1672	Jan Albert Jorman **1673** Johan Karel van Birkenfeld	Holland	-	Groningen (1672) Seneffe (1674) Mont Cassel (1677)	(1678)[50] Private: light grey coat with red cuffs and lining, red breeches and stockings. (1686)[51] Private: light grey coat with madder red facings, brass buttons. Musicians and NCO: crimson coats	*Nationale Regt. 7* in 1772
I-60	1672	Laurens van Veersen **1674** Willem Ter Bruggen **1681** Hendrik Casimir van Nassau-Friesland (colonelcy vacant until 1696), known also as Drenthe	Drenthe	-	Seneffe (1674);	(1674-76)[52] NCO: grey hat with yellow-blue ribbon, red coat with blue cuffs, white lacing, white metal breast armour, blue waistcoat and breeches, red stockings, brass buttons. (1686)[53] Private: light grey coat, dark red facings, tin buttons. NCO and Musician: dark red coat. (1687)[54] Private: medium blue coat, carmine red facings, tin buttons. Musician: blue coat.	1730 *Oranje-Drenthe*; Disbanded 1752
I-61	1672	Johan van Stockheim **1674** Hendrik van Weede	Utrecht	-	Seneffe (1674)	(1686)[55] Private: scarlet coat, pale blue facings, brass buttons. Musician: pale blue coat.	1752, merged with Regiment *le Croyé*
I-62	1672	Willem van Polentz **1674** Leo Frederik van Brumszen **1683** Gustaav Carlson van Bornig-Lintholm **1680** Hans Wolf van Groben **1685** Lodewijk Frederik van Auer	Overijssel	-	Seneffe (1674)	(1686)[56] Private: light grey coat with dark blue facings, brass buttons. Musician: dark blue coat.	Disbanded 1748
I-63	1672	Bernhard von Schleswig-Holstein-Plön	Friesland	-	Groningen (1672)	-	1673, merged with *Holstein-Norburg* (I-88)
I-64	1672	Martin de Manger	Utrecht	-		-	Disbanded 1673
I-65	1672	Dirk van Haeften van Verwolde	Gelderland	-		-	Disbanded 1673

	Raised	Colonel or Denomination	Province	Nat.	Engagements	Uniforms	History
I-66	1672	Jaohann van der Laan	Overijssel	-		-	Disbanded 1673
I-67	1672	Caspar Richard Hundebeck	Holland, later Zealand and Utrecht	-	Grave (1674)	-	Disbanded 1678
I-68	1672	John Scott	Gelderland	-		-	Disbanded 1672
I-69	1672	Ico Gerard Frentz	Holland	-		-	Disbanded 1678
I-70	1672	Assuerus van de Boetzelaer **1676** Charles de Lannoy- **1677** Hendrik van Delwich van Wiebendorf	Gelderland?			-	Disbanded 1678
I-71	1672	Gustaaf van Wittgenstein	Holland	-		-	Disbanded 1673
I-72	1672	Frederik Fagnani	Holland	-		-	Disbanded 1675
I-73	1672	Louis François de Grisperre	Holland	-		-	Disbanded 1673
I-74	1672	Jacob Winkelman	Zealand	-	Since 1674 garrison duty in Surinam	-	Disbanded 1678
I-75	1672	Dionisius Oriordan	Holland	-		-	Disbanded 1673
I-76	1672	Godfried van Straeten	Holland	-		-	Disbanded 1673

	Raised	Colonel or Denomination	Province	Nat.	Engagements	Uniforms	History
I-77	1672	Konrad Christoph von Königsmarck **1673** Frederik van Eybergen **1676** David de Watteville	Groningen, later Overijssel	-	Groningen (1672) Coevorden (1672) Seneffe (1674)	(1672)[57] Private: blue coat.	Disbanded 1678
I-78	1672	Frederick Backer	Zealand	-		-	Disbanded 1678
I-79	1672	Johan Urs de Byss	Holland	-		-	Disbanded 1673
I-80	1672	Floris van Dam van Audignies	Holland	-		-	Disbanded 1673
I-81	1672	Alexander Colins d'Aheree	Zealand	-			Disbanded 1675
I-82	1672	Maximilian Albertus Spindler **1676** Alexander Colins d'Aheree	Zealand	-	Maastricht (1676)	-	Disbanded 1678
I-83	1672	Nicolaas Laurin	Holland	-		-	Disbanded 1674
I-84	1672	George le Vasseur de Huyle et Thouars	Holland	-	Seneffe (1674) Mont Cassel (1677)	-	Disbanded 1677
I-85	1672	Bonstetten	Holland	Swiss		-	Contract deleted
I-86	1673	Godard Adriaan van Reede van Amerongen **1674** Ferdinand de la Verne de Rodes (or Lavergne) **1685** François Nicolaas Fagel	Holland	-	Seneffe (1674) Mont Cassel (1677)	(1673)[58] Private: red coat with blue facings. (1686)[59] Private: scarlet coat with yellow facings, brass buttons. NCO and Musician: yellow coat.	Disbanded 1752

	Raised	Colonel or Denomination	Province	Nat.	Engagements	Uniforms	History
I-87	1673	Gustaaf Ulfsparre **1675** Friedrich August von Braunschweig Lüneburg-Osnabrück	Utrecht	-	Seneffe (1674)	(1686)[60] Private: scarlet coat with yellow facings, brass buttons. NCO and Musician: yellow coat with scarlet facings.	Disbanded 1752
I-88	1673	Rudolf Friedrich von Holstein-Norburg	Holland	-	Seneffe (1674) Grave (1674)	(1674)[61] NCO: black hat with red-white ribbon, red coat with straw yellow cuff white-red laced, red breeches and stockings, straw yellow waistcoat, brass buttons. (1686)[62] Private: light grey coat with madder red facings. NCO and Musician: light crimson coat	Disbanded 1748
I-89	1673	Ahasverius van Lehndorf **1676** Ludwig von Brandenburg-Ansbach **1686** Albrecht Friedrich von Brandenburg-Ansbach	Holland	-	Seneffe (1674)	(1686)[63] Private: ash grey coat, dark blue cuffs and lining, dark blue waistcoat and breeches. Musician: dark blue coat with red cuffs, red waistcoat and breeches. NCO: dark blue coat with red facings; red waistcoat and breeches. Company Officer: ash grey coat, dark blue cuffs and lining, dark blue waistcoat and breeches, dark blue stockings. Senior Officer: crimson coat.	Disbanded 1752
I-90	1673	Melchior van Brodden	Zealand, later Friesland & Groningen	-		-	Disbanded 1675
I-91	1673	George Frederik van Eylenburg **1676** Feijo van Heemstra	Gelderland	-	Grave (1674)	-	Disbanded 1678

	Raised	Colonel or Denomination	Province	Nat.	Engagements	Uniforms	History
I-92	1673	Egidius Christoffel Lutzow **1676** Heinrich IV von Reuss-Plauen	Holland, later Friesland and Groningen	-	Grave (1674)	-	Disbanded 1676
I-93	1673	Friedrich Casimir von Kurland-Semgallen (*Coerland*)	Friesland	Latvian-Polish	Grave (1674) Mont Cassel (1677)	-	Raised by the ruler Duke of Courland. Licensed 1678
I-94	1673	Heinrich IV von Reuss-Plauen	Holland	-	Grave (1674)	-	Disbanded 1676
I-95	1673	François de Courval	Holland	French		-	Formed with deserters from French army. Disbanded 1673
I-96	1673	Carel Christoffel van Horn **1677** Isaaq de Vigny de Warans	Holland	-		(1686)[64] Officer: grey coat, natural leather waistcoat, grey breeches and stockings. Musician: red coat, white cuffs.	Disbanded 1678
I-97	1673	Dominicus Erasmus de Wagenem	Holland	-	Grave (1674)	-	Disbanded 1675
I-98	1673	Christiaan Lange	Utrecht	-	Grave (1674)	-	Disbanded 1675
I-99	1674	Ditmar van Wijnbergen van Horssen	Gelderland	-	Grave (1674)	(1686)[65] Private: light grey coat, carmine facings, tin buttons. NCO and Musician: carmine coat.	Disbanded 1752
I-100	1675	Alexander Colyear **1680** James Douglas **1685** John Wanchope	Gelderland and Holland	Scottish	Mont Cassel (1677) Saint Denis (1678)	(1686)[66] Private: madder red coat with pale blue facings, tin buttons. Musician: pale blue coat. Officers: red coat with blue facings.	*Nationale Regt. 24* in 1783

	Raised	Colonel or Denomination	Province	Nat.	Engagements	Uniforms	History
I-101	1675	William Molyneux-Desnay **1676** Roger Warington (or Widdrington) **1676** Thomas Dolman **1678** Thomas Butler of Ossery **1685** Alexander Canan	Holland	English	Maastricht (1676) Saint Denis (1678)	(1686)[67] Private: red coat with French grey facings.	To England 1689
I-102	1675	Daniel Clare **1675** John Fenwick **1676** Patrick Westley	Holland	English	Maastricht (1676)	(1674)[68] Private: red coat with light green facings. (1686)[69] Private: red coat with pale blue facings. Musician: pale blue coat.	To England 1689
I-103	1675	Henry Lillington **1676** Edward Astely **1677** Henry Bellasyse	Holland	English	Maastricht (1676)	(1674)[70] Private: red coat with yellow facings (1686)[71] Private: madder red coat with pale blue facings. Musician: pale blue coat. Officer: azure coat with red facings.	To England 1689

Artillery

	Raised	Colonel or Denomination	Province	Nat.	Engagement	Uniforms	History
A-1	1677	Regiment *Artillerie*	-	-	Mont Cassel (1677) Saint Denis (1678)	(1670s)[72] Private: grey coat and breeches. (1680s)[73] Private: black hat piped yellow, dark blue coat with red cuffs, blue breeches and stockings, copper buttons, white cravat.	Disbanded 1795

Cavalry Squadrons or Companies

	Raised	Denomination:	Province	Nat.	Engagements	Uniforms	*History*
c-i[74]	1599	**1648** *Eskadron Gardes du Corps* **1660** *Gardes te Paard van de Staten van Zeeland* **1665** *Gardes te Paard van Zijne Hoogheid*	Zealand	-	Seneffe (1674)	(1670s)[75] Private: black hat piped white, scarlet coat with dark blue cuffs, white cravat, scarlet saddle cover laced white. Musician: black hat piped white with red and white plumes, scarlet coat and false sleeves laced yellow, dark blue cuffs, white cravat. Officer: white feathered black cap, scarlet coat with dark blue cuffs, azure sash, scarlet saddle cover laced white. (1686)[76] Private: dark blue coat with white facings, brass buttons, dark blue saddle cover laced yellow.	Also known as *Ouwerkerk* (1672) after the commander, count Hendrik van Nassau-Ouwerkerk. Disbanded 1747
c-ii[77]	1673	*Gardes du Corps van de Staten van Friesland*	Friesland	-	Dijlerschans (1664) Seneffe (1674)	(1673)[78] Private: red cassock with white cross. (1688)[79] Private: black hat piped white, dark blue coat, cuffs and lacing, yellow lace and buttonholes, white cravat, dark blue saddle cover laced yellow.	Disbanded 1795
c-iii[80]	1685	*Eskadron Gardes du Corps*	Holland	-	-	-	Disbanded 1795

Cavalry Regiments

	Raised	Denomination	Province	Nat.	Engagements	Uniforms	History
C-1	1577	**1647** *Gardes te Paard van de Staten van Holland* **1673** Adam van der Duyn van 's Gravenmoer	Holland	-	Seneffe (1674) Mont Cassel (1677) Saint Denis (1678)	(1686)[81] Private: light grey coat with green facings, tin buttons	Become line cavalry in 1672. Merged in 1751 with *Buy Cavalerie*

	Raised	Denomination	Province	Nat.	Engagements	Uniforms	History
C-2	1585	**1635** Frederik Magnus Rijngraaf van Salm	Zealand	-		-	Former cuirassier regiment. Disbanded 1668
C-3	1588	**1641** Cornelis van Aerssen van Sommeldijck **1663** Arent van Wassenaer-Duyvenvoorde **1666** Maurits Lodewijk I van Nassau-La Leck **1683** Everhard Samuel van Lintelo **1684** Gijsbert Ruijsch	Holland	-	Seneffe (1674) Mont Cassel (1677)	(1686)[82] Private: light grey coat and facings.	Disbanded 1720
C-4	1588	**1663** Hendrik van Bentinck van Diepenheim **1666** Rutger van Haersolte **1673** Wolfert van Brederode **1679** Willem Frederik van Nassau-Zuylenstein	Holland	-	Lobith (1672) Seneffe (1674) Mont Cassel (1677)	(1686)[83] Private: light grey coat with pale blue facings, brass buttons.	Former cuirassier regiment. Disbanded 1726
C-5	1591	**1648** Johann van Welderen	Gelderland	-		-	Disbanded 1668
C-6	1598	**1641** Anthoni van Haersolte	Holland	-		-	Disbanded 1668
C-7	1607	**1641** Henri-Charles de la Trémoille Thouars-Talmont	Friesland	-	Dijlerschans (1664)	-	Disbanded 1668

	Raised	Denomination	Province	Nat.	Engagements	Uniforms	History
C-8	1621	**1644** Jacob van Wassenaer van Obdam **1665** Ludolf van Steenhuyzen van Heumen **1674** François Schagen van Sledrecht **1677** Cornelis Aerssen van Sommelsdijk **1683** Mattheus Hoeufft van Oyen	Holland	-	Seneffe (1674)	(1686)[84] Private: light buff coat with red facings, tin buttons. Officer: white coat with crimson facings.	Disbanded 1705
C-9	1625	**1645** Joachim de Saint Georges-Verneuil **1667** Georg Friedrich von Waldeck-Pyrmont Culemborg	Holland	-	Mont Cassel (1677)	(1686)[85] Private: light grey coat with madder red facings, brass buttons. NCO: madder red coat.	Former cuirassier regiment. Disbanded 1723
C-10	1625	**1641** François de la Place-Machault 1665 Godard van Reede-Ginkel	Utrecht	-	Mont Cassel (1677)	(1686)[86] Private: light grey coat facings, brass buttons. Officer: white coat with red facings.	Former cuirassier regiment. Disbanded 1771
C-11	1635	**1642** George Frederik van Nassau **1674** Louis Mario de la Feuillade de la Guette **1677** Frederik Willem van der Borch (Burgt)	Groningen	-	Coevorden (1672) Seneffe (1674) Maastricht (1676)	-	Disbanded 1749
C-12	1645	**1649** Herman Frederik van den Berg **1669** de Bret de Montbas **1672** Jacob van Wassenaer van Obdam en Voorschoten	Holland	-	Staphorst (1673) Seneffe (1674) Mont Cassel (1677)	(1686)[87] Private: light grey coat with madder red facings, brass buttons. Officer and Musician: red coat.	Disbanded 1729
C-13	1665	Johan Maurits van Nassau-Siegen	Friesland	-		-	Disbanded 1668

	Raised	Denomination	Province	Nat.	Engagements	Uniforms	History
C-14	1665	Maurits van Solms	Holland?	-		-	Disbanded 1668
C-15	1665	Josef van Catzler **1673** Johan Joost van Croonenburg **1678** Frans Caspar Casimir Hardunck **1684** Hendrik Bentinck van Diepenheim	Holland	-	Mont Cassel (1677)	(1687)[88] Private: azure-blue coat with red facings	Disbanded 1771
C-16	1665	Zeger van Rechteren van Almelo **1674** Johan Albrecht van Schellaert **1683** Frederick Willem de Heyden	Gelderland	-	Seneffe (1674)	(1686)[89] Private: light grey coat with pale blue facings, brass buttons.	Merged in 1795 with *Regiment Zware Cavalerie 2*
C-17	1665	George Frederik van Schwartsenberg en Hohenlansberg **1672** Johan George van Schwartsenberg en Hohenlansberg **1675** Jarich van Burum	Friesland	-	Maastricht (1673) Grave (1674)	-	Disbanded 1679
C-18	1665	Boudewijn van Soutelande **1671** Boudewijn van Soutelande	Zealand	-		-	Disbanded in 1672
C-19	1665	Frederik Maurits II de la Tour d'Auvergne-Bouillon	Holland	-		-	Disbanded in 1668

	Raised	Denomination	Province	Nat.	Engagements	Uniforms	History
C-20	1668	Ernst Willem van Haren **1673** Douwe van Grovestins, **1673** Hendrik Casimir II van Nassau-Friesland (Gardes Friesland)	Friesland	-	Seneffe (1674) Mont Cassel (1677)	(1686)[90] Private: dark blue coat, carmine red facings, carmine red saddle cover laced white. NCO and Musician: red coats with white facings.	Merged in 1795 with *Regiment Zware Cavalerie 2*
C-21	1671	Frederik Hendrik van den Boetzelaer-Langerack **1674** Wolf Christoffel Truchsess-Waldburg **1680** Claude Frederik 't Serclaes van Tilly	Holland	-	Seneffe (1674) Mont Cassel (1677)	(1686)[91] Private: light grey coat and facings, tin buttons.	Disbanded in 1760
C-22	1671	Walraven van Nassau-Saarbrücken **1672** Wilhelm von der Lippe **1679** Walrad van Nassau-Saarbrücken	Holland	-	Seneffe (1674) Mont Cassel (1677) Saint Denis (1678)	(1686)[92] Private: light grey coat with red facings, brass buttons.	Disbanded 1719
C-23	1671	Daniël d'Ossory	Holland	-	Rijnberk (1672) Nijmegen (1672)	-	Disbanded 1672
C-24	1671	Ignatius Kingma	Friesland	-	Tolhuis (1672) Muiden (1672) Coevorden (1672) Seneffe (1674)	(1670s)[93] Private: grey coat with dark blue facings. (1687)[94] Private: light grey coat lined green.	Disbanded 1688
C-25	1672	*Gardes te Paard van de Staten van Holland* (Gardes Bleus)[96]	Holland	-	Seneffe (1674) Mont Cassel (1677) Saint Denis (1678)	(1672)[95] Private: pale-yellow hat piped gold, dark blue coat, red cuffs and lining, dark blue *casaque* with gold-yellow crowned 'W' on the front, back & on sleeves, red saddle cover laced gold-yellow, white cravat, black horses (1686)[97] Private: dark blue cassock with yellow mustard facings, brass buttons.	Disbanded 1795

	Raised	Denomination	Province	Nat.	Engagements	Uniforms	History
C-26	1672	Armand de Caumont de la Force-Mountpouillon	Holland	-		(1686)[98] Private: light grey coat with red facings, tin buttons.	Disbanded 1702
C-27	1672	Filips Jacob van Brempt **1672** Filips Emminghuysen van Eppe **1683** Otto von der Lippe	Overijssel, later Holland	-	Seneffe (1674) Maastricht (1676) Mont Cassel (1677)	(1686)[99] Private: light grey coat, pale blue facings, tin buttons.	Merged in 1795 with *Regiment Zware Cavalerie 2*
C-28	1672	Ludwig Christian von Wittgenstein **1676** Frederik Ferdinand van Berlo	Holland	-	Grave (1674)	(1686)[100] Private: light grey coat with madder red facings, tin buttons.	Disbanded 1701
C-29	1672	Adriaan Gustaaf van Flodorff	Zealand	-	Seneffe (1674) Mont Cassel (1677) Saint Denis (1678)	(1686)[101] Private: light grey coats, red facings, brass buttons. Officer and Musician: red coat	Merged in 1795 with *Regiment Zware Cavalerie 1*
C-30	1672	Friedrich Casimir von Kurland-Semgallen (Coerland) **1676** Karl Jacob von Kurland-Semgallen (Coerland) **1676** Herman Franck **1681** Bogislaf Sigismund Schack	Friesland	Latvian-Polish until 1676	Seneffe (1674)	(1686)[102] Private: light grey coat, dark red facings, brass buttons. Musician: red coat.	Disbanded 1702
C-31	1672	Ernst van Stolzenberg **1673** Johan Reinhard van Hoornberg **1677** Johan Willem van Holtzappel **1688** Georg von Riedesel	Overijssel	-	Seneffe (1674) Mont Cassel (1677)	(1686)[103] Private: light grey coat, pale blue facings, brass buttons. Musician: medium blue coat.	Disbanded 1761

	Raised	Denomination	Province	Nat.	Engagements	Uniforms	History
C-32	1672	Alexander van Welle **1675** Willem Roeleman van Quadt-Soppenbroek	Holland			(1686)[104] Private: light grey coat, crimson facings, brass buttons	*Regiment Zware Cavalerie 1* 1795
C-33	1672	**1635** Frederik Magnus Rijngraaf van Salm **1672** Johan Theodor Metzger van Weybnom	Zealand	-	Seneffe (1674) Mont Cassel (1677)	(1686)[105] Private: dark grey coat, blue cuffs, dark grey breeches, brass buttons.	Disbanded 1747

Dragoon Squadrons

	Raised	Denomination	Province	Nat.	Engagements:	Uniforms	History
d-i	1673	Nassau-Saarbrucken Dragonders[106]	Friesland	-		-	Disbanded 1679
d-ii	1674	Prins Willem Dragonders[107]	Holland	-		-	Disbanded 1679

Dragoon Regiments

	Raised	Denomination	Province	Nat.	Engagements:	Uniforms	History
D-1	1672	Friedrich Casimir von Kurland-Semgallen (Coerland) **1676** Willem III van Oranje-Nassau (Gardes Dargonders)	Friesland, later Holland	Latvian-Polish	Groningen (1672) Coevorden (1672) Seneffe (1674) Mont Cassel (1677) Saint Denis (1678)	(1672)[108] Private: red cap trimmed with brown fur, grey coat. (1677)[109] Private: grey coat lined orange. (1686)[110] Private: dark blue coat and facings, brass buttons.	Raised by the ruler Duke of Courland. Disbanded in 1795
D-2	1672	Christiaan Brandt **1680** Christoffel Erhardt van der Gröben	Holland	-		(1676)[111] Private: green hat piped orange, green knots and ribbon, green coat lined red, copper buttons. (1686)[112] Private: scarlet coat, pale blue facings, brass buttons. Officers and musician: blue coat.	Disbanded in 1752

Notes

1 Jean Belaupre-Frans Gerard de Wilde, *Les Armees qui Combattirent Louis XIV: les Provinces Unies* (private publication, 1978), part two, p. 18.
2 *Ibid.*
3 Hessische Landesarchiv Marburg (HLM), Wilhelmshöher Kartensammlung, Karten WHK 42/13: *Plan des Feldlagers der Armee des Prinzen von Oranien auf der Mocker Heide bei Nimwegen, 1686*
4 HLM, Karten WHK 42/13: *Plan des Feldlagers der Armee des Prinzen von Oranien auf der Mocker Heide, 1686.*
5 *Ibid.*
6 HLM, Wilhelmshöher Kartensammlung, Karten WHK 42/17; *Feldlager bei Dieren 1687.*
7 Belaupre-de de Wilde, *Les Provinces Unies*, part two, p. 23.
8 *Europeesche Mercurius*, in Jean Belaupre, *Les Triomphes de Louis XIV*, Cabinet des Estampes, Bibliotheque Nationale de France (private publication, Paris, 1970).
9 HLM, Karten WHK 42/13: *Plan des Feldlagers der Armee des Prinzen von Oranien auf der Mocker Heide, 1686.*
10 De Wilde Legacy, Dutch National Military Museum.
11 After a drawing of the ten-Raa-Papendrecht collection, Dutch National Army Museum.
12 HLM, Karten WHK 42/13: *Plan des Feldlagers der Armee des Prinzen von Oranien auf der Mocker Heide, 1686.*
13 *Ibid.*
14 HLM, Karten WHK 42/17: *Feldlager bei Dieren 1687.*
15 HLM, Karten WHK 42/13: *Plan des Feldlagers der Armee des Prinzen von Oranien auf der Mocker Heide, 1686.*
16 Belaupre-de Wilde, *les Provinces Unies*, part one, p. 15.
17 Belaupre-de Wilde, *les Provinces Unies*, part one, p. 14: list of delivery for fabric and accessories for the garrison of Brügge.
18 HLM, Karten WHK 42/13: *Plan des Feldlagers der Armee des Prinzen von Oranien auf der Mocker Heide, 1686.*
19 HLM, Karten WHK 42/13: *Plan des Feldlagers der Armee des Prinzen von Oranien auf der Mocker Heide, 1686.*
20 Koninklijk Huisarchief (Royal Archives) The Hague, A 26-343; contract signed at Leewarden in March 1678, in Olaf Nimwegen, *The Dutch Army and the Military Revolutions, 1588–1688*(Woodbridge, Suffolk: Boydell Press, 2010), p. 354.
21 Belaupre-de Wilde, *les Provinces Unies*, part one, p. 15.
22 *Ibid.* p. 17.
23 *Ibid.*
24 HLM, Karten WHK 42/13: *Plan des Feldlagers der Armee des Prinzen von Oranien auf der Mocker Heide, 1686.*
25 *Ibid.*
26 Belaupre-de Wilde, *les Provinces Unies*, part two, p. 13.
27 *Ibid.*
28 After the painting attributed to Abraham Beerstraten (1668) illustrating the raid on the Medway in June 1667.
29 After the Ludolf Backhuysen's painting illustrating the boarding of the marine infantry at Texel.
30 C.B. Nicolas, *De Mariniersbrigade te kiek* (Amsterdam: Omegaboek, 1986), p. 30.
31 *Ibid.*, p. 31.
32 HLM, Karten WHK 42/17: *Feldlager bei Dieren 1687.*
33 HLM, Karten WHK 42/13: *Plan des Feldlagers der Armee des Prinzen von Oranien auf der Mocker Heide, 1686.*
34 HLM, *Feldlager bei Dieren 1687.*
35 *Ibid.*
36 HLM, Karten WHK 42/13: *Plan des Feldlagers der Armee des Prinzen von Oranien auf der Mocker Heide, 1686.*
37 C.B. Nicolas, *De Mariniersbrigade*, p. 31.
38 HLM, Karten WHK 42/13: *Plan des Feldlagers der Armee des Prinzen von Oranien auf der Mocker Heide, 1686.*
39 De Wilde Legacy, Dutch National Military Museum.

40 Belaupre-de Wilde, *les Provinces Unies*, part two, p. 9.
41 HLM, Karten WHK 42/13: *Plan des Feldlagers der Armee des Prinzen von Oranien auf der Mocker Heide, 1686.*
42 C.B. Nicolas, *De Mariniersbrigade*, p. 30.
43 *Ibid.*, p. 31.
44 *HLM, Karten WHK 42/13: Plan des Feldlagers der Armee des Prinzen von Oranien auf der Mocker Heide, 1686.*
45 *Ibid.*
46 De Wilde Legacy, Dutch National Military Museum.
47 Belaupre-de Wilde, *les Provinces Unies*, part two, p. 10.
48 HLM, Karten WHK 42/13: *Plan des Feldlagers der Armee des Prinzen von Oranien auf der Mocker Heide, 1686.*
49 De Wilde Legacy, Dutch National Military Museum.
50 *Ibid.*
51 HLM, Karten WHK 42/13: *Plan des Feldlagers der Armee des Prinzen von Oranien auf der Mocker Heide, 1686.*
52 Ten-Raa-Papendrecht, collection of the Dutch National Military Museum.
53 HLM, Karten WHK 42/13: *Plan des Feldlagers der Armee des Prinzen von Oranien auf der Mocker Heide, 1686.*
54 HLM, *Feldlager bei Dieren 1687.*
55 HLM, Karten WHK 42/13: *Plan des Feldlagers der Armee des Prinzen von Oranien auf der Mocker Heide, 1686.*
56 HLM, Karten WHK 42/13: *Plan des Feldlagers der Armee des Prinzen von Oranien auf der Mocker Heide, 1686.*
57 *Wytlopiger Journael*, Groningen, 1672.
58 After the correspondence of Godard Adriaan van Reede, in Luc Panhuysen, *Rampjaar 1672, hoe de republiek aan de ondergang ontsnapte* (Leiderdorp: Olympus Pockets, 2011), p. 322.
59 HLM, Karten WHK 42/13: *Plan des Feldlagers der Armee des Prinzen von Oranien auf der Mocker Heide, 1686.*
60 *Ibid.*
61 Ten-Raa-Papendrecht, collection of the Dutch National Military Museum.
62 HLM, Karten WHK 42/13: *Plan des Feldlagers der Armee des Prinzen von Oranien auf der Mocker Heide, 1686.*
63 Belaupre-de Wilde, *les Provinces Unies*, part four, p. 28.
64 From the Haarlem newspaper *De Oprechte Haarlemmer Courant*, May 1674.
65 HLM, Karten WHK 42/13: *Plan des Feldlagers der Armee des Prinzen von Oranien auf der Mocker Heide, 1686.*
66 *Ibid.*
67 *Ibid.*
68 De Wilde Legacy, Dutch National Military Museum.
69 HLM, Karten WHK 42/13: *Plan des Feldlagers der Armee des Prinzen von Oranien auf der Mocker Heide, 1686.*
70 Belaupre-de Wilde, *les Provinces Unies*, part four, p. 30.
71 HLM, Karten WHK 42/13: *Plan des Feldlagers der Armee des Prinzen von Oranien auf der Mocker Heide, 1686.*
72 After the reconstruction in the Dutch National Military Museum, Soesterberg.
73 Jonkh J.W. Imbyze van Batenburg , *Collectie van verschillende illustraties of artilleristen sinds de invoering van uniforme kleding in het Nederlandse leger tot heden 1821* (Collection of different illustrations of artillerymen since the introduction of uniform clothing in the Dutch army up until the present times 1821), copy by F.J.G. ten Raa, in de Wilde Legacy, Dutch National Military Museum.
74 Commanders: 1647 Henry Fleury Culan van Buat; 1666 Casper van Lijnden; 1672 Hendrik van Nassau-Ouwerkerk.
75 After a drawing by Hoynck van Papendrecht preserved in the Military Museum of Delft.
76 HLM, Karten WHK 42/13: *Plan des Feldlagers der Armee des Prinzen von Oranien auf der Mocker Heide, 1686.*
77 Commanders: 1647 Henry Fleury Culan Heer van Buat; 1666 Casper van Lijnden; 1672 Hendrik van Nassau-Ouwerkerk.
78 F.J.G. ten Raa, *Het Staatsche Leger* (Gravenhage, 1940), vol. VI, p. 88.
79 Belaupre-de Wilde, *les Provinces Unies*, part four, p. 37.
80 Commanders: Frans van Emminga; 1689 Jan Hessel van Aylva.

81 HLM, Karten WHK 42/13: *Plan des Feldlagers der Armee des Prinzen von Oranien auf der Mocker Heide, 1686.*
82 *Ibid.*
83 *Ibid.*
84 *Ibid.*
85 *Ibid.*
86 *Ibid.*
87 *Ibid.*
88 HLM, Karten WHK 42/17: *Feldlager bei Dieren 1687.*
89 HLM, Karten WHK 42/13: *Plan des Feldlagers der Armee des Prinzen von Oranien auf der Mocker Heide, 1686.*
90 *Ibid.*
91 *Ibid.*
92 *Ibid.*
93 Recontructions afer painting and items preserved in the Fries Museum (Leeuwarden, Friesland).
94 HLM, Karten WHK 42/17: *Feldlager bei Dieren 1687.*
95 Commanders: Karel Florentijn Rijngraaf van Salm; 1674 Hans Willem van Bentinck.
96 Belaupre-de Wilde, *les Provinces Unies*, part three, p. 23.
97 HLM, Karten WHK 42/13: *Plan des Feldlagers der Armee des Prinzen von Oranien auf der Mocker Heide, 1686.*
98 *Ibid.*
99 *Ibid.*
100 *Ibid.*
101 *Ibid.*
102 *Ibid.*
103 *Ibid.*
104 *Ibid.*
105 *Ibid.*
106 Two companies under *Kapitein* Walrad van Nassau-Saarbrücken; *Kapitein-commandant*: Johan Lodewijk van Frankensteijn; 1676 Mathurin Blandin de Ducheene.
107 Two companies.
108 Ten-Raa, vol VI, p. 101.
109 *Ibid.*
110 HLM, Karten WHK 42/13: *Plan des Feldlagers der Armee des Prinzen von Oranien auf der Mocker Heide, 1686.*
111 Ten Raa, vol. VI, p. 102.
112 HLM, Karten WHK 42/13: *Plan des Feldlagers der Armee des Prinzen von Oranien auf der Mocker Heide, 1686.*

Colour Plate Commentaries

A. Infantry, 1660–69

1. Private of marine regiment *Vrijbergen* (I-35), 1667

One of the best sources concerning the uniform of the first marine regiment is a drawing by Moses ter Borch, who served during the Second Anglo-Dutch war as volunteer in the navy and portrayed several sailors and soldiers engaged in sea warfare. His drawing gives no information about the colours of the clothing but several sources shows some marine soldiers engaged in the raid on the Medway dressed in butternut or grey. This marine soldier wears a long coat with short sleeves tailored in an unusual form, but the same pattern appears in some figures represented in de Hooghe's engraving of the raid. Marines had already received the modern *snaphan* or flintlock musket in the early 1660s.(Reconstruction after a drawing by Moses ter Borch, Metropolitan Museum of Art, New York)

2. Musketeer, *Gardes te voet van de Staten van Holland* (Holland's Foot Guards, I-28), 1662–68

The manual written by Johan Boxel for the training of the Foot Guards regiment in the 1660s includes 54 drawings illustrating musketeers and pikemen in their different drill motions. Musketeers wear cassock and pot helm without exception, with matchlock musket and musket rest as their weapon. Breeches and stockings are the same for all. This is one of the first actual Dutch 'uniforms' in a modern sense, and shows the significant care given to the Life Corps in matter of clothing. The regiment retained the status of Foot Guards until 1674, when was replaced by the regiment *Solms* (I-8).

3. Senior Officer, *Gardes te voet van de Staten van Holland* (Holland's Foot Guards, I-28), 1662–68

Officers in Boxel's manual are represented only in the page illustrating the soldiers in training, and they are represented in early *justaucorps* and round hat. The captain carries a high spontoon, presumably more than 300 cms, while the senior officer leads the training with a simple walking stick. A sash of azure silk was a common alternative to the orange one, especially by the officers close to the anti-Orangist faction. (Reconstruction after the drawings of the *Vertoogh van de Kryghs-Oeffeninge* by Johan Boxel, The Hague, 1670)

B: Infantry, 1672–79

1. Private musketeer, regiment *Königsmark* (I-77), 1672

This regiment appears to have worn blue coats when it was sent to Groningen just before the incoming enemy siege, in the summer of 1672. Because of the shortage of equipment for the troops, the sources relate that swords had been replaced by axes. In 1672, in order to better identify the Dutch troops, William III required the use of grey headgear for the infantry. (Reconstruction after the *Wytlopiger Journael* of the siege of Groningen and the drawings by Joshua de Grave, dated 1675, Rijksmuseum Library, Amsterdam)

2. Ensign, regiment *Aylva* (I-2), 1674

The custom of wearing dress of reversed colour compared to the troops was adopted also by the Dutch infantry officers, who maintained it until the end of the century. The most ancient document relating the uniform of the *Aylva* regiment relates in 1686 coat of grey *carsaay* with dark blue facings, sothis reconstruction is speculative regarding the colours, while the clothing is inspired by the figures by Pieter de Hooch. Except for the pole weapons, sash and uniforms of better quality, decorated with rather more lace on the seams, cuffs and pockets, officers did not carry actual sign of distinction. In early 1680s, officers of the Foot Guards wore gorgets, differentiated by rank as recorded in some coeval sources. The captain' gorget was lined with blue velvet, lieutenants' with black, and ensigns' with white velvet. The company flag was lost at Seneffe, where the regiment suffered heavy casualties.

3. Pikeman, regiment *Reede* (I-86), 1675

In Luc Panhuysen's book on the year 1672, there are several accounts relating the regiment recruited by Godard Adriaan van Reede. When in early 1673 the States-General ordered the formation of new regiments of foot, van Reede, at that time an ambassador in Brandenburg, took his first steps in the soldiers' market. Unfortunately, many things went wrong: captains ran off with the money, the quality of the troops was terrible, and some of them even started a mutiny. Those troops that arrived in Holland were merged with other regiments. In his correspondence with his son Godard, van Reede several times describes the uniforms: red coats with blue cuffs. Thanks to Edwin Groot for this infortmation. (Reconstruction after Luc Panhhiysen and the drawings by Joshua de Grave, dated 1675, Rijksmuseum Library, Amsterdam)

C. Infantry, 1680–87

1. Grenadier, *Gardes te voet* regiment (I-8), 1680–85

According to Frans Gerard de Wilde, the regiment of Foot Guards received their dark blue uniform in the 1670s. The shortage of orange cloth forced the colonel to turn to the less expansive yellow mustard *baay*. This figure is a composite reconstruction after engraving of late 1680s, which probably refer to an earlier date. Foot Guards received flintlock muskets since 1674. (Reconstruction after Battle of the Boyne engraving by anonymous, 1690 and Romeyn de Hooghe, 1689)

2. Musketeer, regiment *Nassau-Ottweiler* (I-11), 1686
In the 1670s, uncoloured kersey was preferred for manufacturing uniforms, being cheaper than coloured fabric. This trend is confirmed in the following decades, when in 1686, the plan of the troops' review tells that except the main part of the Dutch infantry wore grey *justaucorps*. This is the same cloth recorded in the deliveries as grey, light grey, or ash grey *carsaay*. This figure shows the transitional phase of the military uniform, which is already evolving, with minor changes, into the classic pattern unvaried until the beginning of the 18th century. (Reconstruction after the *Plan des Feldlagers der Armee des Prinzen von Oranien auf der Mocker Heide, 1686* and Belaupre-de Wilde *Les Armees qui Combattirent Louis XIV: les Provinces Unies*)

3. Drummer, regiment *Nassau-Ottweiler* (I-11), 1686
Mid-17th century paintings show several Dutch musicians with elaborated and colorful livery, such as the one here reconstructed for this drummer of the *Walen* regiment. The drummers carried a drum weighing 12 pounds which had a height of 58.5 cm and a circumference of about 180 cm. This was rather an old-fashioned instrument and it seems to have been replaced by a smaller model after 1690. (Reconstruction after the *Plan des Feldlagers der Armee des Prinzen von Oranien auf der Mocker Heide, 1686 and Belaupre-de Wilde Les Armees qui Combattirent Louis XIV: les Provinces Unies*)

D. Cavalry, 1660–67

1. Trooper with greatcoat, 1665–69
The earlier descriptions mention 'coats and *surtouts*' and *justaucorps* are mentioned in the 1670s, but both these the words could indicate that at least some regiments received greatcoats in earlier date. Regarding this latter item, a contemporary reference stated that in 1672 Dutch troops were equipped with greatcoats and additional woolen socks as winter clothing. The same items appear in several paintings of contemporary Dutch artists. (Reconstruction after Pieter de Hooch and Wagenaar's *Vaderlandsche Historien*, 1757)

2. Senior officer, unknown cavalry unit, 1664–68
In the second half of the 17th century, buff coats with laced sleeves are the conventional main clothing of the cavalry officers in Western Europe. This figure is based on a portrait of an unknown officer by Juriaen Jacobsz, datable 1664-68. The buff coat completely covered the waistcoat or the doublet worn under, but it leaves visible the elaborate ornamentation of the sleeve of the shirt.

E. Cavalry, 1672–74

1. Trooper, regiment *Kingma* (C-24), 1672
In the painting by Pieter Wouwerman, today preserved in the Rijksmuseum in Amsterdam, are portrayed some mounted officers and troopers who could belong to the Groningen's cavalry regiment *Kingma*, the only mounted unit to participate in the action. At a first examination, the horsemen are dressed

with coats of different colours: butternut, light brown, medium grey and dark blue; a trooper seems to wear a leather coat of buff, but some others in the background wear grey coats with dark blue facings. Another source, an engraving by Lambert van den Bos, represents regular cavalrymen, who form the rearguard of the advancing infantry columns engaged in the storming of Coevorden. Here the colours are absent, but equipment and weaponry appears well detailed. Some troopers seem to wear leather coats while others appear to be dressed in something closer to a cloth *justaucorps*.

2. Trumpeter, unknown regiment, 1673
It is difficult to which regiments belongs this trumpeter however, according to the family's heraldry, this livery could belong to colonel Ignatius Kingma. (Reconstruction after Jan Verkolje, 1673)

F. Cavalry and artillery, 1680s

1. Trooper, *Gardes te Paard* regiment (C-25), 1687
De Wilde and Belaupre gave a version of the uniforms worn by this prestigious units after the research of F.J.G. ten Raa and Jan Hoynck van Papendrecht. These latter reconstructed the uniform after the engraving of Romeyn de Hooghe representing the siege of Naarden in 1673. The Horse Guard wear a dark blue casaque with false sleeves, inspired by that of the French *Maison du Roi* Mousquetaires. A mustard-yellow waistcoat, large brimmed hat with feathers and huge cavalry boots complete the clothing. This uniform is confirmed in other pictures except one: this is the engraving of an anonymous artist illustrating the battle of the Boyne in 1690. Here appear some Guardswearing the same feathered headgear but not the *casaque*, which is replaced by a cassock with large cuffs. This suggests that the first belonged to the courtly dress worn for ordinary duty, but in campaign the warmer and more comfortable cassock was preferred. The Horse Guards Regiment mounted black horses and deployed six companies, which were formed up in squadrons identified by the headgear plumes: red for the 1st squadron, green for the 2nd squadron and yellow for the 3rd squadron.

2. Officer, regiment *Ginkel* (C-10), 1686
(Reconstruction after Romeyn de Hooghe)

3. NCO, Artillery Regiment, 1680
The Dutch National Military Museum preserves the drawings collected by *generaal-majoor* Imbyze van Batenburg, who served in the artillery after 1769. The drawings were copied by F.J.G. ten Raa and Frans Gerard de Wilde and also Richard Knötel turn to this source for his *Grosse Uniformenkunde*. Despite some particulars seem to be old fashioned with the period to which they refer. this is the most ancient source relating the uniform of the Dutch artillery. The 1680 artilleryman wears a dark blue *justaucorps* with red 'Swedish' cuffs, brass or copper buttons, dark blue breeches and stockings, white neck cloth and black broad brimmed hat and white plume. (Reconstruction after by Jonkh J.W. Imbyze van Batenburg)

G. Militia

1. Officer, 1660–65

(Reconstruction after Gerard ter Borch)

2. Militiaman, Blue Company of the Leyden Town Militia, 1660

In this portrait of Captain Gerrit Leendertsz van Grootveld, the militiamen of his company appear in the background. They are mostly dressed in grey or butternut equipped with heavy muskets with rests and a sword. (Reconstruction after Jacob Fransz van der Merck)

3. Militiaman, The Hague Town Militia, 1672

The arrest of the de Witt brothers was carried out by The Hague town militia. In the painting by Pieter Frits appear several militiamen with their officers, recognisable by their polearms. Alongside with the grey dressed figures, there are also red, green, buff and even pink militiamen. Someone wears a coat or *justaucorps* with cuffs, while other figures appear in a doublet or short coat; headdress varies from morion helm to broad-brimmed hat of several colours. On the roof of a house, three militiamen in grey coats with muskets are depicted wearing red breeches and different coloured stockings, and a broad brimmed hat with plumes. (Reconstruction after Pieter Frits)

H.

Infantry regiment *Ingen-Nielant* (I-19), 1672

In his manual of exercise, Johan Boxel gives fragmentary description of infantry flags, but limited to the colours of the field with a few exceptions. The Dutch ensigns with flames, as the one here reconstructed, usually carries a central figure – an armed arm or the seven arrows were the more common subjects – surrounded by branches or garlands in gold or in green, especially of orange fruit. Boxel's descriptions relate 20 infantry colours in all. they are: *Asperen* (I-1) full orange; *Golstein* (I-52) blue with white strikes on the corners; *Wittgenstein* (I-71) full black; *Noordwijk* (I-22) pale blue with a golden garland; *Erskine* (I-32) blue and white divided in four parts; *Mauregnault* (I-34) yellowish colour; *Steelandt* (I-26) red with some whitein the corners; *Scott* (I-68) blue and yellow; *Schotte* (I-36) white; *Dolman* (I-16) red and white divided in four; *Weede van Walenburg* (I-44) black with a golden branch of laurel; *Aquila* (I-38) blue and orange; *Horn* (I-12) red. The list includes further four unidentified regiments: *Sterrenburg* in yellow with golden garland; *Saugé* in full white; *Sidniski* in blue with white flames, *Santen* mixed of yellow and white.

I.

Marine regiment *Vrijbergen* (I-35), 1672

Although the iconography attributed to this regiment a red-white-blue tricolor, Johan Boxel describes the company ensign of dark blue and orange in bands. In the engraving illustrating the raid on the Medway, Romeyn de Hooghe depicts a similar pattern for the ensign carried by the marines engaged in the action.

J.

Infantry regiment *Kirckpatrick* (I-15), 1672

Johan Boxel attributes to this Scottish regiment a blue and yellow ensign. It was also possible that some figures were placed on the flag, like the provinces' coat of arms and the Saint Andrew cross, as appeared on several ensigns of Scottish regiments in Dutch service in the late 17th century.

K.

Utrecht Militia company ensigns

Town militia carried ensigns of a plain field of varied colour since the beginning of the 17th century, together with the province's coat of arms. The militia of Utrecht was no excpetion to this scheme, and on the eve of the French invasion of 1672, the four companies bore white, orange, blue and green ensigns. Similar colours could be found also in the regular army, such as for some infantry ensigns belonging to the regiments of Gelderland.

Regiment *Gardes te Paard* (C-25), 1674–87

Standards with Prince William's crowned monogram appear in several engravings by Romeyn de Hooghe and other artists. This standard is confirmed by de Wilde and Belaupre as carried by this regiment before 1689.

Cavalry regiment *Obdam* (C-12), 1686

Reconstruction after the *Plan des Feldlagers der Armee des Prinzen von Oranien auf der Mocker Heide*, 1686.

L.

Cavalry regiment *Heyden* (C-16), 1690

The regiment lost this and another square blue standard with the same figures and pattern at the Battle of Fleurus (After *Les Triomphes de Louis XIV*)

Cavalry regiment *Oyen* (C-8), 1686

Reconstruction after the *Plan des Feldlagers der Armee des Prinzen von Oranien auf der Mocker Heide*, 1686.

Artillery flags, 1690

The celebrated series *Les Triomphes de Louis XIV* includes also some flags probably used as markers for the artillery batteries. The source does not specify the size, but these flags seem to be much smaller compared to the infantry ensigns.

Bibliography

Contemporary Printed Sources

AA.VV., *Recueil des Ordonnances Militaires pour les Règlement des Troupes qui sont au Service de Leurs Hautes Puissances, nos Seigneurs les Etats Généraux des Provinces-Unies des Pais-Bas*, The Hague (1684), 1701.

de Courtilz, Gaetien, *Histoire de la Guerre d'Hollande* (The Hague, 1689)

Quincy, M. de, *Histoire Militaire du Regne de Louis le Grand Roy de France* (Paris, 1726) vol I.

Le Mercure Hollandois, years 1672–1678; Amsterdam 1673–79.

Books

AA.VV., *The New Cambridge Modern History: vol. 5, 'The Ascendency of France (1648–1688)'*, Chapter 12, *The Dutch Republic* (Cambridge: Cambridge University Press, 1968)

Amersfoort, Hermanus, *Je maintiendrai: a concise history of the Dutch army, 1568–1940* (The Hague: SMG/LAS, 1985)

Belaubre, Jean, *Les Triomphes de Louis XIV*, Cabinet des Estampes, Bibliotheque Nationale, Paris (private publication), 1970

Belaubre, Jean and de Wilde Frans Gerard: *Les armées qui combattirent Louis Le Grand*, parts I–IV, Paris (private publication), 1976

Borselen, Jan Willem van, and Nicolas, Karel, *De Marinier en zijn Uniform. Geschiedenis van kleding en tenues bij het Korps Mariniers*; Mariniersmuseum der Koninklijke Marine: Rotterdam, 2006.

Bosscha, Johannes, *Neërlands Heldendaden te land*, vol. 2 (Breda, 1872)

Carmichael-Smith, James, *Chronological Epitome of the Wars in the Low Countries, from the Peace of the Pyrenees in 1659 to that of Paris in 1815* (London, 1825)

Cénat, Jean-Philippe, *Le Roi Stratège: Louis XIV et la direction de la guerre (1661–1715)* (Rennes: Presses universitaires de Rennes, 2010)

Dam van Isselt, W. E. van, *De Verdediging van Friesland, 1672-1673* (s'Gravenhage, 1931)

Ferguson, James, *Papers Illustrating the History of the Scots Brigade in the Service of the United Netherlands, vol I: 1572–1697* (Edinburgh: T.A. Constable, 1899)

Forbes, Wels, P., *De Nederlandse Cavalerie* (Bussum: Van Dishoeck, 1963)

Hart, Marjolein't, *The Dutch Wars of Independence. Warfare and Commerce in the Netherlands, 1570–1680* (New York: Routledge, 2014)

Howarth, D., *The Dutch Warships* (New York: Time-Life Books, 1978)

Israel, Jonathan, *The Dutch Republic: its Rise, Greatness, and Fall, 1477–1806* (Oxford: Clarendon Press, 1995)

Knoop, W. J., *Krijgs- en geschiedkundige beschouwingen over Willem den derde, 1672–1697* (Schiedam: H.A.M. Roelants, 1895)

Koopmans, Joop W. and Huussen, Arend H. Jr., *Historical Dictionary of the Netherlands* (Lanham, Maryland : The Scarecrow Press, 2007)

Lynn, John A., *The Wars of Louis XIV, 1677–1714* (London: Longman, 1999)

Nicolas, C.B., *De Mariniersbrigade te kiek* (Amsterdam: Omegaboek, 1986)

Nimwegen, Olaf van, *The Dutch Army and the Military Revolutions 1588–1688* (Woodbridge, Suffolk: Boyden Press, 2010)

Nolan, Cathal J., *Wars of the Age of Louis XIV. an Encyclopedia of Global Warfare and Civilization* (Westport, Connecticut; London: Greenwood Press, 2008)

Panhuysen, Luc, *Rampjaar 1672* (The Hague: Olympus, 2009)

Reinders, Michel, *Printed Pandemonium. Popular Print and Politics in the Netherlands, 1650–72* (Leiden: Brill, 2013)

Ringoir, Hendrik: *De Nederlandse Infanterie* (Bussum: Van Dishoeck, 1968)

Rowen, Herbert H., *John de Witt, Grand Pensionary of Holland, 1625–1672* (Princeton, NJ: Princeton Legacy Library, 1978.

Samsoen, F., *La bataille de Saint-Denis le 14 août 1678. L'abbaye dans la tourmente!* (Mons: Belgian Bavarian Society, 2011)

Schama, Simon, *The Dutch Culture of the Golden Age* (New York: Alfred Knopf, 1988)

Schulten, C.M and Schulten, J.W.M.: *Het leger in de zeventiende eeuw* (Bussum: Van Dishoeck, 1969.

Sonnino, Paul, *Louis XIV and the Origin of the Dutch War* (Cambridge: Cambridge University Press, 2003)

Ten Raa, Frederik J.G., *Het Staatse Leger*, Vol. V–VI (s'Gravenhage, 1940)

Articles and Essays

Bottema, Colonel Jan. K. H. L, 'Vaandels van het Staatse Leger', in the quarterly magazine of the Nederlandse Vereniging ter Beoefening van de Militaire Historie 'Mars et Historia'; October 1972, (year 7, nr 4).

Kerkhoven, J.G., 'Het Nederlandse leger tijdens de stadhouderkoning Willem III (1672–1702)', *Armamentaria* 23

Nimwegen, Olaf van, 'Kanonnen en houwitzers', *Armamentaria* 32

Wilde, F.G. de, 'De uniformen van de Schotse Brigade', *Armamentaria* 15

Wilde, F.G. de, 'Grenadiersmutsen in het Staatse Leger 1672–1795', *Armamentaria* 15

Wilde, F.G. de, 'De kledingvoorziening in het staatsche leger', *Armamentaria* 21

Wilde, F.G. de, 'De Mannen van 1688 – Een poging tot reconstructive', *Armamentaria* 23

Wilde, F.G. de, 'De 'Cent Suisses' van het Stadhouderlijk hof (1672–1795)', *Armamentaria* 25

Zwitser, H. L., 'De mariniers in de Nederlandse krijgsmacht', *Armamentaria* 29.

Websites

<http://www.milwiki.nl:80/dutchregiments/index>

<http://web.archive.org/web/20080523162514/http://www.milwiki.nl:80/dutchregiments/index.php?n=Main.HomePage>